Critical Acclaim for Philippe Wamba's
Kinship

"This far-ranging, thoroughly researched, and thoroughly engaging book should become an instant classic. As Wamba illustrates with poignant, sometimes amusing detail, American blacks and black Africans are on very different wavelengths, and their views of each other are often as romanticized, stereotyped, and culturally misapprehended as those on the better documented spectrum of white American and European perceptions of Africa. *Kinship* fills an important gap in the Africanist's library."
—Alex Shoumatoff, author of *In Southern Light* and
The Mountain of Names

"With eloquence and courage, Philippe Wamba confronts many of the myths and misconceptions that have complicated the centuries-old relationship between Africans and African Americans."
—Henry Louis Gates, Jr.

"A strange, wonderful hybrid of memoir and history . . . the best book dealing with the *African* half of the compound *African American*."
—*Kirkus Reviews* (starred review)

PHILIPPE WAMBA was born in California and raised in Dar es Salaam, Tanzania. He is a magna cum laude graduate of Harvard University. Wamba has a master's degree from the Columbia School of Journalism, and his articles have appeared in journals and newspapers in England, Africa, and the United States. *Kinship* is his first book.

KINSHIP

A Family's Journey in Africa and America

PHILIPPE WAMBA

A PLUME BOOK

PLUME
Published by the Penguin Group
Penguin Putnam Inc., 375 Hudson Street, New York, New York 10014, U.S.A.
Penguin Books Ltd, 27 Wrights Lane, London W8 5TZ, England
Penguin Books Australia Ltd, Ringwood, Victoria, Australia
Penguin Books Canada Ltd, 10 Alcorn Avenue,
Toronto, Ontario, Canada M4V 3B2
Penguin Books (N.Z.) Ltd, 182–190 Wairau Road, Auckland 10, New Zealand

Penguin Books Ltd, Registered Offices: Harmondsworth, Middlesex, England

Published by Plume, a member of Penguin Putnam Inc.
Previously published in a Dutton edition.

First Plume Printing, September 2000

10 9 8 7 6 5 4 3 2 1

 REGISTERED TRADEMARK—MARCA REGISTRADA

The Library of Congress has catalogued the Dutton edition as follows:
Wamba, Philippe E.
    Kinship : a family's journey in Africa and America / Philippe E. Wamba.
        p.   cm.
    Includes bibliographical references (p.   ) and index.
    ISBN 0-525-94387-0 (hc.)
            0-452-27892-9 (pbk.)
    1. Wamba, Philippe E.   2. African Americans Biography.   3. Africans—United States
Biography.   4. Wamba family.   5. Kinshasa (Congo) Biography.   6. Afro-Americans—Rela-
tions with Africans.   I. Title.
E185.97.W1346A3   1999
973'.0496073'0092
[B]—DC21   99-21455
                                                                                                    CIP

Printed in the United States of America
Original hardcover design by Eve L. Kirch

BOOKS ARE AVAILABLE AT QUANTITY DISCOUNTS WHEN USED TO PROMOTE PRODUCTS OR SERVICES.
FOR INFORMATION PLEASE WRITE TO PREMIUM MARKETING DIVISION, PENGUIN PUTNAM INC., 375
HUDSON STREET, NEW YORK, NEW YORK 10014.

For Remy Datave Wamba (1966–1979),
Nkaka Luezi Judith Wamba (c.1918–1998),
and my family in Africa, in America, and worldwide

ACKNOWLEDGMENTS

This book would not have been possible without the encouragement and insight of my family (Mom, Dad, Kolo, Saleem—thank you), the advice and editorial assistance of my professor and mentor Sam Freedman, the interest and assistance of Professor Henry Louis Gates, Jr., the energy and enthusiasm of my literary agent Tina Bennett, or the editing and organizational skill of my editor, Rosemary Ahern, and her assistant, Brett Wean. I also depended on the invaluable support and counsel of many friends and colleagues, especially: Katonja Webb, Hisham Aidi, Richard Bazangoula, Debbie Aukett, Marang Setshwaelo, Oz Eleonora, Tsepo Motsohi, Mike Vazquez, Dennis Maryogo, Eddie Cox Solomon. Thanks also to my extended family: Grandfather James and Grandmother Martha, Grandmother Lois, Cousin Chris and the Billups family, the Eisinger family, the Essien-Buchler family, Uncle Butch and Aunt Sharon, Aunt Anne-Marie and the rest of the Wavezwa family, Uncle Andre, Aunt Sylvie and Kiese, Aunt Julienne and the Bazangoula family, Cousin Sadi and family, Uncle Fukiau, Aunt Edie, the Jasper family, the Parker family, and Professors Horace Campbell and Makini Roy-Campbell. My gratitude also goes out to Abbas Abbas, Moumié Maoulidi, Candice Clarke, Pele Kimimino, George Magembe, Lisa Dent, K. Kyriell Muhammad,

Muna Kangsen, Nebiyu Shawel, Victor Mkhize, Kevin Young, Chris Myers, and Marc Mealy. One love. Big up to Dar, New York, Boston, Kingston, Kinshasa and Johannesburg massive.

CONTENTS

INTRODUCTION

This book chronicles a journey that spans history and crisscrosses an ocean. It is the two-way voyage of a family, of individuals, of culture, and of trends and ideas. It is a journey through race, the bedeviling and enduring social phenomenon of our century. And it is my own circular journey from an inherited expectation of racial affinity, through often troubling experiences that challenged this conviction, to a reaffirmed appreciation of the indelible historical and cultural ties that bind black people on either side of the gaping Atlantic.

In telling this story, I have explored both the fertile depths of my own experience and the historical accounts of those who came before, black people who, like me, sought solace and strength in the tides of transatlantic passages. Malcolm X used to say that history is the subject that best rewards all research, and I have followed his advice, delving into my own background as well as the historical record for insights into the complex relationship between black Africans and black Americans. I also once heard Maya Angelou say that literature lets us know that whatever we may be going through, someone has already survived it and written about it. In consulting the African and African American literary traditions, I have met many who, like me, have grappled with the idea that shared skin color should imply a shared heritage, outlook, or destiny—transatlantic personalities who have attempted to bridge gaps and forge new connections while confronting misunderstandings and misperceptions. They are my literary ancestors, and their stories, as well as my own, populate this book.

Kinship is about how and why Africans and African Americans have historically been bound in a voluntary and involuntary cultural and political partnership, yet often too far separated by culture, geography, prejudice, and history to forge a meaningful and functional sense of racial unity. It is also, ultimately, a book about why they should.

In February of 1999, as I was completing this manuscript, an unarmed immigrant from Guinea named Amadou Diallo was shot to death by four white New York policemen. The police, who apparently mistook Diallo for a rape suspect, shot 41 bullets at the 22-year-old man as he stood in the stairwell of his apartment building, hitting him 19 times. The shooting prompted widespread outrage among predominantly black protestors, and apologetic and defensive posturing by the New York authorities, pitting angry activists against a mayor seen by many as insensitive to the concerns of black New Yorkers and far too tolerant of police brutality.

But in a city where criticisms of overzealous police action often seem to dominate the headlines, perhaps more noteworthy than the political conflict occasioned by Diallo's tragic killing are the political alliances formed in its wake. The slaying of Diallo, a West African Muslim who lived in the Bronx, inspired New York's Islamic, African American, and African communities, as well as a broad multiracial and multifaith coalition of diverse individuals and groups, to come together in an unprecedented and unified expression of grief, anger, and purpose.

As the product of a marriage between an African father and an African American mother, I find this emerging process of political cooperation between American blacks and African immigrant communities especially fascinating and encouraging. I feel uniquely situated to appreciate all that separates Africans and African Americans culturally, yet I also recognize the potential rewards of joining forces to address issues of mutual concern. Throughout my life I've felt incredibly challenged by the gulf between the African and African American communities formed by their ideas about each other, and tremendously fulfilled when I've seen the gap bridged in constructive and empowering ways.

This book is about my own journey along the fault lines of

African–African American relations and the wider historical relationship between black Americans and their counterparts in the "motherland." It explores the complexity of this connection, the clash between myths that Africans and Americans hold about each other, and the nature of the passions that seem inexorably to draw black people on two continents towards one another. And using examples from a variety of sources and in a variety of fields, it examines what the African and African American obsessions with one another have wrought in the past and optimistically points to new possibilities in the future.

In bittersweet fashion, the aftermath of Amadou Diallo's tragic death has provided cause for such optimism and, for me, has underlined the importance of my own literary efforts on this topic. The young man's parents, who traveled to New York to claim their son's body, enlisted the aid of African American and African community leaders in the pursuit of justice and were even accompanied back to Guinea by an entourage of black American well-wishers. And as hundreds of sympathetic New Yorkers have paid their respects at the site of Diallo's murder, commemorating his life with flowers and candles, and have protested his "execution" at frequent public demonstrations, a sense of common cause and brotherhood has grown between black American and African communities that have in the past often been mutually suspicious. If anything positive can come of the death of an innocent, perhaps it is this greater sense of African–African American unity, a powerful reaffirmation of historic ties to take us into the new millennium. It's a sentiment I hope this book will help to elucidate and encourage.

A few disclaimers/clarifiers: This book is neither a scholarly work nor purely a memoir. While its narrative is driven by episodes in my life and that of my family, which are presented in chronological order, it seeks to provide a wider historical context for these events, striking a balance between the personal and the general, and making ample and selective use of primary sources and existing scholarship. And since it relies on memoir for its thematic focus, it is far from comprehensive, touching on what is relevant without attempting to be exhaustive. Each chapter has autobiographical and historical segments, and each chapter addresses a specific theme in African–black American relations.

A few names have been changed to protect individual privacy.

Throughout the book, I refer to both *Swahili* and *Kiswahili*; the former denotes the ethnic identity and wider culture of East African coastal communities, the latter refers specifically to the region's most widely spoken language. Similarly, *Kikongo* is a language, *Bakongo* are a people (plural; *Mukongo* is singular), and *Kongo* refers to an African *Bakongo* kingdom which flourished in the fifteenth century. The current Democratic Republic of the Congo (DRC) has gone through several name changes: in 1960, the country, formerly the "Belgian" Congo, gained independence as the Republic of Congo; in 1964 it was renamed the DRC; in 1971 the name was changed to the Republic of Zaire; and in 1997 the name was changed back to the DRC. All four names appear as is appropriate in the context. The DRC's northwestern neighbor is also called the Congo; the two countries are often distinguished by their capital cities: the DRC is referred to as Congo-Kinshasa, while the smaller Congo, formerly "French" Congo, now the Congo Republic, is Congo-Brazzaville.

The Negro is an American. We know nothing of Africa.
                                    —Martin Luther King, Jr.

Hope surged in Kunta. Would the black ones free him now? But he no sooner thought of it than the flame lit their faces as they stood looking at him over the sides of the wagon; they were laughing at him. What kind of blacks were these who looked down upon their own kind and worked like goats for the toubob? Where had they come from? They looked as Africans looked, but clearly they were not of Africa.   —Alex Haley, *Roots*

I've gotten into a lot of trouble for saying I'm American instead of African American. But I've been to Africa . . . and believe me, I'm American.
                                    —Whoopi Goldberg

I think the single greatest mistake of the American black organizations and their leaders is that they have failed to establish direct brotherhood lines of communication between the independent nations of Africa and the American black people.   —Malcolm X

All of us are bound to mother Africa by invisible but tenacious bonds. . . . All of us have roots that go deep into the warm soil of Africa; so that no matter how long and traumatic our separation from our ancestral home has been, there are things we are often unable to articulate, but which we feel in our very bones, things which make us, who are different from others who have not suckled the breasts of our mother, Africa.   —Desmond Tutu

No matter where you come from, as long as you're a black man, you're an African.   —Peter Tosh

MIDDLE PASSAGES

They face each other, the Negro and the African, over a gulf of three hundred years—an alienation too vast to be conquered in an evening's goodwill, too heavy and too double-edged even to be trapped in speech.
—James Baldwin

The ancient woman crawled through the doorway on her hands and knees, moving with the slow and painful determination of a tortoise. She made her way across the porch and around the side of the house to the outhouse, concrete blocks and flimsy sheets of corrugated zinc that shielded the family's simple toilet from view. None of the adults sitting around the courtyard chatting offered to help her; no one really seemed to even see her.

My father, sitting next to me, sighed and stared at the floor. The little kids playing in the dust a few feet away continued with their game, chattering softly to each other and occasionally laughing or shouting. The chickens in the yard scratched at the dirt, pecking at insects, pebbles, and bits of bright plastic. Some young women with colorfully patterned cloths tied around their waists sat together talking in the sunshine that filtered through the leaves of the large tree in front of the house; one of them was braiding the hair of a restless young girl seated in front of her. And my father, my great-uncle, my cousin, and I sat in the porch's wooden white chairs, saying nothing.

We had already exchanged our greetings, and my father and I, who were visiting various relatives in Kinshasa, Zaire, on this Christmas vacation in 1994, had already shaken hands with most of the cousins, aunts, uncles, and in-laws who lived in this particular house, and had already received the drinks a cousin had been dispatched to bring for us. My deeply evangelical uncle had made a sound of disapproval in his throat when I chose beer from the beverages my aunt offered. So now we just sat, nursing our drinks, and seemed to wait. My father was silent. And I, born and partially raised in the United States, and equipped with only halting French and no Kikongo or Lingala to speak of, smiled at my cousin seated across from me, and said nothing.

I had been quiet for much of the four days we had so far spent in Kinshasa, having difficulty making myself understood, and getting slightly lost in the parade of relatives we visited in homes all over the huge city; sometimes I wasn't really sure who lived in what house, whom we had come to see, or how they were related to me, facts that my father, in his typically absentminded manner, often forgot to supply me with. Most of the relatives I met on that trip had me at a disadvantage when they happily embraced me; they always knew exactly who I was, calling me by name, and had been eagerly expecting me, while I would feel awkwardly ashamed that I didn't know their names or who they were in relation to me unless they or my father told me. It was all quite overwhelming, but also very moving, being greeted so warmly by my family, these strangers.

The old woman emerged from the outhouse and made her slow, deliberate journey back to the porch, once again on all fours, once again unassisted by anyone present. She got to the porch and stopped, sitting down on the concrete floor and leaning against the house, catching her breath. She was painfully small and thin, her face etched with deep wrinkles, her small shorn head covered by a head scarf, a once-colorful pagne tied around her waist, and a faded blouse hanging loosely on her wilted frame. She gazed over at us, seemingly expectant.

I looked at my father.

He looked back at me, seeming in that moment to return from very far away. His voice attempted nervous cheer. "That's your grandmother," he said softly.

Though his words only confirmed what I had already suspected, I was struck with disbelief. I had seen old black-and-white pictures of my father's mother: she was a tall, stern-faced woman, strong-looking, with an unsmiling dignity that reminded me of the poker-faced Native American chiefs who stared unflinchingly from nineteenth-century portraits in the American history books I had studied in grade school. I had heard of my grandmother's failing health, but I had trouble accepting that the woman whom I had known only as a proud and impressive figure in a photograph, a woman who had raised my father and his eight brothers and sisters, had been so severely betrayed by time, losing her strength, her vitality, and even the use of her legs. I wondered at how difficult it must be for my father to see her like this. And I felt guilty; I was twenty-four years old, but this was my first time ever meeting her, ever speaking to her. I felt as if I were hopelessly late—if only I could have seen her in her prime, heard her tell the stories and sing the songs that our father had repeated for us when my brothers and I were younger, and watched her effortlessly hoist a basket of cassava onto her head or a plump child onto her back. If only I could have experienced her during her life, had been able to know and learn from her. But all my life we had been separated by distance and circumstance, bound by blood but living worlds apart.

My father got up from his chair and walked over to his mother. He extended his hand, taking her spindly palm in his, and bowed, she gazing at him happily and fondly, his eyes filled with the greatest love and respect. I followed suit, and he introduced me in Kikongo. "This is Philippe Kiatuntu," he said, using the Kikongo name by which I was known only to my relatives in Zaire.

She stared at me with deep, dark eyes that were bright and amused. She spoke, in a soft, high, and warm voice that wheezed slightly with age, and my father translated: "She says finally you've come to see her." I felt tears prickling the corners of my eyes as I smiled down at her, my heart full, frustrated by my inability to communicate.

After the initial greetings, my grandmother made her way slowly into the house, and after a while we followed her to the little room where she lived with my father's older sister, who had been helping to take care of her since my grandfather died and my grandmother moved to Kinshasa from the village where my father grew up. When we entered the room she was perched next to my aunt on the bed, which occupied more than half of the small space; she looked dignified and regal, and indeed I felt like a humble subject in the hushed presence of royalty as I crouched on a stool at the foot of the bed. She stared at me again, smiling slightly. She gestured at her chin, jokingly referring to my goatee, and said something to my father.

He laughed. "She says your father doesn't even have a beard, but you have one." I presented her with the bolt of African fabric and the scarf that I had bought for her in Boston before we left. She clapped her hands in gratitude, immediately yanking her own head scarf off her head, revealing a crown of close-cropped white hair. She asked my aunt to help her put the new scarf on, and when it was in place, she spoke.

"Praise God that you have come," my father translated. "I'm so happy right now, if I weren't so old I would be dancing." My grandmother clapped and wriggled in a little seated jig to illustrate her point. I said that I was also very happy to meet her finally, after having heard so much about her from my father. She continued speaking, and my father said that she was complaining, as she apparently often did, that whenever he made one of his infrequent trips home to Zaire she always asked for us, her grandchildren in foreign lands, but that my father always said that we were unable to come. Now, at last, I, at least, had made it.

"Now you have seen your grandmother, and when you go home you will tell the others about me," my father interpreted. "I am happy now because I have children, and they are here." She gestured to my father. "And they also have children, and they are also here, so I am very happy." She addressed me earnestly. "You must also find a good wife and have many children, too, so that our"—my father's translation faltered for a moment, as he groped for the right word—"so that our species will spread."

I felt a sudden unmistakable rush of love for this small, wizened old woman, a love that eclipsed the regret I felt at not being able to speak her language and the guilt I felt about having taken so long to meet her. None of that seemed to matter. When I was little, my mother had told me that if you handle a baby bird that has fallen out of its nest, its mother will reject it as a strange-smelling impostor because she no longer recognizes it as part of herself. When I visited my grandmother, I know I looked, smelled, and acted like an alien, mute in my inability to speak her language. But she recognized me. She embraced me as her own; and with all that separated us—language, culture, nationality, generations, gender, and our very worlds of experience—we were still inextricably bound and could still reach each other across the divide. Though she, like most of my relatives in Zaire, saw me as a foreigner, I felt that I could never be foreign to her. And I realized that I wasn't too late. Maybe I was just in time.

Our "species," as my grandmother put it, has already spread, and spread far. Of my grandmother's eight surviving children, four are scattered throughout the Democratic Republic of the Congo, one lives in Congo-Brazzaville, the DRC's neighbor to the northwest, two are raising families in the United States, and one, my father, teaches history at a university in Dar es Salaam, Tanzania, where my immediate family settled after living in the United States for nine years.

My father was born in Sundi-Lutete, a Swedish mission in the westernmost province of the Belgian Congo, in 1942. The area had once been part of the Kongo kingdom, which flourished in the fifteenth century, and my father is descended from Bakongo lineages that can be traced back for hundreds of years. He was named after his father, so his own given name and his family surname (his father's name) were the same; his father was called Wamba, so he was Wamba dia ("of," as in "son of") Wamba. My father's father had not actually received the name Wamba at birth; instead, he had acquired it as a young man. It means both "creativity" and "troublesome," and in the days of the Kongo kingdom it was associated with the king's counselors at the royal court—those who dared to tell the truth to the Kongo monarch. Appropriately, both my father and his father had reputations for being creative and troublesome as youths. In one story my father told me to illustrate his father's youthful mischievous streak, my grandfather and some student colleagues, who had been forced to carry a white missionary on a palanquin, cleverly resisted the task. After conferring with his peers in Kikongo while the oblivious white man lounged in his seat on their shoulders, my grandfather and his friends pretended to stumble near a stream, "accidentally" plunging the missionary into the cold water; the European never ordered his teenage charges to carry him again. Though incidents like this probably helped to earn my grandfather the title that became my family name, however fitting the regal appellation was, my grandfather's actual ancestral pedigree was quite humble. His great-grandmother had been a slave, forced to leave her own village of Yanga to live in a neighboring community called Nsundi as payment for a debt (one pig). Indigenous African slavery was very different from the notorious New World version, and though technically "slaves," my grandfather's great-grandmother and her descendants were able to assimilate into their new community essentially as social equals. In fact, by marrying into the village chief's family, my grandfather's clan eventually came to comprise Nsundi's leadership. Nonetheless, when my father was a very young boy, my grandfather and other relatives decided to return to the area of Yanga, their great-grandmother's ancestral home, and left Nsundi to found the village of Zabanga (named after a nearby creek) where my father grew up. My father claims that if I walked through southwestern Congo into Angola, a distance of several hundred miles, repeating my family's tribe, clan, and village to people I met along the way, I would find dozens of distant relatives eager to provide me with food and shelter. And my father's brother in Boston has boasted to me (with characteristic exaggeration) that our family's ancestral lands in the Congo are "as big as Massachusetts." Forget forty acres and a mule; my father's people proudly lay claim to a state-sized chunk of rural Africa.

On my mother's side I am descended from a large African American family with roots in Georgia and Mississippi. Family lore has it that one of my mother's earliest documented ancestors, a woman named Betsy, a slave in Georgia, ran away on the eve of the Civil War after her mistress beat her because a loaf of cornbread she had baked had cracked slightly on top. She successfully escaped with her infant son, Greene, and was sheltered by friendly Indians as she attempted to retrace her mother's steps back to Africa. When this proved impossible (her navigational cues consisted solely of her mother's belief that she had disembarked from the slave ship in Savannah, Georgia), Betsy settled near Sparta and raised the beginnings of my maternal grand-mother's side of my mother's family. Subsequent generations of my mother's ancestors spread from Georgia to Ohio, Illinois, California, and Michigan, where my mother grew up.

My parents, born and raised on either side of an ocean, were coinci-dentally united in 1965, when they met as students at the state university in Kalamazoo. My father came to the States from the Democratic Re-public of the Congo on an international student scholarship, and first saw my mother, a French major, at a campus French Club meeting. She was impressed with his seriousness and cerebral demeanor; he ap-preciated her intelligence and curiosity about Africa. Like many of her peers, my mother had overcome the fear and disdain with which many older black Americans regarded Africa; she saw the continent as a motherland she had never known, and eagerly educated herself about my father's country and culture. Though my father was often at a loss for what to make of the African Americans he met at college, whom he often considered frivolous and unfocused, he felt that he had enough in common with my mother to build a sound foundation for the future. My parents were married in 1966, in an inelaborate Western ceremony attended by my mother's family and assorted friends. The couple stayed on in Kalamazoo, and soon had their first child, a boy they named Remy. Even though my mother's family had accepted my father, one of her aunts still phoned my maternal grand-mother anxiously after the baby's birth. "Is he too dark?" she wanted to know.

The young family anxiously faced a changing world. Africa was rapidly decolonizing—my father's Congo had become independent in 1960—and American blacks were pursuing their rights with renewed vigor in a continuing struggle that was drastically transforming the American political and social landscape. "Black power," "black unity," and "black is beautiful" were for many blacks around the world the Afrocentric catchphrases of the day.

My parents were caught up in these heady political currents and decided to move to Congo in 1968. It was an era of political idealism and anticolonialist fervor in the United States and across Africa: black intellectuals like W.E.B. Du Bois had denounced American racism and moved to Africa, and there was a small exodus of young blacks visiting Africa to recapture their roots. My father, who had secured a job as an adviser to the Congolese minister of social affairs, happily envisioned the part he would play in his country's bright future, while my mother eagerly anticipated her "return" to Africa, looking forward to a glorious "homecoming" to an idyllic continent that occupied a romantic and mythical space in her mind.

For her, the reality was in many ways a shock. Kinshasa, the sprawling capital city, was vibrant and noisy but hardly idyllic. And my father's relatives seemed friendly and welcoming but highly judgmental; on one occasion, an uncle objected rather strenuously to being served a salad—the fact that she hadn't cooked the vegetables before placing them on the table seemed, in his eyes, to disqualify her as a successful bride. My mother felt she was being graded and evaluated every time she cooked or spoke to her new in-laws, as though her acceptance were subject to a rigorous examination process in which her performance of different tasks was observed, noted, and debated.

And there were so many relatives to remember. In most African extended families, distant cousins are all referred to as brothers or sisters, and my mother was rarely sure of the nature of her husband's relationship to the various people who constantly streamed through the house. One day while she was at the market, an unfamiliar young man greeted her joyously, introducing himself as her husband's "brother," a somewhat mystifying claim: my mother believed she had already met all of my father's siblings. He had accompanied her home and enjoyed a meal before my mother found out just exactly who he was in relation to her husband.

She could usually communicate in French, but for that first year, when the discourse shifted to Lingala, Kinshasa's other lingua franca, as it often did, she was completely lost. And to her, Lingala

sounded like a language spoken with almost warlike aggression: greetings were often shouted, and to her untrained ear, exclamations of joy
or celebration often sounded like expletives.

More ominously, she was shocked by the repressiveness of the government under which she now lived. She had always felt that the
black power and African anticolonial movements had been geared
toward gaining power for blacks so that they could better champion
their own destinies, but even with Africans in charge in the Congo, it
seemed that power was still in the wrong hands, used against the weak
instead of for them. Squalid shantytowns comprised large areas of
Kinshasa, while government ministers were chauffeured along the
smooth tarmac of downtown Kinshasa's store-lined Boulevard du
30 Juin in sleek black Mercedes-Benzes, the blue state flag flapping
mockingly from the cars' hoods. Rival political parties were illegal, as
were antigovernment demonstrations, and my mother often heard
hushed descriptions of the government's more odious repression techniques, which included torture and detention without charge or trial.

But even as she was angered and saddened by some of what was
happening around her, she was impressed with the resilience of Congolese, who somehow continued with their lives under such harsh
conditions. She marveled at the market women, who brought loads
of produce from the rural areas to sell in the marketplace every day,
balancing massive bundles on their heads while simultaneously carrying infants strapped to their backs. She admired the enterprising spirit
of the pushcart men who made their livings by heaving commissioned
loads through the busy city streets in their handmade carts. And she
was impressed with a people who always seemed ready to laugh and
dance even in times of great adversity.

Though my mother was bewildered by many aspects of her new
home, she grew quite attached to it, and began to forge friendships
with some of her in-laws, with neighbors, and among other African
Americans transplanted in Kinshasa. Remy, who was then two, also
grew to love his new home, learning to speak French and Lingala and
playing with neighborhood children in the house compound. Still my
mother was relieved to leave Congo in 1971, when my father won a
scholarship to pursue graduate study at a university outside Los Angeles. He had been as disgusted by the Congolese state's misuse of power
as my mother was, and he quickly decided that his contribution to the
nation's development, ironically enough, might be best made from
elsewhere; he eagerly seized the opportunity to continue his education
in the United States.

I was born in 1971 in Pomona, California, where my parents lived briefly while my father finished his master's degree. I was born both African and African American, but it took years for me to understand what that duality could mean, how it would make me struggle to span four hundred years of history, thousands of miles, and worlds of experience. My blackness has been the bridge that has linked my two identities, the commonality that my split selves share. But it often seems a tenuous link. And not just for me. I have traveled the world, with my race as my constant companion and curse, and everywhere I have seen black people bewildered by a strange tension between feeling powerfully bound by what they share and hopelessly repelled by what they do not. It's a strange contradiction, like feeling an instinctive kinship with a long-lost twin only to find that you have nothing in common, and perhaps even hate each other. What happens then? Do you just walk away?

My life has been, then, an experiment in an ideal, the testing of a pan-African hypothesis. And through my experiences as both an African and African American, I have found myself uniquely situated to observe and interpret the various dimensions and complexities of the tangled thicket that is African–African American relations.

As a student of history in high school in Africa and in college in the United States, I learned with interest of Marcus Garvey's Universal Negro Improvement Association of the 1920s, whose central tenet spoke of the inevitability and desirability of African Americans' "return" to Africa. I read of Ethiopian emperor Haile Selassie I's invitation to diaspora blacks to move to Africa to participate in the continent's development. I read about W.E.B. Du Bois's emigration to Ghana, where he died in 1963, and about Malcolm X's important and enlightening trips to Africa in the 1960s. These and many other examples all spoke to me of healthy spiritual and political ties between African Americans and Africans, a notion that seemed supported by my own experiences growing up in a household where Africans and African Americans crossed paths frequently and enthusiastically.

But while my reading told one story about pan-African unity, my experience often provided other, more complex lessons. When my family moved to Tanzania from Boston when I was eight, I was forced to revise many fantasies that I had held about Africa and my place in it as an African American. And similarly, my return to the United States for college in 1989 prompted me to revise many of the myths I had held about African America and my place in it as an African. I came to realize, as my mother had, that African Americans are not always embraced as long-lost kin when they visit or emigrate to the "mother-land." I also came to realize that many African Americans do not look on their African heritage with pride or even a sense of identification; and, as I learned personally and often painfully, many African Americans and Africans not only fail to identify with each other, but look on one another with scorn, resentment, or even hostility.

And even more fascinating to me than the ways in which Africans and African Americans clashed were the ways in which they thought about one another, the ideas that each group had created and assembled about the other. That ignorance and myths were prevalent on both sides was often disturbingly obvious. But I was intrigued by the fact that such established traditions of conceptualizing one another existed and by the functions such traditions seemed to serve. It seemed to me that Africans and African Americans were psychologically captivated by each other, and I came to regard the resulting misrepresentations as expressions of this preoccupation, which manifested itself in my own life in different ways.

I noticed that both Africans and African Americans have a tendency to borrow and celebrate cultural practices and icons from each other, often glorifying ideals that are more rooted in popular mythology than in reality. When I was growing up in Tanzania, African American youth culture had an extremely strong influence on my friends and me; Adidas sneakers, Michael Jackson, and Carl Lewis–style flat-top haircuts were all among the African American icons that we eagerly imitated when we saw them in the African American magazines, television shows, and music videos that found their way to Dar es Salaam. We absorbed and reinterpreted African American songs, fashions, and fads, and often put our own Tanzanian spin on them, singing Michael's songs with Kiswahili lyrics of local improvisation, and adding traditional African steps to African American breakdance routines.

I learned that a similar process takes place among African Americans. When my family would visit the United States from Tanzania my cousin Chris in L.A. used to ask us to bring him East African bracelets of copper and elephant hair, and "dashikis," the term that many African Americans use for the colorful, loose African shirts that in Tanzania mainly appealed to tourists. These items, and other "Afro-centric" gear, were popular among black American youth in the late eighties, at the height of hip-hop's flirtation with Afrocentrism. Some young American blacks also adopted African names (my cousin claimed he had a friend, Michael James, who "Africanized" his name by reversing it, to become "Leahcim Semaj") to go with their African accessories. And I can remember reading an interview with Big Daddy Kane, a rapper who was popular in the late eighties, in which he claimed that his towering high-top fade haircut (which most Tanzanian youth who imitated the style had assumed was an African American invention) came from ancient West Africa.

I began to realize that images, icons, and styles were recycled between Africa and the diaspora with little understanding of their original contexts. On one of my family's trips to the United States from Tanzania, the items most requested by my friends at home were leather medallions with maps of Africa on them. I reflected on how ironic it was that the medallions were worn by trendy African American hip-hop fans in a desire to celebrate their African heritage, and would be worn by my African friends back home in an attempt to emulate African Americans celebrating Africa. And I realized that despite this strange and perhaps distorted adulation of each other's cultural icons, Africans and African Americans celebrated mythical understandings of each other, and perhaps sometimes preferred the myths to the reality.

Africans and African Americans are bound in a multilayered and complex marriage, one often stormily complicated by misperceptions and misunderstandings that have sometimes caused a chilly distance to grow between the two sides. It is a simultaneous closeness and distance that has confounded and fascinated me throughout my life.

As a kid growing up in the Boston area, where my family moved when we left Pomona in 1972, I was often the rapt listener as my father told stories, tales of his youth in Congo and legends and myths he had heard from his mother around the communal fire of his village. He spoke of a clever antelope that constantly outwitted a stupid and clumsy leopard, of a man who used his ability to fly to avoid paying taxes, of a wizened witch doctor who could open doors into the realms of the spirits, and of a drunken uncle who never missed the Communion wine at the village church.

For my brothers and me, all born in the United States and better acquainted with the television culture of our American mother than with the mysterious world of Africa into which our father opened a peephole each night, the stories blurred the lines between fact and fiction and swelled with possibility.

We never really thought it remarkable that our father was from Congo and that our mother's family lived in Cleveland. The fact that

the most important condiment in our fridge was not ketchup but
pilipili, the ferocious, finely ground, scorchingly hot red peppers that
most Congolese refuse to eat without, and the fact that my parents
spoke French to each other, were to us more points of interest than
peculiarities that caused any sort of identity crisis, though we knew
that they somehow made us different from the Johnsons, the only
other black family on our street. We were too young and knew too little about Africa to identify as Africans in any meaningful way, and virtually everything we knew about Africa we learned from our father.
Through the tales he told, the village where he grew up acquired a
mythical and almost magical distance from the Boston suburb where
we lived, and I longed to visit this strange place, Africa, which my father still referred to as home.

My parents planned to move back to Africa in the near future, but
before they had a chance to explore the possibility, my family was afflicted by a terrible tragedy. In 1978 Remy, who was then twelve, was
diagnosed with leukemia, and as his illness advanced he was admitted
to the children's cancer ward at a Boston hospital. My mother spent
nights at the hospital with my brother, and her face began to reveal
her stress. On visits to the hospital, I would spend time with my
brother and then look in on my listless mother, who was sleeping in
an adjacent hospital room, reduced to an invalid in her own right,
emotionally devastated by my brother's illness even as she tried to care
for him from day to day. Remy died in 1979, after a year in and out of
hospitals.

The months following my brother's death were a difficult and
painful period of slow recovery; we all reeled under the cruel blow.
Remy had been my best friend, and I grappled with rage and profound loneliness when he was gone. My parents drew into themselves
for a time, and seemed hard pressed to comfort each other, much less
my brothers and me. Even though my younger brothers were a little
too young to understand what was going on, they sensed the loss and
sadness that enshrouded our home.

In the end it was Africa that intervened to restore my family's hope.
My father was offered a job teaching history at the national university
in Dar es Salaam, Tanzania. He knew it was time to go home, and decided to seize the opportunity. At first my mother was hesitant to
leave Boston, because she felt that leaving for Africa so soon after the
death of her firstborn, who was buried in Waltham, Massachusetts,
would distance her from his memory. But in a series of emotional discussions, my father convinced her that Remy's memory would tran-

scend geography and that he would continue to live inside all of us; my mother agreed, and in 1980 my family moved to Dar es Salaam, Tanzania.

Tanzania was a new playground, brimming with potential discoveries and fresh possibilities, and the move seemed good for everyone's morale. My brothers and I roamed the white sand beaches and swam in the Indian Ocean; we played tag in cashew nut trees and learned Kiswahili from our playmates. It was a glorious time of new experiences and exploration.

At eight I was really too young to suffer consciously from some of the disillusionment with which many African Americans experience their first trip to Africa (as my mother had when she first visited Congo in 1968). And I was too young to grapple in a serious way with issues of identity; when my playmates wanted to know where I was from and to what tribe I belonged, they (and I) were usually satisfied when I said that I had been born in America and that my father was a Mukongo from Zaire (as Congo had been renamed in 1971) and my mother an American. But I can remember a few incidents that forced me to consider the implications of my American background.

On one occasion, soon after we had moved to Dar es Salaam, my mother, my brothers, and I took a shortcut to the store through a neighborhood just outside the university campus, where my family lived in faculty housing. As we walked through the complex of dingy state-owned bungalows, barefoot children playing in the dust saw our American sneakers and jeans and the other subtle signifiers of our Americanness, and pursued us, playfully chanting "Wazungu, wazungu!" I spoke enough Kiswahili at that point to know that "wazungu" referred to non-Africans in general, and to white people in particular. The taunts wounded me. Why did they see us as outsiders when we were blacks returned from America to our rightful homeland? I wondered. After that experience, I took pains to blend in, donning shorts, thong sandals, and T-shirts like most Tanzanian boys my age; after I adjusted my wardrobe in this manner, and after I learned enough Kiswahili to sound like a native, I was rarely "exposed" as a foreigner again.

But I still struggled with the duality of my identity; I was unable to fully transform myself into a complete Tanzanian. In my third-grade class, which was conducted primarily in Kiswahili, the teacher once used the spiritual "Swing Low, Sweet Chariot" as part of an English lesson; when the class laughed at the unfamiliar sounds and joked around jovially, mangling the lyrics and deliberately distorting the melody, I felt personally offended. Didn't they know that this was a song that had been sung by African American slaves and as such should be approached reverentially? I seethed with silent indignation.

A similar chord was struck by my first trip to Zanzibar, a small and beautiful island off Tanzania's coast, where slaves from the mainland had been held in caves before being exported to the Middle East and Europe during the days of the East African slave trade. My brothers, my mother, an African American friend of hers, and I made a week-end trip to the island to see its sites of interest. As we inspected the dank, dark slave caverns, one of many stops on our guided tour, I was moved almost to tears. Maybe my mother's ancestors had been held in this very cave before being taken to America, I pondered sadly. And I wondered if the fact that my family had now returned to our es-tranged homeland mattered to anyone but us. Our guide seemed bored, leading us, a group of tourists, to yet another of his island's many attractions, a cave he must have seen thousands of times. I saw the site as a tragic torture chamber where my own relatives might have suffered hundreds of years ago; I wondered what our guide, or any other Tanzanian, saw. Did they see a blood-drenched pit where their abducted kin had been held against their will, or an ancient ruin where distant and vaguely recalled historical dramas had unfolded long ago, a dullish tourist attraction like the tomb of some nineteenth-century white missionary? And did they see my family as the descen-dants of their enslaved ancestors, or as just another group of tourists, exploitable sources of income? Or, even more sinisterly, were they themselves descended from an African family that had participated in and benefited from the slave trade? Did they therefore see the caves as a perhaps unpleasant, but nonetheless profitable, monument to an important economic engine of history?

The sense of alienation these experiences created was fleeting, how-ever, and within two years of moving to Tanzania I felt at home, learn-ing fluent Kiswahili, playing barefoot soccer with my new friends, and becoming more distanced from my American identity.

My mother also ultimately found this second "return" to Africa a positive experience. She was enchanted by the beautiful East African scenery—the tropical beaches and the palm tree–studded landscapes. She found work as a French teacher at the local international school, which catered to the children of foreign diplomats and foreign-aid agency employees. She began to enjoy the relaxed routine and the slow pace of life in the humid coastal city, making weekly trips to the beach and frequenting local open-air markets. She even learned how to laugh at the frustratingly common shortages of essential commodities like bread and sugar, and managed not to be too exasperated by the frequent electrical blackouts and water shortages.

She learned about Tanzanian culture in a Kiswahili course at the University of Dar es Salaam and through her interactions with Tanzanians she met at work, at the market, and in our neighborhood near the university campus. And she also made friends in the small community of black Americans and West Indians who lived in Dar es Salaam. Many had come to Tanzania in the 1970s, inspired by the then popular black consciousness and pan-Africanist movements, and though the reality of life in Africa didn't usually square with the romantic expectations of black American newcomers, some had settled in Dar es Salaam as teachers and businesspeople, and regarded Tanzania as a newfound home.

My "uncle" Jan was a motorcycle-riding management professor from Milwaukee who sported a magnificent Afro and had dreams of establishing a dynasty in Tanzania; he gave his children African names, filled his house with African carvings in ebony and with other local art, and began construction on an impressive mansion near the beach. He was reluctant to accept some elements of his adopted culture, however: he was too proud to feel comfortable using the Kiswahili greeting *shikamoo*, a salutation reserved for respected elders, which literally means "I hold your feet."

Edie Wilson, a management consultant from Washington, D.C., who had first come to Tanzania in the 1960s, became known as Aunt Edie in my house and in many other black expatriate households in Dar es Salaam. She taught at a management training school in Morogoro, a beautiful mountainous region in eastern Tanzania, and was building a large house there for herself and her children, nieces, and nephews back in the United States. She spoke grammatically flawless Kiswahili but was never really able to shake her distinctive Washingtonian accent.

Uncle Jan, Aunt Edie, and others would gather with my mother to play bid whist, a card game popular among many black Americans, and to exchange experiences as black Americans who had "returned" to a sometimes baffling motherland. The group sometimes spoke disdainfully of blacks who arrived in Africa and were so stunned by the reality that greeted them that they returned to the United States in frustration.

Once, for example, a group of professors from black colleges in the United States came to Dar es Salaam as part of an African tour; many of them had their hair in dreadlocks, wore colorful African patterns, and spoke the impassioned rhetoric of pan-Africanism. But throughout their trip some of them complained about the food, they complained about the heat, they complained about their accommodations, and they seemed to wonder why no one was more helpful. They returned to the United States in bewildered indignation.

My mother and some of her friends took a dim view of such people and regarded them as naive; they seemed to feel that by staying in Dar es Salaam and enduring the relative inconvenience of life there, reconciling their expectations of Africa with the reality, they had earned the right to look down on those who couldn't. But it was a similar idealism that had brought many of them to the continent, and some still harbored a mythical and romantic understanding of Africa.

In 1981 my family was forced to confront a crisis that devastated us all, and, for me, in some ways demystified the often rosy conception of Africa that had dominated my childhood. For our Christmas vacation that year, my parents planned a visit to Zaire. It was to be the first time that my younger brothers, Kolo and James, and I set foot in the country of our father's birth, the first time we met his family. My father, whose vacation began earlier than ours (after two years in state schools, my brothers and I had begun to attend the international school where my mother taught French), went on ahead, resolving to meet us at the airport in Kinshasa.

He never made it. Instead, my mother, my brothers and I were met by members of the Zairean secret police, and a representative from the U.S. Embassy, who greeted us with the news of my father's arrest for the possession of "subversive documents," essays he had written that were critical of the Zairean regime. He was imprisoned for five weeks without formal charge or trial, in a notorious Zairean jail where he was routinely beaten, and was held under "city arrest" (in which he was confined to Kinshasa's city limits) for a year after that. At the time, of course, we had no idea when he would be allowed to rejoin us in Tanzania.

This experience completely soured my perceptions of my father's homeland, and ran a knife through all the naive expectations I'd based on the legends and stories he had told me when I was a child in Boston. Aside from my two years of living in Tanzania, an experience that had been overwhelmingly positive, my understanding of Africa came from my father, who had tried hard to provide my brothers and me with positive images to counter the stereotypical representations we regularly saw in the U.S. media and on television. Perhaps he overcompensated in his efforts; when my family moved to Tanzania, I knew that my neighbors would not be wearing grass skirts and carrying spears like the Sambo character who occasionally appeared in Bugs Bunny cartoons, and I knew enough to be offended by such images; I also knew we'd have running water and electricity, and live in a city. But I had no idea that it was common for black-led governments across Africa to jail or even kill anyone critical of their policies, and to do so with impunity. My father's arrest and the fear and hostility that then pervaded my perception of Zaire savaged the idea of Africa represented to me by him and even called into question my own growing attachment to Tanzania. I felt as though I had been lied to and betrayed. Africa was not a mystical, magical, and beautiful place, as I had thought; instead it was a place inhabited by evil and dangerous men—black men, at that—who had imprisoned and beaten my father and easily could have chosen to kill him. My naive romance with Africa was over.

When I returned to the United States to attend school in 1987, I found that my place in African America seemed equally tenuous. Before I left home I had looked forward to meeting other African American students and to finding a welcoming community among them. Later, during freshman week at Harvard, I attended an introductory meeting of the Black Students Association, but felt out of place; the experiences and preoccupations of the African Americans in the group seemed largely foreign to me. I wanted desperately to feel comfortable, but didn't. Some of my new classmates were excited and interested to hear that I was from Africa, but after a few exchanges, it often seemed that we had little to talk about.

I went to an introductory meeting of the campus gospel choir, attracted by its Kiswahili name, Kuumba, which means creativity. The choir performed in African robes of mud-cloth and kente, the royal Ashanti cloth from Ghana that has become popular among African Americans, and even had "Nkosi Sikelel' iAfrika" ("God Bless Africa"), the South African anti-apartheid anthem, in their repertoire. But it all felt sort of artificial to me. Members of the group asked me what "Kuumba" meant, and few in the audience stood when the choir sang the South African anthem. I decided to save my singing for the shower.

Black members of the freshman class often formed a conspicuously segregated table in the dining hall, and I usually sat at it, but I often had little to say. I began to wonder what I really had in common with these people besides my race, and whether race was such a valid unifier after all. This point was underscored by an encounter with an African American woman I had become friendly with in the first weeks of my first year. During a lull in one conversation she began singing one of Kuumba's gospel songs to herself absentmindedly. She asked me if I knew it. When I said no, she replied, "Oh, yeah, I forgot, you're not one of us." She could have meant that I wasn't a member of Kuumba, but I don't think so.

You're not one of us. The words echoed in my mind throughout my college years, as other events underlined their truth. Who am I? I often wondered. If not one of them, then one of whom?

I was forced to confront the possibility that my expectations of instant rapport and meaningful links between myself and other black students on campus, and therefore pan-Africanism itself, were rooted in a perhaps mistaken notion. Blacks all over the world often assume or expect to share enough with blacks elsewhere to build a significant sense of unity, and such unity is understood to be essential in confronting and combating racism around the world. This is such a powerful expectation that emotions tend to run high when we discuss it, and few dare to critique it. And we often feel devastated or strangely disoriented and indignant when our expectations go unfulfilled.

Despite my disorientation, I was able to find a home in the Harvard African Students Association, a group of twenty or so from all over the continent. HASA was essentially social, sponsoring cultural events and sometimes inviting guest speakers to discuss African issues, but for me it evolved into an extended family of sorts, friends among whom I felt comfortable and who understood me when I spoke longingly of home. Many of them shared my ambivalence toward the Black Students Association, and some even had theories as to why such distance existed between the African and African American contingents at Harvard and at every other campus we visited. A Nigerian friend said that African Americans resented Africans because our ancestors had sold theirs into slavery. Someone else said that African Americans were wary of Africans because we forced them to confront their misperceptions of Africa. And I had heard black American students complain that Africans were "taking over," that we were "overrepresented" in Harvard's black student body and overrunning African American communities. Back then, I never really understood why the rift seemed to exist, but it was something I grappled with constantly, because even though I tended to identify more strongly with my African side, I often felt stuck in the middle, both African and American and unable to bridge the gap between the two. African Americans usually saw me as an African, and though I didn't often admit it, many Africans, both at Harvard and at home in Tanzania, considered me an American, or at best an inauthentic hybrid.

Politics at Harvard offered other puzzles. Early on I sought out the local anti-apartheid group, the Southern African Solidarity Committee, which was mainly devoted to campaigning for Harvard's divestment from companies which did business in South Africa. At the introductory meeting I was astounded to find that the group was almost entirely white. Other blacks came and went in the years of my involvement, but the group remained mostly white, an apparent contradiction I was never able to fully explain or feel comfortable with. I was stunned by the lack of interest with which many of the African American students regarded the activities of organizations like the Southern African Solidarity Committee. I couldn't understand why more African American students didn't express outrage at the situation in South Africa, why more didn't feel that their experiences and destinies were closely paralleled and perhaps even linked to those of South Africans, who combated a system of racialized privilege and oppression so similar to the one that had long endured in the United States. African American leaders and activists were at the forefront of the anti-apartheid movement internationally, but among black Harvard students there seemed a distinct lack of interest in the struggle. Some blacks told me confidentially that they were wary of organizations like the committee because they were predominantly white, but such arguments struck me as ridiculous, perpetuating a cycle in which progressive political organizations remained all-white because they were all-white, and potential black activists remained inactive because they were mistrustful of all-white organizations.

I also found that most African American students just didn't strongly identify with African political issues; they felt that these weren't their battles or their concerns. Few attended anti-apartheid rallies or political panel discussions held by the African Students Association. Once HASA even sponsored a miniconference on Africa in which one of the panelists publicly (and embarrassingly) noted the dearth of brown faces in the audience, wondering aloud if the organization had sufficiently advertised the event and if the Africans and African Americans at Harvard actually spoke to one another. African Americans were enthusiastic activists concerning issues that were closer to home and more explicitly "African American"; they took over one of the administration buildings to protest the university's lack of support for the declining Afro-American Studies Department, and marched to protest a case in which a black Harvard student was falsely arrested by a white Harvard cop (both initiatives in which African students also became involved). But when it came to African issues like apartheid, the civil war in Angola, and the abuses of power by dictators like Zaire's Mobutu Sese Seko, whose regime had imprisoned my own father, African American students showed considerably less interest.

My younger brother Kolo has had similar experiences. He attended a small liberal arts university in a small and sleepy Connecticut town, and we both found returning to the United States for higher education after years of adaptation and assimilation in Africa an often traumatic experience laced with culture shock and confusion. Throughout our studies we often felt the need to commiserate with each other and seek brotherly support in this wilderness of North America. But he was in his third year at college before he first commented to me on the divide that he felt between him and many of his African American classmates.

He called me on one evening at the close of a hectic week, sounding tired and somewhat troubled. I said nothing, knowing that Kolo would get to whatever was on his mind when he was good and ready. After talking briefly of his classes, his music (he plays viola and bass guitar), his job as a teaching assistant, and the perils of the New England snowstorm he had just survived, Kolo told me he had recently attended a political rally to call for a retrial for Mumia Abu-Jamal, an African American death row inmate in Pennsylvania whose conviction for the murder of a police officer has been called questionable by many human rights activists. Kolo's voice slowed as he sidled up to what he had to say. "How was it?" I prompted.

"Cool," he replied. "But I kind of got upset about something." He paused.

"What happened?" I asked.

"Well," he said, softly and tentatively, almost guiltily, "since I got here I've felt like the African American students have been dissing me." He described a list of incidents that he perceived as slights by his African American classmates. How during freshman week he had automatically, as a young black man adrift among unfamiliar white folks, sat at the inevitable "black table" in the cafeteria, but after a few exchanges with his tablemates had lapsed into silence since no one seemed interested in talking to him once he identified himself as an African. How some black classmates wouldn't readily respond to his "Whassup?" when he passed them on the campus paths. How a black woman, in an attempt to explain his ostracism by some African American students, had told him he spent too much time with whites and "acted too white." Kolo told how, recently, on his way to the rally—it was held at a neighboring campus—the only person in a largely black group of protesters who offered him a ride was a white woman in stereotypical nineties neo-hippie gear.

Throughout his undergraduate years Kolo was usually clad in baggy jeans and a sweatshirt, and he sported a crown of dreadlocks, like some of his black classmates. But as the only black student in his academic department (physics), and as one whose relatively non-racialized way of viewing people led him to seek friends among various communities on campus, he was often in the company of whites. He is studious, speaks precise and slightly East African–accented English, and flavors his diction with Kiswahili expressions as well as African American slang. A violist, he was one of a handful of black musicians in the university orchestra, and his CD collection contains music by Mozart and Bach as well as hip-hop by Snoop Doggy Dogg and the Wu-Tang Clan and African music by Manu Dibango and Franco. And early in his undergraduate career he chose to live in International House, a residence shared by many of the college's foreign students, instead of Malcolm X House, the dorm of choice for many black students. Many of his black peers seemed to hold these choices against him.

Kolo had come to discover what many Africans in the United States soon realize: African American attitudes toward Africans are often colored by enthusiastic celebrations of an ideological concept of "Africa," but when confronted with "real" Africans, many African Americans dismiss them as "too white." Kolo had thought about this apparent paradox during and after the rally, and had slid deeper and deeper into a despairing and uncomprehending depression. "Man, I was almost in tears that day," he finished finally.

I was saddened, but not surprised, by Kolo's words. As he spoke, incidents of hostility, derision, and missed connections between Africans and African Americans from my own experience flashed through my mind. I remembered all the hurtful offhand comments and unkind remarks: An African American woman's warning to her girlfriend not to cross a student from Africa lest she "take after you with a spear"; a woman in Harlem who said she disliked Africans because they came to New York in droves and took jobs away from African Americans; a friend from Senegal who referred to African Americans as "Yo's" (because of a stereotypical penchant for the word "yo") and regarded them as lazy, welfare-happy freeloaders; an undergraduate from Ghana who said she felt ostracized by American blacks and angrily questioned their right to be called "African" Americans; my African uncle's look of concern and mistrust and his warning to "be careful" when I told him of my relationship with an African American woman from a low-income black neighborhood in Boston; an African American radio DJ's stereotypical jokes and exaggerated accent mimicry at the expense of Nigerian-born NBA basketball star Hakeem Olajuwon; the sharp divisions and near rivalry between African American and African student organizations at practically every college campus I had ever visited. I had heard Kolo's story before, and had had numerous similar experiences myself, but was not much closer to explaining them as I attempted to console him that day than I had been when I first rudely awakened to the fact that Africans and the descendants of Africans in the diaspora are not just one, big, happy, extended black family.

In confronting conflicts, attitudes, and misunderstandings like these, I had come into an appreciation of the complexity of African-American relations and into a realization of the misperceptions that often informed them. And many Africans and African Americans who come into contact with each other in Africa or the United States have had similarly rude and perplexing awakenings to the existence of disunity, hostility, and confounded misunderstanding between blacks from Africa and African Americans. African American and African leaders and commentators have long acknowledged the tremendous ignorance, stereotyping, and misapprehensions on both sides. One prominent African American civil rights leader admitted that "psychologically, we've been brainwashed to believe that Africa was the dark continent, a place of crocodiles and Tarzan." And the Organization of African Unity's ambassador to the United Nations once conceded regretfully that "when Black Americans believe the images they see in Tarzan movies, this is a problem . . . and it is just as much of a problem when Africans believe all Black Americans are all lazy drug addicts."

Some have tentatively proposed ways to correct such misperceptions. One African American politician suggested that black leaders work to create "more opportunities for us to develop mutual respect and credibility and end the great void in understanding," and others have striven to do that work. In 1991 the "first-ever African/African American summit," with the stated goal of building the sort of links "that the Irish have with Ireland, that the Jews have with Israel," was held in the Ivory Coast and attended by hundreds of African and African American politicians, professors, dignitaries, and professionals. The gathering took place in a euphoric atmosphere, almost giddy with brotherhood and goodwill. The Reverend Leon Sullivan, the African American leader who organized the conference, made a rousing declaration of unity and commitment in the opening speech: "Home of our heritage, land of our past, we can help. We have 2 million college graduates in America. We earn $300 billion a year. Three centuries ago they took us away in a boat, but today we have come back in an airplane!" Coretta Scott King, Martin Luther King's widow, who was also in attendance, proclaimed that "Martin's presence is surely with us today. This summit has within it the possibilities of getting us to the Promised Land."

While valuable in a symbolic sense, the conference was attacked by African and African American critics who felt it was too long on rhetoric and too short on substance. Some spoke of hypocrisy when African American leaders visited the then Ivoirian premier, Felix Houphouet-Boigny, who had been criticized by human rights groups for decades, in his mansion, and praised his political record as "impeccable."

"That is not the real Africa," one Ivoirian conference attendee said of the Americans' trip to the premier's home, where they dined on food imported from Europe. "I hope the Americans know this. The real Africa is in the slums and in the villages. That is our reality."

"I wish some of these Americans would take to the streets with us instead of supporting the old order," mused an Ivoirian student.

Though the conference was originally intended to be an annual event, two years passed before the next one was held, and it foundered on some of the same issues as the first. Many wondered why the second conference was held in Mali, a state whose leader had been accused of election tampering in the country's first multiparty elections, held in 1990, when democracies were slowly emerging elsewhere on the continent. And others still complained of too much talk and not enough practical action. "We have to move beyond romance to finance, beyond causes to contracts," conference participant Jesse Jackson declared with a characteristic turn of phrase. And many realized with frustration what Dick Gregory, the African American political activist and comedian, took home from the first African–African American summit: "We represent a potent political force in the world if we can marshal our resources and reunite," he said then. "But first, we have a lot to learn about each other."

While learning about one another is a worthy goal that most Africans and African Americans seem to share, many have realized that interacting with each other on a personal level inevitably entails a sometimes traumatic debunking of preconceived myths and a reevaluation of expectations of automatic kinship. One African American woman who visited Uganda described her disappointment and surprise at "the wide gap between many of our commonly held perceptions and the reality in Africa," and was saddened to find that some Africans "held indifferent or negative views of African Americans."

On the other side of the ocean, a Kenyan living in Pennsylvania complained that her daughter had been "harassed by a bunch of neighborhood kids, all Black, who had showered her with insults like 'voodoo kid,' 'African dog,' and 'African monkey,' " and lamented that many African Americans are "totally oblivious to the fact that we, as Africans living in America, look upon our African American brothers and sisters as family. And when a member of your family slaps you in the face the pain is a lot sharper than if a stranger had done it."

In addition to bemoaning African American failures to see Africans as kin, many Africans have long complained about a lack of African American empathy for African economic hardship. In the mid-1980s, when famine struck East Africa, a Senegalese U.N. official decried African American indifference to African affairs and expressed an almost indignant sense of reproach that American blacks had not immediately rushed to Africa's aid. "At a time when Ethiopia and other countries are facing the worst drought in living memory, Africans are wondering: where are the black Americans?" he remonstrated.

Africans leveled similar charges against African Americans at a pan-African cultural festival in Ghana in 1994. "There were friendly greetings extended to long lost 'brothers' that many American visitors clearly cherished," one journalist wrote of the event. "[But] there were also candid rebukes for the Americans' superficial knowledge of the continent and the failure of American blacks to pitch in with their wealth and expertise to help Africa." African participants in the festival were also said to denounce the lack of African American involvement in the fledgling African democratization movement, lamenting that "black Americans make noise about Haiti but then come here and hobnob with political elites that often have blood on their hands."

Adding further complexity to the apparent division, an African American countered the charges with a criticism of his own. "Until there is an admission of African involvement in the slave trade, the healing process will be difficult to realize," he said.

Interestingly, as this comment indicates, discussions and conceptions of slavery have also served to divide Africans and African Americans, who often seem to approach the slave trade and its legacy, perhaps appropriately, from entirely different directions.

In one tellingly symbolic confrontation, Africans and African Americans in Ghana became sorely divided over the Ghanaian government's plan to renovate some slave dungeons along the coast and turn them into tourist attractions in 1995. In protest, a group of black Americans staged a two-night fast and sleepover in the dungeons. "The average Ghanaian doesn't understand what we're so upset about," one African American demonstrator grumbled. "They think we're being overemotional troublemakers."

In quite a different clash of viewpoints, at a 1996 conference in Boston on recent reports of slavery in Sudan, the proceedings were disrupted by a spokesman from the Nation of Islam. The Nation's leader, Louis Farrakhan, had recently visited Sudan on a goodwill trip and considered the Sudanese government an ally, despite the fact that it was accused of numerous human rights abuses. So to defend Sudan against charges of condoning modern-day slavery, the NOI spokesman who attended the conference refuted the claims of the members of a conference panel, two journalists who claimed to have purchased slaves in Sudan, and Raphael Abeim, a Sudanese exile and student who said that members of his family were abducted by slave catchers. The Nation spokesman dismissed the reports of slavery in Sudan as a "Zionist Jewish" fabrication, and called the entire panel "hypocrites and damn liars," labeling Abeim a "hanky-headed, scared-to-death nigger."

The incredible irony of having an African American denounce and dismiss the claims of an African who said his family had been enslaved was not lost on the Sudanese student. "It's a shame I have to stand and prove to you that my family has been enslaved," he later responded, with morose understatement.

While zealous black American Africaphiles like Farrakhan have often seemed to cling to a utopian vision of Africa, refusing to accept any criticism of African governments, regardless of what their own people have to say about them, at the other extreme are African Americans who have become so disappointed by African realities that they wash their hands of Africa entirely. One example is Keith Richburg, a *Washington Post* reporter who covered Africa in the early 1990s and wrote an article about his deeply disillusioning experiences there, three years in which he chronicled famines, wars, and other newsworthy disasters for the *Post*. Like many African American travelers to Africa, Richburg had approached his first trip to the continent with an optimistic eagerness, excitedly anticipating his "return" to an ancestral homeland. However, when he was not welcomed to Africa as a long-lost son, and after years of being bombarded by spectacles of poverty, brutality, greed, and corruption, Richburg was understandably appalled; he began to feel very differently about his estranged "motherland." Having experienced Africa as a chaotic wasteland where survival was difficult and life was cheap, he eventually came to conclude that he wanted no part of it. In fact, in what for me was his most heart-wrenching statement, Richburg wrote that while covering the Rwandan genocide that left hundreds of thousands dead in 1994, he felt so moved by the carnage that he thankfully reflected on the accident of history that made him an American and not an African. He gratefully celebrated his ancestor's abduction from Africa as his own deliverance from the possibility of a life of drudgery and death. As he writes,

> If [my] original ancestor hadn't been forced to make that horrific voyage, I would not have been standing there that day on the Rusumo Falls bridge, a journalist—a mere spectator—watching the bodies glide past me like river logs. No, I might instead be one of them—or have met some similarly anonymous fate in any one of the countless ongoing civil wars or tribal clashes on this brutal continent. And I thank God my ancestor made that voyage.

This quote appeared in an article that Richburg later expanded into a full-length book, *Out of America: A Black Man Confronts Africa*. Though in the longer work he softened some of the statements expressing his distaste for the continent of his ancestors, Richburg still lashed out at the very idea of black kinship. "Talk to me about Africa and my black roots and my kinship with my African brothers and I'll throw it back in your face, and then I'll rub your nose in the images of the rotting flesh," he writes venomously.

Reading such statements, I felt angry and sad. I wanted to remind this writer that there was more to Africa than war and chaos; I wanted to tell him that I knew another Africa, a place where hardworking people lived peacefully and purposefully and were as appalled by violence as he was. I wanted to point out that I could just as easily thank God that my father's ancestors had not been enslaved in America, and that I had grown up in Africa and thus been delivered from the "ongoing tribal clashes" that have claimed so many young black men in America's war-torn urban communities; and to let Richburg know that my parents in Africa regard America as a brutal killing field, a jungle they hope their sons will survive. But most of all, I wanted to tell him the same thing I told Kolo when his sadness at having been repeatedly snubbed by his African American classmates began to turn to anger and resentment: Africans and African Americans cannot afford to opt out of coming to terms with one another—we need each other.

Richburg's disillusionment, sadly, is nothing new. Many African Americans who travel to Africa seem to grapple with similar feelings, and jarring experiences of alienation seem an integral part of most personal accounts by black Americans of voyages to the motherland. Eddy Harris, who journeyed across Africa from Tunisia in the north down through western and central Africa to Johannesburg in the south, had mixed emotions about his trip but acknowledged his own estrangement from the places and people he encountered. "My skin is black. My culture is not," he concluded after feeling relieved to reach South Africa. "After almost a year in Africa I have no answers. Only this one question remains: *Who am I?* I have more in common, it sometimes seems, with the Dutch Afrikaner, the Boer. . . . I could no more return to Africa and live than I could live on the moon."

And the knife cuts both ways. A Burundian journalist who grew up idolizing Muhammad Ali toured a handful of U.S. cities in 1998, interviewing the African Americans he met, but became deeply disillusioned by the experience. He had hoped to collect enough stories to return home with a detailed report, so that "Africans could learn more about the black people of America." But instead of finding the "heart beating for Africa" that he had hoped, he learned that many black Americans had little interest in the continent. And after being met with condescension, ignorance, and hostility in inner-city neighborhoods where people were rarely friendly or helpful, he came to feel humiliated, disappointed, and even afraid. "I was terrified in the country of the African American," he concluded in his disheartened final report. "More terrified than I have been in even the most dangerous regions of the African continent."

I have observed many conflicts between Africans and African

Americans, and I've heard the stereotypes, misperceptions, and hostility on both sides. But while I've lamented the missed connections and misunderstandings, I've also seen Africans come together around issues of mutual interest and applauded the forging of new points of contact and unity. I've listened to African Americans spouting fantasies about Africa and Africans, and to Africans repeating their own legends and fables about the blacks of America. But I've also seen the functions that such mythologies have served and the impressive cultural monuments that imaginings and dreams of blacks across the sea have produced. I've heard some Africans and African Americans reject the idea of meaningful transatlantic bonds, but I've also heard many others fervently reaffirm the existence and importance of such ties. And in watching this process of interchange and exchange, and in always being struck by the sheer intensity of the emotions at play, I've retained a belief in the existence of a powerful, intangible, and heartfelt connection binding us, something that is ultimately fundamental to who we are as Africans and African Americans.

African Americans have long sought to derive a sense of self, identity, and pride from their conceptions of Africa and Africans, to develop an antidote to the disoriented rootlessness of a people who slave masters insisted were orphans of a shameful and brutish motherland. And Africans have at various moments in history looked to blacks in America with a similar sense of identification and fraternity, hoping for and offering assistance and support, and identifying and exploring real and imagined commonalities. These potent passions and their lively interplay have fueled cultural innovations, political partnerships, rich mythologies, empowering social movements, and an international system of travel, exchange, circulation, and recycling in which black voyagers, writers, leaders, activists, and artists constructed a transatlantic black kinship.

This emotional obsession has had a powerful impact on many figures in black history, and many have drawn strength and inspiration from it. W.E.B. Du Bois identified "the problem of the color line" as the key issue of the twentieth century and authored pan-African initiatives to mobilize the nonwhite world to fight for global equality. His exploration of the ties between black Americans and Africans was politically prescriptive as well as romantic: he passionately referred to Africa as "the land of my forefathers," but it was primarily the continent's potential political strength that he sought to tap. "My tie to Africa is strong," Du Bois wrote in 1940. "On this vast continent were born and lived a large portion of my direct ancestors going back a thousand years or more. . . . Since the fifteenth century these ancestors of mine and their other descendants have had a common history; have suffered a common disaster and have one long memory. . . . The real essence of this kinship is its social heritage of slavery. . . . It is this unity that draws me to Africa."

The African American writer Ralph Ellison recognized the fires that attracted black Americans to Africa for what they were: "It is not culture which binds the peoples who are of partially African origin now scattered throughout the world," he wrote in 1964, "but an identity of passions." And even while he ridiculed the more utopian black American expressions of attachment to Africa in his masterwork, *Invisible Man* (1952), he seemed somewhat moved by the very emotions he so eloquently described in his interrogation of the ties connecting blacks on two continents. Malcolm X, in his own reinvention of himself and in his political evolution, came into a passionate and proud identification with Africa and was reinforcing personal and political ties with African leaders when he was assassinated.

Feelings have run high on the African side as well. Kwame Nkrumah forged important personal and political ties with African Americans as a student at black colleges in the United States in the 1930s and informed his leadership in independent Ghana with a pan-African sense of political kinship with African American struggles for civil rights and self-determination, welcoming black Americans to participate in Africa's political future. And South African Archbishop Desmond Tutu has expressed his belief in intangible bonds between blacks around the world in more spiritual terms. "All of us have roots that go deep into the warm soil of Africa," he wrote in 1979. "So that no matter how long and traumatic our separation from our ancestral home has been, there are things we are often unable to articulate, but which we feel in our very bones, things which make us, who are different from others who have not suckled the breasts of our mother, Africa."

Many other Africans and African Americans have struggled with the contradictions this abstract sense of kinship has sometimes presented. Some, confounded by the ways in which idealized expectations are often dashed against the hard rocks of reality, were shamed and hurt into rejecting the feelings and assumptions that had led them to explore the relationship in the first place. Some African students like Mugo Gatheru, a Kenyan who studied in America in the 1930s, were dazed by the ignorance, unfamiliarity, and occasional hostility of black Americans they met; they wondered if they had been mistaken in their belief in bonds binding peoples of ancestral African origin. James Baldwin called the cultural and historical chasm separating African Americans and Africans "a gulf of three hundred years— an alienation too vast to be conquered in an evening's goodwill," and seemed deeply disappointed and burdened by the enormity of what he thought divided them, "the memory of the auction block." Much more recently, Keith Richburg's traumatic sense of estrangement from the bewildering and incomprehensible African basket case he covered as a journalist reduced him to a hollowly jingoistic celebration of his own rescue from his ancestors' "brutal" continent, and to gratitude for the disaster that bestowed on them American nationality and cultural identity. "Thank God that I am an American," he exulted, after his sojourn in savage Africa, rejecting the idea that any homeland but mother America could lay claim to his loyalty and identification.

In shaping a sense of who they were as individuals and communities, black people all over the world have looked to one another, building on what they imagined they shared and sometimes defining themselves in opposition to what they felt they did not. This process of looking across an ocean at one another, of reaching out to one another through various mediums, these acts of mythmaking and self-making, are central to black history in Africa and America. It's been a powerful force in my life and that of millions of black people through history. It's pushed us in different directions; at its best, it's inspired us to impressive heights of creativity and empowered us to collectively begin to take control of our lives and histories; at its worst, it has sown seeds of alienation and division, distorting our sense of who we are in relation to one another with so much smoke and mirrors.

But perhaps more significant than the specific ways in which this "identity of passions" has moved us is the fact that it *has*, so profoundly, for so long. Conceptions of Africa and notions of a historical connection to the "motherland" have prompted African Americans to change their own names and that of their ethnic community; they have influenced black music, literature, fashion, hairstyles, language, politics, and culture. And among Africans, ideas about African Americans have sparked similar innovations and processes. The ways in which we have historically related to one another (and to notions and imaginings of one another) form an important part of our shared heritage.

Some scholars have regarded such conceptions as wholly a response to racism, a defensive "circling of the wagons" as negative as the socially constructed prejudices they evolved to confront. Others dismissively characterize the attitudes that have fueled pan-African trends and movements as "romantic racialism" or even a form of false consciousness, myths and fantasies of little or even damaging consequence. But even if notions of black kinship are merely that, their powerful legacy and the passions they arouse have armed them with a significance not as easily dismissed. Perhaps a sense of kinship, which has been a driving force for so much, exists simply because so many black people have felt it and been spurred to act because of it. We've seen what it has wrought in the past. And as we are poised to enter a new millennium, we must revisit the most positive aspects of this legacy to explore what it can build in the future.

The twin histories of African and African American peoples are brimming with both triumph and tears; similarly, the story of the interaction between them has not always been positive. There is much that has divided Africans and the descendants of Africa in America. Their associations, and the collision of their true and false ideas about one another, have sometimes been problematic. But at various historical moments, notions of black kinship and movements based on these sentiments have endeavored to empower black Americans and Africans in the face of a perceived common oppression and exploitation, and to foster rich dialogue between African and African American cultural and artistic traditions. And yet it would seem as if the full potential of such processes has hardly been tapped.

* * *

"The sun never sets on the descendants of Africa," says the East African historian Ali Mazrui. Black people live in every country in the world, speak most of its languages, and reflect the full spectrum of religions, opinions, customs, beliefs, desires, and ambitions. We are technically only united by two things: relatively recent ancestral ties to a common continent, and the obvious physical attributes that attest to them. Some would say that we are actually bound by much more, including common cultural traits and similar experiences with racialized alienation and oppression, as evinced by a long and rich history of cultural and political collaboration and exchange. Perhaps such vague criteria hold no basis for a meaningful and functional sense of unity and cooperation. But I feel that they can and should, even though I am painfully aware of all that tends to separate blacks who come from different parts of the world.

Why should I really expect, or even hope, that things might be different? Why should intercontinental black unity, an idea upheld to some degree on the institutional and political levels, have any real weight on the ground, in personal interactions between actual Africans and African Americans? What really does, or should, unify blacks from Africa and blacks from America beyond the fact that they're "black"? Is common race really grounds for common interests, common goals, common destinies? Cultural and environmental differences do ultimately count more toward defining an individual's character or outlook than skin color, hair texture, or facial features; why, then, would African Americans and Africans, with such different cultural, environmental, and social experiences, see their struggles and destinies as linked?

Despite my firsthand experiences with the divisions between Africans and African Americans, I have retained a perhaps naive and sentimental belief in racial solidarity for very simple, basic, passionate, even trite reasons. After several formative years of living in Africa, I feel the ties that bind me to my adopted home and its people in a spiritual, almost palpable way. This feeling has grown out of twilight walks on East African beaches, inhaling the moist, salty breeze of the monsoon winds blowing across the Indian Ocean and watching Arab dhows bobbing easily on the rising tide. It comes from the familiar smell of rain on a sun-baked red dirt road and the easy humor of Swahili laughter in appreciation of a particularly witty barb during a verbal jousting session. It's a feeling that grows out of my love of the land and its people, a love based on experience.

I am also an adopted child of my mother's country and culture, and I feel a similar sense of connection to them. For some years I've lived in Harlem, the "black capital of the world," on the same street that was home to Thurgood Marshall in the 1950s, in an area once frequented by black celebrities like Zora Neale Hurston, Malcolm X, Willie Mays, and James Baldwin. Now my block is probably more Jamaican than African American, many of the once-respectable brownstones have been abandoned, the most famous people on the street are probably the drug dealers with the biggest reputations. The neighborhood is slowly cleaning itself up; we haven't heard gunfire nearby in many months, and the sidewalks aren't littered with as many colorful crack-vial caps as they once were. After five years here, I feel that in some ways Harlem is almost as much my home as Tanzania. I have come to love the sound of Jamaican patois shouted up and down the block, the colorful sight of hatted Harlem ladies parading to church, the friendly maternal manner of the women who run the corner store, who enjoy a good joke and good gossip and call every customer under thirty-five "baby," the faint smell of fried chicken and marijuana on the summer breeze and the sounds of hip-hop and reggae blaring from street-corner boom boxes, with young voices raised in a call-and-response chorus.

It's an almost instinctive emotional sense of connection, a strange and thrilling sense of intimacy, closeness and of sharing in something important. It's the feeling I had when I met my grandmother and my other relatives in Zaire and they were so excited to see me that they fairly bounced with joy and anticipation. It's not unlike the way I felt when I met some sugar-factory workers in Jamaica whose eyes lit up at the mention of Africa—"He's from the motherland," they whispered to one another with reverence and something like awe—or the over-whelming sensation of pride and kinship I felt standing surrounded by thousands of black men hugging and calling each other brother at the Million Man March. Black people have spread all over the world, but we are still linked by unseverable bonds that imply their own unique demands, rewards, and challenges. I believe that my own family history and the wider history of African–African American relations support my conviction. But at the same time, I'm also aware that transatlantic black relations are nothing if not complex, layered, and twisted in fascinating and sometimes problematic ways.

One strange incident in particular helped to underline this issue for me. It happened in London, where I was traveling with an African American friend of mine. We had gone to a nightclub where we ran into an African American musician whom my friend knew vaguely, through someone else. He played guitar for a relatively popular band known for its colorful fusion of rock, ska, and funk, and was in town for a show. The three of us talked briefly and then parted in the dancing crowd. Later that night, my friend and I ran into the musician again when we stopped to eat in a fast-food restaurant. He was happily drunk by this point, and was leaning over the counter, loudly ordering fried chicken.

Three or four West Indian Londoners leaned on the wall near him, eyeing him coolly. One of them was talking to him, spouting what at first appeared to be good-natured trash-talking, calling him a Yankee and making fun of his accent, the African American musician just laughing tipsily in response. But then the exchange seemed to escalate for no apparent reason, and very suddenly the Londoner's tone became deathly serious. "You fuckin' Yanks come here and think you run the place," he said, cursing angrily. The tension mounted immediately, and it looked as if the two might come to blows. My friend and I stepped forward, concerned, but the musician waved us away. He then did something that still surprises me, something that I will never forget.

Crossing his wrists firmly behind his back, he addressed his furious would-be assailant, swaying slightly on his feet but speaking quite clearly in spite of his drunkenness, and perhaps all the more courageously because of it. "I will never raise a hand against another black man," he said resolutely. "That's what the white man wants you to do, my brother. Why you going to let them get over on you like that? You can kill me if you want, but I will never raise my hand against another black man." The Londoner's friends looked at one another incredulously, and I also caught my friend's eye, both of us frozen in disbelief. We all breathlessly braced ourselves for the finale, wondering what would happen.

I don't know if the Londoner heard or considered what the musician had said, but he hit him with a hard right without any indication of a moment's thought. Crimson sprayed the musician's lips, redder and richer than his loud blazer, and my friend and I, stunned and still dumbfounded, rushed to his aid, but not before the Londoner had hit him again and somehow managed to relieve him of his wallet in the confusion before dashing out the door with his friends. Shaken, my friend and I helped clean the musician up and bundled him into a taxi. We rode to his hotel with him and tried to comfort him as he spoke uncomprehendingly of the encounter the whole way. "Punk-ass niggers," he kept saying sadly through his blood-spotted teeth.

The experience was like a punch in the face to me, too. While I harbored no illusions regarding the prevalence of crime among young, disenfranchised blacks, I wanted to believe that blacks from different parts of the world shared enough to believe in a notion of common international black interests and unity. What I had seen showed me just how hollow pan-Africanist rhetoric could ring. It was obvious that the confrontation had been tied up in issues of class, nationality, culture, and power, but I was more struck, and pained, by the explicit and vehement rejection of one black man's seemingly heartfelt appeal to another. It was not the first time I had witnessed or experienced an incident that made me feel this way. And it certainly wouldn't be the last.

Fortunately, however, the legacy of contact between Africans and African Americans is certainly more than just one of misunderstanding and conflict. Instead, history reveals that far more often than they have clashed, Africans and African Americans have reached out to one another with fascination, purpose, and a spirit of hopeful kinship. And this preoccupation with one another has inspired many significant artistic, political, and religious explorations of the relationship between Africa and the descendants of Africans in America. The psychological ties that bind all black people to Africa are invisible and difficult to even define. But they have played a defining role for the past three hundred years of black history.

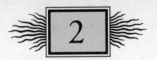

2

THE JOINING OF AFRICA
AND AMERICA

*I want my children to straddle the Atlantic, to feel close to my
people as well as my husband's.*
        —An African American married to a Nigerian (1979)

"Who is that?" the young woman whispered eagerly to her girlfriend, gesturing toward a gray-suited, horn-rim-spectacled
man who sat towards the front of the room. Although she was beginning her senior year at Western Michigan University, the young
woman had spent her junior year studying in Grenoble, France, working to perfect her French as part of her ambition to become a French
teacher. The year abroad had been exciting and enlightening, stretching the horizons of her experience, but she had missed her friends
back in Kalamazoo. She was glad to now be back at WMU, but she
felt like a different person from the one who had left the United States
for the first time a year previously—she was more cosmopolitan, more
independent, and, of course, newly fluent in French. And she realized
that there had also been some changes on campus during her absence;
since her return she had found herself having to ask friends to identify
some of the unfamiliar new faces she saw around her. The man she
now gazed at was clearly a newcomer; she certainly would have remembered him if he had been in the French Club before she left for
Europe.

"Oh, that's Ernest, the new student from Africa," her friend replied
offhandedly.

The young woman nodded, suddenly remembering. While in France she had received a club newsletter mentioning that two students from Congo had enrolled at WMU and joined the club, giving talks on the political situation in their country for the benefit of their new classmates, who were unfamiliar with the newly independent nation. This handsome man who now sat quietly waiting for the French Club–sponsored film to begin must be one of these new additions to the community of WMU French speakers, the young woman reflected. She asked her friend to introduce her to the new student. As they approached the seated man, he rose, standing formally and bowing slightly, and extended his hand.

"Ernest Wamba dia Wamba," he said in a rich baritone, the syllables flowing rhythmically and almost melodically from his lips, as he took the young woman's hand in his.

"Elaine Brown," the young woman said, feeling unexpectedly shy as she smiled and shook hands with the tall stranger. He beamed back at her. He had noticed her when she first entered the room, and was inwardly pleased that she had come over to say hello, although his politely prim demeanor betrayed little of his elation. Speaking in French, she asked his early impressions of the campus, and he responded briefly and favorably. He complimented her on her polished fluency, and she thanked him modestly. As the film the French Club was showing that night was about to begin, they exchanged their pleased-to-meet-yous, parted, and took their seats.

Years later neither Ernest nor Elaine could remember the title or the plot of the movie they watched that night. As they each sat quietly in the anonymous darkness, neither paid much attention to the action onscreen. Instead, they were thinking about each other and wondering when they might meet again.

As in many families, the story of my parents' meeting and courtship was passed on to my brothers and me like a tenderly remembered romantic fairy tale. If distance and time washed away any negative aspects from my parents' idealized descriptions of their pairing, they also converted the narrative of their early relationship into a sort of familial founding myth. In hearing how our parents had met and married, we learned with interest of the events that gave rise to our very existence. And in the telling and retelling of this transatlantic love story, whatever tensions, conflicts, and troubles might have characterized our parents' early association soon dissolved into the past, so the idealized version of the tale became the only one we were aware of.

My brothers and I extracted the details of the story from my mother over card games and bowls of peanuts, and we enjoyed laughing and teasing her as she recalled her first impressions of our father. My father was less inclined to openly dwell with nostalgia on their college romance, but he, too, could be encouraged to cast his mind back to August 1965 and recount how impressed he was with the pretty young woman he met at the French Club movie.

My father, who grew up in a rural village in western Congo and won a scholarship to study in the United States by placing third in national high school exams, had arrived at WMU the previous year. When Ernest and Elaine were introduced, the attraction was immediate. He had briefly dated a friend of hers soon after arriving in Michigan, but they had stopped seeing each other. He was "too serious," my mother's girlfriend said. Having cleared it with her friend, my mother began seeing my father soon after they first met.

My mother had met her first Africans, fellow students, as a first-year at WMU, but there was generally very little interaction between Africans and most of the black Americans on campus. Her first personal connections with Africans were forged in France, where she made a few African friends and was impressed with how intelligent, articulate, and passionate they were about their desire to finish their studies so they could return home and help their people. My mother had grown up thinking of Africa as little more than a "big jungle." Her experience with Africans in France, and an increasing awareness about Africa among African Americans in general, prompted her to reevaluate her perceptions of the continent. In high school she had gone to some Congress of Racial Equality (CORE) meetings and to a few demonstrations, and she had been inspired to become more involved in the civil rights struggle by hearing Martin Luther King, Jr., speak at WMU during her sophomore year. But in France she began to take a serious interest in Africa and became determined to find her way there. Somehow this desire became even more important than her original plan to live and work in the United States, and her relationship with my father seemed an extension of this new interest.

Also, he was unlike any man she had ever dated: extremely bright, well read, well spoken (even though his English was still somewhat shaky), and (as her friend had complained) very serious. When challenged by professors in class, he would answer questions without hesitation and quote passages from books from memory, citing the chapter and page, and he spoke often and eagerly about returning to

Congo after graduation to make his contribution to his country, which as an independent nation was barely five years old.

The young couple went to French Club–sponsored events, African parties (my mother thought they were more fun than the college fraternity gatherings she was used to), sorority events (she was a member of the black sisterhood Delta Sigma Theta), and on study dates to the library. She started typing his papers for him, and he gave her the bulk of his scholarship money to manage. They became very close very quickly.

In pictures of my father as a young man, his tall, slim frame is always draped with a dark gray suit over a white shirt and skinny black tie, he has horn-rimmed spectacles perched on his handsome, unsmiling face, his sharp, narrow shoes are scrupulously polished, and his hair is carefully groomed. He cut a dapper figure on campus, and his intelligence, looks, accented eloquence, and dignified sense of purpose had an intense effect on my mother. By the time he started expressing his feelings for her in French love poems he wrote himself, her heart was already his.

My father was similarly impressed with my young mother. She was smart, generous, and beautiful, tall and graceful with golden skin and soulful light brown eyes. And she spoke fluent French. My father had been popular with girls back in Congo and had casually dated women at WMU before he met my mother, but he had never been involved with a woman so intellectually sophisticated, worldly, and poised. And when he was around her he never felt the unarticulated hostility he sometimes thought he sensed from African American women. As they spent more and more time together, he fell in love with her kindness and with the radiant, selfless spirit that masked a profound but quiet strength.

By Thanksgiving, the relationship was getting "serious," so my mother invited my father to her family's home in Cleveland, Ohio, where she introduced the young African to her father, her stepmother, and her siblings. Her family respected my father immediately, but found him very quiet and reserved. My parents spent Thanksgiving Day in Cleveland and drove out to my mother's uncle's place in Lima the next day. My father was cordial and respectful to all the members of my mother's family, and especially fond of her grandmother, an old Southerner who was very warm to him. But when my mother's cousins attempted to interest him in a basketball game and other outdoor activities, he politely declined, preferring, as usual, to lose himself in his books. And the entire family was mystified by some seemingly odd behavior. On the first morning, when my mother's stepmother asked my father how he wanted his breakfast eggs, he replied, "Just raw," and drank the liquid yolks like milk. It was apparently the first and last time my mother ever saw him do this. Perhaps he was just having some fun with his hosts and their preconceptions by playing up his "strange" African image for his own amusement. When she asked about it later, he just laughed.

After the success of this trip, my parents began discussing marriage. Though the matter wasn't explicitly addressed, my mother knew that marrying my father would mean moving to Congo, because he always took his return home for granted. That was fine with her. As the fires of black consciousness began to sweep black America in the mid-1960s, my mother became more resolute in her desire to make her home in Africa, an ambition that became stronger as she got to know my father and heard about his life and background. He described his family and childhood for her plainly, but with sentimental nostalgia, for he had fond memories of his upbringing. He told her of growing up the fourth of ten children in a village called Zabanga, with a father who was a schoolteacher and church catechist and a mother who raised various crops on the family's land. He spoke of walks in the forest, of singing and dancing with the other kids in the village, and of tending his family's farms with his mother.

To the African American daughter of a research chemist and a social worker who was raised in various American cities, the tales of fishing and hunting, of living within feet of cousins, aunts, uncles, and an extended village clan, and of sitting in the moonlight listening to stories and debates around a communal fire each evening must have sounded incredibly exotic. They certainly didn't sound like the savage Africa she had heard of as a child, but they did strike a chord in that part of her that longed for a pastoral paradise in Africa that she could call home. When my parents' relationship evolved into a sexual one and my mother became pregnant in February 1966, it merely prompted the acceleration of marriage plans that had already been discussed.

My mother's father was shocked when my mother informed him of her pregnancy and imminent marriage, but once he regained his composure he grudgingly supported her decision. Other family members were more wary; an aunt cautioned that African men were wife-beaters who practiced polygamy and wondered if my father didn't already have a wife or two at home. In theory, I suppose, my mother perhaps missed being a second wife by a mere generation: both of my father's parents had grown up in polygamous households, but my grandfather's involvement in the church had made him frown on polygamy and other such "un-Christian" traditions. When my mother's parents visited their daughter and her intended husband to discuss the wedding plans, cultural differences did cause some problems, however. In the absence of his own father, Ernest had asked a fellow Congolese student to act as his intermediary, as is the custom in many African cultures, where it is thought inappropriate for a suitor to address his intended's parents directly. My mother's father had no knowledge of such a tradition and resented the fact that my father would speak to him only through a go-between. Despite the misunderstanding, the wedding was set for a date in May.

When my father informed his family that he was getting married to an African American woman he had met at university, reactions were mixed. Some misinformed family members reveled in the knowledge that all African Americans were very wealthy, and looked forward to the financial advantages of having new, rich American relatives. Others weren't quite sure what to expect, and adopted a wait-and-see attitude. And some were, at first, hostile to the idea. My father had left a fiancée in Congo, but sometime before he met my mother, the woman had become pregnant by another man and had been hospitalized after a disastrous abortion. Though the fiancée admitted everything, my father did not feel obligated to respect the engagement, and he ended the relationship. Nonetheless, his brother and an aunt, who had been very close to the woman, were upset that he was now marrying someone else.

My father's mother received the news happily and looked forward to having some new grandchildren, but his father had to be convinced. It helped that my father was already such a respected member of his family. He had consistently excelled in school; as a teenager he had taken charge of his younger sister and provided for her education; and he had won a scholarship to study further than anyone in his family ever had. He was regarded as sensible, responsible, and capable. When his father expressed his reservations about this stranger Ernest proposed to marry, all my father said was "You know me very well. Do you think I would bring you something foolish?" My father's great-uncle also expressed misgivings. "I thought you were going to marry for us someone who knows how to cook cassava leaves!" he complained. My father replied that cooking cassava leaves could be learned, and one day they would all taste some that his wife had prepared. His doubtful relatives were at last mollified, and my father proceeded with his plans to marry my mother.

The ceremony itself was a simple affair, held in the apartment of an African American pastor in Kalamazoo who performed the marriage, and attended by my mother's immediate family and a few selected friends. My father's family was represented only in the person of the Congolese friend who had acted as intermediary; he was the best man. After the ceremony, the couple and their guests had dinner and then danced at a supper club in Kalamazoo's black neighborhood. The newlyweds couldn't afford a honeymoon, so they just found an apartment in town and returned to the routine of classes and jobs.

Remy was born in October 1966, and the couple greeted his arrival with great joy. The infant seemed to inherit aspects of both his parents; his complexion was a bit darker than my mother's; he had his father's round face and wide mouth, and his mother's eyes. And even as a young child, he showed signs of his mother's sensitivity and his father's seriousness. After Remy's birth, my mother returned to her studies, finishing her coursework and practice-teaching. She graduated in 1968 and took a full-time job at the campus library, where she had had a work-study job as an undergraduate, while my father continued with his studies in philosophy.

Shortly before my father's graduation in June 1968, a Congolese friend with ties to the government suggested his name to the country's new minister of social affairs. Offered a job in the ministry, he accepted gladly and prepared to leave for Kinshasa. My mother and Remy, then just eighteen months old, were to follow later, staying with my mother's father in Cleveland until my father sent for them. Some in my mother's family worried about her moving so far away and fretted that she would be overworked and mistreated, as they assumed most African women were. They had no choice but to accept her decision, but her father still grumbled a little. On the day of my father's departure, my mother packed his suitcases while my father, characteristically oblivious, sat in her father's living room absorbed in a book. As she struggled to load the bags into the car, her father snorted, "He's not in Africa yet," and roused Ernest from the couch to help her.

My mother prepared herself for the imminent adventure by reading as much as she could, although there wasn't much to be found on Congo at the public library in Shaker Heights, Ohio. My father's frequent letters proved a valuable source of information; she also read a book called *Black Rage*, which discussed African American psychology and the self-hatred manifested in such practices as hair straightening. The book had a strong impact on her.

Six weeks after my father left, plane tickets arrived for my mother and Remy. She felt much less apprehensive than her family about what lay ahead, and though my father thought he had done his best to prepare her, my mother still hoped for some sort of special treatment, hoped to be welcomed as a long-lost family member who had finally come home. She also looked forward to conveying to the Congolese she met something of what it was like to be an African American. She was a little uneasy about meeting her in-laws, but felt they were bound to accept her since my father had chosen her to be his wife.

Though there was no welcoming committee of assorted Africans cheering the return of a New World cousin at the airport, my mother's first impressions of Kinshasa were positive. She and Remy joined my father at the home of some friends in a large government house in a beautiful suburb. The wife of my father's friend, also a teacher, was very kind to her, teaching her to cook Congolese dishes (including cassava leaves), taking her on trips to the market, and introducing her to neighbors. On one occasion, my mother's new friend emerged from the kitchen with a plate full of small, oily cylinders of fried meat, explaining that this was one of my father's favorite dishes. Assuming they were made from beef or lamb, my mother eagerly asked to be taught how to prepare the little snacks. Her host obliged by leading my mother into the kitchen, reaching into a bucket, and pulling a single grub from a large mass of wriggling caterpillars that she had bought live in the market. She held it in place on a cutting board and deftly slit it lengthwise, its guts bulging yellow through the long cut, then plopped it into a pan of hot oil. My mother, suddenly less anxious to work on her Congolese cooking skills, declined an invitation to try to duplicate the performance and politely excused herself.

On weekends my parents and Remy would visit my father's relatives around the city, taking taxis and "taxi-buses," rickety vans that were constantly crammed with people, to get there. The various cousins, uncles and aunts who lived in Kinshasa had awaited my mother's arrival with keen curiosity and were pleased to finally meet her. My father had attempted to disillusion those who believed that her entry into the family would mean the advent of vast new wealth, but some still greeted her coming with unreal expectations and were a bit disappointed when she showed up empty-handed. Though most of the relatives could converse in French, Lingala and Kikongo (my father's tribal language) were even more widely used, and my mother was often frustrated by the language barrier. Still, she felt a welcoming sense of kinship with her new family.

Soon, after the initial meetings in which my father's family decided that his new bride was quite acceptable, visits from relatives to the house where my parents were staying became common. Once an uncle and a retinue of cousins arrived, proffering a live rooster as a gift. My mother was happy to be spared having to slaughter the bird, since a cousin offered to, but she did prepare lunch for the visitors and was relieved when the meal was a success, although she could tell that the uncle disapproved of her drinking beer while they ate.

Unfortunately, my mother was at first unable to meet most of my father's immediate family. The demands of my father's job made it impossible to make the day-long trip to his village, a fact he regretted deeply. He had first visited Kinshasa only in 1962, and he found the culture of the big city very different from that of his own Zabanga. If he had been able to bring his wife and child to the village, they would have been welcomed into the clan properly, with appropriate ritual and fanfare. Since an extended trip to the rural areas was impossible, they had to make do with the big-city hospitality of his Kinshasa cousins.

My mother busied herself by applying for a teaching job through the Ministry of Education, and tried to learn Lingala while she waited for something to turn up, a daunting task since the language described in a book she found seemed to have little relationship to the fast-paced gibberish she heard around her. She also began to take stock of her surroundings, noticing sadly that while in shops Africans often manned the counters, the person behind the cash register was virtually always European or Lebanese. She hadn't realized that Congo's much-heralded "flag independence" didn't necessarily always translate into economic independence.

By September my parents had still not found a house of their own and their welcome in my father's friend's home had begun to wear thin, so they moved into a hotel for a brief period and then into a tiny house in a compound owned by a cousin. The little cinder-block house had no indoor plumbing or electricity, and while there was a tap outside, water only flowed from it once or twice a day. Three other families lived in the compound, but the wives in these households spoke little French. Despite the challenging new circumstances, my mother made do.

She got a job teaching at a girls' school nearby, and hired a *domestique* to help out around the house, quite a cultural challenge for a middle-class black American who had been raised to be self-sufficient. Her apprehension dissolved when Basile, a young man, proved to be good-natured and got along famously with Remy. At work she observed with interest how Congolese girls behaved and thought, and she caught glimpses of racism among the Swedish and Belgian missionaries who were her administrators and colleagues. She settled into her new life and began to enjoy it, making some Congolese friends and watching Remy grow into a thoughtful and intelligent child, who quickly learned to converse in French and Lingala.

My parents' new life was soon marred by tragedy, however. My mother became pregnant again and gave birth to a girl, named Judith Luezi, after my father's mother. The little girl, born six weeks prematurely, struggled for breath from the very first and survived only a few minutes. Consumed by grief, the family drew closer together, and the routine of life continued, albeit numbed by the sad, dull ache of loss.

One Saturday afternoon, my parents and Remy were in the house when a large truck pulled up in the road outside the compound and two passengers got out carrying a number of bags and bundles. My father's parents had come for a visit, laden with live chickens and assorted foodstuffs from the village. For my father, it was a joyous reunion, for he hadn't seen his mother and father in several years. For my mother, it was a somewhat tense introduction to her in-laws. Though she felt anxious, the visitors were welcomed happily, and my mother prepared a large dinner for them, scoring major approval points when she blessed the meal by reciting a Kikongo prayer my father had taught her. Her father-in-law, a tall, dignified and gentle man, spoke kindly to her, and she liked him immediately. He established a close rapport with Remy as well. She found my father's mother, on the other hand, rather stern, and whenever they spoke my mother felt as though she were being closely evaluated. To compound my mother's uncertainty and suspicion, her mother-in-law spoke no French and little Lingala, so my mother could not communicate with her directly.

My grandfather stayed a month, my grandmother three, and my mother felt slightly uneasy for much of their stay in the cramped little house. But when they left, she felt as though she had passed some sort of exam, and earned their acceptance and respect.

Shortly after his parents' visit, my father received a promotion at work and the family moved to a larger house. My mother got a new teaching job, one she preferred, at a Congolese-run school, and my parents' living situation improved considerably. By now my mother could speak Lingala, she had established some friendships, and she felt comfortable in Kinshasa. What's more, my father was excelling in his job at the Ministry of Social Affairs. He began as an adviser, then became the assistant director of the minister's office, and was then promoted to director. He brought a conscientious and astute meticulousness to the job, and soon the minister would not sign any document that did not bear his initials, signaling his approval. He earned a reputation for incorruptibility and integrity, refusing to rubber-stamp documents that he regarded as suspect.

Though his star seemed to rise unchecked through the ministry, he became increasingly troubled by the political situation in the country at large. By the late 1960s President Joseph Desiré Mobutu, the country's ruler since a coup d'etat in 1965, had begun to consolidate power by cracking down on "counterrevolutionaries," jailing political opponents without trial, banning demonstrations, and torturing prisoners. My father took to hiding his books on Marxism and radical politics, and began to tread very cautiously at work. It became clear to him that the government was not acting in the interests of the masses of the Congolese people. He began to encounter obstacles when he tried to do his job in the most honest, straightforward way possible, and he realized that in the main these obstacles originated in the presidency. Even as he was considered for yet another promotion, this time to become an adviser to the president on social affairs, he realized he could not work in such a problematic political environment.

As the climate became more and more tense, my father's boss, the progressive minister of social affairs, began to prepare to leave the country. Fortuitously, my father was offered a graduate fellowship from the New York–based African-American Institute to study in California. With mixed feelings, but somewhat relieved to be leaving such a strained political milieu, my parents and Remy said good-bye to their relatives in Congo and moved to Claremont, California, where my father started work on a master's degree in business economics in early 1971 and where I was born. My family remained in California until 1972, when, my father's degree complete, they moved to Boston, Massachusetts; there, my younger brothers Kolo and James were born.

By the time I was born, in June 1971, my parents' marriage was no longer an experiment in cross-cultural understanding. They had already lived together for over five years, in Michigan and Kinshasa, through the infancy of one child and the death of another, through difficult relationships with in-laws and through economic adversity and professional success. While still negotiating the intricate give-and-take that came with sharing their lives, they had already learned how to be together.

And they loved each other. As for resolving cultural differences, they blundered through them without really thinking about it. They never really considered whether their children would be African or American in nationality or cultural outlook, whether they would teach us Kikongo or English, whether we would be raised wholly in Africa or partly in the United States. If my parents had struggled with the weight of all these troublesome questions before they presented themselves as realities, they would probably never have married.

Nonetheless, some unspoken agreements did exist. It was always understood between my parents that my father wanted to make his home in Congo, and my mother, the fledgling back-to-Africa black nationalist, supported this. There was never any thought that they would spend more time than was necessary in the United States, and it was never proposed that my father move away from his family in Congo to join my mother in Cleveland or Detroit. In fact, when they moved to Kinshasa in 1968 they did not intend to return to the United States; that they found themselves back in America three years later was just the way things worked out.

The decision to live in Congo also meant that my mother was expected to integrate herself into my father's culture as best she could. She did this by following the lead of the Congolese women she saw around her. While this often meant accepting a somewhat subordinate role to that of her husband in the decision-making that affected their family, she embraced her position without complaint. And this proved less difficult than her family in the United States might have expected; while on the surface, Congolese women seemed to occupy subservient roles, typically waiting on the men at meals and rarely directly contradicting them, on other levels they seemed quite powerful. My father's boss at the ministry was a savvy, well-educated, and commanding woman. The market women with whom my mother often bargained were aggressive and wily, and certainly unintimidated by the men they crossed paths with every day. And the women in my father's female-dominated family were generally outspoken, strong-willed, and dynamic. Since these women earned my mother's respect immediately, she had few reservations about looking to them to learn her prescribed role in her new society.

She did rebel against Congolese ideals of womanhood in subtle ways, though, drinking beer when some men frowned on it and occasionally wearing pants even though it was considered unladylike and was, in fact, discouraged by the government. In this way she was able to strike a balance she could live with, although it was often difficult. My father, to his credit, helped matters by not trying to pressure my mother to live up to Congolese standards of behavior, and was perhaps more progressive in his attitudes toward and treatment of women than some of his compatriots. In any case, my mother willingly and adaptably assumed a culturally defined role in my father's life, and never really felt constrained by it.

When I consider the implications of my mother's eager willingness to move to Africa, leaving her family and country behind, I realize that my parents' union was more a case of her marrying into my father's family than the other way around. My father refers to my mother's relatives as "our family," but it is clear to me that in many ways he thinks of his own children more as members of his African extended clan than as belonging to my mother's large American family, more as "Wambas" than as "Browns." When my brother Kolo visited my father's village in 1996, the first of his children to do so, my father asked him his impressions in a touching letter that spoke of our family's spiritual ties to the area. "I am very glad to note that you now know very well where I came from and what makes us all some kind of a special phenomenon," he wrote. "The little Zabanga has partially produced all of us. You know what links us together and what keeps us going."

In addition to seeing my father's (and therefore his own) humble origins firsthand, Kolo returned from his trip with pictures of a grassy field that our relatives in Zabanga described as "the proposed site of Philippe's house." It gives me an exhilarating sense of inclusion to think of myself as belonging to a proud African clan and to know that wherever I go I can always return to a rural village in western Congo, where a spot is waiting for me to build myself a home. I celebrate and marvel at my mother's faith and courage in marrying my father and moving to Africa without really looking back, bravery that is understandable in the context of the day's cultural politics and her own personal strength and unequivocal love. But I always wonder if she ever feels that she gave up too much.

Though in some ways my mother seemed willing to allow my father's background to eclipse her own in the raising of her children, in other areas my parents seemed to strike a more or less even cultural balance. In terms of names, however, my father's heritage had the definite edge. Remy Datave took his first name from a cousin of my father's, while his middle name was one of my father's many titles. Judith Luezi was named after my father's mother. I inherited the various parts of my name, Philippe Enoc Kiatuntu Ngila, from my father's uncle and father, while my father invented my brother's name, Kolo Diakiese, a Kikongo construction that roughly means Bond (something joining two things tightly together) of Happiness. James Paul, the youngest, named for my mother's father, grandfather, and uncle, is the only one of my parents' children whose name comes from my mother's side of the family.

While my parents were living in Kinshasa, it was relatively easy to teach Remy to speak French and Lingala: both languages surrounded him. Since the rest of us spent our early childhood in the United States, however, my parents didn't even bother trying to raise us multilingual. When we were growing up, my parents generally spoke French to each other but English to us kids, and while we picked up a few French words, my brothers and I never learned to speak the language until we took formal lessons in high school, and then learned it only barely. Though Remy had been all but fluent in French as a child in Congo, he stopped speaking French and Lingala altogether when he returned to the United States. My brothers and I all regret the fact that we don't speak any Lingala or Kikongo, but in the absence of a real community of speakers in which to have immersed ourselves in Boston, Massachusetts (my father did speak his mother tongue with the few Bakongo who lived in the area, but they hardly constituted a large community), it's difficult to see how we could have learned these languages as children.

Though my brothers and I missed out on an education in Kikongo and French, my parents did self-consciously try to provide us with some knowledge of their respective backgrounds. Since our early upbringing took place in middle-class Boston suburbs whose neighborhoods were home to few black Americans, let alone any Congolese, they both felt it important to impart to us a consciousness of, and pride in, the communities they had come from. My father told us often of his childhood exploits in "the Village," stories of his large family and their countless relatives who lived nearby. He described his fascination with the local flora and fauna, telling, to our excited disgust, of how he would sometimes join adult hunters on quests for buffalo in which they smeared themselves with the animals' excrement to avoid detection by the keen-nosed beasts. He told of setting fires to drive antelope out of the underbrush and mentioned one occasion when he caught a small one by diving and catching its hind leg in his bare hands. He spoke with great respect and love of his parents and told us how much they had taught him, and he kept us in stitches with tales of his uncle, whom he referred to as "the philosopher," a feisty, grizzled old man who subsisted mainly on palm wine and lived to a hundred and twenty-four. And he furnished lessons on his country's political history, speaking angrily of the indignity of having been colonized by "little Belgium" and the harsh treatment his people suffered from the often brutal Europeans. Pictures of African freedom fighters like Patrice Lumumba were displayed prominently around our home, and my father supplied us with narratives of their heroic acts for the cause of African freedom. And he sadly admitted that even though Zaire (as Mobutu renamed Congo in 1971) was now independent, the oppression continued.

For her part, my mother made sure my brothers and I looked up to black leaders like Malcolm X and Martin Luther King, Jr., supplementing the history books she gave us with personal accounts of her own brushes with segregation on trips to see her grandparents in Mississippi, and accounts of her limited involvement in the civil rights movement. She told us about growing up in Pittsfield, Massachusetts, where her family was one of only a few black households, and then moving to Detroit, Chicago, and Cleveland, where they lived in predominantly black communities. She related stories of her proud and strict father, and shared tales of the misadventures of her and her sisters, who sometimes ran afoul of their parents' no-nonsense discipline. And at every opportunity she, along with black friends from the area, would take my brothers and me to picnics, festivals, fairs, and shows with an African or black American theme in Roxbury or Dorchester, Boston's main black communities.

My parents passed other aspects of their respective cultures on to my brothers and me in less deliberate ways, simply by referring to their own upbringing as road maps for day-to-day life. My mother was the primary meal provider, and most of her culinary repertoire came out of her experience growing up black in Chicago and Detroit. Her specialties included macaroni and cheese, coleslaw, black-eyed peas, pepper steak, fried chicken, spaghetti, and meat loaf, with the occasional pot of "peanut butter greens," a delectable concoction she based on a popular Congolese dish, thrown in for good measure. Conversely, when my father cooked, which was admittedly not often, Congolese food reigned; he specialized in huge pots of beans and salt fish, which we ate with mounds of sticky rice or *foufou*, a starchy, doughy Congolese staple my brothers and I learned to love. My father's meals always made liberal use of *pilipili*, and he would encourage us to try as much as we could stand, saying that in Congo children who couldn't eat *pilipili* were objects of scorn.

Both of my parents were enthusiastic fans of music, and when my brothers and I were kids, each played items from their respective collections constantly. If I was arriving home from school and heard the strains of some song wafting down the stairs, I could pretty much figure out who was playing the record before I entered the living room. My mother was into Motown and other black soul and also loved jazz; her favorites included Stevie Wonder, Aretha Franklin, the Jackson Five, James Brown, War, Chaka Khan, Natalie Cole, Donna Summer, Ramsey Lewis, Cannonball Adderley, and Wes Montgomery. My mother played and danced to her music often, sometimes deejaying her own individual dance parties on weekend afternoons when she would use me as a dance partner to attempt to recreate the steps of her youth, the Mashed Potato, the Monkey, the Jerk, and, her favorite, the Bop.

My father also loved to dance, but his tastes ran towards Congolese dance orchestras headed by legendary bandleaders like Tabu Ley, Franco ("le Grand Maître"), Joseph Kabasele, and Sam Mangwana. He also loved Cuban salsa by performers like Johnny Pacheco, funky African jazz by Manu Dibango and Fela Anikulapo Kuti, and the Carribean folk songs of Harry Belafonte. One of my early childhood memories is of my father working in his office in our house on some morning when I was just waking up, and singing his own heartbreaking version of Belafonte's "Jamaica Farewell," his accent, slow pacing and smooth, deep voice giving the song a new unique flavor. "Sad to say, I'm on my way, won't be back for many a day," he sang, transporting me far from our Boston suburb. "My heart is down, my head is turning around, I had to leave a little girl in Kingston Town."

The somewhat odd exceptions to my father's almost complete African-Caribbean musical bias were the lounge-style croonings of Nat King Cole, a perennial favorite, and the lovelorn ballads of Roberta Flack. My brothers and I still know the words to almost every song by both of these artists, the result of years of involuntary exposure. It was only as a teenager that I learned the names of the non-American performers in my father's music collection and grew to actively appreciate their music. When I was a child, my father's music seemed distinctively "foreign": loud, upbeat soundscapes of horns and drums under melodies in strange languages that my brothers and I would jokingly imitate. And my father's dancing style was a far cry from my mother's bop: at home he would typically dance to his music while he rearranged his thousands of books in the living room, smoothly shuffling forward toward the bookcase, rotating his hips in time to the music, and spinning fluidly when the band launched into an insistent soukouss guitar solo.

My father's younger sister and her family moved from Congo to nearby Lynn in the mid-seventies, joining a community of Congolese in the Boston area, a diaspora attracted to America by education, jobs, and the lure of prosperity. My family attended the Congolese gatherings that commemorated holidays and special events quite often. These parties always featured Congolese friends and relations with names like Uncle Bawa, Uncle Sadi, Konzo and Mafwa speaking loudly in Kikongo, Lingala, and French, blaring uptempo Congolese music, and eating lots of Congolese food, often cooked with ingredients brought to the United States by recently arrived Africans. *Foufou*, salt fish, *mbika* (a dish made from pounded pumpkin seeds), *mfumbwa* (a coarse spinachlike vegetable cooked with peanut butter), cassava, and boiled plantains were some of my favorites.

The adults, the men dressed immaculately in pleated pants, pointy-toed shoes, and colorful dress shirts, the women in tight African-print dresses that hugged their substantial hips, would dance to African music until daybreak, and we kids would eat and run around playing until we passed out on the couch or in our cousins' beds. The events had a sense of nostalgia in that what linked the guests was a common and distant place of origin, a far-off, fondly remembered homeland they recreated in microcosm at parties like these. My father and his friends would trade reminiscences and speak animatedly about African politics, enjoying the familiar food and music, and relishing the opportunity to speak the languages they grew up with. My brothers and I were always included as part of the family, as Congolese who would one day return "home" along with everyone else. I was always self-conscious in my inability to speak French or Kikongo, and realized that I wasn't as Congolese as my Kinshasa-born cousin Dina, for example. But I embraced the sense of cultural identification and delighted in the idea of a distant home in Africa that I would someday visit.

For some holidays, my family would drive to Cleveland to visit my mother's father and stepmother or to Detroit to visit her mother and sister. These reunions were similar in spirit to the Congolese parties, but quite different in substance. Legions of cousins with names like

Skip, Beth, Butch, and Chris, and older relatives like Uncle Clarence, Grandmother Martha, and Aunt Sweetie would fill my grandfather's large house for huge meals of fried chicken, collard greens, baked beans, potato salad, cornbread, and homemade preserves, all washed down with sweet iced tea. Remy, my cousin Chris, and I would discuss the latest dances and popular music (Rick James, Parliament-Funkadelic, Chic, and Kool and the Gang, among others) and play video games while the younger kids ran around playing noisily and the grown-ups shared loud jokes and card games. My mother would really unwind at these gatherings, spending laughing, affectionate time with her sisters and younger brother, using exclamations like "Ooh, chile" and terms of endearment like "fool," slipping into fond discussions of old times.

To me, the gatherings on each side of my family felt the same; they had a warm sense of kinship and inclusion, though the sounds, smells, and sights of each environment were quite different. And although balancing two cultures within the same family sometimes involved shifting identities in shifting contexts, in some ways my family managed to situate itself on the boundary between cultural and continental communities. In the joining of two families, cultures, and nations that my parents represented, my brothers and I were bestowed a heritage rooted in both Africa and America.

My parents' romance took shape against the backdrop of the black identity revolution of the 1960s, and in some ways ideas about black kinship and pan-Africanism helped to spark their initial interest in each other and to reinforce their faith in the union's feasibility, even its appropriateness. It's a feeling that was apparently shared by many Africans and African Americans, who chose mates from across the Atlantic in growing numbers throughout the 1960s and 1970s. Early proponents of pan-Africanism had often likened the ties between black Africans and black Americans to a political and cultural "marriage"; by the 1960s, literal marriages connecting the continents were becoming more and more common.

* * *

Relationships and marriages between Africans and African Americans were common enough by the 1950s, when a wave of students from the continent found their way to American universities and mingled with black American classmates, that representations of them began to appear in literature by black writers. One of the earliest and best known of these fictitious romances was depicted in Lorraine

Hansberry's award-winning Broadway play, *A Raisin in the Sun* (1959). The play, which deals with the tribulations of an upwardly mobile black family, features a Nigerian student named Asagai who courts the family's daughter Beneatha. Asagai, a sophisticated and learned Yoruba, makes clear his affection for Beneatha and attempts to teach her about Africa and to take pride in her heritage as a descendant of the motherland.

Though Beneatha knows little about Africa save the stereotypes she has learned from American popular culture, she seems on her way towards reevaluating these attitudes. But her conception of Africa and what Asagai represents for her is nonetheless tied up in romantic imaginings of African splendor. And Asagai seems quite content to encourage these ideas, using his own exotic appeal and that of his homeland to impress and woo her. On a visit to Beneatha's home he presents her with a gift of "the colorful robes of a Nigerian woman" that he had his sister send especially for her, he tells her she has the profile of "a queen of the Nile," and he coins a Yoruba nickname for her, Alaiyo, which he says means "One for Whom Bread Is Not Enough," seemingly referring to her hunger for self-knowledge. Implicitly boasting of his own African "authenticity," he refers to her straightened hair as "mutilated" and accuses her of "accommodating" to a white ideal. And in all that Asagai tells Beneatha about Africa and herself, there is a sense that he doesn't take her interest in the continent seriously. He apparently derives great amusement from her quest for African roots and revels in his power to define Africa for her. "I am only teasing you because you are so serious about these things," he says after poking fun at her "mutilated" hair. "Do you remember the first time I met you at school? You came up to me and you said—and I thought you were the most serious little thing I had ever seen—you said: 'Mr. Asagai—I want very much to talk to you. About Africa. You see, Mr. Asagai, I am looking for my *identity*.'"

Despite the teasing, Asagai has a genuine romantic interest in Beneatha. But though he is plainly enthusiastic about the relationship, Beneatha's feelings are much more confused. Though her mother assumes Beneatha's new interest in Africa derives from her attraction to Asagai ("Lord, that's a pretty thing just went out here," Mama says after Asagai leaves. "Yes, I guess I see why we done commence to get so interested in Africa 'round here"), Beneatha first seeks him out at school in search for her "identity"; Asagai obligingly provides her with Nigerian robes, a Yoruba nickname, and the assurance that she has a heritage she can be proud of in Africa, and he seems to have a profound impact on her. She starts listening to African music, dancing about the house in Nigerian robes, and attempting to sing in Yoruba, even sharing a call-and-response chant in a light moment with her usually vitriolic brother.

But in spite of her enthusiasm, Beneatha's sudden obsession with Africa seems superficial; the limits of her actual knowledge of Africa are made clear time and time again. After Asagai departs her family's home, Beneatha poses in front of the mirror in the robes he has given her, watching herself "wriggle . . . as she thinks a Nigerian woman might." On another occasion, when her sister-in-law Ruth is startled to find Beneatha doing an African dance in the living room, Beneatha explains, "It's a dance of welcome." "Who you welcoming?" Ruth asks. "The men back to the village," retorts Beneatha. "Where they been?" asks Ruth. "How should I know—out hunting or something," comes the indignant reply.

Although admittedly ignorant of African history and culture, Beneatha is consumed by a passionate desire to remake herself in an African image, and she looks to Asagai for the authentic guidance she needs to accomplish this. To Beneatha (and to her family too, but in a different way) Asagai does not necessarily stand as an individual, but is more a symbolic representation of the continent and its culture. And in the context of the play, which deals with the troubled race and class relations of 1950s America, he represents an alternative homeland and way of life for a new generation of African Americans like Beneatha, who sees Asagai as a way out, as a harbinger of a possible new life in Africa.

It is a life Beneatha seems intent on seizing at the close of the play. When Asagai pledges to marry her and take her back to Nigeria with him, he playfully describes their union in mythic terms. "Three hundred years later the African Prince rose up out of the seas and swept the maiden back across the middle passage over which her ancestors had come," he announces grandly. "I will show you our mountains and our stars; and give you cool drinks from gourds and teach you the old songs and the ways of our people," he promises. "And, in time, we will pretend that you have only been away for a day." Though fancifully idyllic, Asagai's description of the life he and Beneatha will lead in Nigeria is appealing, and as the play ends she seems to be realistically considering his proposal, although she has not made a decision when the curtain falls. In this way, Hansberry's *A Raisin in the Sun* introduces transatlantic marriage and relocation to Africa as a real and desirable possibility, as a viable alternative to remaining in the United

States, even while it seems to hint that the black American impulse to go "back to Africa" is often prompted by an idealized understanding and unreal expectations of the continent.

It is not clear whether Lorraine Hansberry modeled the characters of Asagai and Beneatha on actual people or based their relationship on actual events. It is thought, however, that the influence of William Leo Hansberry, the playwright's uncle and one of the earliest black American historians of Africa, helped to add a pan-African scope to her writing, and it is possible that Hansberry had contact with the African students whom her uncle instructed at Howard University. In any case, by the mid-1950s, when Hansberry began work on the play, there probably would have been numerous examples of actual campus relationships between Africans and black Americans on which to draw.

Whatever the possible factual basis of Asagai and Beneatha's relationship, it seems a realistic depiction, for it shares some important aspects with real-life transatlantic romances of the 1960s and 1970s. In this period, most relationships between black Americans and Africans involved African men (especially Nigerians, who outnumber all other African nationalities) and black American women, since the vast majority of Africans who traveled to the United States were male. And many of these unions seem to have reflected the racial politics of a period in which many young African Americans were looking to Africa for a new sense of identity and for reaffirmation, while a generation of Western-educated Africans looked to establish closer ties with blacks in the diaspora.

Like pan-Africanism itself, relationships and marriages between Africans and black Americans are often based on an assumption of cultural affinity, on expectations of shared values and attitudes. But even if Africans and African Americans do share an ancient heritage and some similar cultural values, in many relationships every interaction becomes a negotiation. And while many transatlantic couples do manage to build happy and lasting marriages, many other relationships collapse under the weight of cultural difference, unfulfilled expectations, misunderstandings, and inflexibility.

Most of the detailed accounts that exist of relationships between Africans and African Americans describe the failure of romantic idealism in the face of real cultural differences and belated realizations of incompatibility. And the recurring theme in these narratives is the way in which the seductive power of symbolic Africa can dazzle young pan-African-minded American women into marrying African men whom they don't know as well as they should and then moving to a continent that is very different from what they imagined. Many accounts seem to cast African men who court black American women as snake-oil salesmen intent on playing up their own exotic appeal, and many others refer to the unrealistic demands of African husbands who expect new American wives to adapt to African cultural practices without trouble, help, or complaint. And in general, most representations of failed marriages between Africans and black Americans attribute their demise to unsatisfied expectations on both sides.

The black American poet and writer Maya Angelou described her ill-fated marriage to an African in *The Heart of a Woman* (1981), the fourth book in her multipart autobiography. Described with Angelou's typical honesty and flair, the 1960s romance highlights the attitudes and feelings that often served as the basis for such relationships during that period, as well as the cultural barriers on which many of them ultimately floundered.

Angelou first saw Vusumzi Make, a South African anti-apartheid activist, at a gathering at a friend's home, and immediately found him physically attractive and tantalizingly exotic, with a "delicious" accent and the self-assurance of a warrior. But there was another aspect to Angelou's instant infatuation. As a "born again" black woman with natural hair and a penchant for African head wraps and fabrics, Angelou, like many African Americans of the period, was engaged in a conscious attempt to recreate her self-image by forging a new cultural identity that referred to Africa for inspiration. For this reason, Africans seemed to occupy a special place in her heart, as evinced by her admiration for a friend's African boyfriend. "The man was blue-black and spectacular," she relates eagerly. "His unquestionable dignity gave lie to the concept that black people were by nature inferior. His presence alone refuted the idea that our descendants had been naked subhumans living in trees three centuries before, when the whites raided them on the African continent. That elegance could not have been learned in three hundred years." Not only was Vusumzi Make an authentic African, possessed of a romantic grace and dignity, but he was spectacularly intelligent and engaged in a fight against white oppression in Africa, a struggle Angelou wanted to be part of.

And what's more, shortly after meeting Angelou, Make made his attraction to her assertively clear, insisting that she dance with him at a formal dinner they both attended. "He pulled me to him, and I felt the hardness under the layers of surrounding fat," she writes of the encounter. "He laughed. 'You're afraid of me, aren't you? A big girl like you, an American sophisticate, frightened by a little black man from The Dark Continent. . . . Miss Angelou, you have every reason to be alarmed. I intend to change your life. I am going to take you to Africa.' " Make seemed to deliberately use Africa as an enticement to make himself seem more attractive. And Africa seemed to figure prominently in the rapid erosion of Angelou's initial resistance.

It seems crazy, but after just a few brief meetings Angelou began to seriously consider a marriage proposal from this man, whom she barely knew. At first she vacillated, mainly because she was already engaged to an African American bail bondsman. But her fiancé began to seem dull and pedestrian compared with the fearless African freedom fighter, and Make continued his aggressive courtship. He sent flowers to her workplace with cards addressed to "Maya Angelou Make," and kept up a steady barrage of phone calls and gifts. He finally clinched the issue when he told Angelou how he had escaped from South Africa, a romantic tale of hardship and perseverance in the face of oppression. After being jailed for political activities in South Africa, Make told her, he was released and left for dead in the Namibian desert but survived by eating caterpillars and small animals he managed to kill with a makeshift slingshot. Avoiding towns, finding friends among nomadic hunters and bands of revolutionary guerrillas, Make eventually walked to freedom in Ethiopia, where he was able to contact other anti-apartheid fighters and resume his political activities from exile.

Whether it was completely true or not, Make's dramatic story made a strong impression on Angelou. When he described having to eat grubs to stay alive, Angelou found herself trying "to picture those exquisite hands carrying caterpillars, wiggling to his mouth," and she was captivated and inspired by the hardships that Make had endured in his quest for freedom. By the time Make concluded his story with yet another marriage proposal, Angelou was too overwhelmed to say no. And in the telling of his tale, Make also revealed the nature of his attraction to Angelou.

"When I knew I was coming to the yew ess, I came with the intention of finding a strong, beautiful black American woman, who would be a helpmate, who understood the struggle and who was not afraid of a fight," Make told her. "I heard about you and you sounded like the one. . . . You are exactly what I dreamed on my long march. . . . I am an African with large things to do. . . . I need you. I want to marry you." Angelou looked at Make and saw the embodiment of her own romantic imaginings of a rising, revolutionary

Africa, struggling to rid itself of the yoke of white rule—a seductive image for many black Americans at that time. And Make saw in Angelou the "flesh of his youthful dream," as she puts it. He had already decided before he reached America that he would return to Africa with a black American bride, endowed with all the endurance, intelligence, and vigor he imagined African Americans possessed, a powerful ally in his war against apartheid. Each seemed more attracted by ideas about the other's culture than by the other as an individual, a testament to the power of the passions that fuel the ways in which Africans and African Americans think about each other.

Enticed by the prospect of "a life of beckoning adventure in Africa" (not necessarily a life of love and companionship), Angelou decided to accept Make's proposal. When she told him her decision he held her hands aloft and exclaimed, "This is the joining of Africa and Africa-America! Two great peoples back together again." In this way he consciously underlined the symbolic value of their marriage in their own conception of it; this was not just the pairing of individuals, but the reunification of two long-separated communities. They seemed willing to see themselves, and each other, as cultural prototypes of an imagined identity.

"I would bring to him the vitality of jazz and the endurance of a people who had survived three hundred and fifty years of slavery," Angelou writes of her eagerness to embrace the role Make cast her in. "With me in his bed he would challenge the loneliness of exile. With my courage added to his own, he would succeed in bringing the ignominious white rule in South Africa to an end. If I didn't already have the qualities he needed, then I would just develop them. Infatuation made me believe in my ability to create myself into my lover's desire."

When Angelou announced the news of her imminent marriage to her friends, they voiced some concerns ("He's serious about the struggle, but what else do we know? Are you going to be a second or third wife? How is he planning to look after you?") but were generally supportive. Not that their disapproval would have discouraged Angelou. Her potent infatuation had been further fired by images of Africa that Make sent dancing through her imagination, and she surrendered herself to the romantic promise of return to the continent at the side of her new husband. "At the dining table he spread before me the lights and shadows of Africa," Angelou tells us.

Glories stood in thrilling array. Warrior queens, in necklaces of blue and white beads, led armies against marauding Europeans.

Nubile girls danced in celebrations of the victories of Shaka, the Zulu king. The actual earth of Africa was "black and strong like the girls back home" and glinted with gold and diamonds. African men covered their betrothed with precious stones and specially woven cloth. He asked me to forgive the paucity of the gift he had for me and to understand that when we returned to Mother Africa he would adorn me with riches the likes of which I had never imagined. When he led me into the darkened guest room and placed a string of beads around my neck, all my senses were tantalized. I would have found the prospect of a waterless month in the Sahara not only exciting, acceptable. The amber beads on my nut-brown skin caught fire. I looked into the mirror and saw exactly what I wanted to see, and more importantly, what I wanted him to see: a young African virgin, made beautiful for her chief.

Again, it's clear that the romantic pull of Africa and its huge impact on Angelou's imagination informed and reinforced her feelings for Make. In the end, her intense attraction was directed more to Africa, in all its powerful mystique, than to the short, round South African man who became her husband.

With the weight of such expectations bearing down on such a dubious foundation, it's not surprising that it didn't take long for the heady romance to begin to fade. The couple enjoyed a brief honeymoon in England, where Make attended a pan-American conference. But when Angelou left London for New York to rent an apartment and prepare it for Make's return, she soon found that being the wife of an African can carry expectations of which she'd been unaware. When Make saw the apartment and furniture that Angelou had chosen, he immediately disapproved of her secondhand-store selections. "I am an African," Make protested haughtily. "Even a man sleeping in the bush will lay fresh leaves on the ground. I will not sleep in a bed other men have used." Angelou wisely kept her thoughts to herself. "I didn't ask him what he did in hotels," she tells us. "Certainly he didn't call the manager and say, 'I want a brand-new mattress. I am an African.' "

Angelou soon found that her new husband had high expectations when it came to her performance of household chores as well. "It seemed to me that I washed, scrubbed, mopped, dusted and waxed thoroughly every other day," she says. "Vus was particular. He checked on my progress. Sometimes he would pull the sofa away from the wall to see if possibly I had missed a layer of dust. If he found his suspicions confirmed, his response could wither me. He would drop his eyes and shake his head, his face saddened with disappointment. . . . I was unemployed but I had never worked so hard in my life."

Angelou's friends were amused by the change in her ("That African's got her jumping," they laughed), and one close friend, the singer Abbey Lincoln, lauded Make's firm guidance. "Vus is teaching you that you're not a man, no matter how strong you are," Abbey said approvingly. "He's going to make you into an African woman." Angelou, however, began to wonder if she wanted to be an African woman, if this was what being one meant. "I wanted to be a wife and to create a beautiful home to make my man happy, but there was more to life than being a diligent maid with a permanent pussy," she complains.

The worst of the couple's early conflicts took place when Angelou first voiced her nagging suspicions of Make's infidelity. She had seen telltale evidence before, and she finally confronted him, as aggressively as she knew how. "If you chippie on me, you could get hurt, and I mean seriously," she warned. His response was characteristically arrogant. "Don't you ever threaten me," he said. "I am an African. I do not scare easily and I do not run at all. Do not question me again. You are my wife. That is all you need to know." Angelou found such unresolved finality hard to swallow, but remained silent, beginning to realize that this marriage had begun to present problems she had not anticipated. Surely infidelity was common to all cultures, but she found the idea that she should never question it difficult to accept.

Matters didn't really improve much when Make, Angelou, and her son from a previous relationship moved to Cairo, Egypt, where Make continued his anti-apartheid activities. Though the family lived in a roomy, expensively furnished house and managed to adjust to the new environment, gradually learning to speak Arabic and making new friends, the relationship between Angelou and Make worsened. He was usually inflexible with his culturally defined male conceits, and she had trouble being the unquestioning, dependent, and accepting woman he wanted her to be. And whenever they clashed, Make blamed Angelou's transgressions on her Americanness, characterizing her shortcomings as part of a general failure to be "African" enough. He repeatedly threw the mantra "I am an African" in her face, implying that she, an American, could never understand or properly satisfy him. For example, when it became clear to Angelou that they were having financial difficulties (a man came by the house threatening to repossess the furniture), she went out and got a job to help pay the bills. Predictably, Make was completely opposed to the idea. "You must call . . . and explain that you acted as an American woman, but that I returned home and reminded you that now you are an African wife," he insisted impatiently.

Make also tried to appeal to cultural differences to explain his chronic infidelity. When Angelou spotted evidence of his philandering for the umpteenth time and confronted Make with it, he responded glibly and unapologetically. "I am a man," he declared. "An African man. I am neither primitive nor cruel. . . . A man requires a certain amount of sexual gratification. Much more than a woman needs, wants or understands. . . . As an African man, in my society, I have the right to marry more than one woman." "But that is not true in my society and you knew that when we met," Angelou interjected indignantly. Make was unfazed. "I met you in the U.S.," he said smugly, "but now we are in Africa."

While Angelou was willing to adapt to Make's cultural expectations to a certain extent, accepting her husband's conveniently "African" attitude toward infidelity (an attitude that was by no means universally shared by the other African husbands she knew) was too much to ask. After enduring Make's unfaithfulness for years, Angelou finally decided that she could no longer tolerate it, and she announced that she wanted a divorce. It was an unfortunate end to a union that was supposed to symbolize greater closeness and cooperation between Africans and African Americans. But the marriage and its failure highlighted both the passionate power and the potentially deceptive danger of unrealistic assumptions about identity and black kinship.

Like Maya Angelou, Marita Golden, an African American writer, was attracted to an African man partly for the continent and culture that he symbolized in her imagination, and like Angelou she had a thoroughly disillusioning experience when she married him and moved to Africa. *Migrations of the Heart* (1983) is the chronicle of Golden's short-lived marriage to a Nigerian and her life in Lagos in the mid-1970s.

Golden was born and raised in Washington, D.C., by parents who instilled in her pride in her African heritage. Coming of age in the 1960s, she witnessed the intensification of the civil rights movement and the emergence of Black Power, and was radicalized by the assassination of Dr. King, a "flashing, endless moment" in which Golden's "belief in America seeped through my flesh and formed a puddle at my feet." In college she started hanging out with radical black students, chanting Black Power slogans and sporting a short natural. As she says of the period, "I was no longer a Negro girl. . . . I had chosen to become a black woman."

By the time she enrolled in graduate school in New York and met a Nigerian student, Golden was well prepared to establish a rapport with him as a pan-African-oriented African American who saw little at stake for herself in America and regarded Africans as distant cousins from overseas. Interestingly, it was the exotic sound of the man's accented speech and his "African" self-assuredness that first attracted her, as they had Angelou. Femi was "enveloped in the aura of supreme confidence that blossomed around all the Africans I had ever met," Golden writes. And his "halting British West African accent . . . made everything he said sound irresistible and solemn."

Like Angelou, Golden seemed captivated by the "Africanness" of her new friend's background, seeing him as embodying a distant and exotic place and culture she had read much about but had never really experienced. "He etched verbal pictures of his father, who was a chief, the man's eight wives and many children, his country—at once underdeveloped and lurching toward modern ways—and, most vividly, what he would do when he returned to a place pulsing so audibly through his bones and blood," she relates. "I felt negligible in the shadow he cast. I'd read about my past and now it sat across from me in a steak house, placid, and even a bit smug." In this way, at least initially, Golden's fascination with Femi stemmed from his identity as an African, or even, she implies, as the embodiment of Africa itself. He was her "past." And, like many African Americans influenced by the problack rhetoric of the 1960s, on some level Golden hoped that exploring her African past and reclaiming her ancestral identity would provide the rootedness, the sense of selfhood and belonging that she craved. Femi seemed like the perfect guide to her estranged heritage.

As Golden got to know Femi and met his Nigerian friends and family members in the New York area, she learned more about his home and culture and began to feel comfortable in the inclusive embrace of this surrogate African family. By now a literal orphan, as well as an African American of an often outspoken and bitter generation that had denounced American racism and begun to seek alternative homelands outside America, Golden began to hope that Femi and his people would satisfy her restless sense of homelessness and detachment. When she fell in love, it was perhaps as much with what Femi represented to her in cultural and emotional terms as with his own personality and values. And when she decided to marry him, she immediately began to feel psychologically cradled by her imagined new family, continent, and culture. "Already I had left this cosmic loneliness, the disconnectedness snapping at my heels," she writes.

In preparing herself to become Femi's wife, Golden decided to do some homework; with Femi's encouragement, she made her first trip to Africa, visiting Ghana and Nigeria in an attempt to see what would await her in married life. The trip was a fulfilling and rewarding experience for an African American raised to believe in Africa as an ancestral homeland. She arrived on a flight with other black Americans making the pilgrimage to the motherland, and savored a feeling of spiritual attachment to the land as she exited the plane. She felt an immediate sense of identification with the people she met and relished the sense of belonging she felt as another black face in an independent black country. She quickly became convinced of her ability to live and thrive on the continent.

Golden did, however, hear some disturbing stories about the fates of some African American women who had married Nigerian men. One black American man she met in Ghana advised her to make sure that Femi wasn't already married, warning that black American brides who first arrived in Nigeria often found that they were the second or third wives. The candid words of a black American whom Golden met in Lagos, and who was the wife of a Nigerian, weren't much more encouraging. In response to Golden's anxious question, "How is it to live here?" Sara Bankole replied, "A lot of that has to do with who you think you are when you come. Whether you keep the culture and the people at a distance or try to come to terms with it all. . . . I could tell you stories about women who've come and lasted three months. I could tell you ugly, bitter stories that would curdle the love I hear for your boyfriend every time you say his name. But I won't."

Though statements like these somewhat dampened her enthusiasm, Golden refused to dwell on them, choosing instead to immerse herself in the experience of being in Nigeria and trying to learn as much as she could about Femi's country. In observing Nigerian men in their element, Golden found their blatant misogyny alarming, but she came to better understand the nature of her love for Femi. "Belligerently patriarchal, the men assumed their worth and waited indifferently for the women to prove theirs," she writes. "Yet it was this masculinity that made them so undeniably attractive. Their self-consciousness translated into a rough-hewn charm. Watching their deft, often obvious interplay, I understood why Femi gained my loyalty and why, if what I was told was true, so many black women followed these men back home. Nigeria was their country to destroy or save. That knowledge made them stride and preen in self-appreciation. This assurance became for an Afro-American woman a gaily wrapped gift to be opened anew every day." Perhaps, for Golden and other black Americans of the 1960s, the seductive appeal of Africa and its people had something to do with the patriotic satisfaction of having a nation or homeland to call one's own, a sentiment many blacks at the time did not feel toward the United States. Returning to the United States with a favorable report of her stay in Africa, Golden decided to proceed with her plan to marry Femi and move to Nigeria.

Once married and living in Lagos, Femi tried to find work as an architect while Golden began teaching at a local college. Femi found it difficult to secure employment, and, as he became increasingly frustrated, he withdrew further and further into himself, refusing to share his thoughts and fears with Golden. When she complained to Femi's brother's wife, Golden found that it was common, even "proper," for a Nigerian man not to burden his wife with details of his personal problems. As her sister-in-law Bisi told her, "Uncle will never tell you everything. Do you think [my husband] confides in me?" Golden did not find such revelations helpful, but she resolved to at least try to make her peace with her new place and role in her adoptive culture.

As Golden gradually adjusted to life in Lagos and the routine of her job and life with Femi, she found contentment, if not fulfillment. But tradition and Femi's family soon began to encroach on her marriage, leading to new conflicts and tensions. Femi's younger brother came to live with the couple in Lagos, and he clashed with Golden immediately, making clear his disdain for her even while he enjoyed her hospitality. And the demands of Femi's friends and other extended family members proved equally burdensome. Golden learned that a wife, *iyawo* in Yoruba, was regarded as more than just her husband's partner: she was a nurturing spouse to his entire family. She found that she was expected to feed and entertain guests without question, and she resented the idea of being consigned to the kitchen as an automatic caterer and maid. "Iyawo—wife to husband and spiritual wife to his family," Golden writes bitterly. "The name fit me like a noose."

After struggling to find employment, Femi finally started his own business, and soon the couple's financial situation improved. However, after initial progress, Golden noticed that their income mysteriously began to shrink. When she confronted Femi with her observations, he admitted that since he had no children to support, his extended family had decided to increase the amount of his monthly contribution to the family's collectively held funds. Golden was outraged. "Oyingbo wife or no, I cannot say no to my family," Femi defended himself, using the Yoruba word for foreigner. "But you can say no to me," Golden retorted angrily. "Always you can say no to me. And always your family comes first." To Femi, debate was not an option; the demands of his extended family would almost always outweigh those of his wife. His response to her protests was a stony silence that lasted for weeks. "For the sin of questioning tradition I was cast outside the realm of his thoughts and consideration," Golden writes sadly.

As Golden made friends among other black American wives of Nigerians (she refers to them as "a clan in exile") she found that some of them shared her difficulties with certain aspects of Nigerian tradition. In fact, she realized that the problems plaguing her relationship with Femi seemed all too common. And in listening to the experiences of other African American wives, Golden began to acquire a deeper appreciation of what afflicted her own marriage. "Foreign wives were forced to bend to the collective will of clan, family and custom; or, if brave enough, to stake out an emotional territory of their own that acknowledged the conflicting claims of who they were and where they lived," she writes. "I spoke to black American women and Nigerian men, and . . . . was overwhelmed by their candor and willingness to admit to the ambiguities that characterized their special unions. . . . With startling honesty they all bore witness to the endurance of love and the failure of understanding."

Perhaps as a testament to the ultimate endurance of her feelings for Femi, Golden attempted to preserve her marriage and even became pregnant, giving birth to a son. After the child's birth, Golden's life improved for a while, but Femi soon reverted to his usual reticence, and tradition and custom soon resumed their chokehold. The couple began to drift apart. After one argument, Golden attempted to reason with Femi. "You have to work at a marriage," she complained. Femi's stony response seemed typically dismissive. "It's only you Americans who work at marriage," he sneered. "Africans don't have to." From his perspective, he may have been partly right. Femi and Golden clashed most frequently because differing assumptions led to misunderstanding and conflict; if Femi had married a Nigerian, perhaps his assumptions wouldn't have been so different from those of his wife. And perhaps there would have been no need to "work at" the marriage as much. Whatever the truth of his statement, his refusal to work through his differences with Golden resulted in her further estrangement from him, and, in Golden's opinion, doomed the marriage to failure. Starved of affection, she began having an affair with an African American man who lived in Lagos, and her relationship with Femi continued to worsen. When the oppressive tension finally erupted in violence and Femi struck her, Golden was merely relieved that the last straw had finally come.

Though she felt at home in Nigeria and would have preferred to stay, she realized that she would never win custody of her son if she remained in Africa, so she resolved to flee the country for the United States. She told an African American friend, Anita, of her plan, and secretly enlisted her aid. Interestingly, it turned out that Anita had helped other American women leave their Nigerian husbands, and she led Golden into a room filled with suitcases left behind by women escaping unfulfilling marriages. "Does it always end like this?" asked a wide-eyed Golden, looking at the heaped luggage, tangible testament to the failure of numerous transatlantic marriages. "Not always," replied Anita. "But more often than any of us like to think about." Golden successfully "escaped" Nigeria and moved to Boston, raising her son alone, remarrying, and always wondering if Femi would try to come after her. She eventually put her traumatic African experience behind her.

In essence, Golden's *Migrations of the Heart* is about a woman whose marriage failed under the pressures of overbearing in-laws, an unresponsive husband, and cultural misunderstandings. And in the same way, Maya Angelou's experience can be seen as the story of a woman who struggled to please an unfaithful and arrogant husband and eventually got fed up and divorced him. But in both cases, the relationships were in some way predicated on a mutual sense of identification and affinity that grew out of notions of black kinship through a shared African heritage.

In this way, the difficulties each couple encountered can be seen as calling into question black assumptions of automatic rapport, underlining the complexity inherent in the clash between pan-African perceptions and realities.

By the late 1970s, there were so many marriages between black American women and African men that in addition to being chronicled in books like Marita Golden's, more and more of them began to gain the attention of the black media. In 1979, for example, the African American women's magazine *Essence* devoted several articles in a single issue to posing the question "Can African–Afro-American marriages work?" —a query that in itself seemed to acknowledge the difficulties that many couples had apparently faced. All of the couples who appeared in the issue reported various cultural pitfalls that often beset relationships between Africans and black Americans, but most insisted that transatlantic unions can and do work. And for most of those interviewed, notions of pan-African unity and affinity seemed to have helped inform the decision to marry a spouse from across the Atlantic.

As noted, from the 1950s to the 1970s, most marriages between Africans and African Americans seem to have involved West African men, especially Nigerians, and black American women who typically met on American college campuses. When Africans and African Americans began to have greater contact in different contexts, and as more African women got the opportunity to travel and study in the United States, the "typical" profile of transatlantic couples began to change. In the 1990s media attention focused on marriages between black Americans and South Africans as the next wave in relationships between Africans and Americans, but while the nationalities and genders have shifted, what hasn't changed are the cultural challenges faced by spouses who come from completely different backgrounds.

In the same way that black Americans who followed husbands home to Nigeria in the 1970s had to contend with a new cultural and social milieu, the American spouses of South Africans have faced similar challenges in confronting South African culture and society. An unknown number of black American–South African marriages have reportedly ended in divorce, but most couples have apparently managed to strike a functional balance between sometimes conflicting values and expectations. And their success, like that of the many other transatlantic marriages that have flourished despite cultural obstacles, seems a validation of the pan-Africanist impulse, the horror stories of writers like Angelou and Golden notwithstanding.

Despite the fact that failed African–African American marriages seem more prevalent than successful ones in terms of the literary record, blacks from America and blacks from Africa have continued to pair off in increasing numbers since the 1960s. Some marriages, as we have seen, have crumbled when confronted with contentious cultural assumptions, but many others, including that of my parents, have thrived as cross-cultural partnerships that have seemed to vindicate expectations of understanding and affinity. Some celebrated marriages have even seemed an appropriate embodiment of a pan-African program, as when Miriam Makeba, the South African songbird ("Mama Africa" herself), married the late Stokely Carmichael, the Caribbean-American Black Power leader who later became Kwame Ture, to much fanfare in 1968. Although the marriage was short-lived, many saw it as not only a romantic pairing of lovers but also a symbolic joining of international celebrities who had helped to define the political struggles of their respective peoples.

While the reasons behind any relationship are entirely subjective and personal, transatlantic marriages do not take place in a vacuum, and sentiments of black kinship and positive identification with blacks from across the Atlantic have often seemed to play a role. Africans and African Americans tend to regard each other through lenses colored by myths and fantasies about each other, and in romance this has often served as both the basis for attraction and the cause of misunderstanding. Africa's mysterious allure for many black Americans, and the often glamorous or glorified image many Africans have of black Americans, can serve to pique romantic interest, but without a strong foundation of love and personal compatibility they cannot sustain a marriage. In personal relations, as in all aspects of African–African American relations, myths, assumptions and expectations can form a minefield best negotiated with caution.

Although marriages between Africans and African Americans can often seem fraught with potentially divisive points of dispute, perhaps the most positive and enduring legacy of such relationships are the children they produce. The children of transatlantic unions often seem the appropriate embodiment of notions of black kinship, the living guarantors of even closer African–African American ties in the future. As the African American wife of a Nigerian put it, her children would "straddle the Atlantic," inheriting the cultural identity and knowledge of two nations and uniquely equipped to mediate between them, and a South African man married to an African American woman expressed a comparable perspective. "[My wife] and I are developing an understanding of our differences," he said of the process of negotiation that characterized their first few years of marriage. "We will pass this on to our children, who we hope will gain confidence and have a global outlook." Both African and African American, the offspring of marriages between Africans and black Americans represent a synthesis of perspectives; they're the product of two cultures and usually sensitive to the complexities of each, the virtual personification of dreams of black kinship, born intermediaries between transatlantic communities.

As the children of an African and an African American, my brothers and I often had the impression of moving between worlds and contexts, of bouncing between African and American families and cultures. Most aspects of our lives reflected the duality of our bicultural heritage, and in balancing between cultures we created a cultural amalgam of our own, an African–American identity forged by our family's symbolic joining of two continents and cultures. It's an outlook that served us well as we grew into a childhood understanding of who we were. Our dual black heritage and its ties to two families and traditions were among our parents' greatest gifts to us. And in celebrating the two histories that shaped our identity, we grew into a worldview that spanned the Atlantic.

WHAT IS AFRICA TO ME?

What is Africa to me:
Copper sun or scarlet sea,
Jungle star or jungle track,
Strong bronzed men, or regal black
Women from whose loins I sprang
When the birds of Eden sang?
One three centuries removed
From the scenes his fathers loved,
Spicy grove, cinnamon tree,
What is Africa to me?
　　　　　　　—Countee Cullen, "Heritage" (1925)

Although she grew up to be black and proud, when my mother was a very little girl, she wished that she were white. She used to parade around the house with a towel or an inside-out T-shirt draped over her head, flicking this "hair" casually over her shoulder or out of her eyes as she had seen the white girls at school do. She resented the fact that she had inherited her father's coarse and nappy "bad" hair instead of her mother's naturally straight "good" hair. Like her sisters, she intensely disliked the regular trips to the hairdresser that their mother insisted on, painful weekly ordeals in which their tender heads were tweaked, pinched, and bombarded with harsh chemicals, and their hair washed, pressed, burned, and trussed into temporary straight submission. Being white and having long, flowing tresses would have made life a lot simpler. And white people seemed to run the world, too.

One summer when my mother was eight years old, her grandmother came up to Detroit to "carry" her and her sister Anne "down home." They began the trip sitting near white and black passengers, but when their train entered Mississippi, they had to change to one of the segregated cars. And once in Meridian, my mother was disturbed to see drinking fountains labeled "White" and "Colored," and angry that she and Anne had to sit in the balcony when they went to the movies, while the white kids sat in the good seats closer to the screen. When she asked about it, her grandmother told her that some whites did not like black people and didn't think they should have the same rights. It didn't seem fair, but that was the way it was. The next day my mother was playing in the front yard of her grandmother's house when a young white woman walked by. The woman smiled pleasantly and said hello. My mother stuck her tongue out at her with all the indignant venom she could muster and ran into the house.

My mother's family got their first television set when she was eleven years old, and virtually everyone on TV was white. Whenever a dark face showed up on the black-and-white screen, whoever was watching would yell for everybody to come and see, and my mother and her sisters would gather around the TV with a feeling of anticipation and pride, or, sometimes, with a sense of uneasiness and dread. The family closely watched developments in the early civil rights movement unfold on the evening news, and they enjoyed rooting for black athletes, especially boxers like the dashing Sugar Ray Robinson. But they spurned the embarrassing and all too common antics of black TV buffoons like Amos 'n' Andy. Some of the most humiliating images were in the Hollywood movies set in Africa, which almost always depicted the Africans as ignorant savages in animal skins and bone jewelry, grunting menacingly or comically at the white hero. Among my mother's playmates, one of the surest ways to start a fight was to call someone an ABC—"Africa's Blackest Child." And in school, Africa was never mentioned in a positive light. White people ruled the world, and Africa seemed like the worst place on earth, the furthest from their civilizing embrace. My mother wanted no reminders that there was anything relating her to the big jungle continent that was home to cannibals and brutes.

Things were quite different for my brothers and me, growing up in Massachusetts in the early 1970s, a generation after my mother first dreamed of being white. I grew into my understanding of my race the way I grew into my name, and I've been proud to be black for as long as I can remember. As a kid I think I took it for granted that black was beautiful and that blackness was a badge of excellence; these were self-evident truths I internalized at a young age. There weren't many explicit discussions about race with my parents or siblings in which these values were passed on—instead, my brothers and I grew into a racial pride based on our parents' example and that of numerous black figures who populated our childhood world.

We lived in a predominantly white neighborhood, and all of my elementary school teachers were white. But aside from them, everyone I looked up to was black. My father was the wisest, most dignified man I knew, my mother the kindest and most beautiful woman I knew, my brother Remy was the smartest, most unafraid kid I knew. My more distant heroes included Muhammad Ali, Stevie Wonder, and the Jackson Five. Years later, in college I was alarmed to read that when James Baldwin was a young child he was so bombarded by media representations of whites that he assumed he, too, was white until the disorienting and traumatic revelation of his own blackness. My own experience, decades after Baldwin struggled with the burden of his own identity, was vastly different—my brothers and I learned we were black at an early age and were taught to be proud of it. We certainly did not hate white people, since we were taught to value diversity and had family friends of all races, but when challenged we felt compelled to demonstrate our equality.

And being black in mainly white Boston suburbs in the 1970s was often an embattled experience. On one occasion, the cousins of some white kids who lived across the street were visiting from out of town and casually called Remy and me "niggers." Remy, then around nine or ten, solemnly challenged them to a fight. Remy gave me a pep talk before the fight, explaining its importance: we weren't fighting just for ourselves but for black people everywhere, and we weren't going to allow those white boys to disrespect us like that. It was wintertime, and the three kids who had offended us (one of them was Remy's age and the other two were about my size) showed up at the designated spot brandishing snowballs. Remy shouted at the boys to drop them. He wasn't about to settle this with a minor snowball skirmish; we had been insulted at a profound and basic level, and were out for blood, prepared to take on all three of them and confident in our ability to prevail. The fight itself was brief but furious, an icy free-for-all in which we grappled together on the snow-covered ground. I still have an image frozen in my memory of the oldest of the white kids shoving me hard from behind and Remy lighting into him with renewed fury. It ended when I bloodied the nose of one of our younger opponents and he started crying. Our honor satisfied and the reputation of our race defended, we celebrated the triumph of blackness over bigotry with self-aggrandizing trash talk on our front steps.

Once, I got into a fight with a new kid in the neighborhood (I think he was from India or Pakistan) when he rebuffed my friendly welcome because "his mother told him not to play with blacks." I was more indignant and angry than wounded. I didn't really care that his family had rejected me, but I did think they (or he, at least) should be punished for their views and forced to contend with my existence. He was a little younger and smaller than me, and after that first beating he took to running at my approach, to my unforgiving satisfaction.

As secure in our racial pride as we were, as kids we had little way of knowing that our attitudes represented a shift in recent African American culture, and that our forebears, including my mother, had not always shared this unapologetically problack outlook. In inculcating in us a sense of racial pride, my parents, like many of their peers, were participating in a deliberate celebration of blackness that had gained currency among blacks in America since the mid-1960s, a celebration expressed in all aspects of culture.

My brothers and I still tease my mother about the ten-inch Afro she sports in many photographs from the early seventies, a hairstyle that complemented the African-print skirts and dresses she wore and the African or African-inspired art that adorned our living room walls. Other, older photos in our family albums capture my mother with permed or straight hair plastered against her forehead or teased out wispily around her head, but I have never seen her wear anything but a natural. She gave up hot combs and perms before I was born, after the "black is beautiful" rhetoric of the 1960s forced many blacks in America and elsewhere to reevaluate the Eurocentric standards of beauty that had informed their self-image for centuries.

It was a time when it was cool to wear your blackness loudly. My aunt Anne, my mother's older sister, who lived with us for several years when I was growing up, was an accomplished seamstress and outfitted the entire family in colorful African "dashikis," then all the rage among the problack Afro-American set. I chose the striped fabric for my shirt, and when it was finished I would sport it with my favorite corduroy bell-bottoms, which made a distinctive "zzzip" sound when I walked as the material rubbed together. To complete the effect, I used to comb out my short, nappy hair with a plastic Afro pick that had a Black Power fist for a handle. I was aspiring toward the outsize hair haloes of the dancers I watched on *Soul Train*. My slow-growing hair never reached anywhere near the heights of say, pre–Jheri Curl Michael Jackson's, but I did manage to cushion my scalp with a couple of inches of growth that I would proudly comb out and pat into shape each morning.

My education in blackness also went beyond fashion. My mother once sat me down to debunk the Pledge of Allegiance, telling me it was okay to participate in the daily recitation of the pledge at school, but reminding me that the words "with liberty and justice for all" were untrue and that America had long denied these rights to blacks. I learned the general slaves-kidnapped-and-brought-to-America narrative before I even attended school, and I was smugly incredulous when my mother told me that some black Americans first learned that their ancestors had come from Africa when *Roots* aired in 1977. By the time I watched the miniseries with my family, I was already familiar with the slavery story, but *Roots* still had a significant impact on me. I was angered and traumatized by the terrible treatment of the slaves, and I was especially upset with the failure of the slave ship revolt staged by Kunta Kinte and his compatriots.

My brothers and I brought our racialized attitude to other TV programs. Though we watched seventies kids' staples like *The Brady Bunch* and *Gilligan's Island*, our favorite shows were the black classics *Good Times*, *What's Happening!!*, and *Sanford and Son*. The stereotypical ghetto experience depicted on *Good Times* bore little overt resemblance to our own lives in suburban New England, but we sympathized with the trials of J.J. and the Evans family and felt a kinship with them we did not feel for John-Boy and the other Waltons. My mother was quick to note that the 1950s presented so nostalgically on TV were not *Happy Days* for most black people, and we had little interest in "white" programs like *All in the Family* and *Dallas*. And when my brothers and I watched Westerns, we always rooted for the Indians.

My mother often read to my brothers and me from books featuring black characters, including an illustrated children's version of the *Autobiography of Malcolm X*. When I was very young, one of my early favorites was called *A Is for Africa*, an alphabet book that toured Africa, featuring a different African crop or person for each letter; "C" was for Cleopatra, "H" was for Hannibal, and "I" was for ice cream, since cocoa and vanilla were both African exports.

The lessons in black identity I learned at home often manifested themselves at school as well. I enjoyed my classes at the local public school, even though I was always the only black kid in the class. I never felt victimized or targeted, because I usually basked in the teacher's favor as the good-natured token black kid who could read above the class level. I was a good student, participated in class discussions, and spoke my mind, and I never felt that anything less was expected of me. If anything, I was a prized mascot who was encouraged to excel.

There was little in the curriculum that focused on black people, but I still managed to find ways to express my perspective and interests. When my third-grade teacher told each student in my class to pick a country to cover in a geography report, I chose Egypt because I knew it was the site of a glorious ancient African civilization. When the class went on a field trip to the John F. Kennedy Memorial Library in Boston, I found little of interest until I saw a picture in which JFK was shaking hands with Martin Luther King, Jr.; afterwards, that photograph, and a golden sculpture of a sailboat, based on a presidential doodle, were the only two exhibits I could recall from that class trip. On another class outing, I was deeply moved and a little vocally self-righteous when my class visited a museum commemorating the Underground Railroad and inspected a secret room in the basement where runaway slaves had once hidden.

The lessons of my parents and the prevailing climate of 1970s black outspokenness and pride provided me with a strong sense of identification with Africa. But though my own father was from Africa, and though a celebration of Africa was part and parcel of the problack rhetoric that had shaped me, I really knew very little about the continent. My father's stories of "the village" were mainly the stuff of nostalgia, the recollections of a man who missed his home and wanted to preserve its memory for his foreign-born children. His stories usually made the Africa of his childhood sound like a sort of natural utopia. Of course, when he wanted to motivate us, we'd hear about how strictly disciplined his upbringing had been, how he had had to walk seven miles to get to school and how he had never had an allowance, a bike, a TV or owned any books. But for the most part our father sought to encourage in us a positive consciousness of and identification with the nation and culture of his birth. The stories were brush strokes and impressions that helped me to sketch a picture in my mind, but the things he described were so far outside my middle-class northeastern U.S. experience that I couldn't help but conjure a foreign and fantastic landscape. Even on the rare occasions when my father described negative aspects of his homeland (Belgian colonialism, for example), his memories had the rose-hued glow of distance and affection, and little he said made Congo seem much different from the pastoral paradise I had seen in *Roots*, a bountiful and bucolic place where the only major problems were caused by oppressive white outsiders.

Photos of my Zairean relatives in the family album were informative, but still left much to the imagination. My brothers and I used to flip through these pictures and ask my mother who some of the faces belonged to and why no one in the pictures was smiling. Almost all of the photos were black-and-white and all of them depicted sober-faced Zairean men in pleated pants and wide-hipped Zairean women in patterned dresses posing carefully in front of studio backdrops painted with mountains. Sometimes children standing uncomfortably at attention in their special-occasion clothes appeared in the pictures, and I would search their faces for clues as to what it was really like over there. There were a few pictures from when my parents and Remy lived in Congo before I was born, and these depicted my brother and some of his playmates in the compound of the family's concrete house in Kinshasa. There was also a picture of a market woman balancing a large bundle of wood on her head, a photo apparently taken by my aunt Anne on her visit to my parents in Congo, where she was fascinated by everything she saw. Though I stared intently and with interest at the photos of my father's immediate family, most of the people in the pictures were strangers to me, and remained strangers even when my father attempted to explain how we were related. And the posed studio photos didn't convey much of a sense of *place* to me; they did little to fill the gaps in my knowledge about Africa.

There were, of course, other Africans besides my father in my early life. I saw my father's Zairean family and friends in the area quite often. To my child's eyes, Zaireans seemed good-natured people who loved to eat, drink, dance, argue, and enjoy themselves, but they remained mysterious. And of course, the presence in the United States of all these Congolese did make me wonder why they had all left the Congo, if, as they said, it was so pleasant there. It was clear from my father that his origins in Congo were humble, and that he had not had access to many of the things my brothers and I took for granted. I knew that he had come to the United States to go to school, as had many of our Zairean relatives and friends, but even though everyone talked about returning home, I couldn't see what had prompted so many to seek their fortunes in America when Zaire was presented as a more than worthy alternative.

Africa was a place of my imagination, a mythical environment I constructed in my mind out of raw materials provided by my father, books I had read, and movies and TV shows I had seen. I knew from my father that Africa was more than just a wilderness, which was always how it was portrayed on *Tarzan* and in an ad for the Serengeti wildlife park I saw on TV. But even my parents' ongoing critique of the stereotypical African images that appeared in the media and in books I read could not entirely shield me from the prevailing views of Africa that had long saturated the American psyche. When my father spoke of "the village," years of American television, books, popular mythology, and movies provided me with a welter of associations and images, most of them negative. To my American-educated mind's eye, a "village" was a cluster of grass huts inhabited by Africans in grass skirts and loincloths; I didn't know how that squared with the "village" of my father's experience, but it was this image that his sometimes vague stories evoked.

Though I wasn't conscious of it, like most African Americans throughout history, I ended up having to reconcile my impulse to identify with Africa as a homeland and source of cultural pride with the stereotypes and negative views I inherited from mainstream America. In the end, I knew more about Africa than my white classmates, but was still somewhat susceptible to the prevailing American popular wisdom, which held Africa to be a wild, untamed jungle plagued by famine and bereft of Western technology, infrastructure, and advanced social institutions. While I took the humanity of black people and their potential for brilliance to be self-evident, I still internalized much of American popular culture's imagery of Africa. I found myself locked in the ambivalent state of loving and looking forward to going to a place I knew little about and secretly believed to be backward.

Europeans had called Africa the Dark Continent, a term that expressed their own ignorance of what lay within the continent and their worst fears and assumptions of African savagery. In confronting this sort of legacy, black Americans of the 1970s, in a proud celebration of an African heritage, deliberately strove to unlearn the stereotypes and negative views of Africa that had long fueled African American disdain for the continent. But for many of the blacks who helped to popularize the black cultural reassessment of Africa in the 1970s, Afros, Afrocentric names, T-shirts and other trinkets did little to fill the void in African American knowledge about contemporary African realities. For me as a child in Boston, and for many other black Americans, despite Africa's new prominence as the inspiration for a revolution in African American culture, Africa remained a "dark" continent, shadowed and shrouded in distant mystery. I venerated the glory of the African past in school projects on ancient Egypt, I expressed my cultural identification with Africa in my attire, and I eagerly absorbed my father's sentimental stories of his Congolese childhood. But in the end, my impression of Africa was an imagined one, conjured in my mind with morsels of information given shape by my own naiveté.

A moment stands out in my mind as one that challenged me to come to terms with my own ignorance and conflicted emotions regarding Africa. As a child I would often flip through the books and magazines that overflowed from the desk in my father's study, and once, glancing through a magazine that focused on Africa, I saw a picture that frightened and horrified me. In the photograph, a shirtless African man wearing black pants had his hands bound behind his back, around a wooden post; his body leaned painfully to one side, his arms were twisted in an awkward, unnatural position and I could see how tightly the rope cut into his wrists. His torso and face were marred with ugly red bullet wounds. He was dead. The caption said something about Liberia and civil war. This image left me feeling confused. My father's Africa, as presented to me, seemed idyllic and safe. The Africa my family celebrated in posters, T-shirts, and dress was an ancestral homeland where proud black people were working to uplift themselves; and the Africa I learned of from American popular culture was a lush jungle that was backward, but hardly sinister. There was no place for this cruel and murderous image in the Africa of my imagination, and I struggled to understand its implications.

*   *   *

My childhood ambivalence toward the birthplace of my father was hardly unique. Africa has cast a long shadow in the African American psyche since the very invention of African Americans. Africa was the home from which slaves were forcibly wrenched, the land of their birth, the haven of their families and friends, the place to which they strove to return in life and, as many slaves believed, the place where their souls found peace in death. It was where they were from, and so it was who they were. It is impossible to really appreciate what forced abduction and separation from everything one has ever known must have been like, but telling accounts from across the ages speak to the slaves' strong psychological ties to their homeland. Slave traders reported that shackled slaves would often pitch forward into the African sand before being loaded aboard the slave ship, filling their mouths with African soil, a gritty keepsake designed to maintain a physical link with the motherland to complement the emotional ties that must have weighed heavy on their hearts as they glimpsed the African coast-line for the last time.

We can only imagine what went through the captives' heads and hearts as they huddled in the slave ship's foul hold, listening to the surf splashing against the hull as they sped farther from home, into the unknown. Perhaps they found some small consolation in the crunch of the dirt between their teeth, a tangible reminder of their homeland. More likely, and slave ship records would seem to support this, recollections of Africa served as the basis for plans for escape. It is natural to assume that all of the slaves captured in West Africa and bound for the New World wanted to escape and go home, and there are numerous examples of enslaved Africans attempting to do just that. Slave uprisings aboard American-bound vessels were common but rarely successful; nonetheless, slave ship captains seemed to live in constant fear of revolt and spoke as if the slaves were always planning ways to liberate themselves and return to Africa, up until the point that they were sold in America. The famous and now Hollywood-ized *Amistad* affair of 1839, in which a group of slaves killed two crewmen of the slave ship *Amistad* and ordered the remainder to return them to Africa, was only the best known of hundreds of slave ship revolts.

Another common form of escape was suicide. Slave ships typically lost some members of their cargoes to suicide on each voyage, and it was widely held that slaves who jumped overboard or "willed" themselves to death did so both to deliver themselves from slavery and be-cause they believed that when they died their spirits would return to Africa.

There are also numerous legends in which Africans enslaved in the New World are said to have returned to their homeland using magical means. The legend and image of the "flying African" is an enduring one in the African American storytelling tradition. Legends in the cul-turally rich Sea Islands of Georgia tell of a group of African "Ibos" led by a powerful sorceress who flew home to Africa from a slave ship moored at a site still known as Ibo Landing. Elsewhere, the story goes that field slaves on southern plantations believed that they would be able to fly home if they gave up salt in their diets, but that those who did so were forced to leave without their wives and children, who were fed salty food when they worked in the master's house.

Early African American folklore about Africa usually has this sort of "return" theme; Africa is regarded as a natural homeland, to which all Africans should eventually return, a viewpoint that speaks to the powerful position of Africa in the early African American imagination. The same sense is conveyed by early black spirituals and folk songs, which usually speak of deliverance from the hell of slavery through a voyage to a paradise that, though often unnamed, can be thought of as the free states in the American North or Africa. "Swing low, sweet chariot / Coming for to carry me home," goes the refrain of one of the best-known black spirituals.

That the African slaves' memory and celebration of their estranged home was a mythologized one goes without saying. Africans in America looked back at Africa from their vantage as slaves in a far distant land, remembering their family, lands, and life there with the idealized nostalgia of those whose destiny has been altered by forces beyond their control. Africa was where they belonged, where they were born, and where their place in the world was securely defined; America was where they had been brought against their will and enslaved. Regardless of the reality of their lives in Africa, slaves could not help but filter their memories through this perspective. Africa, remembered in opposition to the hellish conditions of slavery, was a land of freedom and opportunity, a bucolic near paradise where life was governed by ancient customs and values. This was how the first African Americans would have remembered their original home—indeed, this was how they would have had to remember it for its memory to continue to act as a source of reassurance and identity. And this was how they would have represented it to their children, the first generation of Africans born in America.

If the reality of Africa was somewhat obscured or distorted by the traumatic experience of slavery, the rigors of the slavery system itself certainly did not help matters. To prevent slave revolts, the plantation system as organized in America created slave populations that mixed Africans from different tribal groups and discouraged African cultural practices. Slaves were not permitted to speak their original tribal languages; they were not permitted to use drums and were often discouraged from dancing; they were converted to Christianity and forbidden to practice their original religions; and, perhaps the ultimate insult, they were stripped of their African names. While the plantation system put in place the conditions under which a new and uniquely African American culture was created, it also ensured that much of Africa's cultural legacy would be lost to later generations of African Americans.

African acculturation on Southern plantations was more a process of mixing and syncretization than a process in which one culture displaced the other—for instance, the Christianity practiced by African slaves borrowed from African belief systems. But the result of this process was that snippets of African culture and remembrances survived, without the bigger cultural context into which they originally fit. In parts of the West Indies, where runaway slaves were able to retain a sense of cultural continuity with Africa in "maroon" communities, which closely resembled those they had left at home, some African languages and cultural practices survived all but intact for hundreds of years. In America, where escape was difficult and small slave populations had more direct contact with white culture, African cultural survivals were less enduring.

In this way, while second- or third-generation African American slaves might have inherited an appreciation of Africa as a mythologized homeland, they would have had little specific knowledge of the continent and would have perhaps internalized many of the negative associations and stereotypes that dominated white America's understanding of Africa. This sort of ambivalence, a complex sense of simultaneous attraction and revulsion toward Africa undergirded by a general ignorance manifested in stereotypes and myths, has dogged African Americans throughout their history. It can be seen as an aspect of W.E.B. Du Bois's famous theory of African American "double consciousness," the psychological challenge of reconciling an African heritage with a European upbringing and education. African Americans have always had to figure out how to identify with a historical homeland that they have been taught to reject, and the various strategies they have used to do so have found expression in many ways.

The ways in which African Americans have positioned themselves in relation to Africa have long been subject to the push and pull of clashing viewpoints on the continent. And tendencies have shifted with the times, reflecting political and social events in society at large. What *has* remained fairly constant is the mythical space that Africa occupies in the collective African American imagination. African Americans have always had a range of associations and ideas about Africa, but certain themes and images seem to crop up again and again. Words like *jungle, strange, ancient, mysterious*, and *heathen*, words that conjure images drawn from the prevailing American "wisdom" regarding Africa and reflect African American ignorance of the realities of the continent recur frequently in African American imaginings of Africa.

The African slaves were reeducated, taught of the inferiority of their homeland and culture. Olaudah Equiano, a West African who was enslaved as a child around 1756 and later wrote one of the earliest and most influential slave narratives, wrote of Africa with positive recollections, describing a simple and pastoral life among his Ibo kinfolk in what is now Nigeria. However, after just a few years as a slave in the West Indies, America, and England, Equiano came to accept the idea of African inferiority: "It was now between two and three years since I first came to England," he writes. "I now not only felt myself quite easy with my new countrymen, but relished their society and manners. I no longer looked upon them as spirits, but as men superior to us; and therefore I had the stronger desire to resemble them; to imbibe their spirit, and imitate their manners." Equiano was subsequently baptized, and his narrative ends with an account of his efforts to organize a black settlement in Sierra Leone, where he planned to introduce Christianity to his pagan fellows. Equiano's solution to his own conflicted double consciousness was to internalize white culture and values and share them with his fellow Africans.

The African American poet Phillis Wheatley, who was born in Senegal and enslaved in America in 1761, when she was about seven, expressed a similar attitude. After being converted to Christianity and educated in English and Latin by her master, Wheatley began writing poems, and by the time she was a teenager she had published a volume of poetry (the first book ever published by an African American) that was well received in North America and England. She was a novelty: a slave whose literary talents seemed to refute prevalent Enlightenment notions of black inferiority. However, although Africa featured prominently in Wheatley's verse as her acknowledged land of origin, she, like Equiano, accepted the premise of African backwardness. Wheatley celebrated her deliverance from Africa's "dark abodes" in poems like "On Being Brought from Africa to America," which reflected a perspective common among blacks in America at the time:

> 'Twas mercy brought me from my Pagan land,
> Taught my benighted soul to understand
> That there's a God, that there's a Saviour too:
> Once I redemption neither sought nor knew.
> Some view our sable race with a scornful eye,
> "Their colour is a diabolic die."
> Remember, Christians, Negros, black as Cain,
> May be refin'd, and join th' angelic train.

For Wheatley, reconciling her historical ties to Africa with her adoptive American culture became an effort to *transcend* her African
identity; she acknowledged the inferiority of her background, but reminded her readers that it was a circumstantial, not innate, condition
and had not prevented her from finding religious salvation and rising
in civilized American society, and would not prevent others like her
from doing the same.

Wheatley wrote much of her poetry on the eve of the American
Revolution, when many free blacks were poised in optimistic anticipation of full inclusion in the new nation. When the revolution failed
to earn free blacks the rights of citizenship, there was a corresponding
shift in African American attitudes toward Africa, and the notion of
African American emigration became popular. As early as 1809, Paul
Cuffe, a free black Quaker sailor from Massachusetts who had long
championed the cause of full rights for free blacks, began exploring
the possibility of African American resettlement in Africa. Though he
regarded Africa in positive terms, as a potential alternative homeland
for American blacks, Cuffe believed, with Wheatley, that Africa and
Africans would benefit from contact with Westerners. His interest in
the continent was framed in terms of what he and American-educated
blacks could offer the homeland of their ancestors. As he wrote to a
business associate, "I have for some years had it impressed on my
mind to make a voyage to Sierra Leon in order to inspect the situation
of that country, and feeling a real desire that the inhabitants of Africa
might become an enlightened people and be so favored as to give general satisfaction to all those who are endeavoring to establish them in
the true light of Christianity. And as I am of the African race I feel
myself interested for them and if I am favored with a talent I think I
am willing that they should benefit thereby."

Martin Delany, the next great champion of African American emigration to Africa, echoed Cuffe's position in his efforts to popularize
resettlement among free black communities in the Northeast. Delany,
too, cast emigration as an opportunity for black Americans to lead
their overseas brethren out of the darkness. "In Africa we shall be
freemen indeed, and republicans, after the model of this republic," he
told an audience of Baltimore free blacks in 1827. "We shall carry
your language, your customs, your opinions and Christianity to that
now desolate shore, and thence they will gradually spread. . . . Africa,
if ever destined to be civilized and converted, can be civilized and converted by that means only." For these early African American spokesmen, Africa was the motherland where they belonged, both because

they saw no future for their race in America and because they owed it to the land of their ancestors to bring home the superior religion and learning of the West. Here we see one of the dominant and most enduring African American ideas about Africa: the notion that African Americans should "rescue" Africa with their Western religion and expertise. The perspective was grounded in paternalistic ideas of African inferiority. But in the nineteenth century and beyond it formed one of the main ways in which African Americans expressed their identification with Africa—by proposing to move to the motherland and "civilize" her. Interestingly, as we shall see, it's an idea that later gained considerable currency among Africans as well.

The emigration idea did have its detractors, however, especially as the intensification of the abolition movement renewed hope for African American integration into free American society. Frederick Douglass, one of slavery's most eloquent opponents and one of the most important black Americans of the period, summarized what he saw as most African Americans' position on Africa and emigration in the pre–Civil War years in this way: "We are of the opinion that the free colored people generally mean to live in America, and not in Africa. . . . We do not mean to go to Liberia. Our minds are made up to live here if we can, or die here if we must. . . . Here we are and here we shall remain. . . . We live here—have lived here—have a right to live here, and mean to live here." For Douglass, double consciousness or divided loyalty was not even an issue; he felt that African Americans had suffered too much and too long to give up their right to full inclusion in American society. To identify with blacks overseas was well and good, but in Douglass's eyes Africa could never replace the home that blacks had made for themselves in America, and had every right to claim.

With Emancipation and the brief but dramatic political and social gains African Americans made during Reconstruction, the emigration idea lessened in popularity. Blacks who held out hope that the reunited U.S. government would actually follow through on a proposal to give each former slave forty acres and a mule saw little point in chasing the dream of a better life in the land of their ancestors. But when these gains were all but erased in the conservative backlash to Reconstruction, many blacks, with palpable despair of ever being accepted in American society, renewed their hopes in Africa as an alternative homeland. "I see nothing for the Negro to attain unto this country," complained Henry McNeal Turner, a Methodist bishop and early pan-Africanist, in 1902. "I have already admitted that this country has books and schools, and the younger members of the Negro race, like the younger members of the white race, should attend them and profit by them. But for the Negro as a whole, I see nothing here for him to aspire after. He can return to Africa, especially Liberia, where a Negro government is already in existence, and learn the elements of civilization in fact; for human life there is sacred, and no man is deprived of it or any other thing that involves his manhood, without due process of law."

In attempting to gain support for the cause of African American emigration to Africa, African American leaders like John Henry Smyth, a U.S. envoy to Liberia, realized that they had to contend with generations' worth of negative attitudes toward Africa in the black American community. In 1895 Smyth noted of American blacks that "as a class they are averse to the discussion of Africa when their relationship with that ancient and mysterious land and its races is made the subject of discourse or reflection," and he went on to suggest some possible reasons for this. "The remoteness of Africa from America may be a reason for such feeling," he suggested. "The current opinion, in the minds of Caucasians, whence the American Negroes' opinions are derived, that the African is by nature an inferior man, may be a reason. The illiteracy, poverty, and degradation of the Negro, pure and simple, as known in Christian lands, may be a reason in connection with the partially true and partially false impression that the Negroes, or Africans, are pagan and heathen as a whole, and as a sequence hopelessly degraded beings. . . . It is lamentable that two hundred and fifty years have removed us to a far greater distance from Africa than the geographic measurement which separates America from Africa, and to-day that continent is perhaps of less interest to the educated and refined Negro of America than to his thrifty, industrious and adventurous white fellow-citizen." Smyth understood that before his dream of emigration could come true, negative African American ideas about Africa would have to be unlearnt.

The experience of Booker T. Washington, black America's most prominent educator and spokesman around the turn of the century, is particularly telling and representative in this regard. Like most African Americans, Washington held negative views of Africa, shaped by his American education. "The books I read when I was a boy always put pictures of Africa and African life in unnecessarily cruel contrast with pictures of the civilized and highly cultured Europeans and Americans," he wrote in 1909, recalling "a picture of George Washington placed side by side with a naked African, having a ring in his nose and a dagger in his hand." Washington also remembered learning at an early age that "God was white and the Devil was black . . . [and that in Africa] the lowest and most degraded type of man was black, and the blacker he was the further down the scale of civilization I expected him to be."

It is interesting that the forum at which Washington first gained national fame, the Atlanta Exposition of 1895, featured a collection of African artifacts gathered under the unflattering label "uncivilized Africa" and a reproduction of a "Dahomey Village" presided over by what Turner, who was outraged by the display, described as "a big-nosed white man urging the visitors to not miss seeing the wild cannibals from the West coast of Africa." Though voices like Turner's attempted to revise the stereotypical views of Africa held by American blacks like Washington (whose perspective on Africa did change markedly during his life), Washington's misperceptions and those expressed in exhibits like the one at the Atlanta Exposition represented the majority view of the continent, among American blacks and whites alike.

Fledgling pan-Africanists like Smyth and Turner attempted to change African American attitudes toward Africa by stressing the positive aspects of the continent and refuting white claims of African inferiority. While somewhat effective, such efforts often resulted in the popularization of tall tales of African bounty and beauty. In the late 1870s, as the gains of Reconstruction began to crumble, exaggerated myths about the soil and climate of Liberia circulated among American blacks, who passed on stories of the motherland's bacon-growing trees and giant potatoes, which were reportedly so big that one could feed an entire family. Smyth, a committed champion of African American emigration to Africa, spoke glowingly of a land where the people "have no conception of any land greater, more beautiful than their own; any men braver and manlier than themselves, any women better, lovelier and handsomer than African women." And Bishop Turner, ever the emigration promoter, told anyone who would listen of a rich land with "fruits of every beauty," a "mosquito-free" environment where "gold dust can be switched up by women and children in marvelous quantities along the shores of rivers and creeks after heavy rains." It's an interesting "counter-narrative" to the tales of American streets being paved with gold, which helped to prompt so many Europeans to emigrate to the United States in the 1890s.

Another, later proponent of black emigration to Africa, a self-described "Gold Coast chief" named Alfred Charles Sam, characterized Africa as a paradise where diamonds could be scooped freely from gullies, where bread grew on trees and cotton plants grew to the size of trees. And a 1909 letter to a black newspaper from Ethiopia's Emperor Menelik urged black Americans to move to Ethiopia, where abundant land and copious quantities of gold and diamonds made the country "too rich." Stories such as these lingered in the collective African American imagination and took their place in popular African American mythology about Africa.

While many African Americans seemed skeptical of such tales, especially when numbers of would-be African American colonists in Africa returned to the United States with reports of hardship and hunger, the tall tales did play a part in shaping prevailing African American attitudes toward Africa. This was the case even though African American leaders' exaggerations became a joke among those who were critical of emigration initiatives. Turner was accused by some of portraying "the United States as Hades and Africa as Eden," while it was jokingly noted that "even he still holds his residence in Hades, only paying Eden a brief visit once a year."

Although many of them were inaccurate, the stories that African American leaders told about Africa's bounty were revolutionary in that they provided African Americans with a new strategy for dealing with the challenge of double consciousness. While earlier figures like Phillis Wheatley had responded to the dilemma by distancing themselves from the African side of their heritage, spokesmen like Smyth and Turner flipped the script on the myth of white supremacy by stressing the value, and even the superiority, of Africa and African culture. Though they relied on myths to do so, they helped to rehabilitate Africa in the minds of African Americans, presenting them for the first time with the option of rejecting white American culture in celebration of Africa's legacy. That tendency was to endure in African American culture and thought.

The rehabilitation of Africa's image was continued by Marcus Garvey, a Jamaica-born printer and unionist who, perhaps more than any other African American leader, helped to completely redefine the ways in which diaspora Africans thought about Africa and about themselves in relation to it. Garvey rose to prominence in the period during and following World War I, when a newly urbanized black community in America became increasingly alienated in American society as economic conditions worsened and racism intensified. Many blacks hoped that participation in the war effort would earn them the respect and gratitude of the nation for which they fought. When this proved not to be the case, growing numbers of African

Americans sought solace in organizations like Garvey's Universal Negro Improvement Association (UNIA) and sometimes vented their frustration in riots.

Garvey's basic message called for black self-reliance and economic independence and he urged the diaspora's best and brightest to emigrate to Africa and contribute to the continent's development. Though he spoke often of Africa's past greatness and of her potential for future glory, he did acknowledge her present lowly position in the world and, like many African emigrationists before him, saw Africans in the diaspora as saviors, who would lead the continent's development and progress. "If native Africans are unable to appreciate the value of their own country from the standard of Western civilization, then it is for us, their brothers, to take to them a knowledge and information that they need to help develop the country for the common good," he wrote in 1923.

Besides having a political impact, Garvey also provided American blacks with a reassessment of their history and a reevaluation of themselves as black people. He taught that "our race gave the first great civilization to the world; and for centuries Africa, our ancestral home, was the seat of learning; and when black men, who were only fit then for the company of the gods, were philosophers, artists, scientists and men of vision and leadership, the people of other races were groping in savagery, darkness and continental barbarism." He encouraged black people to take pride in themselves and their blackness, and said that "the old time stories of 'African fever,' 'African bad climate,' 'African mosquitos,' 'African savages,' have been repeated by these 'brainless intellectuals' of ours as a scare against our people." He urged blacks all over the world to "emancipate themselves from mental slavery" and refute all the negative ideas they had learned from whites about themselves and Africa.

Judging by his vast popularity, Garvey's message resonated among black people worldwide. Though his dream of repatriation for blacks in Africa was never realized, and though his organization foundered amid allegations of embezzlement and fraud, the UNIA grew into the largest black mass movement in history, and it is difficult to understate its psychological and social impact. Like many of his early pan-Africanist predecessors, Garvey deliberately conjured an Africa that blacks abroad could be proud of; his Africa was a place of majestic kings, ancient learning, and historic civilization, a romantic image that was embraced by blacks all over the world.

The activities of Garvey's UNIA were part of a wider social movement among blacks worldwide, a Harlem-based "black renaissance" in politics, arts, and culture that was redefining blackness and helping to reshape American attitudes about race. In 1925, Arthur Schomburg, the Puerto Rican–born archivist of the movement, described the ideas behind the New Negro ideology, as it was popularly known: "The American Negro must remake his past in order to make his future. For him, a group tradition must supply compensation for persecution, and pride of race the antidote for prejudice. . . . The Negro has been a man without history because he has been considered a man without a worthy culture. But a new notion of the cultural attainment and potentialities of the African stocks has recently come about. . . . Already the Negro sees himself against a reclaimed background, in a perspective that will give pride and self-respect ample scope, and make history yield for him the same values that the treasured past of any people affords." In this respect, the New Negro movement was often a prescriptive effort to "remake" a heritage of which American blacks could be proud. The unspoken implication of this sort of idea was that Africa's actual history—or at least its history as distorted by white scholars—was nothing to be proud of: "New Negroes" who wanted a "worthy" past would have to invent one, to "make history yield" one for them. And this "remaking" often relied on mythology as opposed to scholarship or research.

The Harlem Renaissance poet Claude McKay wrote in exalted terms of the Africa of his imagination, but his characterization remained superficial because his own understanding of Africa relied on little more than stories he had heard and cloudy images plucked from the recesses of his mind. The result exhibited a myopia he sadly acknowledged. In the poem "Outcast," McKay refers to the "dim regions" of Africa, and imagines his estranged motherland as a place of "darkness and peace" to which he would return, but he realizes that the "jungle songs" he envisions himself singing are "forgotten." "Something is lost in me forever, / Some vital thing has gone out of my heart," he laments, recognizing that his ancestors' experience in America has erased all memory of the homeland his forebears knew. And in his ignorance, he recycles images of Africa that differ little from those Booker T. Washington assimilated in school.

Similarly, in "Heritage," another Harlem Renaissance poet, Countee Cullen, gropes for an answer to the question "What is Africa to me?" and comes to the sad conclusion that, while he celebrates Africa as a homeland, his knowledge of the continent and his understanding of what it means to him is strangely limited. As he writes,

Africa? A book one thumbs
Listlessly, till slumber comes.
Unremembered are her bats
Circling through the night, her cats
Crouching in the river reeds,
Stalking gentle flesh that feeds
By the river brink.

It is interesting and telling that, for Cullen, the landscape he can no longer recall is one populated with bats, cats, "barbaric birds," "massive jungle herds," "strong bronzed men," and "jungle girls and boys in love," all stock images of the "Dark Continent" as represented in American popular culture. Cullen acknowledges that Africa is "unremembered," but still paints an exotic portrait of an imagined African scene, plucking the imagery from his own flights of fancy.

Arna Bontemps, another Harlem Renaissance writer, spoke to the same sense of loss and alienation from the memory of Africa in "Nocturne at Bethesda": "Why do our black faces search the empty sky? / Is there something we have forgotten? some precious thing / We have lost wandering in strange lands?" He recognizes that he will probably not see Africa in his lifetime and, playing on a recurring theme in African American literature and culture, envisions his return to the continent after death. "And if there can be returning after death / I shall come back," he writes. "But it will not be here; / If you want me you must search for me / Beneath the palms of Africa." Once again, however, his imaginings of his afterlife sample freely from the exoticized Africa of popular American culture, and he envisions himself "following a desert caravan," "seeking ornaments of ivory," and "dying for a jungle fruit" in a landscape of "shining dunes" and "jungle trees with burning scarlet birds." Poems like these depict Africa as a vaguely conceived jungle paradise where life was simple and bountiful; a positive reassessment of Africa on the poets' parts, but a conjured reassessment nonetheless.

Langston Hughes's verse has similar echoes of a mysterious and idyllic Africa. "Danse Africaine" describes the primeval power of African drumming to stir the African spirit in vague and mysterious terms. As Hughes writes, "The low beating of the tom-toms, / The slow beating of the tom-toms, / Low . . . slow / Slow . . . low— / Stirs your blood. / Dance! / A night-veiled girl / Whirls softly . . . slowly, / Like a wisp of smoke around the fire— / And the tom-toms beat, / And the tom-toms beat, / And the low beating of the tom-toms / Stirs your blood." Poems such as these seem especially telling when juxta-posed with Hughes's poems on Harlem, a place he knows and loves. In pieces like "The Weary Blues," a portrait of a blues pianist in a Harlem club, Hughes captures a detailed sense of place and character; his few poems on Africa, by comparison, are pretty thin in detail, rely-ing on stock imagery and clichés. While Hughes is able to depict a Harlem audience at a jazz club with loving familiarity and color, the scene in "Danse Africaine" is shrouded in mystery and its lone charac-ter is "night-veiled," reduced to a dancing shadow.

Other Harlem Renaissance poets depicted Africa in similarly shad-owy terms. Jean Toomer, one of the most celebrated black writers of the period, pictured an African slave "feasting on a strange cassava" in the poem "Conversion," and Gwendolyn Bennett dreamed of hearing "the chanting / Around a heathen fire / Of a strange black race" in the poem "Heritage." Africa had finally become a place wor-thy of celebration in verse and prose, but what, in the end, did African American writers really know about Africa? Very little.

Some of the Harlem Renaissance writers arrived at a more realistic view of Africa, but they were in the minority. Zora Neale Hurston, widely regarded as the most important black American female author of the first half of the twentieth century, wrote in 1942, after the Re-naissance, of her meeting with an old African American man who had been born in Africa and enslaved in America at a young age. For Hurston, a member of the "niggerati" (to use the phrase she coined) who spearheaded the Harlem Renaissance and espoused an idealized and romantic view of Africa, the experience was a revelation, for some of what she heard did not square with her idealized expectations. "The white people had held my people in slavery here in America," she wrote. "They had bought us, it is true and exploited us. But the inescapable fact that stuck in my craw, was: my people had *sold* me and the white people had bought me. That did away with the folklore I had been brought up on—that the white people had gone to Africa, waved a red handkerchief at the Africans and lured them aboard ship and sailed away. I know that civilized money stirred up African greed. That wars between tribes were often stirred up by white traders to provide more slaves in the barracoons and all that. But, if the African princes had been as pure and as innocent as I would like to think, it could not have happened."

Despite Hurston's efforts to find more accurate representations of Africa, most of her peers in the movement seemed content to uphold "folklore" in the place of empirical research. In the end, a fictitious scene described by the Harlem Renaissance writer Wallace Thurman in *Infants of the Spring*, a novel based on the personalities, events, and ideas of the movement, does not seem so far from the truth. Thurman describes a debate between black writers on the role Africa should play in their work. One character, based on Countee Cullen, says, "The young Negro artist must go back to his pagan heritage for inspiration and to the old masters for form," which prompts another character, based on Thurman himself, to envision "a vivid mental picture of that poet's creative hours—eyes on a page of Keats, fingers on typewriter, mind frantically conjuring African scenes." Nonetheless, conjured up or otherwise, the celebration of Africa in Harlem Renaissance writing did help to rehabilitate the image of Africa in African American eyes, and to expand the dimensions of the mythical space that Africa occupied in the black American psyche.

Though the Harlem Renaissance and its pro-Africa agenda were interrupted by the Great Depression, in the 1930s the Italian invasion of Ethiopia sparked renewed interest in Africa among African Americans, who closely followed the conflict and even mobilized to support Ethiopia in its war against European imperialism. The conflict added some new aspects to the body of popular African American images of Africa. Ethiopia had long held an important position in the African American imagination; Ethiopia is mentioned prominently in the Bible, and the biblical phrase "Ethiopia shall stretch out her hands to God" was often quoted by early pan-Africanists like Edward Wilmot Blyden and W. E. B. Du Bois, who hailed Ethiopia as an ancient center of civilization and learning. Ethiopian resistance to Italian aggression in the Battle of Adowa in 1896, a rare example of African triumph over European colonialism in the nineteenth century, had further heightened Ethiopia's stature in African American eyes; some African Americans even went so far as to claim ancestral ties to the ancient kingdom, a largely fictional idea that was nonetheless appealing. And the romance surrounding Emperor Haile Selassie I and the Ethiopian royal family, which claimed direct descent from King Solomon and the Queen of Sheba, added greatly to the Ethiopian mystique.

The Italian invasion of 1935 was greeted with outrage in the black press and widespread rallies and protests throughout black America. The conflict was regarded by many as a symbolic clash between black and white, and African Americans were quick to offer their prayers, money, and even military service to the Ethiopian cause. The image of the regal Ethiopian, defending his country and impressive heritage against evil invaders, became a popular one in African American newspapers and journals—one major black paper, the *Chicago Defender*, reported that a wily Ethiopian priest had confounded an Italian attack with earthen pots filled with tsetse flies—and Selassie was lionized in the black press as the "only Black Sovereign in the world" and "the natural leader of the (black) Negro race." For many African Americans, Selassie's monarchy seemed the real-life fulfillment of Garvey's idealized vision of a continent governed by African kings of worldly stature and power. The deification of Haile Selassie by blacks in the diaspora was literal among Jamaican Rastafarians, who took his coronation as the realization of a Garvey prophecy and hailed him as an earthly embodiment of God, Jah Rastafari, returned to free the true children of Israel (New World Africans) from bondage in the West.

Garvey himself, living out his final years in London in relative obscurity, supported Selassie initially, but then accused the emperor of refusing to associate with other blacks while on a state visit to England and denounced him as "the ruler of a country where black men are chained and flogged." But Garvey's condemnation apparently did little to stem African American enthusiasm for the leader and his struggle. To many, victory for Ethiopia would mean victory for the entire race, and black leaders called on blacks around the world to defend the "fatherland."

In addition to African American mobilization in defense of Ethiopia, the 1930s also saw the emergence of a number of small "Back-to-Africa" movements and Africa-oriented religious organizations, perhaps most notably the Nation of Islam, but none with the sort of far-reaching mass appeal of Garvey's UNIA. It wasn't until after World War II and the start of the African decolonization movement that Africa captured black imaginations the way it had in the pre-war era.

When the African pro-independence rumblings first began in the early 1950s, African Americans were eager to lend their support. In 1956 Kwame Nkrumah visited the United States and was hailed as a hero in black neighborhoods in Chicago and in Harlem. When Ghana gained its independence in 1957, it seemed as if black America had become re-obsessed with Africa overnight. The emergence of Kenya's Mau Mau anticolonial movement in the mid-1950s further fueled the new fire. Mau Mau seized the African American imagination in strong fashion; to many black American observers, it seemed an exotically African association shrouded in secrecy, a romantic band of marauders who terrified British colonialists with a mixture of

African mysticism and armed force, and it had a significant impact on African American culture. Black American journalists wrote sensational articles about the "secret Mau Mau society" that had "rock[ed] this blood-drenched and terrified colony," and the radical pan-African black American activists Paul Robeson and Malcolm X both developed political ties to Mau Mau leaders. Patrice Lumumba's struggle for independence in Belgian Congo also gained attention in the early 1960s, and the announcement of his murder in 1961 actually sparked a riot among black Americans in the visitors' gallery at the United Nations.

Africa's rapid decolonization, which became symbolically linked to the African American civil rights movement, helped to prompt a revolution in African American politics and culture as the emergence of independent African states raised African Americans' self-esteem and changed the way they thought about themselves as a people. The result was a greater identification with Africa than had ever previously existed, and a cultural celebration of Africa that found expression in fashion, language, food, political outlook, and many other facets of African American life.

African names, sometimes plucked from African naming dictionaries that circulated in black communities, proliferated among African American children born in the early 1970s, including country names like Kenya, Tchad, and Zaire. Distinctly African American names that were inspired by Africa also emerged, names like Shawanda, Lakeisha, or Sheniqua which were African in flavor but conceived in the New World. Muslim names like Jamal, Latifah, and Raheem were also popular among black American Muslims and non-Muslims alike, seemingly valued by many more for their perceived Africanness than to signify Islamic devotion. African American renaming took place on a larger scale, too, as the popular designation for the race as a group went from Colored to Negro to Black (in the 1960s) to Afro-American (in the 1970s). Later, of course, the labels "African American" and even "New World African" became popular as further ways of refining a diasporean sense of self that both emphasized an African origin and acknowledged the history of transplantation to America. This process of reinvention reflected black Americans' changing views of themselves and their place in American society, and an increasing desire after the 1960s to highlight a connection with Africa.

What is perhaps most significant in African American celebrations of an African heritage is that cultural trends that were thought to be inspired by Africa in the end helped to create a distinctively African

American cultural identity. Although Afros became popular among black Americans seeking to evoke Africa, the style became synonymous with 1970s African American culture around the world and was mimicked as such in some African countries and discouraged in others. African Americans who draped themselves in African fabrics, often aspiring toward an aesthetic they assumed was authentically African, conceived their own cultural sensibility as they sampled freely from different traditions, wearing dashikis cut from kente cloth over jeans, or a print from the Congo around the waist and a fabric from Nigeria as a head wrap. Many African American names may have originated as adaptations of African words but often evolved to take on their own unique identity and flavor, sometimes even through mispronunciation, such that a Nigerian name like Nkenge (pronounced "Nn-KENG-ay" in Nigeria) could become the singularly black American "Nikenji." In reaching out to Africa in an effort to recapture an ancestral past, African Americans of the 1970s actually ended up creating a new African American cultural present.

My parents and many of their peers became caught up in this pro-Africa black consciousness fervor in college in the 1960s; my father was involved in a black student takeover of a university administration building to demand a black studies program and more minority hiring, my mother marched in civil rights demonstrations, and my aunt Anne became a member of the Black Panther Party ("The committee to combat fascism," she told me proudly when I asked her about it years later). And both my mother and her sister traveled "back to Africa" in the late 1960s, my mother to start a new family, her sister to visit the land of her ancestors.

I ingested pro-black rhetoric with my baby food, and learned to take outspoken pride in my heritage as an African and African American. But I had no idea that the black cultural trappings that pervaded my life were part of an African American mythology over two hundred years in the making. By the 1970s, the African American challenge of double consciousness had been solved for many black Americans with a deliberate substitution of identification with Africa for identification with America. It hardly mattered that the Africa with which most African Americans identified psychologically often bore little resemblance to the Africa experienced by millions of contemporary Africans—like any myth, the celebration of Africa in the African American imagination served important social and cultural functions, as a source of identity and ethnic pride, and it didn't need to be true to do so. The only problem was that mythical idealizations rarely hold up to comparison with the real thing, as more and more African Americans who traveled to Africa in increasing numbers in the 1960s and 1970s discovered. For my brothers and me, a real understanding of Africa and what it meant to us only began when my family moved to Tanzania in 1980, an adventure that completely debunked our own myths of Africa and changed our lives forever.

And Lo! 1 Was in Africa

When shall I forget the night I first set foot on African soil? I am the sixth generation in descent from forefathers who left this land. The moon was at the full and the waters of the Atlantic lay like a lake. All the long slow afternoon as the sun robed herself in her western scarlet with veils of misty cloud, I had seen Africa afar . . . . The world grew black. Africa faded away, the stars stood forth curiously twisted . . . . Then afar, ahead, lights shone, straight at the ship's fore . . . . "Monrovia," said the Captain . . . and lo! I was in Africa.
—W.E.B. Du Bois

I stepped eagerly from the plane onto the hot tarmac and was immediately engulfed by a moist wall of heat that almost staggered me, a stifling, inescapable airy fire that invaded my pores and wilted my clothes and limbs. I could feel it filling my nostrils and expanding, hot and damp, in my lungs. I could smell it, steamy and acrid, at once slightly familiar yet somehow unidentifiable. And I could see it, shimmering blurrily above the baked black runway. Beads of sweat formed abruptly on my skin, and I suddenly felt extremely tired. My senses felt numbed, as though incapable of registering anything but the overpowering heat.

I watched through a haze of exhaustion as my mother herded my brothers and me across the asphalt toward the small one-room airport building. Inside, the heat was less oppressive and I became more aware of my surroundings. I felt an odd flutter of elation tickle its way through my stomach as I looked around. There were black people everywhere. The baggage handlers in their faded blue jumpsuits, the customs officials in khaki uniforms directing human traffic and stamping travel documents, even a flight crew, hatted pilots and well-groomed cabin attendants, making their way casually through the airport. When we had collected our suitcases and cleared customs, we were greeted by an ocean of black faces assembled beyond the baggage claim area, their necks craning and eyes straining anxiously for a glimpse of a disembarking loved one, apprehensive frowns changing to joyful grins once the relative was spotted. The air was filled with a happy, incessant chatter that was completely indecipherable to me, and even when I picked out the occasional English phrase, the words sounded strange.

Scanning the crowd, I located my father, who smiled when he caught sight of us. My brothers and I ran over to him and he hugged us close. "Welcome to Dar es Salaam," he said, laughing. He introduced us to a new colleague of his, a Zanzibari man named Abdul who had accompanied him to the airport. When the introductions and greetings were completed, we loaded our bags into an old gray Land Rover and piled inside, my brothers and I squirming as we tried to get comfortable on the narrow bench-style seats in the back.

As we drove, I looked out the window and ingested all of the unfamiliar sights and scenes. I watched African men on bicycles pedal smoothly along the edge of the road under palm trees. Overloaded trucks and buses, leaning crazily to one side as though they might capsize at any moment, bellowed down the road with thick black smoke billowing out of their tailpipes. Vendors selling oranges and more mysterious fruits lounged behind their arranged wares in the shade of trees, and women with colorful cloths tied around their waists carried small children on their backs and bundles on their heads as they strode purposefully along dusty paths.

The old Land Rover creaked and clattered and bounced from side to side on the potholed road, our heads wobbling on our necks as the vehicle pitched to and fro. I struggled to stay awake and once again felt consumed by the heat. I was sweating profusely and the hard seat was uncomfortable under my aching buttocks. Clouds of reddish dust kicked up by the Land Rover poured in through the windows and got in my eyes.

I glimpsed the ocean, huge, endless, and intensely blue, through the trees and buildings that lined the road, and I felt strangely excited and replenished. It lay along the horizon, timeless, calm, and indifferent, and its detached distance was somehow soothing. We turned off the main road and headed toward the beckoning sea, and soon we began to hear its hushed, foamy whisper, and to smell and taste its sharp saltiness. A briny breeze began to caress our skin, a warm wind from the east that had swept across Asia and the Indian Ocean, carrying with it the subtly spicy fragrances of Zanzibar and the Comoros, and the unspoken memories of history. It swirled and danced playfully around us, cheerfully welcoming us to this Haven of Peace. When the Land Rover pulled to a stop in front of the hotel where my family would be staying for the next five months, I leaped from the rear of the vehicle and stretched, opening my arms wide and reaching fingers out towards the pale blue sky as I hungrily inhaled the salty, humid air. It was good to finally be home.

It was almost a year after Remy's death when I first learned that my family would be moving to Africa. Despite the months that had elapsed, the grief still weighed heavily on all of us. After the funeral I had listlessly returned to school, and my abrupt disdain for my classes and uncharacteristically poor performance had landed me in sessions with the school psychologist. My mother wandered our apartment in West Newton with a wounded look in her kind, light brown eyes. Even Kolo and James, then four and two respectively, were emotionally affected by the pervasive sadness that overwhelmed us. And my father, usually a quiet and pensive presence in my life, was even more withdrawn than usual. He found constant reminders of his firstborn son everywhere, and kept thinking he saw Remy's eyes staring at him out of the faces of children he saw in the street. He realized that the whole family was in need of healing. And, as it became more and more spiritually difficult for him to remain in the United States, he began to long for Africa.

Serendipitously, he was offered a teaching job at the University of Dar es Salaam in Tanzania; a colleague who taught there had recommended him to the administration. After discussing the offer and resolving that my father should accept, my parents decided that he would set out for Dar alone and send for us later.

When the decision was made, my mother gathered my brothers and me around her and told us we would be moving to Dar es Salaam, a city in the East African country of Tanzania. The prospect of a new home was deliciously exciting to all of us, and moving to Africa made sense to us since our father had always talked so nostalgically about his homeland and how we would one day travel there. I relished the notion of finally experiencing at first hand the "Africa" I had heard so much about, even if I was somewhat apprehensive at the idea of leaving my friends and all that was familiar behind. And my brothers and I also responded eagerly to the return of the light of hope and anticipation to our mother's eyes. Equipped with new purpose and the promise of change, she gradually recovered her smile. The stifling, unarticulated sadness with which we had lived for months dissipated in the face of a new energy that suddenly charged the air around us and chased some of the gloom from our home. When my father left for Tanzania, my brothers and I happily began to look forward to a new adventure in Africa.

In preparation for the trip, my mother led my brothers and me on a fact-finding project in which we gathered information on Tanzania and on East Africa in general. We consulted our Encyclopaedia Britannica and discovered that Tanzania was a small country that had been colonized by Germany in the late nineteenth century and become a British colony after World War I. It had gained independence as Tanganyika in 1961, and then merged with the coastal island nation of Zanzibar in 1964 to become "Tanzania." We located the country on one of my father's atlases and found that Dar es Salaam was right on the Indian Ocean; we eagerly envisioned leisurely days on tropical beaches. We found out that the name "Dar es Salaam" had been coined by Arab traders who had frequented the East African coast in the thirteenth century and that it meant "Haven of Peace," an allusion to the deep, calm waters that made it one of the best natural ports in the world.

We learned that Kiswahili and English were the official languages, and my mother purchased an English-Kiswahili dictionary and a Kiswahili book for children entitled *Jambo Means Hello*. We would spend hours on our living room couch flipping through the book and attempting to pronounce the strange words. We learned that *habari?* was a greeting that meant "How are you?" and we took turns quizzing each other in mock conversations in which we struggled to enunciate Kiswahili salutations with our clumsy American tongues.

I told my class at school that my family would be moving to Africa and my friends were excited and full of questions. Would we live near lions and monkeys? Would we live in mud huts? I answered the questions as well as I could, assuring my classmates that we would indeed live in a house in the city with electricity and indoor plumbing, and that we would not live among lions and other wild animals—but in truth I wasn't sure. I didn't really know what to expect. Some friends seemed envious. "You're so lucky, you'll get to wear shorts all the time, and climb trees, it'll be great," one said. I agreed with him out loud and enjoyed his envy, but deep inside I didn't know what it would be like, or even if I would like it, and that bothered me. I kept my reservations to myself.

Our actual departure was uneventful. It was the first plane trip I could remember (I had flown to Boston from California when I was a baby), and my brothers and I were thrilled to be flying and wrangled for the window seats. We flew British Airways through Heathrow Airport in London and spent a few hours in transit, touring the stores, buying small souvenirs, and fidgeting with impatience for the last leg of our trip. When our plane finally made its approach into Dar es Salaam, my brothers and I gazed raptly out the window at the completely foreign landscape dotted with palm trees. We were gripped with jubilation. Our excitement was only temporarily faded by the sweltering heat of a typical Dar es Salaam afternoon.

The Hotel Africana Vacation Village, where my family stayed until the University of Dar es Salaam provided us with housing on campus, was a cluster of self-contained room units gathered around a central administration complex that contained a dining room, a bar, a disco, and an outdoor swimming pool. Most of the hotel guests were Europeans on vacation, but there were a few other families in our position, people who had come to Dar to work and live and were staying at the hotel while they awaited housing in the city. As a tourist hotel, Africana was relatively isolated from Tanzanian culture and society at large, a getaway where guests could sun, swim, and sit without ever having to come into significant contact with local people. Usually the only Tanzanians in sight were the waiters, cooks, and other hotel employees who frequented the grounds, or families who came to the hotel on weekend outings. In this setting, I made my acquaintance with Tanzania's natural landscape long before I learned anything about its people or culture.

I was smitten by the ocean from the very first. My brothers and I would play on the beach for hours, splashing in the warm, salty water, walking way, way out at low tide, and building elaborate forts and castles in the sand. We explored the tide pools that dotted the shoreline and collected hermit crabs in ice buckets we pilfered from the hotel rooms. We made friends among the other kids staying at the hotel, and among the hotel staff. One waiter in particular was an amiable presence at meals, which he would announce by playing a jovial little song on a large wooden African xylophone situated outside the dining room doorway. He would address me as "my friend"(I later learned this was a common way to speak to a stranger in Tanzania) and smiled when I was unable to respond to phrases in Kiswahili.

My brothers and I thoroughly enjoyed our time at the hotel, but my mother quickly became bored and began to search for ways to occupy her time. My father boarded a special university vehicle to go to his office on campus every morning, and soon my mother found work as an English-French translator at an embassy downtown and began leaving shortly after my father. Kolo and I pretty much wandered the hotel and beach on our own every day, but a baby-sitter, the cousin or sister of one of the hotel waiters, was hired to take care of two-year-old James. Her name was Asha, and she spoke little English. As we struggled to communicate with each other through gestures and simple English and Kiswahili words, my brothers and I learned our first basic Kiswahili expressions and phrases, while Asha picked up some English, notifying us that it was time to eat with the words "Lun time."

The first time I ventured away from the hotel was with my father, on what was also my first visit to the university campus that was to be my home for the next seven years. We took the daily Land Rover from Africana to the campus, which was situated on a hill on the outskirts of Dar es Salaam. We got off the bus at a stop near an elementary school (there were hundreds of schoolchildren bustling about in their uniforms of blue shorts or skirts and white shirts), and walked along a dirt path through grass that was almost up to my knees. Large grasshoppers cavorted in the grass, making a clicking sound with their wings as they flew from stalk to stalk. We followed the path from the bus stop to a paved road leading into a cluster of identical two-story gray stucco houses, and as we walked along the side of the road to number F24, the house we had been assigned, I took stock of my new neighborhood.

Chickens scratched around in the dust, and small barefoot children played in front of some of the houses. A team of bare-chested young men, each armed with a long scythe, was spread out on a little park adorned with two white wooden benches, slashing at the grass with smooth strokes, sending tufts of green flying skyward with each arc of the sharp blades. Young women hung wet laundry on clotheslines or laid it flat on patches of grass, chatting idly and moving with slow, fluid motions in the noonday heat. Skinny dogs lounged on their sides in the shade of mango and avocado trees, and occasionally a car made its way carefully along the road, slowing to gently lurch over the speed bumps it encountered every few hundred feet. Number F24 stood at the end of the paved road on the right; my dad unlocked the door. The house, like all those in the neighborhood, was made of plain gray concrete and equipped with a dining room, a living room, and a small kitchen downstairs, and a bathroom and three bedrooms upstairs. It was furnished with the university's standard issue: a steel-framed couch and chairs topped with flimsy blue cushions, a large dining room table, and six narrow beds with thin foam mattresses. Our residence in the house had been delayed because the university's housing department was still fixing the place up after its last tenants, but as far as we could tell the only item missing was a toilet seat.

After inspecting our new home, my father and I walked through the university campus to his office in the history department, and I felt the interested gaze of the neighborhood's kids upon me as we left. On the day I first visited Chuo Kikuu Cha Dar es Salaam (the University of Dar es Salaam) the campus was commemorating its tenth anniversary, and I watched some of the celebration from my father's office, where I crouched behind his desk and peeked through one of the ventilation holes that lined his office wall. My father left to teach a class, but I remained transfixed, watching in fascination as performers in traditional dress whirled and gyrated in the first *ngoma* (the word literally means "drum" and is the generic term for any traditional Tanzanian dance presentation) performance I had ever seen. Before my campus visit, my father had promised that we would see a blind drummer who could play ten drums at once, and I was enthralled as I watched his hands flying from drum to drum, maintaining an impossibly intricate rhythm while energetic dancers struggled to keep up. I was so engrossed that I didn't hear one of my father's colleagues come into the office to check on me, and he left to look for me elsewhere, not realizing I was tucked out of sight behind the desk. It was my first real introduction to Tanzanian culture, and though I was conscious of my position as an outsider looking on foreign and unfamiliar events, I was excited by the colorful costumes, the driving rhythms, and the fast-stepping dances. I returned to Africana that evening filled with a new eagerness for my Tanzanian life.

Although my brothers and I reveled in our beach setting, my mother grew increasingly restless. She wanted to get established in her own home, to cook and go shopping for herself, to decorate rooms that were ours, not merely borrowed from a tourist hotel. Every day, my father checked on the progress of our assigned house with the university's maintenance department, but was usually informed of some new maintenance task that had to be performed before we could relocate. It was our first taste of the frequently confounding Tanzanian bureaucracy, which often seemed to needlessly complicate and lengthen what we felt should have been simple processes, and we could not figure out why there was such a delay.

We finally left Africana to take up residence in house number F24 on Darajani Road. My dad explained that "Darajani" meant "by the bridge"; the road and neighborhood were named for their proximity to a small bridge across a riverbed that came to life during the rainy season.

With our move onto the university campus, our Tanzanian adventure began in earnest. My brothers and I were sought out by the neighborhood kids on the first day we arrived. Curious faces approached us in the road outside our new house and new barefoot friends accompanied us inside to investigate the toy treasure trove we had brought from the United States. Some of the kids had a little English, but in general they spoke to us in Kiswahili. We found ourselves trying to repeat the unfamiliar phrases, and in so doing we began our induction into the local culture.

The minds of young children are malleable, absorptive sponges, and, at three, five, and eight, respectively, James, Kolo, and I enthusiastically soaked up the language and culture of our new environment. I don't think we even missed the television we had watched every day in the United States. Over our parents' objections, we quickly shucked our shoes in favor of the freedom and excitement of going barefoot around the neighborhood, and we learned to climb mango, cashew nut and guava trees like the rest of the kids.

We took long walks along the riverbed near our home, raiding the fruit trees and sugarcane that grew wild there and often catching sight of the snakes, mongooses, monkeys, lizards, and hundreds of birds that lived there.

I began to play soccer with the other boys my age, on a sand-and-grass–patched little field ringed with thorny bushes that claimed the careers of many freshly pumped balls. Whenever our store-bought, inflatable soccer balls failed us, we resorted to using small homemade bundles of paper and plastic that we would kick around until it was too dark to see. I had played on a youth soccer team in Boston, but my real education in the sport began in Dar, where it seemed that every neighborhood had a team of barefoot ball jugglers who idolized international stars like Pele and Maradona, and local football heroes like Zamoyoni Mogella. Our neighborhood, like all the others in our area, had an informal soccer team that we had organized ourselves, challenging other neighborhoods to matches we took quite seriously. We treated our almost daily scrimmages like strenuous practice sessions. We would run drills for ourselves and compete in "one touch" games, in which each player could only touch the ball once per possession (to improve team passing), games in which you'd have to hit the goalpost to score (to improve accuracy), and *"dana dana"* (ball juggling) contests. Sometimes our neighborhood team would ally with another to take on a formidable opponent from a more distant community, and all of our matches were hard-fought affairs that sometimes resulted in postgame skirmishes. Our soccer games formed an arena in which neighborhood friendships and loyalties were forged in glorious boyhood battles.

Soccer quickly became my primary passion, but I also learned how to play Tanzanian marbles (a soccer-derived game, in which you tried to knock marbles into your opponent's goal), Tanzanian hide-and-seek (we called it *"Kombolela!"* or *"Tapo!"*—words you shouted when you broke cover to kick a can, liberating all of those who had been found and caught), and even "girls' games" like "Lede," a Tanzanian version of dodgeball. (I always wondered if the game's name, which you shouted when you were prepared to dodge a hurled ball made of socks, was a corruption of "ready.") "Bao," an African board game of strategy and mathematical calculations, became a more cerebral passion. A friend and I would sit for hours on the steps behind my family's house, moving beads around a board in which thirty-two shallow holes were scooped, trying to gain an edge in prolonged conflicts in which momentum would shift back and forth before one of us prevailed by capturing all of the other's beads.

I was always amazed with my new peers' creativity in devising new sources of amusement. My new friends taught me how to build foot-long toy cars of wood, wire, and rubber and "drive" them around with sticks ingeniously rigged with string to actually steer the little front wheels. Or we would find abandoned car tires and roll them along as fast as we could up and down the road that ran through the neighborhood. After days of rain, we would dig near the riverbank and fashion little sculptures and pottery out of the rich gray clay we'd find just below the sandy surface. We would cut up scavenged inner tubes to make sling shots and sling rifles to hunt wood pigeons (for roasting on outdoor fires) and monitor lizards (for sport). And using a time-honored method I saw as pure genius, we would catch wild lovebirds, the colorful East African parrots, to keep or sell as pets. All you had to do was collect the sticky sap from a certain bush, boil it until it formed a gray wad of gluey gum ("ulimbo"), wrap it around a long, slender stick, and place it high in a tree that the birds were known to frequent. Then you just had to sit back and wait for an unsuspecting lovebird to get hopelessly stuck on what looked like the perfect perch.

To sustain me on my exploratory escapades around my new neighborhood, I eagerly sampled from a panoply of new foods. As a young child in the United States, I had been a finicky, stubborn eater, but I found a new appetite in Dar es Salaam. I had never before tasted such luscious mangoes, pineapples, avocados, and bananas, and had never even seen guavas, papayas, and young green-husked coconuts before, or the other strange fruits no one seemed to have a name for in English. I quickly developed addictions to *kashata*, a sweet coconut candy, and *maandazi*, airy balls of fried dough, but it took longer to get used to *ugali*, a stiff cornmeal porridge eaten with a spicy sauce, or *kumbi kumbi*, the roasted termites that were a popular seasonal snack. Instead, *Ndizi na nyama*, a hot plantain and meat stew that is a typical Tanzanian dish, *pilau*, a savory mix of rice, potatoes and meat, and *mshikaki*, morsels of goat meat roasted over a fire, became some of my instant favorites.

During my first year in Dar es Salaam, Tanzanian guides helped to provide me with an education in a new way of life, and my extensive interaction with my new companions also helped me to learn Kiswahili. To supplement the words and phrases I was quickly picking up from my friends, I began to take daily private Kiswahili lessons from a teacher who lived next door. And, to my initial unhappiness, I also began attending the local primary school, an experience that was at first traumatic. On my first day in Darasa la Tatu A (Class 3A) I donned my new uniform—blue shorts and a white shirt—and walked reluctantly to school. I had no idea what to expect. I was bewildered by all the attention I received from my new classmates, who bombarded me with greetings and questions in rapid-fire Kiswahili that I could not understand. I assume most of my classmates were just being friendly, but I was unable to distinguish their enthusiasm from hostility, and after just a few minutes of sitting at the small wooden desk I shared with two other students, listening to all the excited chatter and laughter and feeling certain that my classmates were mocking me, I vowed never to return.

The classroom was made of unembellished concrete blocks and had no electricity, and there must have been sixty loud kids in my class alone. Chaos reigned until the teacher finally arrived, and all of the students rose to greet her, chanting "Shikamoo, Mwalimu" ("Good morning, Teacher") in melodious unison. When my presence was brought to her attention she assigned a fellow student named Sandi, who had lived in Zambia and spoke some English, to guide me through the day. So much was unfamiliar, and I was thankful for the help.

The schoolwork, except for math (which I had always hated) and

English (which I found inanely easy since it was designed for non-native speakers), was almost completely incomprehensible to me. But I did enjoy music, a simple affair in which the teacher wrote some lyrics on the blackboard and waved her arms to establish the rhythm, at which everyone began to sing with unrehearsed exuberance, adding harmony and embellishments at will. I think on that first day we sang "How Many Days in the Week" (half the class posed the question, while the other half sang out thunderously, "Seven days," in an energetic call-and-response chorus that we repeated until the teacher seemed satisfied).

I learned the hard way that all students were required to bring a small broom to school with them to help clean up the school grounds. The penalty for nonparticipation was a couple of whacks on the leg or hand administered by the teacher in front of the class, with a stick selected especially for the occasion. I took my punishment silently, although I felt I could not be blamed for my ignorance.

I also learned to line up with the rest of my class at daily assemblies, when we marched and responded to military-style commands barked by the older students: "Mguu upande!" (Legs apart!) "Mguu sawa!" (Legs together!) "Kulia geuka!" (Right face!) "Kushoto geuka!" (Left face!) And at the end of each day, we sang the national anthem, "Mungu Ibariki Tanzania" (God Bless Tanzania), while the Tanzanian flag that flapped above the school during the day was ceremoniously lowered and folded. At the close of that draining first day, my class filed out of the classroom and I stood outside uncertainly while the teacher said something to Sandi. He turned to me and announced carefully, "Now is the time to go to the home." I walked away, feeling the eyes of my classmates on me, going over the day's events in my head. I was still daunted by the prospect of returning the next day, but I was no longer set against it.

Kolo attended the nursery school close by and had similar experiences. Shule ya Vidudu (literally, School of the Little Ones) was mainly a play group; the kids would learn songs, frolic on playground equipment, and listen to stories told by the teacher. Kolo seemed to enjoy his days at the school and would come home repeating songs he had learned there, childish ditties like "Napenda Mambo Yote ya Shule Kabisa" (I Love Everything About School) and patriotic anthems like "Bendera ya Tanzania" (The Tanzanian Flag). Though school was usually fun, Kolo did fall from the teacher's favor on one occasion, when he neglected to finish the milk provided as part of his snack. Many Tanzanians enjoy their milk slightly curdled, like yogurt, and when Kolo turned up his nose at it, he was reported to the teacher. "Kolo amekosa" (Kolo has done wrong), the informant said accusingly, indicating his cup of unfinished curds.

Despite committing our share of blunders, my brothers and I quickly adjusted to our new surroundings. And our growing fluency in Kiswahili helped us unlock the secrets of the new culture that surrounded us.

The language was the most significant barrier, and once we began to grasp the fundamentals of Kiswahili, our acclimatization proceeded that much more rapidly. Our progress was difficult and gradual, but in an environment where Kiswahili was usually the only language that was universally understood, we had no choice but to learn and to learn quickly. The words sounded like jumbled mouthfuls at first and my ears initially had trouble organizing the syllables that tumbled out of people's mouths into logical phrases and sentences. But slowly, so tediously that I was hardly aware of my own improvement, words that had once sounded unpronounceable became simple, and my stuttering speech gained fluidity and pace. And as my fluency grew, so did my understanding of the culture that the language reflected.

Kiswahili is in essence a Bantu language, a member of the largest African linguistic family, but it has a lot of Arabic vocabulary and even some words from Hindi, Portuguese, German, and English, a legacy of all the cultures that over the centuries came into contact along the Swahili coast. Kiswahili is partly rooted in a brutal history, because it evolved into the lingua franca for an entire region through the East African slave trade, in which millions of Africans were marched from the interior to the coast along caravan routes that became littered with human bones. But despite its history as a language forged at the points of contact and conflict between disparate peoples, Kiswahili seemed well suited to the culturally mixed milieu of Dar es Salaam and seemed to help provide the cohesion that unified the nation. The stereotypical boast in Tanzania was that though Kiswahili was spoken across East Africa, it was "born in Tanzania, grew up in Kenya, and died in Uganda." Tanzanians prided themselves on speaking the most refined, fluent, and beautiful Kiswahili of all, and I discovered that Kiswahili eloquence, linguistic flourish, wit, and the facile command of proverbs and sayings were highly prized.

The first thing my brothers and I learned about the intricacies of Kiswahili linguistic culture was the importance of the dozens of elaborate Kiswahili greetings, steeped in ritual formality and an indispensable part of any chance encounter. "Shikamoo" was reserved for those older than you and expressed your acknowledgment of the status earned through old age and experience. Even preverbal children were taught to symbolically say "Shikamoo" by reaching to touch adults' heads in a silent expression of respect, and my brothers and I quickly learned to reflexively repeat the phrase whenever we saw grown-ups, whether acquaintances or strangers.

We learned that whenever we crossed paths with a family friend, the meeting was sure to last for several minutes as we completed the cycle of greeting that followed the obligatory "Shikamoo" and its response, "Marahaba." "Hujambo?" (How are you?), these exchanges would begin. "Sijambo" (I'm fine), I would reply. "How is your father?" "He's fine." "How is your mother?" "She's fine." "How are your brothers?" "They're fine." "How is everything at home?" "Fine." "How is school?" "Fine." When these questions were exhausted, we would promise to say hello to everyone at home, and then finally resume whatever we had been doing when the adult appeared. The answer to the opening questions, by the way, was always "Fine," even if you were sick or suffering from some recent tragedy. You could divulge your misfortune later, once the ritual cycle was complete.

Kiswahili, like any language, carries embedded within it the cultural values of the society it sprung from, and as my brothers and I learned to think in Kiswahili, perhaps in some ways we learned to think like Tanzanians. Early on I noticed telltale signs of this transformation. Swahili culture, like that of most African societies, places a strong emphasis on respect for elders and on the social hierarchy of age, a stress largely absent from contemporary American culture. Interestingly (and logically, I suppose), I found that if I asked James to run an errand or do me a favor in English he was much more likely to dawdle, but if I asked in Kiswahili he would usually comply without complaint, like a dutiful Tanzanian little brother. And more and more, my brothers and I found ourselves switching to Kiswahili to express ideas that eluded us in English, or to convey an emotional flavor or spice we instinctively felt we could not capture in English. *Eti,* an untranslatable word used frequently in casual Kiswahili speech (almost in the way an American teenager might use the word "like"), began to creep into our English sentences, along with expressions like *nini* (literally "what," often used like "whatchamacallit") and *Ala!* (from "Allah," an exclamation of surprise like "Oh, my God!").

I learned to savor what I saw as the peculiarly Tanzanian sensibility of certain Kiswahili words and expressions, especially those that to me reflected the importance of community and personal relations in

Swahili culture. Teachers and parents would often remind us to look out for *mwenzako*, your "fellow," or your "peer," a word that to my ear carried with it a sense of ownership, expressing the idea that your friends belong to you, as you belong to them, and for this reason are your responsibility. *Pole* didn't just mean "sorry" in the American sense of apologizing for personal actions that had harmed someone else; it was an all-purpose expression of sympathy for a hard day at work, illness, hunger or whatever; it meant that one person's misfortune was a burden shared by his fellows. *Tumefiwa* ("We have been bereaved") was a succinctly powerful way to say, "A member of our family has died," and implied that the loved one's death was experienced (as opposed to witnessed) directly and personally by everyone in the family. It expressed a sense of the family's strong ties to the departed.

Kiswahili slang and humor proved an equally rich source of cultural instruction. I spent countless afternoons sitting around with neighborhood friends and listening to spirited exchanges designed for the amusement of the assembled audience. Guys would jokingly insult each other's mothers in filthy rhymes, or use inspired wordplay to ridicule aspects of their opponent's appearance—the shape of his head, his protruding ears, or his missing teeth. Sometimes this banter would lead to conflict, but much more often the battles ended with everyone collapsing in breathless, paralyzing laughter. The most skillful verbal combatants could think on their feet with amazing speed, spinning impromptu narratives starring their opponents and their families, and using sly allegorical allusions instead of explicit attacks to communicate their insults. Soon I could understand the insinuations along with the others and was laughing just as hard at jokes that had at first escaped me.

As I began to learn the subtleties of Kiswahili I began to internalize aspects of Swahili culture, and soon developed a new way of looking at the world. Mine was not a wholly American or wholly Tanzanian perspective; rather it reflected the influence of different traditions. My brothers and I took to speaking to each other in a uniquely Americanized Kiswahili, or would directly translate Kiswahili expressions into English, often to humorous effect. "He can't you!" I would shout to encourage Kolo as he faced an opponent in a basketball game, a literal translation for a Kiswahili phrase that actually meant "He can't handle you" (*Hakuwezi*). "Nilimsalimia [I greeted him], but he just dried up," Kolo might complain to me, using an English translation of a Kiswahili slang expression (*alikausha*) to explain how a friend had ignored him. Sometimes it seemed that my brothers and I shared a cultural identity that no one but us would ever understand, but as we became more and more comfortable in Tanzania we learned to shift easily between cultural contexts.

Some aspects of our new home were more difficult to adjust to, of course. There were chronic shortages of basic goods, such as sugar, bread, cooking oil, toilet paper, and toothpaste, and my mother would often find herself searching the city for these commodities. Gasoline (locals called it petrol) was sometimes scarce, and all drivers carried gasoline ration cards on which gas station attendants checked off the forty liters that were each car's weekly allotment. To help save gas, the government also instituted a Sunday afternoon driving ban that was well intentioned but rarely enforced.

Every so often the water faucets would unexpectedly run dry, days on which everyone in our neighborhood would fetch water in buckets from wells nearby. During such shortages my family would use water as sparingly as we could, bathing with buckets of water we heated on the stove, and flushing the toilet only when it *really* needed it. Since the university campus was on a hill outside the city, we were particularly hard hit by dips in the water pressure, and when we were deprived of water for extended periods, people would joke that the *chuo kikuu* (the main university) had become the *choo kikuu* (the main toilet). We would wait suspensefully for the water to return, and it finally would, as unexpectedly as it had departed, coughing from the faucets in a sudden splash of muddy brown.

Power outages were also common. We would be sitting in the living room after dinner, reading or doing homework, and suddenly the lights would go off, the music from the tape recorder would stop, and the fridge would go silent. Sometimes you could actually hear the collective groan from people all over the neighborhood. My brothers and I didn't really mind the power cuts, in part because they were a great excuse for undone homework. Since the electricity would usually be off all over the city, it would get extremely dark, and we would rummage for candles and flashlights. My father would tell us stories in the dark, or, if it wasn't too late, we'd go outside and sit with our friends, talking and sometimes playing drums under a beautifully starlit sky that was all the clearer in the complete darkness. Eventually the power would return with a spontaneous surge of light and sound, usually greeted by cheers that echoed all over the neighborhood, and we would go back to what we had been doing before the lights went out.

Other aspects of Tanzania were more unsettling. As residents of the university campus, where most of the homes were occupied by professors and other university employees, we were surrounded by members of the nation's small middle class, but we did not have to go far to see the poverty that afflicted most Tanzanians. The campus was surrounded by predominantly working-class enclaves like Saavei (named for its proximity to a state college where they taught surveying), Mwenge, Ubungo and Makongo, small communities largely comprising dirt roads and basic shacks. Spindly, malnourished children wandered the street in ragged shorts, their round little bellies poking out beneath dirty T-shirts. My brothers and I would venture into these neighborhoods to visit friends who lived there or to run errands for our mother—to buy eggs and other items, or to get a shoe repaired. I was always disturbed by the obvious hardship and felt guilty for my own privilege, even though I realized that by American standards my family was rather poor, and that we were virtually paupers compared to the government ministers, businessmen, and diplomats who formed Tanzania's elite. I was vaguely aware of *ujamaa*, Tanzania's socialist policy of cooperative economics, and of its goal, some form of economic equality, but when *wakubwa* (big men) drove Mercedes-Benzes and lived in mansions while the majority of the population dwelled in shacks and couldn't afford shoes, I couldn't see how it was working.

The symptoms of poverty were everywhere. Buses, the sole means of transport for most of the city's population, were always vastly overcrowded, listing to one side as a hundred crushed into space designed for fifty. My brothers and I learned to use the *dala dala*s (so named since at the time they charged a fare of one dala, five Tanzanian shillings), and even managed to perfect the athletic leaps onto moving vehicles that were often a requisite of *dala dala* travel. But moving around Dar es Salaam by public transportation was usually a time-consuming and arduous process, and we sometimes heard reports of terrible accidents in which overloaded buses had crashed. Whenever we could, we preferred to get rides with our parents or friends. But for the majority of Tanzanians there was little alternative to the troubled public transport network.

The local health care system was similarly overwhelmed. It was common to see polio and leprosy victims hobbling along on makeshift canes, and whenever we went to the campus's free clinic there was always a long line of people awaiting treatment, mostly malaria victims slumped feverishly in their seats while flies buzzed around the hot, smelly waiting room. For the first year after we arrived in Tanzania, my family took weekly doses of chloroquine to stave off malaria attacks, and these were reasonably effective, although all of us suffered through the disease at least once. But since most Tanzanians could not afford regular prophylaxis, malaria was practically as common as the cold, and it was the nation's (and Africa's) number one killer. And since the parasites responsible for the disease repeatedly developed resistance to the drugs used to treat it, malaria kept coming back stronger and in more virulent forms.

Tanzania's widespread poverty also resulted in widespread crime. Kids often stole garments from clotheslines, buses were haunted by pickpockets, and some deserted paths were patrolled by muggers. More ambitious heists were also common, and every now and then a campus family would be robbed of everything by armed thieves who struck at night. We hired a night watchman and got a dog, but despite these precautions we endured more than one robbery attempt and once had our car windshield stolen.

To me, the customary treatment suspected thieves received was almost more disturbing than the prevalence of crime itself. I witnessed many mob beatings of accused thieves. All it took was for one or two people, usually women who claimed to have witnessed the act, to give the excited cry of "Mwizi!" (Thief!), and for the accused to take off running, and it was on: able-bodied men and boys would suddenly converge from all directions to chase the sprinting offender, and if they caught him, he was in deep trouble. I have heard many stories of thieves being killed by mobs, but all the beatings I saw ended with the accused being escorted to the police station (he received a fresh beating from onlookers in each neighborhood the entourage passed through), where he was handed over to officers who looked eager to continue the torture. I would follow these processions but never participated in a mob beat-down; I always worried that the accused thief was telling the truth when he said, "Siyo mimi!" ("It wasn't me"), as they all inevitably did. Many of my friends, however, delighted in beating thieves and would leap excitedly to their feet when they heard the call.

However ambivalent we were about some aspects of our new home, during those early years in Dar my whole family seemed to feel a sense of excitement and promise. My father seemed to especially enjoy being back "home," even though Tanzania, as we were often reminded, was something of a pale substitute for his actual home, Zaire.

As if to compensate for the country's perceived shortcomings, my father regaled us nightly with stories and songs from his village. After dinner we would sit around the dining room table eating boiled peanuts or sugarcane and listening to my father spin tales about the toad who made a whistle, the dog who played dead, the woman who followed a handsome stranger home from the market, and the antelope who ate the leopard's children during a famine. The stories were almost mysteriously surreal, filled with unearthly events and odd characters, and all of them had accompanying Kikongo songs that we learned to sing even if we never had more than a basic understanding of their meaning. My father stocked the living room with drums and other instruments he bought at the local crafts market, and we would sing and play accompaniment to his songs while he played along on the marimba, an African thumb piano.

My mother also seemed pleased with her new life. She became quite proficient in Kiswahili, and began to relax in the slow pace of life in our neighborhood and to feel at home there. She also began to familiarize herself with the city, making trips into town to buy groceries in a 1972 Volkswagen Beetle my parents purchased from a departing British couple. Eventually, many people began to take her for an African, a mistake she always took as a compliment.

I sometimes accompanied my mother on her expeditions into the warren of crowded, potholed streets that was downtown Dar es Salaam. "Town," as we called it, was about a half-hour's drive from our home on campus, a ride that took us past Mwenge, a noisy produce market and transportation hub, along Bagamoyo Road, one of the city's primary thoroughfares, through residential areas, and across Selander Bridge, where the stench of sewage merged with the salty ocean breeze to welcome you to downtown. Downtown itself was a bustling collection of drab, somewhat dilapidated buildings housing shopping emporiums run by Indian and Arab merchants, government offices, travel agencies, restaurants, and bookstores. Few structures were taller than five or six stories, and those that were, like the Embassy and Kilimanjaro hotels, loomed above their peers like mahogany trees surrounded by acacias. The hot, dusty streets were always filled with cars (Land Rovers and Peugeots were among the most popular), and the sidewalks were always awash with people—men in safari suits, veiled women in colorful *khanga*s, schoolchildren in uniforms, streetwise vendors in shorts and sunglasses, and lepers in rags, reaching for handouts with fingerless hands. Though it could be pleasant to sip a cold Pepsi in front of the central post office while watching the sidewalk parade my mother always ran all her errands as quickly as she could and then withdrew to the comparative peace of our campus home.

She made friends among our neighbors, my father's colleagues, and among the community of African Americans and West Indians who lived in Dar es Salaam. Black expatriates in Dar tended to seek each other out, and it was usually easy to spot them, by their features, dress, and accents. On more than one of my mother's trips to town she was approached by wide-eyed African Americans eager to meet a compatriot, usually these were tourists, students, or Peace Corps volunteers newly arrived in the country. My mother would take the newcomers home, feed them, and then introduce them to the other members of the local black expat community. The group included a transplanted Washington, D.C., native, a black family from Milwaukee, a Trinidadian family who lived near our neighborhood and became close friends of ours, an African American family who ran a butcher shop, and various students and aid agency employees who found themselves in Dar on year-long assignments. It was common for Uncle Jan or Aunt Edie to come by the house with a new African American friend in tow, and at the resulting gathering the talk would inevitably turn to Africa and the experiences of African Americans on the continent.

Dar's African American community included old-timers who had left the United States in the early 1960s, as well as more recent "repatriates" who hadn't set foot on African soil until the 1970s or 1980s. Many moved to Tanzania to become permanent residents and planned to never again live in the United States; others were merely visiting, spending a few months or a year in Africa before returning to their families, jobs, and communities. They came from various parts of the diaspora and various social and class backgrounds, and they came to Tanzania for various reasons. Some sought to make a contribution to the country's development as professors, teachers, and aid workers, some looked to establish lucrative African business enterprises, and others sought more insubstantial psychological rewards in a quest for an African identity. But virtually all of us were united by a pan-African racial outlook. We viewed Africa as a logical place for blacks to settle, as a possible homeland for blacks around the world. And I think we all felt we had a personal stake in Tanzania as a nation; when we endured inconveniences like gasoline shortages or other symptoms of underdevelopment it was often with a sense of belt-tightening patriotism. We realized that we would always, at least partly, be outsiders in Tanzania, but this was still our adoptive home, and we took pride in it and hoped we were helping to improve it. This conviction was so strong among my mother and her friends that it went largely unsaid; we took it for granted that as blacks we had a special allegiance to Africa, the black continent, and a right to claim it as our own. And though most of Dar's black expatriates seemed to have overwhelmingly positive experiences in Tanzania, I know that all must have been forced to test the endurance of this belief practically every day.

Tanzanians were usually welcoming of black newcomers, usually approached them with some sense of identification and brotherly enthusiasm, even if they didn't always know what to make of blacks who sometimes seemed more like white people. Among educated Tanzanians there was a general understanding of Africa's history of slavery, and of African Americans as its product, but there was rarely as intense an appreciation of racial affinity and unity among Africans as there was among black repatriates. Most Tanzanians associated African Americans with the images of Michael Jackson, Lionel Richie, Mike Tyson, and Jesse Jackson that found their way into local popular culture, and perhaps they took pride in the achievements of these fellow blacks, but they also recognized African Americans as culturally and ethnically distinct from Africans. And while the United States was associated with imperialism and exploitation and often resented because of it, most Tanzanians accepted the popular depiction of America as a rich paradise where life was easy and wondered why African Americans would choose to leave cushy Western lives for less pampered existences in Africa. In Kiswahili slang, America was "Juu" (Up There) and Tanzania "Chini" (Down Here), the implication being that to come to Tanzania from the United States was to descend from the giddy heights of privilege to the lowly depths of poverty. From the perspective of most Tanzanians in Dar es Salaam, members of various regional ethnic groups thrown together in the diversely cosmopolitan capital city, identity and affinity were perhaps more shaded by language, ethnicity, geography, culture, and social status than by skin color.

Nonetheless, the slave trade and the racist basis of the German and British colonial systems that had ruled Tanzanians for nearly a century had indeed prompted a local appreciation for the dynamics of racial oppression and generated a sense of "blackness" or "Africanness" as a socially defined and subjugated political identity.

Under the colonial system, Africans endured the humiliating

attitudes of European paternalism, which regarded "natives" as savage children who had to be Christianized and Europeanized and were unfit to rule themselves. Because of this legacy, many Tanzanians, particularly politically minded nationalists of the independence generation, were suspicious of whites. But others seemed to have internalized the notion of white superiority and seemed to look up at whites with self-effacing veneration. Whites were a curiosity to many Tanzanians and in certain areas were still regarded with the awe they had often inspired during colonial days; but they were distant oddities to most. Whatever their attitude toward white people, most Tanzanians rarely had more than passing social contact with them. In general, save for the brave few who made the effort to reach beyond their expatriate community, the whites who remained or settled in Tanzania after independence, a small percentage of the general population, lived as an elite and socially segregated group who frequented European sporting and social clubs, and usually reserved their most intimate African interactions for their employees and servants.

The social distinction between blacks and whites was an obvious one in Dar es Salaam; but the city was also home to large East Indian and Afro-Arab communities and was a magnet for WaChagga, Wanyamwezi, Wahaya, Maasai, and members of Tanzania's hundreds of other tribes, a powerful cosmopolitanism that made for many different and complex layers of interaction. For example, members of other ethnic groups often stereotyped WaChagga as money-hungry entrepreneurs and criticized Wahaya for their perceived clannishness, while Indians, who formed an affluent merchant class, were often resented by Africans who regarded them as an arrogant economic elite. Also, in Tanzania religion tended to dovetail with politics, such that while Muslims and Christians lived together peacefully, they often found themselves pitted against one another politically. Amid such complexity, the black-white divide was only one of Dar's social distinctions and rarely the foremost cleavage in people's minds.

Though racism and a sense of racial identity were realities in postcolonial Tanzania, in a majority black but ethnically diverse country run by Africans, the dynamics of racial division were quite different than they are in America, so even when experiences with racial oppression served as the basis for empathy between Africans and African Americans, it could be a misleading sentiment. Blackness was something Africans shared with black expatriates that they didn't share with white ones, and it did serve as the basis for some mutual sense of identification. But there was still much that served to distinguish

African Americans from their local counterparts, both culturally and in terms of what they felt they could expect from each other.

Black expatriates who lived in Tanzania long enough to learn Kiswahili and the nuances of Tanzanian culture were able to forge close friendships with Tanzanians, but those who only stayed in Dar for a little while often found language and culture impenetrable barriers that kept them from interacting with locals in any meaningful way. Uncle Jan, who had hosted and become familiar with a number of diasporean "repatriates," was an especially fertile source of anecdotes on cross-cultural misunderstandings between newcomers and locals, episodes he seemed to find endlessly amusing.

One of his favorite stories was about a Jamaican Rastafarian who was traveling through Tanzania when his car broke down near a rural community. The man walked into the village seeking help, but could not speak any Kiswahili, and found no one who could understand English. The villagers he approached were completely bewildered by the sudden appearance of this odd-looking stranger and, unable to comprehend a word he said, made some conclusions on his identity based on his looks. Though the men of some African ethnic groups traditionally wear their hair in braids or long, matted strands (like the Maasai of northern Tanzania), to many Africans, dreadlock hairstyles are a sign of mental illness, sported primarily by ragged neighborhood madmen who are too far gone to clean themselves or comb their hair. In the streets of the capital, jaded urbanites would hardly have been alarmed by the Jamaican's appearance (some children might have even shouted "Peace and love!" or other Rasta slogans when they saw him), but in this rural enclave it was a different matter.

The way Uncle Jan told it, when this tall Rastaman emerged from the darkness, many of the villagers who saw him took his long locks as an indication that he was crazy, took his marijuana-reddened eyes as evidence that he was *mnyonya damu* (a bloodsucker, or African vampire), and his incomprehensible speech for evil magic spells designed to harm those who heard it. In short, they concluded that he was *mchawi* (a malevolent witch doctor). They leaped on him, restrained him, and tied him up, ignoring his cries of surprise and protest. Then the villagers summoned some policemen from a nearby outpost to come and retrieve their prisoner. Fortunately, the officers spoke English, so the Jamaican was able to explain what had happened and was released. It was a frightening example of the explosive potential of cross-cultural misunderstanding, and sadly ironic in that the confusion was in part caused by a hairstyle that the Jamaican wore to celebrate his ties to Africa. Nonetheless, my brothers and I thought the story was hilarious.

A friend of my father's once told me about another Rastafarian who had settled in Tanzania, a Jamaican who called himself Jah Bube. He believed he was on a divine mission to found a repatriate settlement in Tanzania, an endeavor he documented in a long, illustrated, Scripture-laden tract that described the citadel he hoped to create and the strict religious ideals that would govern the new society. He had approached a number of local leaders, as well as members of Tanzania's black expatriate community, to ask for help in his ambitious plan, but some dismissed him as a crank. After discussions with President Julius Nyerere and other politicians, Jah Bube was granted a large plot of land in rural western Tanzania, the proposed site for the glorious city he prophesied. Though he had secured the land he needed, Jah Bube's plans seemed to run aground as he attempted to line up a contractor to help him start building a new metropolis and to round up some followers to populate it. Promises of assistance fell through, and he ran into financial difficulties. He began trying to raise funds by selling copies of his oracular treatise and soliciting donations, with mixed success. Every now and then you'd catch sight of him around Dar es Salaam, striding along the side of a road, his dreadlocks trussed tightly in a white head wrap and his wife and daughter trailing dutifully behind him. My father's friend had purchased one of Jah Bube's books, but he said he did it mainly because he hoped the money would help to sustain Bube's wife and daughter, whom he viewed as the silent hostages to the grandiose vision of a man with big ideas but little apparent organizational acumen and no stable source of income.

Sometimes my brothers and I found ourselves translating or mediating between African Americans and Tanzanians, an experience that often highlighted the gap in culture, language, and expectations. They would struggle to communicate, but all too often they ultimately just wouldn't hear one another. On one occasion an African American student in a study-abroad program at the university was at our house when the "fish man," a middle-aged Tanzanian who went door to door on his Chinese bicycle selling fresh fish, stopped by. Speaking through my younger brothers, the student asked to buy some prawns, haggling for the best deal through her interpreters. When the price was settled and the fish man unloaded the shrimp, the trouble started. The student, perhaps prompted by an American expectation of being able to buy packaged, processed food, maintained that the fish man should clean the individual prawns, preparing them for cooking by re-moving the heads and shells, and that the established price automati-cally included this service. The fish man, sounding as though this was the first time he had ever heard such a thing, disagreed quite strongly, and protested loudly, his brow furrowing under his Muslim cap. "Hii ni shauri ya cook! Shauri ya cook!" (That's the cook's job), he kept as-serting stubbornly. The disagreement got louder and more heated as both parties refused to compromise. My brothers gave up trying to translate and tried not to laugh, while a Tanzanian friend of theirs at-tempted to straighten things out. "Mnajua nyinyi hamuelewani" (You know, you guys don't understand each other), he said, diplomati-cally stating the obvious. The fish man finally relented, scraping the shells off the tiny crustaceans in a huff, but he was clearly unhappy with the arrangement. My brothers escaped from view and collapsed in laughter.

Though such moments of misunderstanding were common, Kolo, James, and I also had occasion to observe many examples of impor-tant connections forged between African Americans and African lo-cals. My brothers and I were once listening to the national radio station when we heard an African American woman being inter-viewed about her recent visit to northern Tanzania. She eagerly re-counted how she was welcomed with open arms by Maasai tribesmen who called her a long-lost daughter and made her an honorary mem-ber of the clan, giving her a name, a title, and cattle. Although I knew her experience was far from typical, I was touched by the fairytale quality of her story and thought it a fitting welcome for a cultural repatriate, the stuff of idealized diaspora dreams of return.

* * *

As black "returnees" to Africa in the early 1980s, my brothers and I were stragglers in a small African American "Back-to-Africa" exodus that had peaked in the 1960s and 1970s, when thousands of black Americans traveled to Africa to visit and settle in newly independent countries like Ghana and Tanzania. Though the 1960s were a period of significant African American travel and settlement in Africa, the decade was only one phase in a tradition of African American "return" to Africa that dates from the eighteenth century.

It seems obvious that African captives enslaved in the New World would have desired and attempted to return to the homes from which they had been wrenched, and centuries of literature, history, music, and art attest to Africa's enormous stature in the African American psyche. Early documented examples of slaves who managed to return to Africa are scarce, but we know of a few who succeeded in gaining their freedom and were reunited with loved ones in West Africa. Job ben Solomon, a Muslim Fulani nobleman, was abducted in Gambia and enslaved in Maryland in 1731. He wrote to his father, begging him to intercede on his behalf. The letter never made it to Africa, instead ending up in London, where it somehow reached and sparked the interest of James Oglethorpe, a wealthy philanthropist. Oglethorpe purchased the young slave and delighted in his novelty as a literate African of royal heritage, showing ben Solomon off as an "Arabic scholar" and introducing him to various dignitaries, including the English queen Caroline. Ben Solomon was such a hit that it was decided that he should be set free. Ben Solomon was returned to his village in Gambia in 1736, more because his sponsors hoped he would champion British interests in the region than out of any sense of charity, and he later hinted at the emotional impact of his return in a letter to a friend. "I must leave you to guess . . . the Raptures and pleasures I enjoy'd," he wrote. "Floods of Tears burst their way."

Ben Solomon's case was obviously exceptional, and it wasn't until decades later that the idea of black repatriation to Africa began to be seriously discussed as a possible solution to what some farsighted social commentators already recognized as a brewing social problem. By the mid-eighteenth century there was already a significant community of free blacks in northern American cities like Boston, and they campaigned against slavery and for the full rights of citizenship. When the American War of Independence failed to gain civil rights for blacks in America, some proposed emigration as a solution to the racial divide in American society. The slave owner and American founding father Thomas Jefferson, who somewhat hollowly claimed ethical opposition to slavery, wrote of his "suspicion" of black inferiority in 1781, and, seeing no way of forging one nation from two unequal and incompatible peoples, suggested that blacks be sent to live elsewhere. The idea became popular among a number of prominent white pundits of the late eighteenth century.

In the 1780s, Britain stumbled on repatriation as a solution to an embarrassing situation that presented itself after the American Revolution. Blacks had fought on both sides of the war, usually in the hope that the side they chose would be victorious and grant freedom to the slaves who had assisted them. When Britain was defeated in the conflict, thousands of former slaves who had sided with the empire settled in Canada and England, rather than return to certain retribution in a newly "liberated" America. The thousands who thronged the English capital, where they lived in terrible poverty, came to be known as the Black Poor of London, and their presence became a perpetual nuisance and national fixation. In 1786, Henry Smeathman, a naturalist who had traveled extensively in West Africa, proposed that London's destitute blacks be settled in Sierra Leone, an area he described as "fertile, healthy and pleasant." Smeathman offered to escort the settlers to their new home (for an appropriate fee) but died before the plan could be implemented. The scheme was rescued by Granville Sharp, a British religious leader who had long been an opponent of the slave trade, and by the support of blacks who petitioned in favor of "Smeathman's humane plan."

In April 1787, a ship carrying 411 eager settlers (including around seventy white women, the wives of black settlers) left Plymouth, bound for West Africa. As the first large-scale effort to repatriate former slaves, it was an historic event, marked by an appropriately high-minded sense of mission and pioneering spirit. Sharp encouraged the settlers to found "the Province of Freedom," to conduct themselves according to the laws and religion of England, and to pave the way for future emigrants. However, this first "Back-to-Africa" voyage set the standard for later initiatives not as an ideal model but in that it was plagued by disasters that were all too often repeated in subsequent re-settlement attempts. The troubles began before the ship even lost sight of England; a delay of several months resulted in the outbreak of fever aboard the ship, and fifty passengers died. Fourteen more died of illness en route, but a month after setting sail the somewhat depleted and haggard settlers landed at the mouth of the Sierra Leone River and established a rudimentary settlement they named Granville Town.

More trouble followed. The settlers had arrived just before the rainy season, too late to plant crops or build permanent dwellings. They were ill equipped to endure the deluge, and a mere three months after landing, more than a hundred of them had died of fever and dysentery. The seeds that had been brought for planting spoiled, and the soil under their coastal settlement seemed much less fertile than advertised. To make matters worse, the elaborate system of discipline and government that had been devised by Granville Sharp soon deteriorated into resentful infighting and backbiting. The colonists were reduced to trading their stored food, clothes, and weapons with the local Temne tribespeople in order to survive. The situation seemed eloquently summarized by a settler named Elliot, who updated

Sharp on the colony's progress: "I am sorry, and very sorry indeed, to inform you, dear Sir, that this country does not agree with us at all," he reported forlornly. "And without a very sudden change, I do not think there will be one of us left at the end of a twelvemonth." Sharp did little but lament the settlers' unhappiness. "I have had but melancholy accounts of my poor little ill-thriven swarthy daughter, the unfortunate colony of Sierra Leone," he remarked in response to the complaints.

Matters actually got worse. Granville Town became increasingly lawless; faced with few options for survival, some of the colonists, ironically, began trading in slaves. And there were conflicts with the local Africans, skirmishes largely based on a misunderstanding between the colonists and the local chief from whom they had "purchased" their land. The newcomers were unfamiliar with African attitudes toward land ownership and assumed that the £59 worth of goods they had given the chief entitled them to outright ownership of the settlement's twenty square miles. The local king, on the other hand, referring to a traditional land tenure system in which land was not bought or sold but used with the permission of the regional chief, saw things differently. As he understood it, he had allowed the colonists to settle on his lands as a favor; he began to reconsider his generosity as they became more troublesome.

In 1788 the colonists were ordered off the land altogether. They paid an additional £85 to placate their disgruntled landlords, and signed a treaty with them in August 1788, a document recognized as the legal origin of the colony of Sierra Leone. The agreement did not end the tensions, however. The local king, apparently encouraged by slave traders hostile to the repatriates, continued to harass the colonists, and the aggression escalated into full-blown hostilities by late 1789, when a British warship attacked the coast in defense of the colony. The African king's response was to raze Granville Town, scattering its inhabitants in the bush.

Other black colonists would later return, and the colony of Sierra Leone would eventually endure, but the destruction of Granville Town signified the inglorious end of the first major attempt to resettle New World Africans on African soil, an experiment ironically cut short by native Africans who were less than welcoming of their returned "cousins," who encroached on their land and were in league with imperialists.

In 1792 the colony was reestablished by former slaves who had settled in Canada after the American Revolution and petitioned the British Sierra Leone Company to sponsor their repatriation. Over a thousand settlers arrived in the area in January 1792, but their experience was tragically similar to that of their Granville Town predecessors. They arrived during the rainy season and had inadequate shelter. Fever soon broke out. One settler, the wife of the British agent who led the settlement process, painted a vivid picture of the widespread suffering. "Alass! alass! in place of growing better, we seem daily advancing toward destruction," she wrote sadly. "It is customary of a morning to ask 'how many died last night?' Death is viewed with the same indifference as if people were only taking a short journey, to return in a few days."

Almost a hundred settlers died in that first rainy season, but the colony managed to survive. Homes and a church were built on land deserted by the locals, and the colonists began planting gardens and raising livestock. And amid the disappointments and death there were some encouraging moments; Zachary Macaulay, who became the colony's governor in 1793, reported that one settler, a former slave who had been abducted in the area years previously, was actually joyously reunited with his mother.

New World Africans continued to pour into the colony, strengthening and diversifying it. First came 550 Jamaican maroons in 1800, then thousands of slaves freed at sea by the British navy after the abolition of the slave trade in 1807. The newcomers helped to fortify a growing coastal settler community that thrived as a trade outpost through which British goods made their way into the African interior. By 1850 over 40,000 newcomers had settled in Sierra Leone in a firmly entrenched community around Freetown, a "Creole" society made up of Americanized and Europeanized blacks who are said to have prided themselves on their Christianity and Victorian mores and who tended to look down on the local Africans, among whom they attempted to spread the gospel.

Though there was significant cultural mixing, the settlers evolved into a distinct political and social elite upholding British interest as the colonial administrators (the colony became a protectorate under Creole control in the late 1880s), and earned themselves the resentment of the natives. The tensions erupted in open conflict in 1898 when Creole enforcement of a British tax on local dwellings prompted African resistance in the Hut Tax War. The Creoles and their British backers prevailed, but the war soured Creole-African relations, perhaps permanently. Contemporary Sierra Leonean society, which is still characterized by a class distinction between Creoles and natives, continues, to some degree, to be afflicted by mistrust and rivalry. It's an odd legacy for an experiment in repatriation informed by notions of black nationalism, self-determination, and uplift; New World African settlers in Sierra Leone in the eighteenth and nineteenth centuries did succeed in forging a viable black "returnee" community on African soil, but they did so largely at the expense of the local population.

There were numerous subsequent repatriation efforts, but some repeated many of the same mistakes. In 1816, Paul Cuffe, the Quaker sailor mentioned earlier, took thirty-eight African American settlers to Freetown in a well-publicized trip that helped to popularize the notion of repatriation in America. Cuffe died in 1817, and little is known of the fate of those he led to Sierra Leone, but his voyage seemed to spark several others.

In 1820 Daniel Coker, a black minister who eagerly looked forward to spreading Christianity among Africans, led a group of ninety free blacks to found a new colony in Sierra Leone. The voyage seemed ill fated from the first. Their ship, the *Elizabeth*, got stuck in the ice of New York harbor, and languished there for a week before finally setting sail for West Africa. When they finally landed at Sherbro Island, some way down the coast from Freetown, the settlers thanked God for bringing them to their "mother country" and communed with some of the local Africans. The good cheer didn't last, however. Like their predecessors, this group of immigrants arrived right before the rains, and soon many were stricken with fever. Those who could fled to Freetown, and the new would-be settlement disintegrated.

As the free black population in America grew, so did white support for repatriation. The year 1816 saw the creation of the American Colonization Society, an organization conceived to sponsor and support black settlement initiatives in Africa. Founded and dominated by whites who sought to export what they saw as a troublesome minority with whom they could never coexist, the society was denounced by many blacks who viewed its ideas and goals with suspicion, but it did play an important role in encouraging African American emigration to Africa. The Society became an unlikely and problematic ally to African American leaders who sought to direct black American efforts to settle in Africa. African Americans who viewed Africa as the past and future home of American blacks were motivated by a desire to "uplift the race," but in seeking to organize a black "return" to the continent, they courted the assistance of racist whites who would be happy to see them leave and anticipated their departure as the appropriate return of an inferior race to their backward homeland. African Americans who wished to leave the United States and the whites who helped them do it essentially had the same goal, but it seemed an uneasy and strange pairing between people who were ordinarily antagonists on most other matters.

In 1819 the U.S. government, bowing to increasing pressure from international abolitionists, ordered the U.S. Navy to seize all American ships involved in the slave trade, and dispatched agents and thirty-three black emigrants to West Africa to scout out a site on which to settle slaves liberated at sea. Using their considerable powers of coercion to win the support of the local chief (allegedly, the U.S. agent in charge of the mission held a gun to the chief's head until he agreed to lease the land), the American representatives founded the Republic of Liberia. Like Sierra Leone before it, the new settlement was a colony established by an imperial power specifically as a home for former New World slaves. And like Sierra Leone, the fledgling colony was plagued by problems from its very inception.

Repeating a by now familiar pattern, the colonists found that they were ill equipped for life in the new environment; many suffered from fever, and their food stores soon dwindled alarmingly. Among the more trying ordeals that afflicted the colony were an invasion by a swarm of bees (one woman was said to have been stung between three hundred and five hundred times), attacks on their livestock by leopards and other predators, and raids on the settlement by the local Africans. Nonetheless, despite the hardship, a year after its establishment the community boasted one hundred and fifty members and was thriving. In fact, through the Colonization Society journal established in 1825, the settlers wrote with zealous enthusiasm of their experiences in Liberia. Many settlers gave voice to their feelings in poems, like this one:

> *The sun had far mounted the sky,*
> *When my pathway on ocean was o'er*
> *And none was so happy as I,*
> *When delighted, I leaped on the shore.*
> *In freedom and joy did I stand,*
> *And pour forth my thanks to my God,*
> *Who thus led me back to the land,*
> *My fathers for ages had trod.*

Others spoke eagerly, in proudly racialized terms, of how superior their new home was to the America they had left. "What my sensations were upon landing I can hardly describe," wrote one. "You here behold coloured men exercising all the duties of offices which you can scarcely believe, many fulfill the important duties with much dignity. We have now a republic in miniature. . . . I long to see young men, who are now wasting the best of their days in the United States, flocking to the land as the last asylum to the unfortunate."

Before departing for the colony, Lott Cary, a Baptist missionary who was later appointed Liberia's governor, had declared, "I am an African, and in this country [America] however meritous my conduct and respectable my character, I cannot receive the credit due to either. I wish to go to a country where I shall be estimated by my merits, not by my complexion, and I feel bound to labor for my suffering race." Cary seems to have felt that in Liberia he had found such a country, for shortly after arriving he asserted, "There never has been an hour or a minute . . . when I could wish myself again in America."

Other settlers expressed their satisfaction with their new home by prevailing on their peers back in the United States to follow them to Liberia. "We know nothing of that debasing inferiority with which our very colour stamped us in America," they wrote in an open letter to "the coloured people of the United States." "It is this moral emancipation—this liberation of the mind from worse than iron fetters, that repays us, ten thousand times over, for all it has cost us."

Interestingly, however, none of the colonists' writings acknowledge what the repatriation process cost their new neighbors. The local Vei tribe sustained heavy losses in conflicts with the colonists, who readily repelled African attacks with a cannon provided by the U.S. government. Apparently the lives of hundreds of resident Africans were necessary casualties in the African American quest for "moral emancipation" and "liberation." Ironically, Cary, the missionary "bound to labor for his suffering race," died in an accidental explosion of cartridges he was making to use in battle against the local Africans.

Despite the ongoing battles, the Liberian colony endured and grew into an independent black nation in 1847. Naming its capital Monrovia (after then American president James Monroe, a strong proponent of black emigration) and adopting a national flag with a striking resemblance to the U.S. Stars and Stripes, the country became something of an American satellite state in Africa and a symbolic homeland for thousands of American blacks, a leading destination for African American emigrants on into the 1960s. However, like Sierra Leone, despite a degree of syncretization and mixing, the new nation was characterized by a sharp social and cultural division between Africans and Americo-Liberians, with the newcomers establishing themselves as a political elite who were not above exploiting and subjugating the native population. It's a conflict that still echoes in Liberia's troubled political landscape.

While the American Civil War and the Northern promise of freedom for America's blacks decreased the popularity of black repatriation to Africa, by the 1870s the consolidation of white supremacy across America through lynchings and a racist backlash against post–Civil War social reforms led to widespread black disillusionment and gave the back-to-Africa movement new vigor. Martin Delany, a prominent black doctor, judge, editor, author, and early pan-Africanist, emerged as one of the era's most important emigrationists, helping to establish the Liberian Exodus Joint Stock Steamship Company in 1877. By selling stock the company raised enough money to buy a ship, the *Azor*, and in 1878 it set sail for Liberia carrying 206 black emigrants. Twenty-three passengers died en route, but the rest made it to Liberia and settled there successfully. The deaths—the result of food and water shortages, disease, and the absence of a doctor on board—soured perceptions of the company back in the United States, however, and it soon went bankrupt, never managing to sponsor another voyage.

In the 1890s the chief black spokesman for repatriation was Bishop Henry McNeal Turner, the vice president of the American Colonization Society, who traveled through the South trumpeting the virtues of West Africa and encouraging emigration. A bitter critic of the United States (he referred to the American flag as a "dirty and contemptible rag" and to the U.S. Constitution as "a cheat, a libel"), Turner spoke in exalted and exaggerated terms of the beauty and bounty of Liberia and found a considerable following among poor black farmers in the South. Turner eventually toured Africa to significant acclaim and managed to build ties between his African Methodist Episcopal Church and churches in Africa.

In another odd alliance, Turner received support for repatriation from a group of racist white Alabama businessmen who wanted to encourage blacks to leave the country and formed the International Migration Society in 1894. Altogether, the society sent around five hundred emigrants to Liberia, two hundred in the *Horsa* in 1895 and three hundred in the *Laurada* in 1896, but the newcomers' reactions to their new home were varied.

W. R. Haffer, one of the settlers who reached Liberia on the *Horsa*, wrote his mother in Arkansas complaining that "something to eat is scarce over here. . . . We eat twice a day, when we can get it. . . . ever since we have been here we have been in a suffering condition and starving." Less than a year after their arrival, a hundred of the *Laurada*'s passengers had died of fever. The disasters that befell the *Laurada* emigrants and stories of hardship that filtered back to the United States (often gleefully publicized by African American editors who opposed repatriation) gained Turner and the society damaging publicity, and his efforts to resettle blacks in West Africa were cut short. From 1890 to 1910 around a thousand black Americans actually settled in Liberia—hardly a mass exodus, but a significant number nonetheless. If Turner's pro-Liberia propaganda did not spark a mass movement of black American returnees, it did prompt many blacks, predominantly poor farmers from the rural South, to attempt to find their way to the motherland.

Alfred Sam, who claimed he was a Gold Coast chief and recruited black emigrants in the South with utopian descriptions of what awaited them in Africa, was another emigrationist leader of the 1900s. Though denounced as a charlatan by British colonial authorities in the Gold Coast and African American intellectuals alike, Sam nonetheless managed to round up five thousand shareholders in his Akim Trading Company and sixty passengers for his ship, the S. S. *Liberia*, which sailed for West Africa in 1915. Though by most accounts the newcomers were welcomed warmly by the Africans they met when they landed in the Gold Coast, the British authorities imposed several restrictions on the new settlers, whom they regarded as potentially disruptive troublemakers. And many of the emigrants found fault with Chief Sam. "I am sorry to say that this Negro, our so-called leader, Chief Alfred C. Sam, has only lied and frauded the people out here," complained one. "He fooled our people; he said the cattle here were eight feet high. I learned there isn't a cow in the place—this was a fraud. . . . this is one of the dirtiest things our race has gotten into since the world began." Sam had actually purchased a piece of land for the settlers, but the new residents found their tract of jungle quite inhospitable. The difficult conditions earned Sam the colonists' ire and he eventually ended up fleeing the settlement in disgrace. His bitter followers scattered, and, once again, a new black American colony in Africa dissolved.

Sam's repatriation initiative was one of the last in which African

Americans were organized en masse to resettle in Africa. Though organizations that sought to return African Americans to the land of their ancestors continued to exist into the 1920s and 1930s, none would have much success in actually sending settlers to the continent. The most spectacular failure in this regard was Marcus Garvey's UNIA, which generated unprecedented popularity for the repatriation idea and revolutionized African American and African attitudes toward Africa and blackness but failed, due to mismanagement and legal obstacles, to settle many UNIA members on African soil.

The Great Depression and World War II effectively squelched most repatriation impulses in the 1930s and 1940s, but in the late 1950s, with the start of the African decolonization movement and the rise of black nationalism, African Americans began once again to look to Africa as a lost homeland to which they wanted to return. Hundreds of black returnees traveled to and settled in Africa in the late 1950s, 1960s and 1970s, but in this era of exodus, settlers and visitors ventured to the motherland as individuals, in families or in small groups, not as settler communities sponsored by colonization or repatriation societies. Arriving in Africa as an individual rather than as a member of a large group allowed for a more personal process of "reacquaintance" with the motherland, but did not necessarily make for less pronounced feelings of disorientation and disillusionment.

The independence of Ghana in 1957 was a major event in the history of black nationalism and the back-to-Africa movement. The leader of the fledgling nation, Kwame Nkrumah, had been educated in the United States and had made a strong impact on the African Americans he met there, many of whom became caught up in the romance of the Gold Coast's struggle for independence. When Ghana became independent, many African Americans celebrated the event as the long-awaited emergence of a liberated black homeland, and Nkrumah's pronouncements encouraged them in this belief. "Long may the links between Africa and the peoples of African descent continue to hold us together in fraternity," he said in 1958. Nkrumah welcomed African Americans to settle in Ghana and ended up employing a number of New World blacks in his government. And at his invitation, the venerable Dr. W. E. B. Du Bois moved to Accra to oversee the compilation of an Encyclopedia Africana; Du Bois became an honorary Ghanaian. As one African American who settled in Ghana in the 1950s reported, "When Ghana became free it gave us a fantastic sense of pride, it gave us the same taste of pride that other Americans had. Before that there was no bridge we could cross over to

Africa. Sure, we had Garvey's Africa and all other kinds of Africas. But we were surrounded by Germans and Italians and Poles who all talked of the Old Country, and Jews were hearing about their homeland and so on. But when we looked at Africa, we found nothing there. The white man had depopulated it, so it was Garvey and all the rest of them that invented people for it. But now, why here was a homeland that was real, and they were real people in the United Nations and all."

Though Accra became the haunt of a large circle of transplanted African Americans, many of whom settled in Ghana permanently, every member of this new generation of returnees doubtless contended with culture shock and a sense of alienation. The celebrated black novelist Richard Wright had visited Ghana before independence and wrote of being overwhelmed by an uneasy sense of unfamiliarity and even fear. "I was gazing upon a world whose laws I did not know, upon faces whose reactions were riddles to me," he wrote of his experience. "Faced with the absolute otherness and inaccessibility of this new world, I was prey to a vague sense of mild panic, an oppressive burden I could not shake off."

Many accounts by later returnees also express this feeling of isolation and strangeness, perhaps at least partly inspired by decades of exposure to American stereotypes of Africa's exotic and somehow menacing mysteriousness.

This sense of alienation that many repatriates describe is part of the dawning realization that all New World Africans who resettle on the continent are soon forced to confront: though black and therefore descended at least partially from African stock, diaspora blacks are not African, and in many ways are quite culturally distinct. "When you *really* realize you are not African, it's the loneliest moment of your life," says one African American who settled in West Africa. "If you can withstand that, you can make it here. It goes on being lonely, and it's how you adjust yourself to that loneliness that matters, not how you adjust to Africa."

Priscilla Stevens Kruize, an African American who settled in Ghana in the 1960s, had a similar experience: "Before I came here I thought that I would be accepted. But it isn't like that at all. . . . this Ghanaian friend of mine . . . makes me feel very American, although I certainly never wanted to feel American." For Kruize, her outsider status was reinforced by the fact that Twi-speaking Ghanaians referred to her and other African Americans as *abruni*, a Twi word applied to foreigners. "It means 'stranger,' 'white.' It doesn't mean *exactly* white, it means more 'not from the family,' " according to Kruize. "I really don't fit. I cannot fit. My conduct is all different from theirs and they can't cope with me because of my background . . . I realized that I was very lonely and I had nothing in common with many Ghanaians."

Other repatriates found that African Americans' reputation had been sullied in some African circles due to the misadventures of previous settlers, like the Americo-Liberians who became an unpopular political elite in the nineteenth century. "I discovered that this emotional idea of identification that I had was a little bit out of whack," says Bill Sutherland, an African American who settled permanently in Africa, in Ghana and then Tanzania, in the 1960s. "The emotional attachment of the man in the street here was still the same. If you were Afro-American and you came over and talked to somebody, there would be a real warmth of expression. But among more politically aware people there was a wary look that spelled caution."

For many New World African returnees, the realization that many Africans do not share their pan-Africanist enthusiasm was also alienating. One Nigerian judge met an African American civil rights leader at a conference in Lagos and seemed bored by the American's bitter denunciation of U.S. racism. "I am simply not interested," he icily told his counterpart when the American began to remove his shirt to show off scars inflicted by white policemen. "That young American assumed that he and I had some special common bond," the Nigerian reflected later. "But all we really have in common is that we both have black skins, and that's evidently more important to him than it is to me."

The stream of African Americans that continued to flow into Africa in the 1960s and 1970s suggests that Africa had remained very important to diaspora blacks during their three-hundred-year exile, and many newcomers were stunned by African failures to reciprocate their Afrocentric zeal. One African American arrival greeted Africans at the Dakar harbor where he disembarked with an impassioned speech extolling the virtues of pan-Africanism and expressing his joy to finally be "home," but was met with an underwhelming response. "Give us a dollar," said one member of the African throng when the African American had finished his oration. "You from America. You got plenty dollar. You be Big Man. America rich country. This be poor country. We need dollar. You give dollar."

As a West African diplomat in London put it, "[African Americans'] problem is to 'acculturate,' if one might use such an expression;

they must make a change. The first generation never really makes the change. Many come with a certain idea of Africa in the abstract. For those who do, it is rather like going down a set of steps and finding there is one more at the bottom they hadn't seen. It gives them a nasty jar."

Some African American settlers were able to overcome this initial shock and arrive at more realistic views of Africa and their place in it. Patience, humility, and a willingness to learn about African cultures were huge assets in the acculturation process. As Robert E. Lee, a longtime resident of Ghana, says, "If you really want to belong to their society you can do it. But if you don't speak their language and if you don't agree with whatever their customs are, there is no point of your being around. Why should they want you?"

His point is echoed by an old Liberian of the Grebo tribe who spoke disparagingly (and instructively) of his country's original New World settlers. "They didn't ask the news," he complained, using a fitting colloquial expression to illustrate the settlers' arrogance. "They didn't try to find out what the customs were. They thought it was bad that Grebo left their dead on a small island, not burying them, and they said we must bury them, and we said no, and there was a big palaver and then a big fight. They didn't ask." His summary of the attitudes of more recent returnees is similar. "They don't ask the news, do they?" he says.

Despite all the misunderstandings, miscommunications, and often traumatic experiences of disillusionment, for many African Americans who manage to remain in Africa beyond the first giddy and revealing months, the repatriation process is ultimately positive. The experience of an African American doctor who settled in Ghana in the 1950s seems somewhat representative of the circular journey through identity and culture that many New World Africans make after settling on the continent. "The longer I live here the more I realize what we have in common; we just don't know how to express it," she says of her growing closeness to her African peers. "But I'm patient. In the beginning I just assumed we had these affinities, then I went through a long stage of believing that there were so many irreconcilable differences, and now again I feel there are affinities."

My family and I plotted a similar course in our arrival and settlement in Tanzania, moving from an assumption of automatic acceptance by our African fellows to a more complex appreciation of what we shared as black people and what we did not. And in our discovery of the nuances of local cultures, as we learned Kiswahili, made Tanzanian friends, and learned to navigate the physical and social landscapes of Dar es Salaam, my brothers and I grew into a new "African" identity, grounded more in reality than in the dreams of Africa that had spurred our journey across the Atlantic. We had arrived in Africa secure in a belief in our own inherent "Africanness," but had quickly realized the limitations of this imagined, inherited assumption. And as we debunked our own preconceptions about Africa with the evidence of personal experience, we learned new truths about the continent and, in so doing, laid claim to a proud and personal stake in a place we came to regard as "home." A year or so after moving to Tanzania, my younger brother James, who was then around five, took to describing himself as "half Tanzanian, half Zairean, and half American," a humorously appropriate expression of a sense of personal complexity that Kolo and I had also come to share.

As our ideas about Africa began to change in light of our experiences as newcomers to Tanzania, so did our assumptions about African attitudes toward African Americans. In fact, our increasingly complex sense of self was partly shaped by our realization that to most Tanzanians, African Americans were hardly "African," except in physical appearance. In a way, the simplistic notion that black skin implied an immediate sense of belonging in Africa was untenable in an environment in which few Africans seemed to share the idea. As African American arrivals in Africa burdened by expectations of instinctive kinship, my brothers and I found ourselves confronting Africans whose perceptions of us were clouded by a great deal of ignorance and a wealth of stereotypes, in the same way that our own prejudgments about Africa had distorted what we thought we knew about our new home. In negotiating a process of acculturation into Tanzanian life, my family relied on the guidance of new friends who introduced us to their nation and culture and helped us to understand them. As we learned about our hosts, we also tried to teach them about ourselves. And as abruptly as we realized that there was much we had to learn about being African, it was also quite obvious that there was a great deal we could teach about being African American.

Our Fellow Blacks in America

There are legends among the tribes that our brothers and sisters were taken across the wide sea, and that one day they would return. And when they return they would be supermen.

—Patrice Lumumba

One day when my mother was shopping at the Ubungo market, selecting fresh produce from colorful piles on tables in the open-air stalls, she overheard a European woman having difficulty communicating with one of the vegetable salesmen. My family had been living in Tanzania for nearly two years, and in that time my mother's Kiswahili had become reasonably fluent, so she volunteered her translation services, facilitating the transaction between the African and his white customer. When the white woman made her purchase and left the market, the man turned to my mother, staring at her curiously. He asked her where she came from, wondering aloud how it was that she spoke *kizungu* (the language of *wazungu*, whites) so fluently, while her Kiswahili was a bit accented. When my mother said "America," his brow furrowed with puzzlement; he took in her short Afro and brown skin, struggling to make sense of them. "Ina maana kuna watu weusi huko?" [So you mean there are black people over there?] he asked, surprised and pleased. My mother was shocked and was barely able to hide her amazement. Regaining her composure, she provided the man with a short summary of three hundred years of black American history. The man said he had thought that all Americans were white, and he listened with interest as my mother described the mass abduction of millions of Africans who were enslaved and stranded in America. The man clucked sympathetically, as though the tragic events she related had happened a few days ago, and he seemed satisfied and edified by her explanation. But my mother kept wondering how it was possible in the 1980s for an African in Dar es Salaam, Tanzania, not to know of the existence of African Americans.

In two years of living in Dar es Salaam, my family had rarely encountered such utter unawareness. And while the Ubungo vegetable salesman's ignorance perhaps suggested the existence of widespread misperceptions about African Americans among Tanzanians at large, his happiness at the idea of a large population of exiled Africans on American soil may be the more representative response. Whatever misapprehensions many Tanzanians might have had about African Americans, what was perhaps more significant about their impressions of black Americans was the fact that they often felt a certain level of kinship with them.

Although my brothers and I were called *wazungu* on more than one occasion after our arrival in Tanzania, most Africans did not simply regard us as strangely dark-skinned white people. They knew that we had come from the United States, and it was clear when we first arrived that we spoke American English, not Kiswahili, and seemed to share many of the cultural traits of white Americans who traveled to Tanzania. But many Tanzanians we met seemed to reserve a different category for black expatriates. And because we were black, I think Tanzanians had higher expectations of us than they did of white foreigners. Some of my early acquaintances kept speaking to me in Kiswahili, despite my repeated pleas of incomprehension—they seemed to expect that I should already know the language or have some natural affinity with it that would allow me to learn with lightning speed. And early on I came to realize that many Tanzanians seemed to feel that they could rely on my family for assistance or understanding that they would not usually ask of whites.

My mother had found such pan-African expectations even stronger in Congo when she lived there in the late 1960s. At the time Kinshasa was home to a small community of black Americans, and in general they were regarded by the locals as welcome additions to the society, individuals whose presence in Congo made sense in light of their ancestral ties to the continent. One black American friend of my parents, an electrician named Robinson, was especially well liked and respected in Kinshasa, where he lived for many years and made a number of close friends. When he died there after nearly thirty years in Congo, his wife buried him along the road to Matadi, fulfilling his lifelong wish to be laid to rest in Africa. Thanks to the long-term presence in Congo of black Americans like Mr. Robinson, African Americans enjoyed a positive reputation in the country, even if some Congolese resented their relative, and often conspicuous, wealth. And although they sometimes came in for criticism for their prosperity in the midst of widespread poverty, they were seen as members of the international pan-African family, returned to Africa to assist with the continent's development. Similar sentiments weren't always as strong in Tanzania, but they did exist there as well.

In shaping their ideas of what they could expect from us, the Tanzanians my family met relied on what they already knew or thought about America and black Americans. And as far as many Tanzanians were concerned, the United States was a wealthy paradise on earth whose inhabitants were universally rich.

Once my brothers and I were watching the film *The Defiant Ones* on video at a family friend's home in Dar es Salaam. Our friend's Tanzanian "helper" (the preferred local term for maid) watched the movie with us while ironing clothes from a pile heaped on the dining room table. My brothers and I quickly became engrossed in the action on screen: Sidney Poitier and Tony Curtis as two convicts making a desperate escape attempt while chained together. The forced pairing of a proud black man and a racist white man compelled to work together to achieve their freedom was a suitable symbol of the troubled race relations that held America in thrall, a metaphor that was not lost on my brothers and me. Dividing her attention between the television set and her ironing, the helper asked occasional questions about the film, and I tried to answer them in my not-yet-fluent Kiswahili. When she asked why the two men were fleeing the pursuing police and I explained that they were criminals, she exclaimed that she hadn't known that they had crime in America. She had assumed it was strictly an African problem. After gasping in shock, I hurriedly explained that this was far from the case, but it occurred to me that in addition to assuming that America was a crime-free society, she had completely missed the film's depiction of the troubled interaction between blacks and whites in American society. From her perspective, America seemed like an essentially perfect place; so, if there were blacks there, they were as privileged and wealthy as the whites, and had little in common with blacks in Africa. My brothers and I found this notion quite common among Tanzanians.

Though black Americans were usually regarded as American in their wealth and cultural outlook, many Tanzanians still hoped and assumed that they would be sympathetic to the struggles and sufferings of Africans. The tone for such attitudes was often set by the Tanzanian government, which had been self-consciously pan-African in its worldview since independence, inviting black Americans to settle in Tanzania and supporting black struggles for equality in America. In the mid-1960s the Tanzanian government went so far as to offer asylum to black American fugitives who claimed they were wanted by the U.S. government for political reasons, and even refused American requests to extradite the refugees. And later in the decade, Tanzanian president Julius Nyerere signified his support of the American Black Power movement by allowing the Student Nonviolent Coordinating Committee (SNCC) to open a branch office in Dar es Salaam. (Ironically, however, in 1970 the Tanzanian government demonstrated its disdain for black American culture by discouraging Tanzanian women from wearing their hair in Afros.)

Tanzanians acquired information about black Americans not only from the symbolic activities of the government in promoting pan-African ideas but also from the international media, which often showcased the accomplishments of black Americans whose names were familiar around the world. In the 1950s, glossy magazines like *Ebony* and *Jet* helped to instill in black Americans a sense of pride and heightened self-esteem by providing positive images of prominent blacks. In the same way, media representations of black Americans resonated with Tanzanian audiences pleased to see coverage of celebrities who looked like themselves. In the early 1980s, black America's leading poster child in Tanzania was probably Michael Jackson, whose music and then Afro-topped image were probably recognizable to a majority of people around Dar es Salaam. Since most Tanzanians thought of Michael, Diana Ross, and Lionel Richie if they ever thought of black Americans, they had a somewhat skewed picture of the position and condition of average black Americans. Even if educated Tanzanians had heard of American racism and knew of the historical mistreatment of blacks in America, for many the logic still ran as follows: if the United States was a rich country, and if blacks, like Michael Jackson, were making good, then all black Americans must also be well-to-do. This notion was difficult to shake despite frequent protests by my brothers and me; it was an extension of a generally held view of America as a paradise of incredible wealth, abundance, and harmony, a popular myth all over the world.

Though the international popularity of black Americans like Michael Jackson was largely responsible for influencing African attitudes toward African Americans, Tanzania's historical experience with slavery probably also played a role. Colonized by Arab traders as early as the thirteenth century, the coastal region that is now mainland Tanzania was crossed by routes along which slaves captured in the interior were marched to ports along the coast. The port of Bagamoyo, whose name fittingly means "Lay Down My Heart," became one of the major departure points for slaves bound for Zanzibar and then headed for the Middle East, Europe, and, sometimes, the Americas. In the nineteenth century the British missionary David Livingstone campaigned against the trade throughout the region but slavery was not officially abolished until well into the twentieth century. The slave trade financed the lavish lifestyle of the Omani sultans who inhabited palaces in Zanzibar, and it served as the basis for a social hierarchy in which a slave-trading class lorded over an exploited local populace. Centuries of pent-up tension erupted in the 1964 Zanzibar Revolution, in which many of the descendants of slave-trading families were slaughtered. The British colonial authorities attempted to intervene by pointing out that the targets of mob rage were not those who had personally carried out the slave trade, but angry Zanzibari revolutionaries replied that "the son of a snake is also a snake."

Despite the cathartic revolution and the creation of a new, representative government and political system, Tanzania has yet to exorcise all of the demons of its past, or even to fully confront slavery and its impact on Tanzanian society. Except for a simple memorial at Bagamoyo and the slave caves and dungeons that are tourist attractions in Zanzibar, there is no major monument in Tanzania to the millions of Africans who were kidnapped from East Africa over a period of several centuries. Still, the popular consciousness of slavery among Tanzanians at large meant that African Americans who visited Tanzania were often regarded affectionately as the returning survivors of a shameful and devastating episode in African history.

As supposedly rich Americans with ancestral ties to Africa, black Americans in Tanzania were often looked on as privileged cousins who were expected to assist their less fortunate African relations to progress as they had. And my brothers and I often fielded questions from Tanzanian friends who wondered why, if Bill Cosby and Eddie Murphy were so rich, they didn't help Africans out of their financial crisis. That so many black singers would gather behind Lionel Richie and Michael Jackson to sing the song "We Are the World," raising millions in the "USA for Africa" famine relief initiative, was commendable, but wasn't it the duty of rich cousins to help their less prosperous relatives?

Despite such visible assistance efforts, many Tanzanians assumed that most black Americans cared nothing for Africa or Africans. And many Tanzanians felt that they couldn't blame black Americans who enjoyed lives of affluence in the United States for looking down their noses at Africa. In 1984 Jesse Jackson looked to many Africans like a realistic contender in the American presidential election, while the black American lifestyle depicted on *The Cosby Show* (circulated on videotape in Dar es Salaam, it became highly popular in the 1980s) evinced wealth that was far beyond the means of most Tanzanians, and black entertainers and athletes seemed the toast of American society. In light of such evidence, to many Tanzanians it seemed that black Americans were so culturally Americanized and well off that they shared little with Africans save the color of their skin. Still, many Tanzanians hoped the phenotypic similarities would count for something.

But while Tanzanians certainly seemed to identify with black Americans and to feel and express a sense of racial kinship with them, it was clear that they regarded us as different from themselves, perhaps akin to a peculiar tribe of blacks from a foreign land. Most Tanzanians acknowledged ties that bound blacks together, but while African American repatriates could generally expect real warmth and enthusiastic inclusion, they could not generally expect to be regarded as Africans, no matter how long they remained on the continent. This fact was, often ruefully, recognized by black American visitors early on, and it found expression in many ways.

Still, African Americans in Africa did manage to claim African identities for themselves, and to deeply root themselves in the life and culture of the societies in which they settled. When my mother arrived in Kinshasa in the late 1960s, she was immersed in the new culture and soon absorbed enough of its essentials to negotiate it. And Remy, whose introduction to Congo came at two, learned to speak French and Lingala as a young child and to see himself as a Congolese. When playmates who were aware that he and his mother were newcomers to Congo called Remy *mundele*, the Lingala equivalent of *mzungu*, a white person, Remy would respond proudly in fluent Lingala, "Ngai naza mundele te!" (I am not a *mundele*!)

Many African Americans in Tanzania also seemed to have successfully assimilated into local cultures sufficiently to claim a real kinship. My brothers and I grew to love visits to Aunt Edie's house in Morogoro, a town nestled in the Uluguru mountains of eastern Tanzania. Three hours from Dar es Salaam, Morogoro was a convenient getaway for holiday weekends or short school breaks, and often when school closed for a few days my mother would load us into the car and we would leave the coastal humidity of the capital for the warmth of Aunt Edie's hospitality and the agreeably cool climate of her surroundings. On mornings in Morogoro, my brothers and I would gaze out the window at the beautiful emerald hills, decorated gently with tufts of white cloud, and feel excited by the promise of the coming day. Some days at Aunt Edie's were spent on walks along red dirt roads, through eucalyptus forests and past sisal plantations, idle hikes on which we breathed the fresh mountain air and drank in the stunning natural scenery. Others were devoted to sprawling lazily in her living room, watching videotaped TV shows from the States or trying to create convincing meanings for imaginary words we concocted in our customary Scrabble marathons. And there was always good food: spicy meat stews and chapati served up by Aunt Edie's helper, or American feasts of greens, fried chicken, and macaroni and cheese, Aunt Edie's personal specialties.

Aunt Edie had arrived in the country in the 1960s, and so was one of the senior members of the African American community in Tanzania. To me, she always seemed the perfect embodiment of the idealized "back-to-Africa" scenario. She was a pan-Africanist and a staunch supporter of Julius Nyerere, and was well known and well respected among people in high places in Dar es Salaam and Morogoro. A child of the civil rights movement, she had been deeply influenced by pan-Africanists like Chancellor Williams, and had decided in the early 1960s to make her home in Africa. Unlike some of the black Americans who made it to the motherland around the same time, she hadn't looked back.

Aunt Edie made her contribution to Tanzania's national development as a management professor and business consultant, and, an outgoing socialite, she established a vast network of friends and acquaintances throughout the country. Locals seemed to appreciate the fact that she spoke excellent Kiswahili and understood the niceties of Tanzanian culture, unlike many other foreigners who settled in Africa. It was impossible to go anywhere with Aunt Edie without running into someone she knew, and she always paused for the obligatory extended cycle of greetings and pleasantries. Also, it was easy to get directions to her house because many people on the streets of Morogoro knew exactly who you were talking about if you asked for Mama Wilson.

Tanzanians tended to pronounce her name "Eddie," possibly because "Edie" sounded to many like a Muslim man's name ("Idi"), but I never heard her correct anyone. She spoke of Tanzania as "our country," and though she made occasional trips to the United States, she clearly planned on living in Morogoro permanently. As a popular, valued, and thoroughly acculturated member of the community, she seemed to have earned the right to think of herself as a bona fide African, and she did.

But whether Tanzanians thought of Aunt Edie as an African was a different matter, and the same went for the rest of us black Americans and West Indians in Tanzania. For many diaspora blacks who had "returned" to the continent, settling in Africa represented the culmination of a lifelong quest for self-realization, a journey through race and identity in which "colored" people became "Negroes," then "black" people, and finally claimed an "African" identity by returning to the ancestral fold. But however important this process was to many black "returnees," its intricacies were often lost on Africans. Like many African American transplants to Africa, Aunt Edie claimed a new African identity even while educating Africans about a specifically black American experience and its relation to Africa. Every year during Black History Month she hosted screenings of *Roots* for people in her local community, and she was a proud and knowledgeable conveyor of African American culture. But Tanzanians often seemed to approach questions of racial identification and affinity from a slightly different perspective.

On one of our customary walks around Morogoro with Aunt Edie, we passed various neighbors, who all called out familiar greetings, and Aunt Edie responded easily and affectionately with the self-assurance of someone at home among friends. A little farther up the road we passed a group of playing children, and they turned from their game and waved happily. Like everyone else we had met, they knew who Aunt Edie was. And to prove it, they ran up to her and greeted her respectfully in Kiswahili. Then, as we began to move away, one little boy, as if to show off his knowledge in front of his friends, began a playful chant. "Negro! Negro!" he shouted, and soon the other children joined in, trailing cheerfully after us as we strolled slowly away, singing out hopefully the whole while. "Negro! Negro!" Aunt Edie turned and smiled at them. "Yes, that's right, children," she said in Kiswahili. The children piped down and returned to their game, and we resumed our walk. But the cries echoed naggingly in my ears.

* * *

While Africa and Africans have occupied privileged positions in the imagination and consciousness of African Americans and other diasporeans, there is much to suggest that the obsession has been less than mutual. In fact, Africans' seeming ignorance of or indifference to the fates of those abducted and sold into slavery has long been a source of bewilderment and pain to many African Americans who wonder how the slave trade's rape of Africa was allowed to happen and why more Africans did not seem to actively oppose it. Didn't West African contemporaries wonder where their enslaved compatriots were being taken? And wasn't there anything they could have done to prevent it?

Many African Americans have been shocked and saddened to detect in Africans a seeming lack of interest in slavery and the plight of Africans in America. Others who have traveled to Africa have discovered, to their surprise, that many Africans do not even seem to be aware that African Americans exist. And far too many are persuaded by experience to accept as fact the disdainful pronouncement of a Ghanaian educator who seemed unimpressed by the friendly overtures of African American visitors to his country. "You know, for the last three hundred years we haven't thought about them too much, if at all," he said, bluntly summarizing his apathetic view of black Americans. "And I don't suppose they've thought about us in any real sense."

While it is obvious that African Americans have thought about Africa a great deal during their centuries of separation from the continent, it may be slightly less obvious that Africans have indeed intensely pondered the fates of the Africans enslaved in the Americas and of their descendants. There is little recorded evidence of the position that African Americans have historically occupied in African thought, but enough accounts, anecdotes, legends, myths, and ideas have circulated to construct something of a history of African perceptions of black Americans. And, interestingly, just as African American ideas about Africa have been based on myths rather than on empirical evidence and experience, African conceptions of African Americans are dominated by rumors and folklore that have often obscured realities about the nature and condition of Africans in the Americas.

If it stands to reason that Africans freshly abducted from villages and homes in Africa would lovingly and longingly recall the countries and families of their origin, it would also seem intuitively likely that the families from which they were stolen would remember the departed prisoners with heavy hearts and mourn their absence. While few contemporary accounts of African commemorations of enslaved kin exist, their memory has endured through the ages. In the mid-1970s when Alex Haley managed to track down the village from which his African ancestor Kunta Kinte was kidnapped, he found Kinte's fate enshrined in the local collective memory. A griot, a traditional oral historian, was able to provide a detailed narrative of the fateful day when Kinte was captured while cutting wood for a drum he was making for his younger brother. In the West African retention of Kinte's memory, Haley's first African American ancestor was commemorated as a tragic hero who had been stolen from the family but was never forgotten.

Maya Angelou had an equally heartening experience as a resident of Ghana in the 1960s. Once, on a trip to a remote Ghanaian village that had been ravaged by slave traders in the eighteenth century, Angelou was confronted by an African woman who claimed to recognize her. When the woman was made to understand that Angelou was an American, she tearfully gave voice to an anguish centuries old: she was the descendant of villagers who had watched while most of their kin were shackled. The tale of their abduction and suffering had been passed on through the generations with a warning to never forget. And with the appearance of this American woman whose build and features were so like her own, the woman now felt sure that her abducted ancestors had survived, even thrived, on American soil. Angelou was embraced as a lost descendant of that very Ghanaian village, welcomed tearfully by self-described cousins, and assured that Africans had not forgotten her stolen people.

The anthropologist Melville Herskovits found a strong tradition of commemoration of abducted kin in his field research in Dahomey (now called Benin) in the early 1930s. Dahomey had been hard hit by the slave trade; entire villages and regions had been depopulated by the rapacious slave catchers, and the American academic found that those stolen more than a century before were still remembered with a tragic reverence by their African relations. Herskovits's guide on the trip, a Togolese named Felix, told him how many of his ancestors had been enslaved by Portuguese traders.

The people who were taken away . . . had never been heard from. His family did not know whether any of them had lived long enough to leave descendants. But these relatives, wherever they had died, were still members of the ancestral generations, and that is why today, when Felix's family in the city of Anecho in Togoland give food for the dead, they call also upon those who had died far away to come and partake of the offerings.

Herskovits himself witnessed ceremonies in which abducted ancestors were invoked, rituals in which a family reconfirmed its ties to all of its kin, including those who "had never been heard from." "At these customs food is given to the spirits of the recent dead, and to those of all the other ancestral generations," Herskovits recounted. "To those who died at home, and to those who met their end in distant lands; to those whose names are known and remembered, to those who have been forgotten, and to those whose names the family in Dahomey had never had the opportunity to hear."

Though the individual fates of those abducted were not known to their relatives in Dahomey, Herskovits found that those left behind had understood that the enslaved were taken to Western countries, which were referred to by their local names during the ceremonies. Not only were offerings made to ancestors at home and abroad but also prayers were said to protect those who had remained in Africa and to exact vengeance on the slave traders. "Oh, ancestors, do all in your power that princes and nobles who today rule never be sent away from here as slaves to Ame'ica, to Togbome, to Gbulu, to Kankanu, to Gbuluvia, to Rarira," intoned a Dahomey priest during one ritual, listing the Western countries where slaves were thought to have been taken. "We pray you to do all in your power to punish the people who bought our kinsmen whom we shall never see again. Send their vessels to Whidah harbor. When they come, drown their crews, and make all the wealth of their ships come back to Dahomey. . . . Long live Dahomey! You who have not succumbed to slavery here, act so that those . . . who died . . . be kept in the memory of all Dahomeans."

West Africans enslaved in America were not always remembered so affectionately by those left behind, however. The slave trade would not have been possible without the collaboration of African chiefs, kings, and agents who cooperated with European traders for personal profit and other self-interested motives. For some collaborators, enslavement became a way of eliminating political opposition or getting rid of troublesome rival clans. Hence, during the trade and through the twentieth century, some Africans adopted a "good riddance" attitude toward their kin on American shores. "You have nearly all the people of this family in your country," a Dahomean who seemed sympathetic to aspects of the trade told Herskovits, referring to a clan that was particularly devastated by the slavers. "They knew too much magic. We sold them because they made too much trouble." "This family has strong men," said another interviewee, speaking of a second Dahomean clan whose members were abducted. "They are good warriors but bad enemies. When they troubled our king, they were caught and sold. You have their big men in your country."

One of the Dahomeans whom Herskovits interviewed attributed his people's high consciousness of their countrymen in foreign lands to the return of a few abductees in the nineteenth century. According to local legend, the mother of a boy who later became king was sold into slavery in the late eighteenth century, toiling among other Dahomean slaves on plantations in Brazil and, later, North America. "When Gezo became king he was not happy," the story goes. "He said, 'I am king. I can do anything I like, yet my mother is a slave.' He went to his Portuguese friend Da Souza, and Da Souza went across the seas and searched everywhere until he found her. She came back with six other Dahomeans, and from them Gezo heard what happened to Dahomeans in America. That is how we know."

Since relatively few New World slaves actually made it back to Africa, firsthand accounts of how abducted Africans fared in the New World were very rare during this period, and most Africans had to rely on rumor and legend for information on the fates of their abducted relations. And, as time, distance, and circumstance made memories of Africa more distorted and mythical for Africans in the New World, so African depictions of Africans who had been taken to the Americas seem to have early on acquired a mythological ring.

Information concerning the status and condition of Africans in America that informed and fueled African ideas about African Americans made its way to the continent through correspondence, newspapers, periodicals, and books provided by seamen and members of black American organizations who were stationed in Africa. By the 1870s, accounts of black Americans were often disseminated around the continent by sailors, migrant laborers, and traders who traveled into the interior bringing word-of-mouth reports they had heard on the coast.

And by the 1890s, African American churches began to establish missions in Africa and to send representatives to the continent. Most of the Africans who lived in communities where black American missionaries were assigned now had their first encounter with the New World Africans who were immortalized in local lore. The newcomers generated considerable interest and even spawned new myths and legends. When black American missionaries first arrived in the Transvaal in the 1890s, the southern African locals were astounded by the respect they commanded from the local white authorities. Visiting black Americans were given the status of "honorary whites," and were not bound by the segregation and social restrictions imposed on the local Africans. Such special treatment led some locals to see black Americans as more powerful than Africans, as blacks who were on a par with whites because they were privy to white knowledge.

Early black American visits to South Africa also showed the local Africans the heights to which blacks could rise. In 1890 an African American performance group, the Jubilee Singers, arrived in South Africa for a three-year concert tour. The professionalism and talent they displayed in their shows became a benchmark for many African aspirations, and the treatment the singers received from the local authorities (segregationist rules were relaxed for the group) impressed on local Africans the possibility of political and social reform. As a South African newspaper, *Imvo Zabantsundu*, reported, "Their visit will do their countrymen here no end of good. Already it has suggested reflections of many who, without such demonstration, would have remained skeptical as to the possibility of the natives of this country being raised to anything above perpetual hewers of wood and drawers of water."

Even more influential than the Jubilee Singers' visit was that of Bishop Henry McNeal Turner, the head of the African American AME (African Methodist Episcopal) Church. When he toured South Africa in 1898 to promote his church's missionary activities in the region, Africans were amazed to see a black bishop. Many had never thought it possible for blacks to occupy such an exalted position. Equally astonishing to the locals was Turner's reception by the Transvaal's Afrikaner president, Paul Kruger, who welcomed Turner to his residence saying, "You are the first black man whose hand I have ever shaken." An eyewitness, Charlotte Manye, described the scene at one of the bishop's speeches, capturing the near hysteria that gripped his audience: "Bishop H. M. Turner . . . was welcomed as never a man was received before," she wrote. "Some called out 'now the promise is fulfilled,' others saw him as a Moses to deliver them from chains of sin and superstition."

As the African American National Baptist Convention and the AME and AME Zion churches began to set up missions around Africa in the 1890s, Africans marveled at the wealth and resources of black-led organizations that could finance churches and schools, had memberships of several hundred thousand, and owned property in the United States. And black American churches were often more popular among Africans than those run by Europeans because black missionaries tended to not be as patronizingly racist as white missionaries. Black churches generally allowed Africans to occupy positions of responsibility (white churches usually did not), and, unlike most white missionaries, black missionaries often socialized with members of their African congregations as equals.

Also, to many Africans, black churches demonstrated the impressive feats of which blacks were capable. As an African reporter exclaimed proudly in the *Gold Coast Chronicle* in 1901, the black American churches proved "that the black man was not the incapable being he was taken by some to be but that he had something of originality too in him." Another contemporary African commentator greeted the establishment of an AME Church school in the Gold Coast in 1899 with similar enthusiasm. "Our fellow blacks in America . . . have for the first time in the history of our nation stretched out the hand of kinship to us across the seas," Kofi Asaam, a lawyer and church activist, said excitedly, "and are ready to educate and Christianize us and make the land of our common ancestors a glorious habitation in the eyes of the world."

Africans were also encouraged in the belief that black Americans possessed great power and would wield it on Africa's behalf by the pronouncements of diaspora spokesmen like Bishop Henry McNeal Turner and Edward Wilmot Blyden, the Barbados-born proponent of pan-Africanism and black repatriation. Blyden and Turner subscribed to a "Providential Design" theory, preaching that God had had a divine purpose in allowing Africans to be enslaved in America. The theory was closely identified with the Biblical Psalm 68, which includes the verse "Princes shall come out of Egypt; Ethiopia shall soon stretch out her hands to God." To many Christianized black Americans, the psalm seemed a prophecy foretelling how black Americans ("Princes") would return from America ("Egypt") to lead Africa ("Ethiopia") to independence and modernity, and leaders like Blyden and Turner popularized the idea among Africans. There was a "divine purpose in permitting their [African-Americans'] exile to and bondage in this land [America]," Blyden asserted in 1890. "Slavery would seem to be a strange school in which to preserve a people." Turner echoed this sentiment in 1895, saying, "I believe that the Negro was brought to this country in the providence of God to a heaven-permitted if not divine-sanctioned manual laboring school, that he might have direct contact with the mightiest race that ever trod the face of the globe."

Many Christian Africans were quick to embrace the "Providential Design" theory. "America is not the destined home of the Negro," the *Lagos Standard* declared in 1903. "He is an alien and a stranger there. In his removal to that distant land, we can discern the hands of an All-wise Providence. His enforced exile has been for a purpose, and when that purpose is accomplished, like the ancient Israelites, he will once more be led out of Egypt to return to his original home. . . . Sooner or later, by some means or another, the destined end, we fully believe, will be effected, and God's hidden purposes will be revealed in the fullness of time."

The theory did have its detractors in Africa and America, however. In Africa, some critics disputed the African-Americans' "superman" status, arguing that American blacks were not really superior to Africans and were hardly in a position to lead Africa anywhere. "The Afro-American has lost his original tribal morality," an African reporter at the *Central African Times* opined in 1900, expressing a sentiment echoed elsewhere in Africa. "His freedom is that of the wild ass in the desert and under it his character and intellect have no chance for development."

The *Lagos Weekly Record* went so far as to say that in actuality Africans had outdone their American cousins. "Indeed we are bound to say that the native African, from our limited knowledge of his achievements within the past thirteen years, has shown himself to be superior to the Negro in America and has accomplished more with his five talents singlehanded and alone than the American Negro has with his ten talents and the financial aid of a great body of the dominant race in this country," the paper contended in 1899. "The thousands of dollars spent for Negro education in the United States have not as yet begun to show tangible results."

Despite the voices of dissent that refuted black American accomplishments, African perceptions of African American superiority, wealth, and power endured long into the twentieth century. The persistence of notions of black American affluence and influence in American society was doubtlessly encouraged by African perceptions of American society at large. For many educated Africans across the continent, chafing under the colonial rule of various European powers, the United States was seen as an extremely rich, liberal, and demo-cratic country, the cradle of liberty, where individual rights were re-spected and economic opportunities abounded for all. To those who accepted the myth of the American utopia, it seemed obvious that the descendants of Africa on American soil would have excelled once lib-erated from slavery.

George Mwase, a Malawian scholar, probably spoke for many con-temporary Africans when he said, "America as far as I am aware is the best country, where a Negro of Africa . . . would permanently settle there, and enjoy the beauty of the country with his fellow Negroes." A similarly rosy picture of the United States was expressed in the *Sierra Leone Weekly News* in 1908. The paper reported that blacks in America had economic and political equality and were "entrepreneurs," who ran banks, insurance companies, beauty parlors, and farms in the American South. What's more, the paper said, in America white ladies "give their hands and hearts" to blacks.

Magazine reports on prominent black Americans encouraged Africans to believe in the opportunities open to blacks in America. A missionary in South Africa described the excitement of a South African who saw a picture of the famous African American singer Paul Robeson and dreamed of making his own fame and fortune in America, where anything seemed possible. "For days afterwards [he] lived in a world of fantasy," the missionary reported. "He would go to America. He would sing the Manyika songs. His voice was good and he could master the language. He would acquire great wealth, open a shop. He would buy a gramophone, a house, furniture, a motorcycle. No—a car!" In the words of another white missionary in South Africa who observed the popularization of American myths among the lo-cals, "Natives received impressions of an idealized America, which they took to be almost entirely peopled by blacks."

African perceptions of America and the black American position within it were so positive after the turn of the century that some Africans even expected black Americans to establish their own inde-pendent state in the New World. "There looms up before us now in the future, AFRICA IN AMERICA," the *Sierra Leone Weekly News* re-ported in 1909. "It is not impossible that in the Southern States, espe-cially in the Black Belt—there may arise an *imperium in imperio*—a Negro empire separate and distinct." U.S. propaganda also encouraged positive perceptions among Africans of America and the position of blacks within it. In 1910 the *Sierra Leone Weekly News* was happy to re-port that the American President Taft had said, "The Negro race is a great and growing race ... a race ... with whose progress and improvement this country must always be bound and united. ... the white race and the Negro live contentedly together."

More realistic portrayals of America did exist, but these seem to have been in the minority. In 1903 the *Lagos Standard* reported on the prevalence of lynching in the southern United States, and noted that since the 1880s, when a number of blacks had been elected to public office in the United States, black American political influence had dwindled considerably. And in 1908 the *Sierra Leone Weekly News* angrily quoted the Governor of Mississippi as having said, "I am just as much opposed to Booker Washington, with all his Anglo-Saxon reinforcement, voting as I am to the voting by the coconut headed, chocolate coloured, typical coon who blacks my boots." Also, African experiences with white American missionaries in Africa who were as condescending as European colonialists tended to buttress such reports of white American racism.

World War I brought Africans into even greater contact with black Americans, and after 1918, more information than ever before began to find its way to Africa. By 1920, a number of African American journals had begun to circulate among educated Africans, including *The Crisis* (the official publication of the NAACP), the *New York Age*, the *Washington Bee*, the *Colored American*, the *Crusader*, and, most prominently, the *Negro World*, the official paper of Marcus Garvey's UNIA. Periodicals were often sent to coastal cities, then brought to the interior by travelers and traders. Sometimes articles were read aloud to groups of listeners who then shared oral reports about African Americans with Africans in more remote areas. And there are several documented cases of Africans being arrested for possessing or distributing copies of the *Negro World*, which espoused Garvey's "Africa for Africans" platform and was therefore a threat to colonial authority.

Through black American periodicals and other communication, Africans learned of African American leaders like Booker T. Washington, who came to have a significant impact on Africans looking to the diaspora for leadership and inspiration. In the 1920s Harry Thuku, a Kenyan who later became a national leader, was impressed by reports he received from America. "The Negro race in America has been successful in producing many large-hearted men like Booker T. Washington," he said after reading about the black American educator. "We regard such men as our saviours." He also fondly referred to Washington's Tuskegee Institute as "our asylum where the hunted downtrodden and oppressed Negro may hasten to seek help or advice." Similarly, in 1920 the *Gold Coast Leader* referred to African Americans as "our intelligent brethren on the other side of the Atlantic." The literary writings of the "intelligent brethren" also began to gain an audience among educated Africans. With the rise of the Harlem Renaissance, the problack ideas of the New Negro movement began to resonate with many African intellectuals, who looked to the black American writers as literary "big brothers." In fact, the ideas and stylistic approaches of the Harlem Renaissance helped to spawn the Negritude movement, an African literary school which, like the New Negroes, sought to celebrate Africa and blackness in literature. Léopold Senghor, the Senegalese poet, scholar, and president who was the first African ever elected to the Académie Française, was one of the movement's founders and acknowledged his debt to black American writers. Speaking at Howard University in 1966, Senghor reflected on the origins of Negritude and offered "well-deserved homage to the poets whom we translated and recited and in whose steps we tried to follow: Claude McKay, Jean Toomer, Countee Cullen, James Weldon Johnson, Langston Hughes, Sterling Brown." Commenting on influences that shaped Negritude, Senghor wrote, "Studying at the Sorbonne, I began to reflect on the problem of a cultural renaissance in Black America and I was searching—all of us were searching—for a 'sponsorship' which would guarantee the success of the enterprise. At the end of my quest it was inevitable that I would find Alain Locke," the famous black American philosopher and educator who pioneered the Harlem Renaissance.

With the spread of ideas of African American power and brilliance and the advent of such diaspora-led initiatives as the Pan African Congresses of 1919 and 1921, many Africans began to call for African American leadership of the fledgling African independence movements. In 1921, on the occasion of the W.E.B. Du Bois–organized Second Pan-African Congress, the *African World* wrote, "It is evident that for a time the lead must be taken by the American Negro. Upon him . . . rests a large part of the responsibility. If he, working with other groups, meets this responsibility then the Congress can and will be made a great and powerful international weapon for the bringing of justice, long denied, to the 400 million coloured people of the world."

The image of African-Americans in Africa was also given a boost by James E. Kwegyir Aggrey, a Ghanaian who studied in black American schools and traveled around Africa as a delegate of the American Phelps-Stokes Commission, which presented lectures on education in

Africa in the 1920s. Aggrey preached the value of technical and vocational education and development within the colonial system; more important, he provided for many Africans an example of what Africans could accomplish in America. Hastings Kamuzu Banda, Kwame Nkrumah, and Nnamdi Azikiwe, the first leaders of independent Malawi, Ghana, and Nigeria respectively, all credited hearing Aggrey speak with prompting their decision to study in America. What's more, for some Africans, Aggrey seemed proof of the enduring myth that Africa would be liberated by African Americans. When Aggrey spoke at Transkei in the early 1920s he "was supposed by some to be the herald of an invading band of Negroes—they thought all Americans were Negroes—who would drive the Whites of South Africa into the sea." And Aggrey himself seemed in some ways to promote this idea. "God sent the black man to America. Was this all a matter of chance?" he said in 1921. "You who are philosophers know there is no such thing as chance; God always has a programme. He meant America to play a special part in the history of Africa."

Even more substantial than Booker T. Washington or Aggrey's influence in Africa was Marcus Garvey's. Garvey's UNIA grew into a huge New York–based mass movement among West Indian and American blacks in the 1920s, and gained considerable support in Africa as well through circulation of the *Negro World* and the establishment of UNIA offices in various African cities. Garvey's impact in Africa can be gauged by his representations in various African newspapers.

Echoing the "Providential Design" theory of the 1900s, the *Gold Coast Leader* seemed to view Garvey's rise as the fulfillment of God's will. "It is but asserting the commonplace when we say that the expatriation of some of our people to America and to the West Indies in times past, was in the order of Providence, to hasten a national consciousness," the paper wrote in 1920. "And today our brethren there are turning with longing eyes to the fatherland." Also in 1920, the *Sierra Leone Weekly News* referred to Garvey as "a modern Joshua," while the *Colonial and Provincial Reporter* said "the voice of God now seems to utter through Marcus Garvey" and referred to him as "Paramount Chief of the Negro Race or, in other words, 'His Supreme Highness the Potentate.'"

Many other Africans all over the continent responded happily to Garvey's message and the prospect of a mass return by diaspora blacks who would lead the continent from colonial bondage. Charles Chidongo Chinula, a student in Malawi, recalled in a 1920 letter that "in those days we read Marcus Garvey's newspapers and learned that many American Negroes would be carried back to Africa in ships. We believed that Garvey was a great man and that he was there to help all of us." In 1921 the British district commissioner of an area in rural Nigeria reported that Africans in his district were "excited by rumors that a black king was bringing a big iron ship full of black American soldiers to expel all the whites from Africa." And an AME Church missionary said in the 1920s that "the young men of Sierra Leone are giving up first-class jobs and waiting for the Black Star Line to touch the shores." Similarly, Africans on the Nigerian coast are said to have camped on the beaches and lit bonfires to guide the ships of "Moses Garvey."

Some Africans, however, were hostile to Garvey's vision, questioning the feasibility of his plan and wondering how Americanized Africans from the New World could integrate themselves into African societies. "Before the American Negro can hope to be of any other than temporary assistance to the Negro race in general . . . they must acquire the African point of view," the *Gold Coast Leader* warned in 1920. "Suppose for a moment 15,000 American Negroes really descended upon Africa," the *African World* hypothesized. "What would be the result but acute tribal antagonism between the reforming newcomers and the more or less contented indigene?"

Kobina Sekyi, a Gold Coast politician who was hostile to Garvey's program, had similar reservations. "In fact our brethren from beyond the seas, with their American ideas and ideals, would confuse us a good deal more, because then we should have here not only a medley of English and Akan-Fanti ideas and ideals, but a worse potpourri of American and English and Akan-Fanti modes of life and thought. This would surely be confusion worse confounded; and this would probably mean jumping from the frying pan into the fire," he wrote in the *Gold Coast Leader* in 1922.

The *Nigerian Pioneer*, possibly currying favor with the British colonial authorities, took issue with Garvey's antiwhite posture. "Marcus Garvey is trying to light the fire of racial hatred, whilst the sane men on both sides are endeavoring to work together for the good of Nigeria," the paper complained in 1920. Blaise Diagne, a Senegalese "Frenchman" and deputy to the French parliament, was even more harsh in his criticism of Garvey. "The black bolshevism of Mr. Garvey can only lead to ruin and devastation," he asserted in 1921.

Despite the intense (although limited) opposition in Africa to Garvey and his UNIA, his important psychological impact on Africans is perhaps best summarized in a Sierra Leonean's letter to the *Negro*

World in 1921: "Some of us Negroes did not know that we have a soul in ourselves, and did not feel that we should be respected as other men as the whites are, until we began to read the sentences of the Honorable Marcus Garvey in the Negro World."

In addition to having an important influence on African intellectuals, Garvey's movement sparked a huge following among less educated Africans, many of whom regarded his back-to-Africa ambitions as the embodiment of traditional legends that referred to the triumphant return of a crusading army of American blacks. One legend from lower Congo described how Africans enslaved in the New World had created a powerful society. "The white men dumped these Africans on a big island where they abandoned them," the story went. "After many centuries of isolation, the African descendants, who came to be called black Americans, developed a prosperous industrial country with a strong army. When the white men came back, they were surprised to see that the black Americans had developed an industrialized society. Before such a reality the white men were forced to accept them as equals." When distorted versions of *Negro World* reports describing Garvey's repatriation efforts reached rural areas of Africa, many Africans came to see him and his black American followers as the powerful diaspora blacks described in legend as the liberators of Africa. The apocalyptic language prevalent in UNIA writings, such as the poem "The Tragedy of White Injustice" (1922) only served to reinforce this idea:

> There shall be conquests o'er militant forces;
> For as man proposes, God disposes.
> Signs of retribution are on every hand:
> Be ready, black men, like Gideon's band.
> They may scoff and mock at you today,
> But get you ready for the awful fray.

The anticolonial Kitawala movement in Rhodesia in the 1920s, a spiritually based initiative that fused traditional religious beliefs with Christian prophecies, seems to have been inspired partly by Garveyist ideas. The Kitawala leader Joseph Sibakwe promised his followers that Northern Rhodesia's white government would be replaced by black Americans, while a Kitawala preacher from Lusaka assured his flock that "the negroes of America had heard of their ill-treatment and were coming to drive out their white oppressors, that there would be a fierce war between the blacks and whites . . . and they would become rulers of the country." Such reports became so prevalent in southern Africa that a Cape Town clerk named Joel Mnyimba claimed in the 1920s that he "waited everyday for those Americans to come free South Africa."

Gravey-influenced myths of a conquering black American army also became associated with the Rhodesian Watch Tower movement, like Kitawala an anticolonial campaign in which charismatic preachers combined Christian theology and traditional religious practices to organize masses of people against the colonial authorities. At Urungwe in 1929 a Watch Tower preacher told his Shona flock of the imminent arrival of an avenging army of American blacks. "In about six months a flight of aeroplanes will come from America—sent by a person who lives under the water there—manned by black people, who will make an aerial reconnaissance of the whole country," the preacher predicted. "These Negroes will recognize their own people and will then return to America. Shortly after this they will return and bring war in their train. The white people will then be driven out of the country and the natives will be freed from all taxes and European control." And in 1932, a Southern Rhodesian preacher named Luka Jarawani told his followers, "The time is at hand, America is coming to rule the country. The white people are going back to their own country. . . . The Americans will soon come and you will be happy when they come because you will be free of all troubles the white people have caused you."

An anti-Belgian movement in Congo led by the preacher Simon Kimbangu in 1921 is also said to have been influenced by Garvey. The Kimbangu movement adopted the colors of the UNIA flag, and popular Congolese lore held that Kimbangu would be assisted in ousting the Belgians by African Americans. In fact, Kimbangu may indeed have actually had political contact with UNIA representatives, as we shall see.

With the outbreak of World War II, when American army units including black Americans were stationed in Africa, some Africans assumed that the predictions of preachers and local tradition had truly come to pass. Black American soldiers were greeted joyously by crowds of Africans, and hailed as though they were conquering heroes.

Although the idea of black Americans as supermen who would vanquish colonialism was widespread in various parts of Africa during this period, by the 1930s it had to compete with the very different images of black Americans that appeared in contemporary American media. As Hollywood films made their way to the continent, Africans saw a host of stereotypically undignified and offensive depictions of black Americans, and many Africans were prompted to attempt to disassociate themselves from American counterparts who, on film at least, seemed servile and self-deprecating. The Ugandan writer John Nagenda recalls that in his youth the words "Nigger or even Negro" were serious insults, "for it was an unfriendly act to point out your racial relationship to American Negroes." He attributes this disdain to the prevailing image of black Americans in American films, that of a "flashing-teethed, eye-rolling, broken shouldered, perpetually perplexed nigger [who] brought drinks to Clark Gable." It seems an extraordinary irony that in Africa in the 1930s it would have been an insult to "point out an African's racial relationship" with black Americans, while in the United States it was exactly the other way around.

In any case, negative portrayals of black Americans on film had become so common in Africa by the 1950s that Nnamdi Azikiwe expressed concern over the movies' effects on Nigerians' self-image. He even advocated the censorship of films depicting blacks "in a derogatory and humiliating manner, because they tend to create a spirit of resentment and bitterness on the part of Africans, thus embarrassing race relations in this part of the world."

Though many Africans were angered by the "Stepin Fetchit" stereotypes of American film, many others seemed to see the depictions as appropriate representations of a people descended from slaves. Many African Americans who have visited Africa or crossed paths with Africans elsewhere have felt as though Africans looked down on them because of their historical experience with slavery. A typical African American complaint leveled at Africans who travel to America is "They're too proud," which usually translates as "They think they're better than us." Maya Angelou bore the brunt of such distaste in a Ghanaian office when she took a secretary to task for being decidedly unhelpful. "American Negroes are always crude," the secretary said when Angelou became aggressively confrontational. The unspoken implication was that she expected nothing more from one descended from slaves.

A corollary to the assumption among some Africans that the "tainting" influence of slavery has made American blacks servile and crude is the notion that after centuries in America, African Americans have assimilated typically "American" cultural values and a slavish devotion to America and white authority. In 1969 Hastings Banda qualified an invitation to black Americans to settle in Malawi with this: "I don't think they would fit in. We haven't got a cinema, you know." The implication was that black Americans, with their American obsession with entertainment and leisure, would never be happy with relative hardship in Africa. When the idea of black American settlement in Kenya was debated by the Kenyan Assembly in 1968, one minister opined that black Americans "do not . . . even like to be called Africans and they would not like to come back to Africa." And Emile Zinsou, onetime president of Dahomey, was open to the idea of black repatriation in his country in the 1960s but worried about "the black American's complete loyalty to the United States." Though most Africans lauded the racial pride expressed by black leaders like Malcolm X, and by Du Bois and Garvey before him, others felt that too many black Americans, victims of slavery-induced self-hatred, were ashamed of their heritage and sought to emulate whites, making themselves blindly complicit in white efforts to victimize Africans.

Negative perceptions of black Americans among West Africans were also founded on the controversial "colonization" of Liberia and Sierra Leone in the eighteenth century. The emancipated New World slaves had run roughshod over local populations, and many Africans were hard pressed to distinguish between white colonizers and the black settlers who looked like Africans but behaved like Europeans. Black Americans who settled in West Africa in the 1960s and 1970s often found themselves the focus of suspicion thanks to the misbehavior of Americans who had preceded them by over a century. As Bill Sutherland, who moved to Ghana in the sixties, discovered, "There had been a great deal of alienation from Afro-Americans in West Africa because of the Liberian situation: the fact that over a long period of history 'Americo-Liberians'—ex–American slaves resettled in Liberia—had behaved in the same way colonial rulers had elsewhere."

Though most Africans seemed to expect to have a natural affinity with black Americans because of their shared appearance and heritage, these expectations were repeatedly dashed by New World blacks whose behavior and culture seemed indistinguishable from those of whites; many Africans began to think of black Americans as "black white men," African in appearance but whites nonetheless. Langston Hughes reported ruefully that he was called a "white man" on his first trip to Africa in the early 1920s, a label prompted by his American cultural outlook as well as by his fair complexion and straight hair. And black Americans who settled in Africa in the 1960s often found themselves saddled with African labels that were the same as those used for whites: *oyingbo* (Yoruba), *abruni* (Twi), *mundele* (Lingala), and *mzungu* (Kiswahili), for example, all of which mean foreigner, stranger, or white man.

Despite the persistence of these sorts of attitudes, it is impossible to easily generalize about African perceptions of black Americans, because negative and hostile perspectives have long existed alongside more positive conceptions. In the absence of significant contact with black Americans, Africans relied on kernels of truth, myth and legend to construct ideas about their kin in foreign lands. As contact between Africans and black Americans increased, especially through African visits to the United States, actual experience began to take a larger role in shaping African notions of black Americans.

During the 1950s and 60s, important transatlantic ties were forged between Africans who studied in the United States and their African American classmates, and, as many Africans returned home with positive memories of their interactions with black Americans (even if the close contact often forced them to revise their stereotypical expectations), pan-African sentiments began to color African attitudes toward African Americans. Many educated Africans had come to see black Americans as an extension of the African family, as a "lost tribe" to whom they owed allegiance and from whom they could expect it. During the independence struggles of the post–World War II era this idea translated into black American involvement and assistance in African anticolonial movements, and once independence was won, many African leaders expressed their outrage at the mistreatment of American blacks in the segregated South.

However, even while many African observers of the 1960s identified with African Americans in political terms, many still struggled to come to terms with black Americans on a cultural level, and much of the pan-Africanist writing of the period expresses this ambivalence. If many Africans saw black Americans as natural allies in a world cleaved by what Du Bois called "the problem of the color line" most still recognized that black Americans were *American*, and seemingly had more cultural similarity to white Americans than to Africans.

By the 1960s a generation of African intellectuals seem to have come to regard black Americans as a community of displaced Africans marooned on American soil, and this attitude provided the basis for pan-African political initiatives. But most Africans also realized that black Americans were very distant cousins at best.

Despite the strengthening of political and cultural ties between African and black American intellectuals and leaders, the mainstream

American media remained the dominant source of information on black Americans for most Africans "on the ground." And, as criticism of American treatment of blacks began to intensify around the world in the 1960s (during the Cold War the Soviet Union made a point of denouncing U.S. racism at every opportunity), the U.S. government made a concerted effort to provide international audiences, especially in Africa, with images of black American affluence and success.

In 1968 a Kenyan politician felt prompted to note happily that black Americans were "doing very well," and went so far as to say that he "would not be surprised if before long we see the President of the United States an Afro-American." Similarly, on his first trip to Africa in the 1970s the black American political activist Randall Robinson was amazed by the images of black Americans that predominated in Dar es Salaam. "Although material opportunities had been denied to the vast majority of African-Americans, Tanzanians had been given quite a different impression," he reflected after a visit to Dar's U.S. Information Service Reading Room. "Books, magazines, and large posters could be found illustrating the conspicuous and broadspread success of America's people of African descent. I had visited the reading room to learn what Tanzanians were learning about me and was stunned to discover in Tanzania how well I was doing."

Representations of this sort are partially responsible for one of the most enduring African perceptions of black Americans: Many black Americans who have visited the continent are surprised to be confronted with the belief that all, or at least most, black Americans are wealthy, a stated assumption often followed by a request for money. This common misconception possibly originated with a distortion of the famous and unfulfilled "forty acres and a mule" proposal. In Ghana Maya Angelou met a man from Mali who wanted to know if it was "true that after slavery White Americans gave their money to the Blacks and now all Blacks were rich[.]" Whatever its origin, the popular view of America as a paradise of universal abundance and the image of prosperous African Americans provided by American propaganda and in glossy black American magazines like *Ebony* definitely perpetuated this idea.

Of course, the flip side of exaggeratedly positive portrayals of black Americans in American media are the exaggeratedly negative representations of American blacks that cast them as pathologically poor, underachieving and violent. Ideas of black American affluence and glamour exist simultaneously with notions of black American poverty and desperation. The apparent contradiction disappears when you consider the biases of the American media, which have tended to glorify the prosperity of Bill Cosby, Oprah Winfrey, and Michael Jordan while at the same time highlighting the tribulations of a black underclass, rarely depicting the more typical experiences in between.

With the advent of new technologies that have made it easier and easier to disseminate images and information, Africans have learned progressively more about black Americans, but since most information is provided by television, magazines, and film, representations of African Americans find their way to Africa distorted and decontextualized. To the majority of Africans on the ground, and for the youth especially, African Americans are probably best symbolized by film, music, and sports superstars.

By the 1990s, urban Africa had become seemingly saturated by African American popular culture, with African American television shows on TV stations in many African cities, rap music by Tupac Shakur, the Notorious B.I.G., and other performers on local radio waves, and posters of basketball superstars like Shaquille O'Neal on walls and kiosks. Young urbanized Africans have fashioned their dress after American rappers and have even imported and reinvented the slang, style, and symbols of popular youth culture in America. While the myth of the diasporean supermen who would return to deliver Africa from bondage seems an idea of the past, an African tradition of identification with and emulation of African Americans seems as strong as ever.

As African American repatriates to the motherland, my family seized every opportunity to teach our new compatriots as much as we could about ourselves and other blacks in the diaspora. This often meant refuting the stereotypes many Tanzanians held about black Americans, and in some cases was a process of informing Africans of our very existence. My family did much to increase knowledge about American blacks among the Tanzanians we encountered, and in so doing we helped forge stronger ties between locals and the African American community in Dar. But while we enjoyed success in sharing information about ourselves with our new friends and neighbors, we still had much to learn about Africa. And a mere two years after moving to Africa, we faced a crisis that threatened my family's very survival and confused almost everything I thought I knew about the continent of my ancestry.

6

AFRICA'S TYRANNY

In every family, bad boys—difficult children—are not absent. . . . The chief that I am is not only for the good citizens, but also, and perhaps even more, for those who are less so. And if a chief must know how to punish, I believe that a pardon is sometimes necessary. There is not only the prodigal child who deserts the paternal roof whose return one day is passively awaited, there is also the lost sheep who leaves the herd that the master is going to find.

—Mobutu Sese Seko, granting amnesty to
Zairean political prisoners in May 1983

My mother shook us awake and began to gather the bags from the floor in front of our seats. "Come on," she said. "It's almost time to go." Our flight hadn't been announced over the loudspeaker yet, but I knew she wanted to beat the inevitable stampede for the departure gate. She had complained on the ride to the airport that Air Tanzania flights were often overbooked.

My brothers and I stirred groggily. James moaned softly, his excitement about the trip momentarily dampened by his premature awakening. "I want to sleep," he said crossly. My mother had literally dragged him from his bed that morning, and he had slept all the way to the airport, beyond the outskirts of Dar es Salaam. Even though we had had a chance to doze in the departure lounge before our flight left, we were all still sleepy. Kolo stretched tiredly. I yawned and slowly stumbled to my feet.

Passengers began to assemble around the glass door that led onto the hot runway where the plane waited. Potbellied men in safari and business suits and women in colorfully patterned dresses and wraps pressed around us, jostling for position. Mom grasped James's hand tightly and protested anxiously as a heavyset man with bulging eyes wedged himself between them.

"Please—my sons," she began.

The man grinned back and mimicked her. "Oh yes, sons," he said, guffawing as he continued to force himself into the crush of bodies. I put my arms on Kolo's shoulders and elbowed my way closer to our mother, glaring up at the oblivious interloper.

The departure gate was clogged by the sweaty throng, but some passengers managed to squeeze through. This trickle of bodies quickened into a steady stream as the zealots at the front of the swarm approached the plane, assuring themselves of the seats of their choice. My mother managed to force my brothers and me through the doorway ahead of her, extricating us from the crowd still pressed up against the glass. As we hurried across the tarmac, she tried to keep us clustered around her, tugging at James's sleeve when he began to stray. He was captivated by the aircraft, gazing up at it in awe, and had to be reminded to keep walking.

Finally inside the jet, Kolo and James lobbied for window seats while Mom and I sat along the aisle. We watched a commotion that had erupted toward the front of the plane, where a stout woman wearing a bright maroon *kitenge* argued with a flight attendant in loud Lingala. The woman had her hair styled in the antennalike braids that were so popular in central Africa, individual stems of hair bound with black thread so that they stood up stiffly, like quills. James thought they looked scary. "What's she saying, Mom?" he asked, staring at the woman with wide eyes.

"I think she's complaining because her brother didn't get a seat or something," my mother said.

I was surprised that she could still understand Lingala. It had been a decade since she had lived in Kinshasa. This December trip was to be her first return to Zaire since she, my father, and Remy had left in 1971, back when the nation was barely eight years old and still called the Democratic Republic of the Congo. For Kolo, James, and me, it would be our first trip to Zaire. We were suitably excited, although we didn't quite know what to expect.

My mother was looking forward to the visit. She seemed as eager as we were when she answered our questions about who we would see in Zaire and what we would do there. When she'd first arrived in 1968, she was entirely unprepared for what seemed to her an overwhelmingly loud and aggressive city. She'd been startled by shouted Lingala greetings between housewives, which to her sounded like invitations to combat, and she'd mistaken cordial exchanges between men on the street for declarations of war. It took weeks for the clatter of unfamiliar sounds to begin to sort itself into streams of meaningful words. And in addition to the language barrier, my mother's introduction to her new home was complicated by the fact that my father's family had (or so it seemed to her) scrutinized her actions with the intense care of new employers dubious about the recruitment of an unproven outside candidate.

Despite the culture shock and the nerve-racking inspection by her new in-laws, my mother had made some friends in Kinshasa and had come to appreciate the city's spirit and flavor. Still, she told me, she'd been relieved to return to the United States. The politically charged atmosphere and what she saw as the increasing abuse of power by the state had made it difficult to stay in Kinshasa. She had loosely followed events in Congo with some interest as a student, greeting the nation's independence from Belgium with enthusiasm in 1960. Patrice Lumumba, who led the Congolese independence movement, had become a household name among politically conscious black Americans; like Kwame Nkrumah, he was an embodiment of Africa's anticolonial struggle. My mother had been as horrified as many other African Americans when Lumumba was killed in 1961. It was hard for her to tell from afar what had really happened and who was responsible, but finally it was Joseph Désiré Mobutu, a former army colonel, who became the new leader of the Congo. And though my mother's first impulse had been to applaud and support the proud new president of an independent black nation, once she moved to Kinshasa she found that there was a deeply unsettling side to Mobutu's rule.

She had heard so many stories about people who were being watched, grisly tales of torture and detention, and rumors of strange "disappearances." She had constantly heard grim accounts of a prison in Kinshasa that people seldom emerged from. In Congo, it seemed, there was no rule of law; government soldiers routinely broke up demonstrations by firing on unarmed civilians, and killed with impunity. My mother had found this extremely disturbing, even painful. She felt that the government was squandering the gains of the anticolonial movement right before her eyes, dashing the hopes of a generation of Congolese who dreamed of building a more equitable and democratic society after the Belgians departed.

The repression my mother observed around her, the stories about people being spied on and arbitrarily imprisoned, and other examples of the government's increasing authoritarianism contributed to a growing anger and frustration in both of my parents. They ostensibly left Congo so that my father could continue with his studies, but my mother had always felt that in leaving when they did, they may have escaped just in time. She didn't think she could live there any longer, not under the prevailing conditions. And she feared it was just a matter of time before my often outspoken father attracted the suspicious, prying attention of the security forces, who watched closely for signs of dissent.

My parents and my brother Remy left Kinshasa in 1971 and returned to the United States. From Pomona, California, where my father finished graduate school, they kept up on the situation in Congo and were alarmed to watch the government become even more authoritarian. In 1971 Mobutu changed the country's name to Zaire, a Portuguese corruption of a Congolese word for river (*Nzadi*), and then changed his own name to Mobutu Sese Seko Kuku Nguendu wa Zabanga (something like "The Rooster Chief Who Will Rule Forever"). He created a new state ideology, "Mobutisme," a somewhat arbitrary set of principles he concocted himself, and decreed that all "Zaireans" were obliged to become members of the national party, the MPR (Popular Revolutionary Movement). Opposition parties were banned and critics were persecuted. Mobutu began to enrich himself by embezzling millions from international mining contracts. And he ruled with the support of the United States, France, and Belgium as a staunch and ruthless anti-Communist who was good for business.

Our father's contempt for the Zairean government was well known to my brothers and me. In the ten years since he had lived in Kinshasa, years spent teaching at Brandeis and Harvard and the University of Dar es Salaam, my father had spoken loudly and critically of Mobutu and his government and the Western countries that supported him, at the family dinner table and in more formal ways. His essays on neocolonialism and political repression in Zaire were often published in academic journals, and he had gained considerable prominence in the international circle of progressive scholars to which he belonged. He would have never been able to do this work if he had stayed in Zaire, but his activities had now made returning more difficult. The Zairean regime kept a close eye on dissidents at home and abroad and was often quick to punish critics.

My father had been back to Zaire only once since 1971, on an emergency visit to his sick father's bedside. On that trip he had entered the country through neighboring Congo-Brazzaville, taking a ferry across the wide Congo River, which separates the two nations, exploiting the lax border controls along the riverbank, and passing casually into Zaire. He planned to enter by the same route this time, to avoid potential problems with suspicious immigration officials at the airport.

Our father's mother had been complaining for years that her son had never taken my brothers and me to see her and that he had abandoned her, leaving their village for the capital and then leaving Kinshasa for the United States and Tanzania. This Christmas trip was my family's long-awaited pilgrimage, for my brothers and me an introduction to a homeland and family we'd never known and for my parents a rediscovery of old ties. My father, whose vacation had begun a month earlier than ours, had gone to a conference in the United States and planned to meet us in Kinshasa, where he would arrive the day before us. We were to spend the next couple of weeks visiting grandparents, aunts, uncles, and cousins and getting acquainted with the country where my father was born.

My father was usually very conscientious, though he did have bouts of professorial absentmindedness; sometimes he would drive our battered Volkswagen the mile to his office, then walk home at the end of the day, forgetting he had left the car in the university parking lot. And on another occasion my brothers and I often laughed about, he cut himself while cooking and then medicated and bandaged the wrong finger. Still, despite these moments of forgetfulness, my mother knew he would be careful not to draw any attention to himself when entering Zaire.

As the plane taxied down the runway and paused for a moment, gathering itself for take-off, James tapped my mother on her shoulder and grimaced in pain. He had a history of infections and other ear problems, and his ears always became irritated when flying. My mother reached for the gum in her carry-on bag and distributed it among us, and we chewed it to ease the pressure on our ears. As the plane gained altitude we settled in our seats and tried to get comfortable, each of us alone with our thoughts, cradled by the soothing drone of the airplane's engines. My brothers and I soon drifted off to sleep.

*   *   *

James, Kolo, and I blinked tiredly in the bright fluorescent lights of Kinshasa airport, stumbling along the red-carpeted corridor after our mother. She walked along quickly, searching the faces of passersby.

"Mom, where's Dad?" asked James, yawning. She didn't answer, but continued to scan the crowd. A group of men in ominous army greens walked towards us, talking among themselves.

"Something's happened to Ernest, something's happened to Ernest," my mother thought, her mind racing. She told me later that she had taken pains to conceal her concern, but I immediately felt that something was wrong; I could see it in the way her eyes flitted about the room nervously, and in the way she looked at the soldiers. My brothers, however, seemed oblivious, and they slouched sulkily, tired and cranky after the long trip. One of the soldiers, a tall, thin man with a thick mustache above a wide grin, asked to see our passports and directed us into a small, spare room.

"Isn't your husband here to meet you?" the grinning soldier asked sweetly in French. My mother felt her stomach clench in fear. "Something's happened to Ernest," she thought again. I couldn't understand the soldier's words, but for a moment my mother's fear flickered on her face, and I looked at her frustratedly, trying to find clues that would tell me what was happening.

After briefly examining our passports, the soldiers escorted us to the baggage claim area, saying nothing more. My mother glanced around nervously, still looking for familiar faces; if Ernest couldn't make it, surely he would have sent his uncle, or . . . someone, she thought.

She noticed a tall white man with brown hair and a mustache standing at the bottom of a stairway. When we reached the base of the stairs, trailed by our uniformed entourage, the man stepped forward and introduced himself. He worked at the U.S. Embassy in Kinshasa. He had been sent to meet us because my father, a Congolese married to an American citizen, had been arrested the day before. Now, he continued, the Zairean security forces wanted to question my mother.

She felt as if she were spinning, as though the white concrete walls of the airport and the cloudy white lights overhead were converging around her suffocatingly. She felt a cold, hard sensation in the pit of her stomach. Her expression did not change. She pulled us closer around her, but I could tell that she felt very, very alone.

My father's detention was a defining episode in a lifetime of engagement in the cause of political freedom for his people and nation. And as such, his experience was an allegory for the sad betrayals of independence that have been played out all over the continent, where patriots often become enemies of the state and today's freedom fighters are often tomorrow's dictators.

When my father was born, in 1942, his country was still called the Belgian Congo. It had been a Belgian colony since the Berlin Conference of 1884–85, which essentially divided Africa among the European powers, and had endured a notoriously brutal colonial experience.

As the Congo Free State, the territory was subjected to barbarous acts of political coercion under Belgium's King Leopold II, whose troops terrorized the local population, enslaving them as porters and forcing them to collect rubber on pain of torture or death. Millions of Congolese were killed under the king's bloody rule, and the Force Publique, the army of mercenaries and conscripts responsible for putting down rebellions and extracting as much wealth as possible from King Leopold's personal fiefdom, became notorious for collecting human hands as gruesome trophies to tally the dead and intimidate the locals. Recalling this sort of cruelty, my father used to shake his head angrily, and call King Leopold a "psychopath."

Such activities in the Congo Free State eventually sparked enough international opposition to prompt the intervention of Belgium's civilian government in 1908, which took over administration of the region and renamed it the Belgian Congo. Though not as brutal as King Leopold, the new colonial authority continued to exploit the territory for its vast deposits of rubber and minerals, and forced its colonial subjects to pay taxes and undergo a Christian "civilizing" process that taught them basic literacy and European values, but denied them further education until the 1950s.

The legacy of colonialism weighs heavily on the shoulders of my father's generation, and profoundly informs its outlook. My father grew up hearing horrific stories of the savagery of King Leopold's colonial rule and remembers the racist arrogance with which whites treated him as a young student. He was one of a generation of Congolese targeted by the Belgium civilizing mission, but he came of age in a time of African awakening. The disgruntlement that would erupt in the anticolonial movement of the 1950s was already being articulated. Like many of his peers, my father became politicized at an early age and grew into an adamant opponent of colonialism, favoring complete Congolese independence. As a student he became active in the local youth chapter of ABAKO ("Alliance des Bakongo"), a regional political group, and closely followed political developments unfolding on the national stage.

In 1958, Patrice Lumumba, head of the National Congolese Movement, the country's first national party and a longtime opponent of Belgian colonialism, demanded independence from Belgium in a landmark public speech, and after a series of violent demonstrations, the Belgians finally agreed to outline a four-year transition schedule for self-government. Local politicians and a growing mass movement stepped up the pressure on the Belgians, however, and forced them to speed things up. Popular legend had it that Lumumba had expressed the unacceptability of having to wait four years by deliberately arriving late to a meeting held to discuss the decolonization process; when he finally sauntered into the conference hall and the irate Belgians demanded to know why he was so disrespectfully tardy, Lumumba calmly noted that they were angry because he had made them wait just a few hours, yet they wanted the Congolese people to wait years for their freedom. They must have gotten the point, because the Belgian authorities held the country's first democratic elections in January 1960, and Lumumba, whose party had a power base in the Congo's largest province, was elected the country's first prime minister. Independence was formally granted on June 30, 1960, and 16.2 million Congolese celebrated the birth of the Republic of the Congo. My father greeted the news with elation and eagerly anticipated making a contribution to the development of his independent country. With a variety of academic interests and talents, my father was unsure what field to pursue, but he decided to continue his studies as far as they would lead him.

Like most Congolese, my father was shocked and crestfallen when the Congo's first democratically elected government collapsed less than a year after its formation. After Lumumba won the election of January 1960, some rival politicians refused to recognize his legitimacy. Moise Tshombe, a Congolese businessman from Katanga province with close ties to Belgium, attempted to form a breakaway state by proclaiming Katanga's independence, prompting fighting between his followers (supported by Belgian mercenaries in his employ) and forces loyal to Lumumba. As the conflict intensified, the Congolese army mutinied, order disintegrated nationwide, and a United Nations peacekeeping force was deployed to protect Europeans and attempt to stem the hostilities. In the ensuing power struggle, the U.S. government, which had come to view Lumumba as a potential Soviet ally and a threat to U.S. business interests in Congo, moved to support Lumumba's political adversaries. Tshombe, Joseph Mobutu (then the twenty-nine-year-old army chief of staff and a former Lumumba aide), and other Lumumba foes plotted with the CIA to orchestrate Lumumba's ouster.

Mobutu took power in a coup in September 1960, placing Lumumba under house arrest. Lumumba's plea for help from the United Nations was ignored, and he was eventually brutally killed by his Congolese and Belgian enemies in an elaborate scheme conceived and financed by the CIA. Lumumba's allies, based in eastern Congo, launched a rebellion to challenge the forces that had murdered the prime minister, and the country became torn by a civil war in which the superpowers vied for control of Africa's most valuable Cold War prize.

Rural Bas-Congo, my father's home province in the west, was pretty far removed from the conflict, but my father followed events closely. He had been deeply affected when Lumumba was killed and now felt at a loss to understand the intricacies of the struggle now gripping the country. It was all very confusing, depressing, and disappointing. My father tried to focus on his studies instead of dwelling on the disheartening turn Congo's march towards freedom had taken.

In 1964 my father won a scholarship to study philosophy and economics at Western Michigan University. As a university student in America he continued his political and intellectual development, taking an interest in radical politics and African independence struggles. He also became involved in campus politics as a member of Black Action Movement (BAM), a student group. As the civil rights struggle intensified in the late 1960s, campuses across the nation became hotbeds of protest, and WMU was no exception. When Martin Luther King, Jr., was assassinated in Memphis, Tennessee, in April 1968, my father and two African American friends coordinated the student response. They led a takeover of the campus administration building and headed the student negotiating team that presented campus administrators with a list of demands designed to increase black representation on the university faculty and curriculum. This initiative became the basis for the creation of a black studies program at WMU some years later.

After graduating in 1968, my father eagerly took a job at the Congolese Ministry of Social Affairs.

The political situation seemed to have stabilized in my father's absence. The war that had gripped Congo when my father left for the United States had ended with the defeat of Lumumba's allies. The UN forces had departed in 1964, and though Mobutu had initially returned power to Joseph Kasavubu, the president of the Congolese parliament, in 1961, he had retaken control of the government in a CIA-backed coup d'état in 1965.

Mobutu had come to power on the crest of the rising wave of Cold War intrigue as the United States' perceived best hope for an anti-Communist Congo that was friendly to U.S. business interests, and he had been promised American support as Congo's new leader. By 1968, Mobutu was firmly entrenched in power.

From his vantage point in the Ministry of Social Affairs, my father observed firsthand the early abuses of power by the Congolese state. The late sixties were a period in which Mobutu was relatively popular: he had instituted a cultural revolution that championed African values, and had stewarded a healthy economy that had made steady gains since independence. But he ensured his firm grasp of power by repressing opposition. The state controlled the media, rival political parties were illegal, political opponents were jailed without trial, and antigovernment demonstrations were violently disrupted.

My father once told my brothers and me a vivid story about a nephew of his, a young student by the name of Pierre who became one of many victims of state repression. Pierre, a gifted student, often came to see my father in Kinshasa, when my parents and older brother lived in Congo. Pierre admired and respected his worldly foreign-educated uncle and often asked him for advice and help with his schoolwork.

One day, Pierre told my father that he was going to participate in a student march to pressure the government to improve the poor conditions at the national university campuses, which were understaffed, undersupplied, and prone to long closures because of the inadequate facilities. My father advised him against it, but Pierre joined the demonstration anyway, without telling anyone.

Mobutu had banned antigovernment demonstrations. The army was ordered to disperse the marchers. They did so by opening fire on them.

Most of the students flattened themselves on the ground, but Pierre remained on his feet and attempted to encourage the others to stand up and resume the march. He was struck in the head by an army bullet and killed.

My father heard what had happened when a friend of Pierre's delivered the news, his shirt drenched with Pierre's blood.

My father saw the repressive policies of the Congolese government as a betrayal of the promise of the anticolonial struggle. Mobutu seemed to have become another Leopold. Pierre's fate, and the similar fates of many other friends, relatives, and countrymen of my father, helped to prompt my parents' decision to return to the United States in 1971. And when he finished his graduate work in California, my father decided that instead of returning to Zaire our family would remain in the United States. We moved to Boston in 1972.

As a professor at a number of Boston universities in the 1970s, my father began to publish essays and articles on African politics and the tyranny of the Zairean regime. He began to associate with other Zaireans in the Boston area, and together they founded the Committee for Zairean Research and Studies. One of the members of the group was one of my father's longtime mentors and a prominent Zairean dissident, Thomas Kanza, a professor at Boston University and a former member of Lumumba's short-lived government of the early 1960s.

By the late 1970s, my father's writings and the work of his research group had begun to gain the attention of the Zairean government, which monitored the activities of Zaireans abroad through a network of informers. In their eyes, Kanza was a well-known "subversive"; my father's association with him undoubtedly cast him in a similar light. The Zairean secret police were notorious for compiling lists of their "most wanted subversives," and Kanza was thought to head it. My father had apparently also earned a place on that list.

In 1979, the Zairean government, which had helped to sponsor my father's education in the United States, began to demand that he return to Zaire.

My father feared that he would be detained if he returned home, and Remy's leukemia diagnosis and subsequent hospitalization only complicated matters. He asked to be allowed to remain at his son's bedside. But the stream of written demands to return that arrived regularly from Kinshasa made it clear that his refusal to come home had further angered the Zairean authorities. And as a non-U.S. citizen who did not have a green card, he felt especially vulnerable to the pressure.

My family eventually found refuge from the Zairean government's ultimatums when my father accepted the job in Dar, where the residence permit his job afforded him meant the Zairean government could not force him to leave. The University of Dar es Salaam was regarded by many African scholars as a progressive center of learning and had attracted many great minds in its history. My father made many friends and became a respected figure on campus and in scholarly circles continent-wide, gaining a reputation for his clearly reasoned lectures and writings, which were often critical of the repressive tendencies of governments like Zaire's.

He was able to make a satisfying life for himself in Tanzania, but he always longed for his real home. I could hear it in the wistfulness of his tone when he spoke of his birthplace and family, and I could see it in the look of eagerness on his face when he saw Zairean stamps on his mail. But his growing recognition as a critic of the Zairean government made the prospect of return more and more remote.

Despite the risk, my father felt compelled to travel to Zaire in 1980, when he received word that his father was ill. Emboldened by his success, my parents planned another visit for Christmas of 1981. The trip was presented to us kids as our true homecoming, our return to our father's country, where we would meet hundreds of new relatives and acquaint ourselves with our paternal heritage. We were going to spend a few days in Kinshasa and then take a bus to Zabanga, the little village that figured so prominently in my father's stories of his childhood. My brothers and I greeted the prospect of finally traveling to Zaire with eager excitement. We were still basking in the happy newness of Dar es Salaam, and felt things could only get better. We were totally unprepared for my father's arrest.

When we were met by the armed soldiers at the airport, I was numb with disbelief and very frightened. My very first impressions of Kinshasa took shape in a hazy bad dream in which my brothers, my mother, and I wandered a strange city, stalked by leering, uniformed men, looking frantically for a familiar face.

My mother was similarly stunned. Years later she told me that she had experienced the events following my father's arrest as if from outside herself, observing the action from a detached and objective distance. She watched as she received the news of her husband's arrest from the U.S. embassy representative who met us at the airport, watched herself conceal her fear from her children and the security men who had come to interrogate her. She watched as she visited my father in jail the day after our arrival, observing the haggard look on her own face and the fear and anger in her husband's eyes. And she watched herself crisscrossing Kinshasa trying to contact her husband's relatives and to get help from old friends, some of whom wanted nothing to do with her for fear of also becoming targets of the secret police.

Despite her disorientation, my mother managed to focus on the situation at hand. She began writing a journal to keep each day's events and objectives in mind and in order, and tried to methodically determine what she needed to do. Her early entries are almost businesslike, possessed of a dispassionate and orderly distance, although at times they verge on venting the despair we had all begun to feel. "Sunday December 20, 1981," begins my mother's second diary entry, which describes our first prison visit with my father.

We arrive Kitambo shortly after 10 and wait till 12:30 or so for Ernest to arrive. We are all finally taken to an office where we can talk. Ernest describes his situation: *very serious* because of what they found him with; the President will be informed today. He is incarcerated in that place we have heard so much about at Mont Ngalima where there is an underground prison and from where many people never return. He is always beaten during interrogations. He sleeps on the floor in an unhygienic cell, rarely sees the light of Day. He is fed once a day. He must get special permission to wash or use the toilet, which is in a different location. He has not been able to change his clothing or brush his teeth for 2 days. I am to contact Ernest's family as soon as possible. Am given a map of where uncle lives. We wait for the adjutant to arrive. At 3:45 it is decided that he is probably not going to come, it being Sunday, and that we must come back tomorrow. We leave and look for a taxi to Ernest's uncle's place. The taxi breaks down on the way and we go on foot. We follow the map and ask for directions. We search till 6:00 not finding the place. We take taxi back to town. Money is very low. We can't eat dinner. We undress and go to bed totally demoralized.

On each of those first frightening days in Kinshasa, my mother led my brothers and me out of our downtown hotel on a mission to accomplish the tasks she had set. We would try to contact friends and relatives, taking taxis or cramming into *fula-fulas* (large buses or trucks) and hiking tiredly along the potholed warren of roads that threaded the sprawling city. On that first unsuccessful attempt to locate my father's uncle's home, we roamed somewhat aimlessly until dark, asking around, trying to get directions from red-eyed men who smelled of liquor and insisted that they knew where they were going, even though we usually ended up more lost. In addition to trying to locate family, we made daily trips to the prison where my father was being held, although we rarely got to see him. And we always stopped by the U.S. embassy to try to send messages to the States and Tanzania. After hours of tiring legwork around Kinshasa, and usually with little to show for it, we would return once again to the expensive hotel where the American from the embassy had deposited us after my mother's interrogation on our first night in the country.

We finally got in touch with my father's relatives and found his uncle's house in Kingasani, a Kinshasa suburb, on the third day. It was a relief to contact family, and it was good to meet all the relatives who populated the house, especially some of the cousins who were close in age to my brothers and me. Our relatives had heard what had happened to my father, but had not known how to find us. Exclamations of surprise and relief greeted our sudden arrival, as relatives my mother had met more than ten years before rushed to embrace us. But the reunion took place under an ominous shadow of worry and uncertainty.

My mother moved my brothers and me into my uncle's house and, while my brothers and I played in the streets of Kingasani with our newly met cousins, continued to make daily visits to the prison where my father was being held. Sometimes she was able to see him only from a distance; she always brought him some food my aunt had cooked, and also passed on a blanket provided by the International Committee of the Red Cross (she had gone to their office in Kinshasa to ask for help) and some toiletries. My mother was rarely allowed to meet with the prison's commanding officer, however, an elusive man who was never able to tell her the exact charges against my father. She began contacting friends and relatives in Tanzania, the United States, and Europe, letting them know what had happened and asking for their help. She made frequent visits to the Tanzanian and American embassies in Kinshasa and contacted Amnesty International to recruit its assistance. When these initiatives yielded promises but few immediate results, she made the difficult decision to leave Kinshasa for Dar es Salaam, where a base at our home, a network of friends, and greater access to money and potentially helpful institutions would make the struggle for my father's release easier.

My memory of the events immediately after my father's arrest is sketchy. I was ten, and my early impressions of Zaire are cloaked in overwhelming fear and bewilderment. I knew who Mobutu was; I was well aware of my father's attitude toward the Zairean government, and knew vaguely of their apparent aversion to him, but somehow his arrest was a complete shock. To me, politics occupied a realm of ideas that had few actual manifestations in real life; I didn't really see how criticizing Mobutu could actually lead to being imprisoned by Mobutu.

Also, at the time I spoke very little French, and my memory of my mother's exchange with the soldiers who greeted us at Kinshasa airport is one of impressions, not of actual sentences. I knew immediately that something was terribly wrong, but my mother had to explain the situation to my brothers and me, which she did at our hotel room after she was interrogated. Because I was only ten, the workings of the adult world often seemed encoded in a complex jargon to which I was seldom privy, and my perceptions at the time occupied two levels: the level of what I observed and decoded on my own, and the level of what my mother told me. A few days after our arrival in Kinshasa, we visited a Zairean friend my mother knew from her years in Kinshasa; even though I couldn't understand what was being said, it was clear to me from his agitated gestures and strained tone that he was afraid to help us.

And when we were allowed a short visit with my father the day after our arrival, the only occasion we got to actually be with him, he hugged us to him, but his stony face, creased with deep grooves on his forehead and around his mouth, never brightened. He and my mother spoke in hushed French using short, curt sentences. I could tell that he was frightened and extremely worried and reluctant to show it. And when a security officer entered the room to escort us out, something in the way that the man interacted with my father told me that he had been beating him.

What had happened to Pierre in the story my father told had seemed to me an event in the distant past; this was here and now, and I could scarcely grasp what was happening. I felt frightened and wanted to leave Kinshasa from the moment we learned about my father's arrest. And even though I didn't want to leave my father in Zaire, I was greatly relieved to return to the relative familiarity of Dar.

In Dar, my mother joined my father's colleagues and friends and helped organize a crusade for his release, the "Free Wamba Campaign." She and other members of the group published a newsletter, *Zairean Detainee*, chronicling the events surrounding my father's arrest, and distributed it among his associates around the world. Even my brothers and I got involved, sitting at our dining room table, taking the pink or green photocopies of the newsletter from a mountain in the center of the table and folding, addressing, and stamping them.

The campaign circulated petitions decrying my father's arrest and sent them to the Zairean embassy in Dar es Salaam, laden with thousands of signatures. My mother was interviewed by the national newspaper, and my father's arrest was announced on the national radio station and the BBC. My mother contacted her relatives in the United States and urged them to write their congresspeople for help. A former professor of my father's who had once been an adviser to Ronald Reagan when he was governor of California made some calls on his behalf. And Amnesty International adopted my father as a prisoner of conscience, pressuring the Zairean government for his release.

When I returned to school a few weeks after our return to Tanzania in the spring of 1982, I was a bit of a celebrity; all of my classmates had heard about the news and were sympathetic and curious. I felt proud of him as I explained the reasons for his detention, careful to underline the fact that he had done nothing wrong. But at home we worried for his safety. My mother didn't tell us much, but her silence was uneasy; she kept us updated on her efforts to win my father's release, but did not speak her fears.

I didn't ask my father what detention in a Zairean prison was like until many years later. I doubted that he would want to talk about it, and I was probably also afraid of what I might hear. When we finally did discuss his experience, it was distant enough for him to laugh about it. But it had been harrowing. He had been arrested with two friends of his from secondary school, men whose only crime was that they were waiting to meet him at the ferry port in Kinshasa where he disembarked. His friends were soon released, but he had no way of knowing that because once in prison, he was separated from them, stripped naked and searched, and confined to a small cell, alone.

He was grilled by his captors regularly. They insisted that he was a member of a dissident organization that sought to overthrow Mobutu, and they demanded that he provide names of others in the group. They pulled phrases and sentences from the "subversive" essays they had found on him (a review of a book by an anti-Mobutu dissident and an article which was critical of "Mobutisme") and asked him to explain himself. My father tried not to answer their questions directly, and he took to equivocating and arguing about semantics, a strategy that infuriated his questioners. When he failed to respond to their satisfaction, he was beaten.

My father was fortunate that the Red Cross had just recently seen to it that the electric shocks previously in use at Mont Ngalima prison no longer were. Instead, when an answer my father provided was not well received, he was forced to lie on his front and whipped between five and ten times on the back with a soldier's thick, buckle-laden belt. If he continued to be uncooperative, he would have to spend twenty-four hours in solitary confinement.

Despite the beatings and psychological torture, sometimes, in small ways, he felt that he managed to get the best of his tormentors. During one long interrogation session in which he persisted in artfully evading accusatory questions, his questioners began to get frustrated. One of my father's jailers declared angrily that he wouldn't be able to use "philosophy" on them. His evasion technique seemed to work, however. Seemingly bored and fed up with my father's circular explanations and verbose distortions, the interrogators changed tactics, asking him to respond in writing to a series of written accusations and questions. Even better, thought my father, and he spent several pages and hours on the first part of the first question, once again seeking to confuse the issue with a cloud of philosophical double-talk. Not only did these elaborate dissertations help him avoid incriminating himself, they also provided a valuable distraction from the solitary, empty hours when he wasn't being interrogated. With nothing to do in his cell (he was not permitted to have books or a pen and paper, except when he was responding to the written queries), my father would try to keep himself occupied by exercising or meditating, but he usually ended up just sitting there, his idle mind becoming cluttered with unspoken thoughts and worries.

He occasionally got to see other prisoners, and he always welcomed the chance to speak to someone other than his jailers. Though most of the inmates were "criminals" rather than political prisoners, all of them seemed bound by the unity of the collectively oppressed, and some of them, veterans of imprisonment, offered my father tips on how to survive. One knew all of the guards and interrogators well, and was describing the cruelty of one especially feared questioner when my father was startled to realize that he knew the man to whom his new friend referred, a colleague of his from secondary school. When my father's fellow prisoner heard this, he shook his head with foreboding. "You know him?" he asked, seemingly alarmed. "That means you're really going to get it." He was right. When my father faced his old schoolmate across the interrogation table, he saw recognition but no sympathy in the man's eyes. And if my father's high school classmate felt any compunction about questioning and hitting a former acquaintance, it was not evident in the zeal with which he approached the task.

As the days of my father's detention stretched into weeks, he gradually hardened himself to the cycle of idleness, interrogation, punishment, and humiliation. He thought of us, his family, often, with a sad longing that was heavy on his soul but nonetheless helped to fortify him against the physical and mental onslaughts. In his head, he reviewed books he had read, sometimes drawing strength and inspiration from phrases he recalled, especially those from the prison narratives of writers such as Nigeria's Wole Soyinka. He became determined to resist the mounting pressure and tried not to dwell on the fact that many who entered Zairean prisons as suspected enemies of the state never reemerged. And in steeling himself against the constant abuse, he managed to will himself to survive.

Fortunately, the mounting pressure from the U.S. government and international human rights organizations succeeded just five weeks after my father was first detained. Mobutu made a speech grumbling about foreign interference in his country's internal affairs, but my father was released from jail in January 1982 and allowed to stay with his uncle in Kinshasa. He emerged from his cell barefoot and bedraggled. He had lost a lot of weight and gained new physical and psychological scars. But he was happy and relieved to be free, and surprisingly unresentful. Though no longer in prison, he was not permitted to leave the city, however, and was required to report four times a week to a security administrator. He was also often tailed by surreptitious security agents when he left the house. Still, he felt that the physical danger was over. In Dar es Salaam we celebrated my father's release with a party at a friend's house, my youngest brother dancing hysterically after a taste of wine given him by some irresponsible reveler.

The Free Wamba Campaign moved to secure my father's complete and unconditional release, but momentum seemed to slow once he was no longer in immediate danger, and the agencies and organizations that had pressed for his release seemed less energetic in continuing their demands. For the Zairean government, the issue seemed to be one of saving face; my father had essentially been released because a large enough international support network had consistently and aggressively demanded it. By freeing him, the Zairean government had capitulated to foreign directives; so, to maintain face, they dangled my father's complete freedom before him tantalizingly, drawing the process out for as long as they wished.

He was no longer interrogated when he checked in at security headquarters. In theory, he just had to be seen briefly by a certain official, but sometimes this meant three hours of waiting, only to be told that the person was not there—"come back tomorrow." When he did get to see the administrator he was supposed to, he would often have to sit through lectures and threats. "Tell your friends in the United

States to stop making so much noise," one security officer used to tell him. "The more noise they make, the longer we are forced to keep you here." Some officials admonished him for his dissidence and insisted that his animosity towards the Zairean government was misguided; a person with his intelligence should be working for them, not against them, they said.

Having to check in was especially a hassle for my father because he would have to take Kinshasa's notoriously crowded, dilapidated, and unreliable buses to the security office and back to his uncle's house, which made the visit an all-day affair and a drain on his very limited financial resources. It seemed clear that the system was designed to be a humiliating inconvenience, a way of asserting control and power over him even though he was no longer in jail. He had, however, no choice but to cooperate. The empty routine of the often useless visits to the security headquarters filled weeks, which were anxious and otherwise idle. And there was no real end to them in sight; my father and my family had no real sense of when he might finally be allowed to leave Kinshasa.

My brothers and I returned to Zaire with our mother in June 1982, en route to the United States where we were going to spend the summer visiting relatives and continuing the campaign to free my father. It was a joyful reunion. He was able to show us around Kinshasa, we visited some of his old friends, and for the first time my brothers and I met our paternal grandfather, who made the bus trip to Kinshasa from Zabanga to see us. He was a tall, stately man who struck me as being very calm and gentle. When he appeared, Kolo exclaimed, "It's our grandfather!" ("Nkaka yeto yena!") in Kikongo and ran to him. (No one in my family seems to know who taught him that phrase.) My grandfather hugged us all and beamed.

But even as we enjoyed the first time we'd spent with our father since his detention, the undercover security officers whom he pointed out to us from time to time, trailing us in a white sedan, were a forbidding reminder of his incomplete freedom.

As we left Kinshasa for the United States, my mother finally succumbed to the stress and exhaustion of my father's detention. She became very ill on the flight, showing symptoms of a disease later identified as viral hepatitis. She later told me that she had been convinced that she was going to die, and was worried about my brothers and me. She concealed her concern well: my brothers and I were, of course, deeply troubled by her illness, but I took heart from the fact that she was well enough to make a joke of her use of an entire row's airsickness bags. I assumed leadership of the family during that trip, reassuring my brothers, negotiating the travel-related bureaucracy during a transit stop in Europe, and trying to ensure that my mother rested as much as possible. It wasn't a role I was entirely unfamiliar with; I had welcomed mourners to my older brother's funeral because my parents were too grief-stricken to do so, and in the months when my father was unable to leave Zaire, my mother looked to me to assume greater responsibility at home. When we arrived in Boston she was admitted to the hospital, and was able to recuperate within a few weeks at the home of some relatives. We returned to Tanzania at the end of the summer, to the routine of school, play, and the political activism of the Free Wamba Campaign.

In addition to prompting my increased maturity, my father's detention marked the start of my politicization. For the first time, politics, which had previously only occupied an intangible universe of ideas, had taken an active and concrete form in my life. My home became a crossroads for political activists involved with Zairean politics and human rights issues, and I sat in on meetings of the key organizers of the campaign, trying to follow as the group discussed strategies. I sat in the living room with my mother as she welcomed my father's colleagues and friends from around the world, who stopped by to offer their support and advice. One memorable visitor was a Zairean pilot and dissident who offered to smuggle my father out of Zaire in a "borrowed" Air Tanzania jet; to my disappointment, my mother politely refused.

The experience also led me to think about things I had never before considered. Once my mother was discussing my father's detention and subsequent "city arrest" with a neighbor, a Danish mathematician who taught at the university. He gave my mother some mathematics textbooks to pass on to my father, who, though an historian and economist, liked to practice solving math problems (a passion that has always baffled me). "Is he a very strong man?" the mathematician asked my mother as he handed her the books, looking at her seriously above his thick glasses.

"Yes," my mother replied, "he's very strong." She said it so proudly.

I assumed they were talking about physical strength, and later I asked my mother what she had meant. She explained that she was talking about mental toughness, and that one of the hardest parts of my father's detention was the fact that it was such a psychologically trying situation. While in prison he was not permitted to read or write, and when he was restricted to Kinshasa, idle months in which he whiled away the hours at his uncle's house between the mandatory interviews with security officials, he simply had nothing to do. He felt he was in a state of physical and mental paralysis, a condition made all the worse because he felt powerless to change it.

It made me angry to think about this, but it also filled me with a sense of awe. I wondered what it was like, being detained just for speaking your mind, and whether I might ever find myself in a similar situation. I tried to imagine what it was like to be in prison, languishing in a cell for weeks with nothing to do and no one to speak to, being separated from family and friends and subject to the cruel, arbitrary whims of hostile jailers. And I wondered whether it was worth it. My father had made a choice to criticize the Zairean government, and if he hadn't done so, perhaps none of this would have happened. But even though at times I resented the fact that he was not with us when we needed him, more than that I was proud of him for standing by his beliefs the way he had.

My father's eventual return home, in December 1982, was anticlimactic in many ways. By that fall, my family regarded his release from city arrest as just a matter of time, and my mother's work of applying political pressure on the Zairean government, sending letters to U.S. congressmen and to human rights organizations and making regular visits to the Zairean embassy, had begun to feel routine. She kept abreast of developments in my father's case through the U.S. embassy in Dar es Salaam, where she had been permitted to send and receive telexes and telegrams to and from Kinshasa. When we received word that my father would finally be coming home, it was more with a sense of tired relief than with exuberant joy. The year of his absence had hardened us, too. The university, impatiently awaiting the return of its professor, had threatened to evict us from the house they provided. (Since my father was a foreigner and was sometimes regarded as too outspoken by the university authorities, his plight was not always looked on sympathetically by his employers.) My mother had struggled to support us on her single paycheck, and my brothers and I had long fallen into the no longer awkward habit of setting only four places at the table. We had steeled ourselves against disappointment so often, as we eagerly awaited word from Zaire each week, that we were mistrustful of and ill prepared for good news. My mother first told me that my father would be coming back ("Dad's out" were the simple words she used) after she picked me up from a soccer practice at school. It wasn't the first thing she said when I got into the car, we were well on the way home before she told me, and she said it very cautiously, almost offhandedly, as though she almost didn't believe it herself.

My father returned to a different household from the one he had left; he found his children more mature and self-sufficient, and he found all of us much more cynical. And in my youngest brother, James, especially, he found a deep anger, both with those who had prevented his return and with him for having been absent for a year. James was four when our father was arrested and it was difficult for him to understand why Dad could not come home; for years after the fact, his bitterness about my father's absence was still an unspoken barrier between them. As for myself, I would never fully recover from the deeply disillusioning shock of my first visit to my father's land.

With the arrest of my father, an Africanist historian who had taught at several U.S. universities and at one of the most respected campuses in Africa, an international network of friends, family members, activists, academics, politicians, and students responded quickly to call for his release. My father had been a part of various political struggles while a student and professor in the United States, and many of those he had worked with in the 1960s and 1970s now moved to support him in his time of need. Nearly twenty years of forging ties and contacts with like-minded colleagues all over the world paid off as the worldwide outcry helped secure his release. Many of those who helped were relatives or family friends with little real knowledge of African politics. Others were academic associates who were more familiar with my father's work than with him as an individual. And others were activists who had never even heard of him until his name appeared on lists circulated by organizations like Amnesty International and in journals like *Index on Censorship*.

The campaign was truly international, and in many ways it was also pan-African, coordinated by his black American wife and his African, black American, and West Indian colleagues in Dar es Salaam. They alerted people all over Africa, Europe, the United States, and the Caribbean, seeking support in their efforts to free my father; my mother shuttled between Dar, Kinshasa, and Boston, spreading the word and trying to generate political pressure on the Zairean government. Members of her family and activists in the American black community urged the U.S. government to intervene on my father's behalf, and a global coalition of Africa-oriented political groups launched letter-writing, petition, and speak-out campaigns, targeting the Zairean government from pan-African nerve centers all over the world.

In rushing to the aid of an African scholar unfairly imprisoned by a tyrannical regime, the African Americans and other black activists who joined the Free Wamba Campaign were joining and sustaining a deep-rooted tradition of diaspora involvement in African political struggles. African Americans have played an important role in influencing U.S. and international policy in the Congo specifically and in Africa in general, and have long worked alongside Africans in a variety of political initiatives. African American political involvement in the Congo at various points in time has in many ways been representative of processes taking place in the continent at large.

In the nineteenth and early twentieth centuries, black American voices were among the loudest raised in protest of Belgian inhumanity in the Congo. In the 1880s George Washington Williams, an African American war veteran, minister, politician, and historian, decided to visit the Congo Free State to assess its suitability for black resettlement. In the hope of securing King Leopold II's assistance, he contacted the ruler and requested permission to tour the colony. Though Leopold initially supported the idea, he changed his mind when he began to worry about the effects that educated black outsiders might have on his Congolese subjects. The king's agents attempted to thwart Williams's trip, but he made his way to the continent despite the obstacles they erected. Touring a number of African countries in 1890, and making his way along the Congo River to the Congolese interior, Williams was shocked by Belgian mistreatment of the locals; he described the colony as "the Siberia, of the African continent, a penal settlement."

Documenting his observations in "An Open letter to His Serene Majesty Leopold II, King of the Belgians and Sovereign of the Independent State of Congo" (1890), Williams was the first to alert the international community to the atrocities committed by King Leopold II's emissaries in the territory. Though it maintained a tone of politeness and civility, the "Open Letter," which was immediately distributed among the international media and world leaders, openly denounced the brutal tactics of Belgian imperialism. Williams wrote that he was "disenchanted, disappointed and disheartened" to observe the evidence of Belgian misdeeds and pointed out that in Congo natives "everywhere complain that their land has been taken from them by force; that the Government is cruel and arbitrary, and declare that they neither love nor respect t[h]e Government and its flag. Your

Majesty's Government has sequestered their land, burned their towns, stolen their property, enslaved their women and children, and committed other crimes too numerous to mention in detail. It is natural that they everywhere shrink from 'the fostering care' your Majesty's Government so eagerly proffers them."

Williams called for the signatories of the Berlin Conference, which had awarded Belgium control of the region, to look into his charges and take appropriate action: "I now appeal to the Powers, which committed this infant State to your Majesty's charge and to the great States which gave it international being; and whose majestic law you have scorned and trampled upon, to call and create an International Commission to investigate the charges herein preferred."

Though Williams was relatively unknown in international circles, his charges proved embarrassing to King Leopold, who represented himself as a benevolent colonialist and had skillfully manipulated the Congo's public image to encourage investment in the region. The irate accusations of a black American who claimed to have witnessed unspeakable horrors in what had up to now been portrayed as an idyllic and bountiful forest were bad for Leopold's reputation and bad for business. Williams's "Open Letter," which was reprinted in a number of international newspapers, helped to spark outrage among Western critics of imperialism and prompted some to call for American annexation of the Congo or at least the end of Leopold's rule in the territory. "I indulge the hope that when a new government shall rise upon the ruins of the old, it will be simple, not complicated; local, not European, international, not national; just, not cruel; and, casting its shield alike over black and white, trader and missionary, endure for centuries," Williams wrote optimistically. He quickly became one of the most vocal opponents of imperialism in Africa. "My cry is for *Africa for the Africans!*" he declared on several occasions, using a slogan that Marcus Garvey would popularize over a decade later.

The pressure on King Leopold, and on the United States to withdraw support from him, was sustained by an African American missionary named William Henry Sheppard. Sheppard was trained at the Hampton Institute in Virginia, a black college where he heard the pan-African scholar Edward Wilmot Blyden speak in 1882. Perhaps inspired by Blyden's address on black America's duty to Africa, Sheppard resolved to devote his life to church work, and he was ordained as a Presbyterian minister at Stillman College in Atlanta. After preaching in Atlanta and in Montgomery, Alabama, Sheppard became discouraged by Southern racism, and requested assignment to an African mission. Loath to place a black man in charge of an entire missionary outpost in Africa, the Presbyterian Church paired him with a white missionary, Samuel Norvell Lapsley, and the two departed for Africa in 1890.

Sheppard and Lapsley established a mission at Luebo in the Kasai region of the Congo Free State, but the white missionary, who was prone to illness, died in 1892. After his death, Sheppard moved the mission from Luebo to Bakubaland, a fabled kingdom in the Congolese interior that had apparently never before been visited by outsiders because all routes to it were closely guarded secrets. Allegedly gaining access to the Bukuba domain by secretly following a guide sent ahead on the pretext of collecting eggs, Sheppard was eventually welcomed by the Kuba king. His facility with the language, which he had learned from Kuba travelers, and his dark-skinned appearance were said to have led some Kuba courtiers to greet him as a reincarnated Kuba prince. Sheppard quickly made himself at home among the Kuba, and even enjoyed some missionary success, primarily earning converts among slaves he purchased and freed. Though more white missionaries were later sent to supervise him, Sheppard remained a focal point of the mission, and was well respected by the local Africans.

In 1900, Sheppard began to report atrocities he attributed to African forces in King Leopold's employ. He claimed to have witnessed the destruction of villages, mass killings, widespread pillaging, and even cannibalism, and the infamous severed hands that came to symbolize the Congo Free State's brutality—all crimes perpetrated in the name of Belgian rubber production. When confirmed, Sheppard's reports led to a political outcry in the United States and Britain. Prompted by them, British critics of Belgian imperialism founded the Congo Reform Association in 1904, an organization created to pressure King Leopold to institute reforms. Sheppard himself became active in the American branch of the society, calling attention to such Belgian practices as the use of slave labor on rubber plantations, the massacre and mutilation of local villagers, and the wanton devastation of entire communities.

In addition to attracting international scrutiny to Belgian activities in Congo, the American Congo Reform Association (ACRA) gained the support of Booker T. Washington. After being contacted by the ACRA, Washington pledged to help "in calling the attention of the country to the awful conditions prevailing in the Congo." He took a firm stance against Belgian imperialism in an article published in 1904, writing that "wherever the white man has put his foot in the Congo State the black man has been degraded into a mere tool in the great business of getting rubber." Washington also made appearances in 1905 and 1906 (sometimes joined by anti-imperialist agitator Mark Twain) calling for reform in the Congo and urging Americans, and blacks especially, to join in condemning King Leopold. "The oppression of the colored race in any one part of the world means, sooner or later, the oppression of the same race elsewhere," he warned. The mounting pressure earned King Leopold the U.S. government's censure and helped to prompt the Belgian Chamber and Senate to wrest control of the colony from King Leopold in 1908.

Though Leopold's legal claim to the Congo had ended, in 1909 Sheppard and another missionary who had criticized Belgian rule there were sued for libel by the king. Attempting to salvage some credibility after the international scandal produced by Williams and Sheppard's exposés, the Belgians tried to refute Sheppard's accusations in court. Sheppard had written of "armed sentries of chartered trading companies who force the men and women to spend most of their days and nights in the forest making rubber, and the price they receive is so meager they cannot live upon it," charges that Leopold denied. Despite the protests of Leopold's legal team, they were unable to disprove the ministers' allegations, and the charges were dismissed. It was a final victory for Sheppard, who retired from missionary service in 1910.

After all the damage done by Williams and Sheppard, Belgian colonial authorities were understandably wary of black American activities in the Belgian Congo. And though their concern about the influence of black American ideas on the Congolese often seemed overstated, there did seem to be some basis for uneasiness. In 1920 the Belgian vice governor general worriedly informed his superiors at home that he had heard reports of a black American who was distributing incendiary documents among educated Congolese. The man in question was a clerk named Wilson, and the document in question was a letter proclaiming the foundation of "the Black Star Line Limited," a black-owned, New York–based steamship company that Wilson said would bring black Americans to Africa and help liberate the continent. Wilson, a black American working in Congo, was supposedly the head of a black American organization in Kinshasa that followed the teachings of Marcus Garvey and circulated copies of the *Negro World* amongst the locals.

The Belgian colonial administration was anxious enough about the specter of a black American–led plot to overthrow Belgian colonial authority—an idea that became more and more popular in Congo as rumors of Garvey's plan spread among Africans—that in 1921 it was recommended that black Americans not be allowed into the Congo at all. As a sort of compromise, after 1921, all Congo visas issued to black Americans had to be screened and approved by Belgian intelligence authorities.

As an additional precaution, Wilson, the black American thought to be Garvey's local representative, was expelled from the colony. However, Belgian authorities continued to uncover copies of the *Negro World* in Kinshasa, and Garveyist ideas continued to make their way into remote areas: even when black Americans were physically barred, their ideological influence still caused political problems for the Belgian colonial administration. Local political movements arose that seemed deeply inspired by Garvey's rhetoric. Paul Panda Farnana, a Congolese educated in Belgium, was apparently spurred by Garvey's teachings when he founded the Union Congolais de Bruxelles and began to agitate for African self-rule. Similarly, Andre Yengo, another early Congolese leader, may have had contact with Garveyists prior to establishing his "Congomen" organization, which advocated armed rebellion against Belgian control and sought to create a black church, much like the UNIA. And, most explosively, Garvey's ideas seem to have informed the religiously based anticolonial struggle of the charismatic Kongo prophet Simon Kimbangu.

Kimbangu spent some time working in Kinshasa before he returned to his village and began the religious revival that challenged Belgian authority in 1921, and he is thought to have come into contact with Garvey's writings and perhaps even black American Garveyists while in Kinshasa. The essence of his movement was religious in nature; he first earned followers as a spiritual healer and prophet who sampled from Protestantism and traditional Kongo beliefs. But as his struggle intensified and became more political in outlook, it seemed to draw significantly on Garveyist ideas. Like Garvey, Kimbangu sought to create a religion that was in tune with Africans' spiritual needs and cultural background, and he foretold the imminent defeat of white imperialism. The red, black, and green of the UNIA became the colors of Kimbangu's emblem, and he echoed Garvey's pronouncement that blacks in the Americas would redeem Africa, a notion espoused in a Kimbanguist hymn:

> *If the king of the Americans comes*
> *To restore the King,*
> *The chiefs of this world shall pass away.*

If the King of Americans comes,
The troubles of this world shall pass away.
If the King of Americans comes,
The King of the blacks will return.

Kimbangu's campaign was cut short by his capture and imprisonment in 1921, and during his trial he admitted to having communicated with and been influenced by an unnamed black American. Though the threat of Kimbanguism was contained by his incarceration for life, Belgian authorities were alarmed by his admission of black American inspiration. In response, they again resolved to crack down on black Americans in Congo and to prevent the entry of others. And they also attempted to discredit and disrupt the Pan-African Congress scheduled to take place in Brussels in September 1921, to them an extension of the same "subversive" forces at work in Congo. The conference was organized by W.E.B. Du Bois, who had long had an adversarial relationship with Garvey, and Blaise Diagne, a Senegalese *évolué* (assimilated Frenchman) who had bitterly criticized Garvey. Nonetheless, the Belgian Ministry of colonies was convinced that Garvey was behind not only the congress but also anti-Belgian activity in Congo, and it vented its hostility in attacks in the press accusing conference participants of being Communists and Garveyists and through bureaucratic harassment and pressure. The tension further strained the congress's already shaky unity, and the Third Pan-African Congress suffered from an inability to reach a consensus on a number of topics, including the UNIA.

The Pan-African Congress of 1921 was the third in a tradition of international conferences that had begun in 1900 (the second was held in Paris in 1919), forums in which Africans and blacks from the diaspora agitated for colonial reform and sought to strengthen pan-African political ties. W.E.B. Du Bois had helped to organize the first three, but by the fourth congress, in 1927, Africans had begun to enjoy a more prominent role. By 1945, when a fifth Pan-African Congress was held in Manchester, England, the event was dominated by Africans, signaling a shift in the dynamics of pan-African political cooperation. During the 1920s and '30s, black American involvement in Congolese politics waned in the face of Belgian obstacles discouraging American blacks from having contact with Congolese, but African Americans continued to express political solidarity and support for African struggles at large. African American newspapers like the *Pittsburgh Courier*, the *Chicago Defender*, *The Crisis*, and New

York's *Amsterdam News* devoted considerable coverage to Africa and the Caribbean, and exchanged information and views with journals in London, Johannesburg, and Lagos. In the wake of the UNIA's pioneering efforts, African American organizations took on an international outlook, seeing black Americans as part of a larger nonwhite world community of oppressed people. And the Italian invasion of Ethiopia in 1935 became a cause célèbre for millions of African Americans who rushed to support the Ethiopian struggle against imperialism morally, politically, financially, and even militarily, as black Americans volunteered to fight in Africa's defense.

The Council on African Affairs (first formed in 1937 as the International Committee on African Affairs and reorganized as the CAA in 1942) became the African American organization at the forefront of campaigns against colonialism in Africa and worldwide in the 1940s. Initially led by Max Yergan, an African American activist who had worked in South Africa for many years, the organization was revitalized and acquired a more radical vision in 1942 when the incomparable Paul Robeson became its chairman. Robeson's international celebrity as a singer and actor helped to bring the CAA's message to a wider audience, and at the Council's peak thousands were attracted to its mass meetings in New York. The ubiquitous W.E.B. Du Bois, who was seemingly involved in every progressive black movement of the first half of the twentieth century, Alphaeus Hunton, Mary McLeod Bethune, and the black sociologist E. Franklin Frazier also became active members of the CAA. The Council took a leading role in efforts to mobilize African American communities in support of African political causes and drew explicit parallels between international struggles against colonialism and African American campaigns against racial discrimination in the United States. "Our fight for Negro rights here is linked inseparably with the liberation movements of the people of the Caribbean and Africa and the colonial world in general," asserted a CAA statement of the early 1940s.

The CAA served to galvanize African American support for anticolonial struggles in Nigeria, the Gold Coast, and India, coordinated food drives to help famine victims in South Africa, and attempted to force decolonization onto the agenda alongside the defeat of fascism as an objective of World War II, highlighting the hypocrisy of Western powers who claimed to be fighting for freedom but refused to free their colonies. The Council insisted that protests against oppression in Africa and America be rooted in a critique of the exploitative nature of global capitalism. At a New York rally in 1946, Robeson noted that the uranium the United States had used to build the atomic bomb was taken from the Congo, and warned that U.S. corporations were "interested in Africa for the wealth they can extract from it and from the labor of the people there. You can be sure that their ideas for the future of Africa do not include freedom." While such statements became popular among many African Americans and assured African anticolonialists of the support of American blacks, they did not win the favor of the U.S. government.

By the 1950s, with the rise of the Cold War and McCarthyism, the CAA's agenda came under severe attack from the U.S. government and mainstream African American political organizations. In 1950, Paul Robeson was stripped of his passport and labeled "un-American" because, as the government explained, he had been "extremely active in behalf of the independence for the colonial peoples of Africa," apparently an unpatriotic pastime. Du Bois was arrested and had his passport seized in 1951, and in 1952, the U.S. attorney general's office subpoenaed many of the CAA files detailing its contact with African organizations like the anti-apartheid African National Congress. In the wake of international protest at the restrictions imposed on Robeson, the State Department even allegedly attempted to discredit him by circulating a story that he had suffered a mental breakdown.

Other organizations and individuals who had been critical of U.S. policy came under similar fire. Activists of all races who spoke out against the government or in support of anticolonial struggles risked blacklisting, harassment, or imprisonment, and many were effectively silenced. In the new political climate, the culture of critique that had animated African American news coverage and activism began to give way to a banal jingoism in which American society was celebrated in opposition to Soviet communism. As more and more African American leaders and journalists began to assert that "Negroes are American" and refused to take issue with U.S. foreign policy or Western imperialism, the notion that American blacks shared any political solidarity with other oppressed groups seemed to fall from favor. While the excesses and exploitation of colonialism in the Belgian Congo and elsewhere had been denounced by African and American political organizations and newspapers in the 1940s, by the 1950s, some of the same groups and journals had abandoned all criticisms of colonialism and capitalism.

In 1954 the *Pittsburgh Courier* reported happily that the Belgian colonial authorities and mining companies were "increasing the purchasing power of the natives," improving their economic status to such a degree that they "do not desire African nationalism, unrest, Communism, industrial disturbances, or the organized crime seen elsewhere in Africa." Similarly, in 1955 the *Chicago Defender* wrote in praise of Belgian rule in the Congo, asserting that the colony was "progressing slowly without bias" and expressing relief that the "huge overland frontier in the heart of restless Africa, rich with uranium and other raw materials vitally needed by the free world" had not suffered "native unrest, terrorism, and anti-colonialism." And equally alarmingly, the *Defender* remained uncritical after quoting a Belgian official as saying, "You must understand that some of the people with whom we deal are primitive, very primitive." The Belgian went on to castigate the British for allowing Africans to attend universities, arguing that it was a mistake to burden "very primitive emotions" with "advanced political ideas." Instead of taking offense, the *Defender* reporter seemed to agree with the Belgian's assessment: the Belgian colonial government could refer with "justifiable pride to the work they are doing to raise the standards of a primitive people," the reporter concluded enthusiastically.

Though by the 1950s Congolese and other colonized Africans could not expect mainstream African American organizations or newspapers to seek to defend their interests (or even to disseminate accurate information on Africa's internal conditions), African American political solidarity with Africa continued to find expression in nonmainstream organizations that dared to criticize Western imperialism. The Nation of Islam, a religious group formed in the 1930s, became one of the leading sources of African American denunciations of colonialism and calls for pan-African unity; though primarily a spiritual institution, the NOI's anti-U.S. political orientation made it a space in which dissent could be openly articulated in the confrontational terms that made the Nation famous and exceptionally popular among many disenchanted African Americans.

There were limits to the NOI's willingness to take on a political role, but a dynamic young minister named Malcolm X managed to make a radical political discourse a central part of the Nation's program. In the mid-1950s, after emerging from a stint in prison during which he converted to Islam and became politicized by his voracious reading of history, Malcolm X rose through the ranks of the Nation of Islam leadership and established a reputation for firebrand oratory and uncompromising condemnations of white supremacy. In 1954, he spoke supportively of the Mau Mau uprising in Kenya, and by 1958, he had already made the acquaintance of one of the decade's most prominent pan-Africanists when he and other Harlem leaders hosted a reception for Kwame Nkrumah, the Ghanaian prime minister. In 1959, Malcolm X made his first trip to Africa and the Middle East, where he established contacts with African leaders that he would later reinforce, cultivating pan-African alliances that enabled him to become much closer to African struggles for liberation than many other black American leaders of the 1960s.

One of the African leaders that Malcolm X came to admire was Patrice Lumumba, who became an icon of the African anticolonial struggle for many blacks in America.

Lumumba earned much of his popularity among black Americans on a coalition-building trip to the United States in July 1960, a visit on which he also asked the U.S. government for economic aid. Speaking at Howard University, the young leader paid tribute to black American accomplishments, describing them as an inspiration to Africans. "Africans built America," he told his black American audience in Washington. "They are the reason America has become a great world power. If Africans can achieve that in the new world, they can achieve it in their own continent." After Lumumba's address in Washington, he spoke at Reverend and Congressman Adam Clayton Powell's Abyssinian Baptist Church in Harlem, another forum for pan-African exchange in the 1960s. And following his remarks there, Lumumba attended a meeting of African, Arab, and Asian leaders hosted by Malcolm X and the Nation of Islam. It was the only instance in which Lumumba and Malcolm X, two titans of international black struggles for equality and freedom, had occasion to meet, and the new friendship was noted with alarm by the U.S. intelligence establishment.

At the time Malcolm X was forging contacts with other African leaders as well. Later in 1960, some months after his meeting with Lumumba, Malcolm X led delegations of Muslims to New York airports to welcome Kenneth Kaunda of Zambia and Sekou Touré of Guinea, who were arriving in New York for the UN General Assembly. And soon afterwards Malcolm X spoke at a rally in Harlem alongside Kwame Nkrumah, a former Harlem resident, who addressed the crowd warmly. "The 20 million Americans of African ancestry constitute the strongest link between the people of North America and the people of Africa," Nkrumah told the excited audience. "I am informed that black American leaders are beginning to grasp the tremendous advantage that is conferred on the United States by their presence in this country." Lumumba had been expected to address the rally as well, and some listeners waved signs saying "Welcome Lumumba!" although the Congolese leader never materialized. He had hoped to be in attendance at the United Nations when Congo's independence was formally recognized, but while so many African leaders were meeting in America, Lumumba was in Congo under house arrest, the victim of a conspiracy conceived by the United States and enabled by the U.N.

When news of Lumumba's murder finally spread in February 1961, a month after it actually took place, his international supporters raised a tremendous outcry, with rioters attacking U.S., British, French, and Belgian embassies and consulates all over the world. A number of African American organizations, including the United African Nationalist Movement and the Liberation Committee for Africa, sponsored marches in New York City, and hundreds of demonstrators interrupted a Security Council session, angrily blaming the United States, the U.N., and Congolese traitors for Lumumba's murder. African American protestors also vented their frustration by pelting Belgian diplomats with eggs in Washington, D.C., and other black activists laid Lumumba to rest at a symbolic funeral in Harlem.

James Baldwin described the murder as "surely among the most sinister of recent events." And as the situation in Congo deteriorated, with the superpowers jockeying for position in the region and U.N. troops seemingly doing little to restore order, Malcolm X drew a parallel between imperialism there and Jim Crow in the American South. "You cannot understand what is going on in Mississippi if you don't understand what is going on in the Congo," he said. "The same schemes are at work in the Congo that are at work in Mississippi. The same stake, no difference whatsoever."

Most of the details on the plot to kill Lumumba and the role of the CIA and Congolese turncoats like Moise Tshombe did not become public until some years after the murder. And in the United States the only newspaper that carried the complete sordid account of the affair when the story broke in 1964 was *Muhammad Speaks*, the Nation of Islam's official journal. In the 1960s, the paper became one of the African American community's greatest sources of critiques of U.S. policy and information on Africa. Though the United States would deny that it had had any involvement in the death of Patrice Lumumba, the efforts of leaders like Malcolm X and information outlets like *Muhammad Speaks* helped to keep the fate of the Congolese people at the forefront of the African American consciousness at a time when many mainstream black organizations were silent on African issues.

In addition to seeing African American communities passionately support the cause of freedom in the Congo, the 1960s also saw African leaders of independent countries taking a new interest in African American political struggles. With the emergence of so many new independent African nations in the 1960s, Africans who wielded power at home for the first time could begin to offer political support to black campaigns in America. By the mid-1960s, when a majority of African countries had already become independent, a number of African governments moved to at least verbally champion black American efforts to secure full civil rights and equality.

In 1960 a Nigerian government official attending a conference in Philadelphia declared, "The interests of twenty million American Negroes are entwined with those of two hundred million kith and kin in Africa," setting the tone for a decade of unprecedented active African engagement in black American concerns. In 1963 African leaders assembled for a pan-African summit in Addis Ababa roundly condemned the police beatings of peaceful civil rights demonstrators and the killing of four little girls in the bombing of a church in Birmingham, Alabama, earlier that year. The conference participants endorsed a resolution asserting "the deep concern aroused in all African peoples and governments by the measures of racial discrimination taken against communities of African origin living outside the continent and particularly in the United States."

The widely publicized unrest in Alabama also led Ugandan president Milton Obote to write an official letter of complaint to U.S. president John F. Kennedy in which he referred to embattled black Americans as "our kith and kin." Similarly, at an Organization of African Unity meeting in Cairo in 1964, African leaders reiterated their opposition to "continuing manifestations of racial bigotry and racial oppression against Negro citizens of the United States." It seemed that a Nigerian diplomat was correct when he wrote that America's mistreatment of its black population and the rise of Southern violence "have been a matter of as much concern to African leadership in Africa as they have been to the American Negro directly affected here."

More than any other African American activist, Malcolm X made a point of trying to capitalize on African leaders' commitment to

African American civil rights, efforts that intensified after he was expelled from the Nation of Islam in 1964 and freed from some of the constraints of his role as an NOI minister. In April 1964, Malcolm X made his second trip to the Middle East and Africa, this time making the holy pilgrimage to Mecca. He also visited Egypt, Morocco, Algeria, Ghana, Nigeria, and Tanzania and secured the backing of various African leaders for a petition he planned to bring before the United Nations denouncing the U.S. treatment of American blacks. "The United States condemned the colonial powers of European countries, but as the leader of the Free World, it is holding back 22 million people who have to beg and crawl to be recognized as human beings," Malcolm X accused in a speech after his return from Africa. "We want to put this country on the world stage. Our goal now is the complete recognition and acceptance of the Negro as a human being by any means necessary." In the months that followed, Malcolm X continued to work even more closely with African leaders and returned to Africa again in July 1964 to attend an Organization of African Unity conference, where he again sought support for his U.N. petition.

In November 1964, American military intervention in the ongoing civil war in the Congo prompted united expressions of condemnation from Malcolm X, Dr. Martin Luther King, Jr., various other African American leaders, and the governments of Kenya, Algeria, Ghana, Chad, Tanzania, and Guinea. And in a further expression of solidarity, many African leaders delivered on promises to support Malcolm X's U.N. petition by denouncing the United States as a "colonial power" that subjugated African Americans as second-class citizens, reprimands that were obviously embarrassing for the U.S. government.

Malcolm X's ever closer ties with African leaders had made him the leading African American pan-Africanist of the period, but unfortunately we will never know to what extent his relationship with progressive African leaders of the 1960s would have continued to flourish. Malcolm X was assassinated on February 21, 1965, and one of the most promising pan-African careers was cut short in a hail of bullets. Like Lumumba, Malcolm X was murdered by rivals who almost certainly acted with the complicity of segments of the U.S. government. And by the end of the decade, a number of the African leaders who had become some of Malcolm X's closest allies had either been killed or deposed with the alleged encouragement or collusion of the CIA.

Despite the demise of Malcolm X, a loss that was deeply mourned in Africa as well as America, African interest in black American battles for equality continued through the 1960s. In 1966, African representatives at the United Nations vocally supported Julian Bond when the former SNCC official was barred from assuming his seat in the Georgia legislature because of his opposition to the Vietnam War. In 1967 U.N. delegates from Tanzania and Guinea facilitated SNCC's participation in a discussion on racism, colonialism, and apartheid held in Zambia. For the first time, a black American organization "had the opportunity to raise questions and discuss within a forum of the United Nations some aspects of our general condition in the United States," according to SNCC official James Forman.

In keeping with this sense of kinship and common cause, throughout the 1960s a number of African heads of state, including the leaders of Tanzania, Liberia, Ghana, Congo, Malawi and Dahomey, made it a national policy (at least on the rhetorical level) to welcome skilled black Americans to settle and work in their countries. (Interestingly, Mobutu, in a move reminiscent of the Belgian colonialists who had been so concerned about the possible activities of black Americans in Congo, qualified his invitation to black Americans to work in Congo by warning that they would not be welcome if they had come to "make politics.") Other leaders were less eager to encourage an African American exodus back to Africa, insisting that emigration would not solve black Americans' problems. But most African heads of state, and many of their countrymen as well, took a strong interest in the political aspirations of black Americans and worked to support them, at least verbally and symbolically.

Not only did the emergence of independent African states in the 1960s present Africans with the opportunity to offer unprecedented political assistance to black Americans, but also, with the advent of African leaders of sovereign black nations on the international stage, black Americans shared in the triumph of the African anticolonial struggles, campaigns that they had actively supported. And with the end of European political rule in many African countries, black Americans were now able to mobilize their efforts on behalf of African governments instead of against imperial powers. Black American lobbyists and organizations pressured the U.S. government to adopt policies favorable to African nations, and black American professionals were employed by the new governments, for example, Ghana's, to assist in national development. And pan-Africanist scholars, activists, journalists, and politicians continued a long and positive tradition of black American engagement in African political life.

However, sometimes the rise of black governments in Africa also complicated black American efforts to offer political support. In some instances, black Americans who had raised their voices against European colonialism seemed to become slightly disoriented. In the protest against colonialism, the objective and enemy had been clear. It was relatively easy to build a consensus among black American activists on the necessity to oppose European colonialism and to campaign for African self-rule. But with those battles largely won and new black governments taking charge all over the continent, it seemed to become more difficult for many blacks to tell good leaders from bad ones. To many, the installation in Africa of African governments was what blacks around the world had fought for. Some black Americans found themselves unwilling to heed accusations of poor governance and oppression when the alleged culprit was a black leader, regardless of what charges were leveled against him by his opponents at home.

In the 1970s, when Idi Amin Dada earned a reputation in much of the world as a ruthless totalitarian and alleged cannibal, denounced by black and white critics alike, some African American visitors to Uganda still returned home insisting that Amin was just misunderstood. In 1973, Roy Innis, the head of the Congress of Racial Equality (CORE), traveled to Uganda, supposedly to investigate allegations of Amin's brutality, but was so shielded from evidence of state repression and apparently blinded by his own defensive race pride that he ended up describing Amin as a "congenial and responsible" leader who was being targeted by the racist West.

Similarly, when Mobutu Sese Seko firmly entrenched himself in power in the 1970s, with tactics that rivaled those of Caligula, some black Americans who had been outspokenly critical of Belgian oppression in Congo became strangely mute concerning tyranny in Zaire. This refusal to criticize obvious abuses of power was perhaps best exemplified in a spectacle that embodied African American infatuation with the imagery and romance of independent black Africa and at the same time highlighted the unwillingness of many black Americans to confront political repression by some African leaders.

The 1974 "Rumble in the Jungle" between George Foreman and Muhammad Ali was a landmark in many ways, the first major international sporting event to be held in Africa, an unprecedented collaborative effort between black Americans and Africans, and, for Zaire, a "coming out" party of sorts, the decade-old nation's high-profile introduction to the world. But at a time when Mobutu, the self-declared president-for-life, was having his name written into Christian hymns in the place of God's and routinely imprisoning and murdering political opponents, it is unfortunate that the world paid more attention to the world championship boxing match than to the ongoing abuses of human rights in Zaire.

One would hope that truly progressive black activists in the diaspora would evaluate African governments with regard to their popularity at home and the nature of their relationship with the people they are supposed to serve and represent. But while many pan-African activists have indeed consistently aligned themselves with the African people against the forces of imperialism, global capitalism, and African tyranny, many others have unfortunately perpetuated a pattern of uncritical black support for African strongmen. In the political complexity of the postcolonial context, all too often black Americans who have claimed to support freedom and democracy in Africa have blindly applauded African leaders who exploit and oppress their people simply because they are black and cast themselves as black nationalists or anti-imperialists.

In the 1970s, despite the endurance of the Cold War and the hostile political climate, a number of African American grassroots organizations like the Patrice Lumumba Coalition and the African Liberation Support Committee continued to engage in African solidarity work, but they sometimes foundered in the face of the intricacies of new African political realities. Disputes between different African factions in newly independent countries often served to divide African American activists who were unsure of which side to support, as in the case of Angola, which became torn by civil war in the mid-'70s, a conflict that drove deep wedges between segments of the black American pan-Africanist community. Organizations like TransAfrica, an African American advocacy group formed in 1977, were successful in building an African American consensus against South African apartheid, a campaign in which black Americans played a leading role in the 1970s and '80s, but had much greater difficulty in trying to mobilize an African American constituency to target regimes like Zaire's.

By the 1980s, the international pan-African movement that had so explicitly linked the struggles of Africans and African Americans throughout the first half of the twentieth century, inspiring African Americans to passionately support African anticolonialism and Africans to call for African American equality, had lost much of its momentum. Small grassroots organizations denounced African dictators like Mobutu in scattered demonstrations, and African American leaders like Andrew Young attempted to encourage the United States to adopt more progressive policies toward nations like Zaire from within the government. But what was missing was the sort of dynamic mass movement that had attracted thousands to rallies in Harlem in the 1920s and '40s, and had shaken the centers of Western power in outspoken proclamations of unity and outrage in the 1960s.

Though the fight against colonialism had been largely won by the end of the 1960s, in many cases the struggle for true African freedom had only just begun. But with the seemingly widespread waning of African American and African interest in maintaining and continuing to nurture the powerful progressive pan-African alliances that had proven so effective in that decade, the movement seemed to fall into a fitful slumber. And while many black American and African leaders dozed or looked the other way, dictators like Mobutu Sese Seko presided virtually unchallenged over the pillage of their countries and the oppression of their people.

*   *   *

Despite the splintering of international black alliances and the decline in progressive activism since the 1970s, when my father was imprisoned by the Mobutu regime in December 1981, my family was able to effectively revisit the best aspects of the pan-African tradition of the 1960s by mobilizing an international network to agitate for his release. As my mother and my father's colleagues spread word of his detention, letters of sympathy poured in from all over the world. Petitions demanding his immediate freedom garnered thousands of signatures and read like who's who lists of Africanist academics and pan-African activists. Organizations as far flung as the Association of the African Community in Jamaica, the New Jersey–based Committee of Concerned Africans, the Steering Committee of Africanists in the Netherlands, an association of lecturers at the University of Dakar, Senegal, and the Australian *New Africa News* journal all issued statements protesting my father's arrest. Newsletters circulated by the Free Wamba Campaign celebrated the international clamor as "a spirit of protest" and lauded its impact: "The 'new spirit' . . . is worldwide," the newsletter asserted proudly. "It unites students, teachers, and workers from all walks of life, and it is becoming organized. And it proclaims: WE SHALL NOT TOLERATE THE VIOLATION OF FUNDAMENTAL HUMAN RIGHTS."

But while my father survived a Zairean prison with the help of hundreds of relatives, friends, and colleagues, we knew that the furor raised on his behalf would do little to change conditions in Zaire itself. The urgency of his situation had galvanized an international community and spurred it to act, but it would take much more than petitions and letter-writing campaigns to end the oppression in Zaire. Some time after my father was released, my mother's sister in the United States told us how she had watched her TV with disgust while Mobutu was being warmly received at the White House. Reagan had smiled and embraced his African ally like an old friend. The Free Wamba Campaign had made itself heard and won my father's freedom by generating enough pressure to make the Mobutu regime take momentary note. But now it was business as usual for the leopard skin–hatted despot, whose authoritarian rule in Zaire would continue to endure for more than a decade.

Home safe in Dar es Salaam, my father began to recover from his traumatic experience, resuming his teaching at the university and trying to respond to all of the letters of concern and congratulations that had awaited him on his return. His imprisonment had not silenced him, and he continued his outspoken criticism of Mobutu—far from feeling intimidated, if anything, he was even more determined to remain engaged in the cause of Zairean freedom after such an intimate taste of tyranny. It was several years before my father felt that he could safely return to Zaire, but after missing his father's funeral in 1987— something he always deeply regretted—he felt compelled to make a cautious trip back to see his aging mother, a journey that was mercifully without incident. As the Mobutu regime's power began to slowly unravel in the early 1990s, my father was able to visit relatives and to participate in conferences surrounding the political reform that Mobutu was finally forced to implement, but he often did so with a sense of uncertainty and trepidation, an uneasiness that was shared by my family. We had no way of knowing it in 1982, but my father's detention would not be the last time he came into such direct confrontation with a dictatorial regime.

Although I was thrilled and relieved to have my father safely back among us, my family's brush with Zairean authoritarianism left me feeling somewhat disillusioned and cynical. I resented the power of tyrants like Mobutu to imprison or even kill people seemingly on a whim, and I despaired of ever being rid of such villains. But the experience underlined the imperative of action to rectify the political crisis gripping African countries like Zaire, and in the wake of my father's return from the year in which he was forced to remain in Kinshasa, I began to wonder how I, too, could make a contribution to the struggle for freedom in Africa. Of course, at the time I had barely completed primary school, but in the years that followed I took an intense interest in African history and politics, and felt inspired by the courage and conviction of African freedom fighters who waged the continent's wars of liberation. But I was never really able to shake a sense of bitterness and betrayal. I would carry it with me through my high school years and back to the land of my birth.

In the White Man's Country

Shall I sing your song, Africa,
In this strange land of hate and love?
—Akinsola Akiwowo,
"Song in a Strange Land" (1951)

When my father first arrived to study in the United States in 1964, he was a little overwhelmed. At twenty-two, he had barely ever left his rural province, much less his country and continent. He had heard stories about the United States from a Congolese colleague and mentor who had studied there, and from an American teacher who had taught him mathematics at his Swedish mission secondary school. And a friend had provided him with the addresses of some acquaintances who might be helpful. His expectations were minimal: to get a college diploma and return to Congo to teach secondary school. But he immediately realized that there was much he would have to learn and experience before he could achieve his objective.

Having scored well in Congo's national exams, my father had become eligible for one of three scholarships to study in the United States offered by the African-American Institute, a New York–based foundation involved in African development work. The American psychologist who interviewed each of the scholarship candidates had been surprised that he wanted to pursue a career as a high school teacher; she said his strong results suggested that he could eventually excel in teaching at the university level. My father hadn't really ever considered teaching college as a possibility. He had always been encouraged by his parents to take his studies as far as he could, but he hadn't really had much of an idea of how far that could mean.

As a student in Congo, my father gathered his first impressions of the United States from stories told by travelers and foreigners. One early source of information about America was a doctor who worked at a medical center near my father's village. Dr. Washington, the first African American he ever met, treated my father's mother for diabetes, and my father enjoyed talking to him about life in America. Dr. Washington told him about racism in the United States and said that the white missionaries who came to him for treatment in Congo would never do so in America. When President John F. Kennedy was assassinated in 1963, Dr. Washington spoke at my father's school, attempting to put the crisis in context for his African audience. And Dr. Washington sometimes asked about the possible roots of African American words and cultural traits. My father told him that his family was probably descended from Bakongo, because Dr. Washington said he had a relative named Ngouba, which meant peanut ("Goobers," Dr. Washington noted) in Kikongo. Though the doctor didn't always make America sound like the best place for a black man, his stories about his country, and the tales of America's abundance and opportunities that circulated among my father's friends, made my father look forward to going there. And his relationship with the doctor made him eager and curious to meet more African Americans.

My father's first stop in the United States was Sandanona, Vermont, to study English for five months at the Experiment for International Living, a school for foreigners about to attend American colleges and Americans about to head overseas to work abroad. He found English a bit difficult at first, but could soon communicate adequately. He had ample opportunity to practice, as the school assigned him a white host family in Keene, New Hampshire, who coached him in the nuances of American language and culture. The family was very friendly and welcoming, but the wife had a tendency to ask very probing questions that sometimes made him uncomfortable. He learned much later that she had been working on a master's thesis on Ralph Ellison's *Invisible Man* and the black psyche. My father couldn't help but wonder if her inordinate interest in him stemmed from his usefulness as a research subject. And though most of the people he met in Vermont and New Hampshire were very amicable and polite, he was struck by American ignorance of world geography and Africa. He once told a woman in Keene that he was from Congo and she asked if he knew her daughter, who lived in Freetown, Sierra Leone. And another American he spoke to couldn't remember whether Congo was in South America or Asia.

His early experiences with African Americans, of whom there were few in Vermont and New Hampshire, were usually more encouraging. He contacted black American friends in New York whose addresses he had been given by his colleague in Congo, and he visited them as often as he could. A black American named Blanche Bailey, a politically conscious woman with a pan-African outlook, was especially helpful and kind, and made an effort to introduce him to America. He became quite close to her and her family in the Bronx, and his positive relationship with them helped to compensate for the few disappointing experiences he had with black Americans who assumed that Africans were "uncivilized" and backward.

He found another black American friend in his roommate at Western Michigan University. To my father the young black man who greeted him at the dormitory looked huge. Though my father's roommate was younger, he towered over my father, and soon took to affectionately calling his new African companion "kid." My father made more friends among the black American students, and also became close to the several other African students at WMU. Though he sometimes felt ignored or ostracized by some black Americans in social contexts (he spent a few uncomfortable evenings as a wallflower watching others dance at some black parties), he was more successful on an organizational and intellectual level. In fact, at WMU my father began to create a network of pan-African contacts that he would maintain for decades to come.

Often these links were established through his involvement in campus politics and activism. At one point during his undergraduate career he was the vice president of the African Student Association (which, among other activities, found itself having to mediate between Yoruba and Ibo students estranged by the civil war in Nigeria). And he was an active member of the U.S. chapter of the General Union of Congolese Students and of the student group BAM. Also, through Blanche Bailey and others, he was connected to a large pan-Africanist community in New York.

My father's role in a number of black student protests was a highlight of his years at WMU, but the most significant pan-African alliance he established in America was obviously his marriage to my mother. If my father had few expectations when he left his home in Congo to attend an American university, he certainly did not anticipate that he would meet and fall in love with a black American woman. In spite of some misunderstandings and miscues, not only did my father forge long-term friendships and working relationships with members of the black American community, he married into it. His journey to America changed the course of his life.

In early 1987, after seven years of schooling in Tanzania, I prepared to graduate from the eleventh grade. The International School of Tanganyika "upper" school, where my mother taught and where I had been a student since the sixth grade, followed the British educational system, and my classmates and I would take University of London "Ordinary level" exams in June. After O-levels, most IST students would go on to do the school's two-year International Baccalaureate program, or leave Dar es Salaam to continue their education elsewhere.

I had done well in high school. Although I had always struggled with math and physics, I was especially strong in English and history, and my parents encouraged me to continue my studies in these subjects. I was not immediately eager to leave Tanzania, and I thought of enrolling in the University of Dar es Salaam to study history or political science. But my father was well aware of the university's troubles with facilities shortages and frequent closures, and he and my mother advised me to take advantage of my American citizenship and avail myself of the ample educational opportunities the United States had to offer. Although I had come to regard Dar es Salaam as my home and would leave behind many friends, I decided to repeat my father's journey from Africa to America for further education.

As my graduation from IST approached, an English teacher who had been one of my favorite instructors suggested a school she thought would be good for me. Miss Archer, an Englishwoman, had taught at an international school in Singapore before coming to Tanzania. The school where she had taught was a member of a worldwide educational system called the United World Colleges (UWC), two-year upper-level pre-university secondary schools around the world that offered internationally oriented education to students interested in world affairs. At the time that I applied there were seven UWC campuses worldwide, each offering rigorous academic study balanced with a commitment to community service and the promotion of "international understanding."

In high school I had become a prodigious reader of history. I had participated in student United Nations conferences and gained an understanding of the world's political workings, and I had considered becoming somehow involved in African politics and development.

The UWC seemed an ideal next step towards my vaguely defined professional ambitions, so I prepared an application to the Armand Hammer United World College of the American West in Montezuma, New Mexico, and some months later excitedly received word of my acceptance with a generous financial aid package. I was saddened by the prospect of leaving Tanzania, but I looked forward to continuing my education elsewhere and to the adventures that I was sure awaited me in the somewhat alien land of my birth, the United States of America.

On the eve of my departure, family friends and well-wishers gathered around, presenting gifts and solemn advice. Aunt Edie offered an old typewriter and made me promise to write my mother. Uncle Jan, swallowing my hand in his muscular paw and flexing mightily, volunteered some typically hard-nosed hints: "Don't be afraid of confrontation," he counseled gruffly from under his thick moustache. "It simply means people have taken notice of you. Antagonism is better than fading into the background like some bland peanut-butter man." And Mzee Robeson, an elderly black American man who had probably said ten words to me in the entire time I had known him, proffered a message of ominous intensity. "Be careful over there," he said, shaking my hand and looking me in the eye. "It's a jungle." I laughed nervously, but he did not smile.

I wondered if there was more to this gathering than my triumphant send-off to college. Perhaps there was a reason why my mother's black American friends transplanted to Tanzania greeted the news of my scholarship and imminent migration to the United States with a pride tempered by concern. I thought I saw an unspoken reticence expressed in the anxious eyes that scrutinized me, maybe assessing my readiness for an ordeal they sensed ahead. My father's African colleagues had congratulated me with offhand ease, asking what I planned to study, joking about the "brain drain" and the winters I would suffer, while my own Tanzanian friends made obvious their envy, referring longingly in exalted terms to my journey *majuu* (up there). While it was evident that my "relations" who gathered to see me off shared in my parents' pride, they also seemed interested in preparing me for reentry into a world they knew all too well. A world they had chosen to leave. Perhaps the same misgivings that had prompted their departure from America now inspired their uneasiness as I made my return there. I was about to reverse the middle passage they had made years earlier, a voyage many of them must have viewed as deliverance.

Of course, I was too giddy to seriously consider any of this as I prepared to leave my family, friends, and adopted home. At the airport my mother cried tears of apprehension and pride, but I felt a strange elation as I waited to board my flight overseas, an excitedly oblivious lightheadedness that must have inoculated me against the emotion of the situation. When I hugged my mother and noticed her tears, I laughed and told her not to cry, I would be fine. I joked with my brothers and the friends who had accompanied me to the airport, and when it was time to go I walked toward the departure gate waving cheerfully, my backpack slung jauntily over one shoulder. I was sixteen and blissfully bereft of the understanding that that moment signified the end of my childhood. It was only years later, when I next returned home, mature, jaded, and much more experienced, that I realized that my life would never be the same again, that I could never go back to the joyful simplicity of being a child in my parents' house.

The Armand Hammer United World College was isolated in the mountains of northern New Mexico, in a small community called Montezuma, seven miles from the town of Las Vegas, NM. Students were selected to attend the college by national committees in seventy-five different countries; they spoke dozens of languages and were united in an idealistic wish to change the world.

In the first week, as students arrived from all over the world, they milled around the campus introducing themselves and stating their countries of origin; I was often at a loss for what to say, short of embarking on an extended narration of my family's journeys from country to country. Still, I quickly warmed to the friendly openness of this unlikely community of international teenagers marooned in the wilds of the southwestern United States.

The academic curriculum consisted of a challenging six-course program that allowed students to sample from a broad palette of disciplines, offered at "higher" or "subsidiary" levels. My higher-level subjects were English, history, biology, and art; I took math and French at the subsidiary level. Classes were international in outlook, covering material from around the world, and extracurricular activities often had a similar emphasis. Students attended and participated in weekly "coffee table" discussions devoted to contemporary political topics, and every Monday at "World Affairs" invited dignitaries would speak on various international issues.

Academics was complemented by community service; students would venture into local neighborhoods of nearby Las Vegas to visit the elderly or mentally ill, or work in children's recreational programs. All of us were required to do community service work, and a general desire to make the world a better place was among the college's guiding principles. Behind the scenes, the United World College was less high-minded, and though most students seemed to take the goal of "international understanding" to heart, they weren't really much different from other teenagers. After hours, students smuggled alcohol into their rooms for impromptu late-night drinking sessions, and weekend nights were often celebrated with loud sweaty dances in the campus center. The college's infamous Guideline 4, which technically prohibited sex between students, was probably fractured on a nightly basis. And while everyone complained about academic pressure, most people could be persuaded to put off study in favor of midnight dips in the nearby hot springs.

The United World College was a very close and comfortable little community, where many lifelong friendships were forged and many students identified lifelong intellectual passions. It was easy to forget that our idyllic microcosm bore little resemblance to the "real" world outside. But as an insulated two-hundred-member family in which students felt safe and at home, the College provided students with the freedom and support to explore our ideas and identities among like-minded peers. For many of its students, the school was to become a cocoon in which political convictions and personal ambitions and ideas were first explored and solidified. And for me, it became an experience in internationalism on one level and pan-Africanism on another.

There were about thirty African students at the college, fewer than ten West Indians, and only a couple of African Americans. And, seemingly from day one, the black students formed a large, visible campus clique. Early on we formed an unofficial "African" table in the dining hall, and on some evenings we would meet to discuss African politics, nostalgically cooking and consuming huge African meals at the house of a teacher from Barbados, the college's only black faculty member. Though in general everyone at the college got along, and though smaller, multinational circles of friends did exist, students from Latin America, Americans, and Europeans all formed their own large continental cliques as well. For us Africans it seemed somehow natural to want to gather with those with whom we felt we had the most in common. We would trade stories about our homelands, celebrating the similarities we found between different African cultures and jokingly ridiculing the differences. We would speak African languages with those with whom we shared them (the only other Kiswahili speaker in my year was a Kenyan named Peter), and share "culture shock" anecdotes about our sometimes confounding experiences in America with listeners who we felt would understand. The African Americans and West Indians who attended these parties did not always have as much sense of cultural commonality, but they seemed to feel their place was with us anyway.

In America, the stench of racial prejudice is often overpowering, and experiences with American racism in the nearby community of Las Vegas, New Mexico, went a long way toward strengthening racial solidarity among the black students at the United World College. Sometimes trips into town would make the college feel like an oasis of social tolerance in a forbidding desert of bigotry. A town of ten thousand mainly working-class and middle-class whites and Hispanics, Las Vegas was where all the students went to shop for basic necessities, to do community service, to have dinner at one of the handful of restaurants, or to catch a movie at the single theater. UWC students could expect friendliness from the majority of town dwellers, who were generally good-natured and appreciated our community service efforts, but a few were sometimes hostile. And black students who visited the town would sometimes hear racial epithets or experience other manifestations of racism.

A mere week after I arrived in New Mexico, two new friends—a West Indian and an African—and I ventured into Las Vegas to do some shopping. We had made our purchases and were waiting outside a store for the campus school bus to pick us up when a group of guys in a passing car launched some empty beer cans at us and leered out the windows, their faces made ugly with anger. "Niggers!" they yelled, as the car careened past. We numbly watched it go. It was not the first time that word had been hurled my way. And though my companions might have been more used to hearing equivalent insults in different languages, the shout and its meaning were all too familiar. Barely seven days on American soil, and the three of us, from Dar es Salaam, Curaçao, and Nairobi respectively, had already been quickly unified by that one bitter, all-important jeer of welcome.

On another occasion, an African American friend and I were walking down a Las Vegas sidewalk in a residential neighborhood when we saw a figure watching us through the screen door of a house we were passing. Without a word, the silhouette reached out an arm and opened the door. A huge German shepherd bounded out of the house, leaping toward us and growling menacingly. We didn't stick around to see if the enraged dog would be able to jump the fence that separated us. As we ran, through the barking I thought I heard taunting laughter chasing behind us.

One of the community service projects I worked on at the college involved coaching a soccer team of children from Las Vegas. Two Africans, my friend Michael from Curaçao, and I coached fifth-graders in soccer basics; we established a good rapport with most of the kids. But some of them happily referred to us as "niggers" and seemed genuinely taken aback when we explained that this was unacceptable. While some seemed titillated by the term's obvious transgressive emotional power, others seemed puzzled that we would take offense. After all, it was the word some of their parents had used when the kids had pointed out their coaches after practice.

In addition to experiences like these, I heard many similar stories from often bewildered African students. I had, of course, experienced this sort of abuse before (although it was a distant memory after seven years in Tanzania), but for many of the Africans at the college, some of whom had never had extensive contact with whites, crude racial attitudes were a novelty. Whether racism was familiar or not, however, I think experiences with it served to pull our campus clique closer together. A bond usually develops between people who feel that they are under siege, and though we all felt comfortable among our peers on campus (even if some white students who had never before met black people curiously asked to touch our hair), the apparent hostility of America at large highlighted the importance of supporting one another.

Brushes with American racism also served to further politicize us. Perhaps we felt that if we could do little to confront the racial attitudes that seemed to run rampant in Las Vegas, maybe we could at least address racial issues on campus. When the Red Cross organized a campus blood drive from which all sub-Saharan Africans were excluded because of the alleged preponderance in Africa of a strain of AIDS that was not detectable by standard tests, some African students countered by calling for a student boycott of the drive. We eventually met with a Red Cross representative and presented our complaints, arguing that a general ban on sub-Saharan blood stigmatized Africans as "AIDS carriers." We wrote a list of probing questions to the United Nations health office that had supposedly recommended the policy, but we never received a reply. In the end it was a partial victory, because while the blood drive was still held with the policy unchanged, we brought our feelings on the issue to the attention of the student body, who were widely supportive.

In addition to protesting what we felt was the possible racism of the Red Cross, African students led the local anti-apartheid movement. We raised consciousness in Las Vegas through rallies and cultural performances; a South African student taught us the miners' "gumboot" dance, a perennial favorite among anti-apartheid activists and African student associations. And we raised funds for a school in Tanzania for exiled South Africans with a swim-a-thon, in which swimmers sponsored by local businesses earned money by completing laps in a Las Vegas pool.

We also sought to share aspects of African culture with our peers and the locals. The college designated a "national day" for each continent, an opportunity for students to share their culture with the rest of the school and community. We approached "African National Day," a day of presentations, food, and activities celebrating African culture, as a chance to display our heritage with pride, to show our peers some of the good and bad of where we were from, and also to debunk some of the stereotypes and negative images often associated with Africa. But more than that, our African clique, which included the Caribbean and black American students, seized our day as an opportunity to reinforce the ties that bound us as Africans, to laugh together and revel in our special distinctiveness, our insidership in the pan-African club. Throughout the day we regaled our audiences with African sounds, flavors, and colorful fabrics, screened African films, and offered our fellow students the opportunity to participate in African games and dances. The day culminated in a cultural show that featured skits, dances, and songs and, a highlight for many of the participants, an elaborate "traditional" African ceremony in which all the actors spoke to each other in their own native languages, a nuance lost on some members of the audience, who assumed that we could understand each other. At the end of the show we all danced onstage to the Peter Tosh song "African," skanking to drums and bassline, and proudly singing the lyrics: "No matter where you come from, as long as you're a black man, you are an African." The entire day was well received by our audience, but I think we, the hosts, had the most fun.

We would often reflect on the irony of the fact that we had had to come to America to make friends with Africans from all over the continent and to truly understand the common threads that ran through African culture. But perhaps it was our collective sense of isolation in the land of the whites that prompted our ready transformation from an assortment of Kenyans, South Africans, Swazis, Jamaicans, Ugandans, Sierra Leoneans, Senegalese, Bahamians, Antilleans, and black Americans into a group of self-identified "Africans."

Though my time in Montezuma was largely spent in the company of Africans, on holiday trips to my mother's sister's home in Los Angeles, I explored my American side, going to movies with my cousin Chris, hanging out at the Fox Hills mall, immersing myself in the latest African American dances, fashions, slang, and music. Through my cousin and time spent with his African American friends, I was often exposed to black American views and expectations of Africans. Black popular culture of 1988 often seemed obsessed with Africa; the black nationalist rap group Public Enemy was among the most popular hip-hop acts, and Africa medallions and red-black-and-green beaded necklaces were favored fashion accessories. Nonetheless, I found that many black Americans still held stereotypical views of Africa and Africans.

When Chris introduced me as his "African cousin" Phil, surprised reactions were sometimes followed by displays of unwitting condescension. To many, my being "African" seemed to mean that I would not know how to speak English, that I had never been in a car, and that by coming to the United States I had escaped a life afflicted by war, poverty, and famine. For others, however, as an African I possessed an exotic black "authenticity" that they seemed to admire. So while one of Chris's friends spoke to me as if I were a deaf child and another disparagingly referred to me as Chris's "dark" cousin from Africa (perhaps loading all her assumptions of African backwardness onto that one word), others asked what life was like in the motherland and whether I could hook them up with some copper or elephant-hair bracelets or cowrie-shell necklaces.

I became fascinated by these seeming contradictions. Chris explained the recently renewed interest in Africa among some black people with his own historical theory. "Black people get blacker every thirty years," he said, referring to the seemingly cyclical rise and fall of pan-African sentiments in black American history. I did my own research to try to reach my own conclusions. I wrote my International Baccalaureate "extended essay" in history on the Black Panther Party and black nationalism of the 1960s, interviewing a few former Panthers, including my mother's sister Anne, and reading extensively in African American politics and history. I was impressed by the Panthers' strong identification with African political struggles and the movement's African icons and imagery: in one memorable photograph, Huey Newton, the Panther chairman, was seated proudly in a regal African chair, a shotgun in one hand and a spear in the other. I shared some of my findings with my schoolmates at a "coffee table" discussion on race in America, and I learned much about my own heritage as an African American and the history of pan-Africanism. But I still wrestled with the simultaneous preponderance of disdain and adoration for Africa among blacks in America.

As my time at the United World College began to draw to a close, I visited the campus guidance counselor to discuss plans for my future. His comments were very encouraging: he said that my grades, background, and citizenship would probably help to gain me admission to a number of universities, and with the financial assistance I would need to attend. He encouraged me to apply to Harvard and other Ivy League schools, because of their educational reputations and their ability to provide substantial financial aid packages, and because he thought I could get in. My parents supported the idea, and I prepared applications to Harvard and a number of other American colleges.

When I received word of my acceptance to Harvard University in the spring of 1989, I felt giddy with elation and pride, but a little apprehensive. How would I fare at the famously rigorous school? I wondered. Why had they accepted me, anyway? And even though I had been awarded a large scholarship and was eligible for student loans, I knew that the relatively small contribution my parents were expected to make would still pose problems. They earned their salaries, tiny by American standards, entirely in Tanzanian shillings, a soft currency that consistently lost ground against the U.S. dollar. Would we be able to afford it? Despite my concerns, my parents were delighted with the news of my admission, and they tried to allay my fears about the cost. Somehow we would work it out. I resumed my studies, getting ready to graduate and anxiously anticipating my next imposing academic hurdle.

The remaining months of the school year crept by as students got ready for year-end exams and completed their arrangements for further study. Most would attend American universities, but some were headed for Europe and others were returning to their home countries. We would be scattering all over the world, and even while we looked forward to the graduation that would signify our successful completion of two years of demanding study, we also realized that it would mark the dispersal of a close extended clan. The graduation ceremony itself was a tearful rite of passage, the end of one era and the beginning of another. After receiving our diplomas, the new graduates assembled for a final group photo. And after the pictures were taken, stunned friends milled about, hugging and crying, as parents and graduation guests looked on, unable to understand the depth of the emotion displayed before them.

In my college recommendation my UWC history teacher wrote, "Philippe straddles the Africa of his father and the America of his mother," but I think I emerged from Montezuma with a stronger sense of what it meant to be African than American, and a strong identification with the seven formative years I had spent living in Tanzania. I had forged a family among the African, West Indian, and African American students at the United World College and had enjoyed the inclusion and belonging I had felt during African National Day, at the dinners the African students used to organize, and in the lively debates that always raged at our "African table" in the cafeteria. While my experiences with the African Americans I met in Los Angeles had often been somewhat confounding, I graduated from the UWC emotionally confident of the validity of pan-African cultural affinity. I hoped to create another campus family at my next educational destination.

My introduction to Harvard University, my home for the next four years, was on a late-summer reconnaissance trip I made alone from my father's brother's house in Lynn, Massachusetts, where I was staying until school opened. Even though I was curious and eager to look around my new school, I felt strangely nervous.

The subway from Lynn jerked to a halt with a screech of brakes and a wheeze of hot air, sighing like my mother when I had said good-bye. "Hahvahd Skweah," the tinny voice crackled over the loudspeaker. I stepped from the train and rode the escalator to the street. Gathering my courage and thoughts, I stepped onto the sidewalk, into the clear September air—too dry to remind me of home—and entered Harvard Yard through Johnston Gate ("Johnston," not "Johnson," the brochure had insisted at least three times). I took in the ivy-covered brick buildings and the statue of the university's benefactor and namesake, and surveyed the dozens of students seated on the grass in the courtyard, chatting to one another amicably, clad in khaki shorts, polo shirts, and leather boat shoes.

Refusing to publicly consult my campus map, I walked through the Yard until I quite accidentally happened upon the dormitory I had been assigned to. A fat blond guy wearing jeans and a paint-splattered T-shirt was fiddling with the door, apparently trying to fix something.

"Is this Matthews South?" I asked, interrupting him.

"Yeah, why?" he asked, looking up from his work.

"I think I've been assigned to live here," I said.

The fat guy looked me up and down with new interest. "You mean you go here?" he asked, seemingly impressed. "What did you do, get a sports scholarship?"

When I next arrived on campus, to move into my dormitory room and report for orientation, I was escorted by Congolese family members from Lynn: two uncles, an aunt, and one of my cousins. My uncles, as usual, were immaculately outfitted in pressed shirts, pleated slacks, and shiny shoes, while my aunt cut an impressive figure in a colorful African dress, complete with a towering headdress. They spoke loudly to one another in French and Kikongo, and I noted with satisfaction that among the legions of parents unloading futons, TVs, and carpets from station wagons and limousines and saying good-bye to bright-eyed teenaged white kids, my family stood out in bustling Harvard Yard like an OAU delegation at a St. Patrick's Day parade.

After picking my key up from a tent in the courtyard, I led my family to my dormitory, my uncles carrying my two suitcases, while my aunt walked beside me, commenting on the buildings, the students, the parents, and anything else that caught her eye. I discovered Matthews Room 40 on the second floor and found one of my roommates already there. Andrew was taller than I, with sandy blond hair and blue eyes. He wore khaki shorts, a faded red T-shirt, and boat shoes. "Hi," he said.

"Hi," I answered, and introduced him to my family. I took my suitcases into one of the bedrooms, the one in which he hadn't spread boxes, suitcases, rugs, and shopping bags in a mountain of wealth that made my own two suitcases seem somehow inadequate. After I had gotten myself settled in my new room, my family said their good-byes and told me to visit them every weekend. When they left I felt very lonely, but tried not to show it as I made small talk with Andrew. He was from a town just an hour or so from Boston, so he knew the area well. He had never heard of Tanzania before, but when he had learned where his new roommate was from, he had done a little research; he had expected me to have an English accent, on account of having been colonized by the British.

That evening all the students from our wing of the dorm met for an informal get-to-know-one-another session in the room of our proctor, the graduate student in charge of guiding and disciplining us.

I had decided that I liked Andrew and felt that I had been rather fortunate on the roommate front, and looked forward to meeting other potential friends. I circulated among the assembled students, shaking hands, talking, laughing. Toward the end of the evening I introduced myself to a white woman I hadn't spoken to yet. She took my hand and smiled, but I had the impression that she was nervous. She asked me where I was from, and when I replied that I had grown up in Tanzania, I was pleasantly surprised: her eyes lit up with recognition. "I have a friend who once went there," she explained. She paused. "So what's it like there?" she asked curiously. "Because the parts where my friend was weren't exactly civilized."

I was momentarily stunned into speechlessness. I tried to keep my voice neutral as I responded that I lived in Dar es Salaam, the capital city of almost two million people, and that yes, it was quite "civilized," but she looked doubtful.

In the weeks that followed, I was often exposed to such attitudes. I often found it hard not to get defensive or angry when confronted with people who seemed to wonder if I was used to wearing clothes or how I had made it out of Africa alive. I generally tried to seize opportunities to educate my new classmates, but sometimes I found myself irritated enough to yield to sarcasm ("No, we don't usually wear clothes, they gave me these at the airport") and didn't care when people found this off-putting.

To my unhappy surprise, the African American students I met were not necessarily any more interested in or informed about Africa than their white counterparts. I automatically gravitated toward the black students I met in those early weeks, and did establish some friendships that lasted throughout my college years and beyond. But sometimes the cultural distance between my upbringing in Tanzania and that of African Americans from U.S. cities and suburbs seemed an obstacle to empathy. Most black students I met seemed intrigued to meet someone who had lived in Africa, and asked a lot of questions about conditions in Tanzania. But at other times I thought I could see eyes begin to glaze over with boredom when I said where I was from.

Selecting friends and joining social circles is like shopping for commonalities, and students quickly began to be drawn toward different sets. Students from particular cities or regions of the United States tended to stick together, students who had met before through different regional or national high school organizations were usually happy to resume old friendships, and those meeting for the first time would feel each other out to assess each other's background and interests, searching for common ground.

The campus clubs and organizations made this process of self-categorization even easier. Many black students of West Indian ancestry soon established friendships with the other members of the Caribbean Students Association, and a number of black fraternities and sororities (each identified with its own social stereotypes) recruited members on campus. There were black singing groups, black theatrical troupes, black academic associations, and black literary magazines, all seeming to cater to different tastes and interests within the university's diverse black population. And in addition, many black students joined the Black Students Association (BSA), a large, all-encompassing organization that became an umbrella for all of the various cliques that made up Harvard's black community.

I attended very few BSA meetings. While it always felt good to look around an auditorium and see dozens of black people amassed in the belly of one of America's oldest and most elitist institutions of higher learning, I tended to feel somewhat socially isolated in the crush of chattering black bodies. It wasn't so much that I had nothing in common with the other BSA members—I'm sure my eight years of childhood in the Boston area provided a bevy of cultural memories I shared with other American students. It was more that the setting was unable to provide for me what it did for many of the other black students: a comfortable and familiar feeling of understanding and belonging that took the edge off their homesickness. I think I shared the interests, concerns, and perspectives of many BSA members, but at the gatherings I often felt something missing.

I was able to find a haven in the Harvard African Students Association. HASA reminded me of the group of African students I had left in New Mexico. It included maybe twenty Africans from all over the continent, some of whom, like myself, had been born in the United States or had lived there for a significant portion of their lives. HASA held African cultural events, organized conferences, and sponsored speakers who addressed African-oriented topics, but it was also a social club for Africans at Harvard. We would have regular meetings over dinner and attended parties and events sponsored by African students at other local campuses. In college I made friends among the other history and literature majors, among other members of the freshman soccer team, among residents of my dormitory, and through my various extracurricular activities and jobs (I worked my way through a dozen different positions throughout my always lean undergraduate years). But the members of HASA became almost like family.

While Africans and African Americans at Harvard certainly associated enthusiastically on a social level, HASA and the BSA often seemed to address completely separate agendas and constituencies. HASA invited a speaker to talk about the civil war in Angola and sponsored a conference on African history and civilization; few black Americans seemed interested in attending these events. BSA-sponsored functions tended to deal with celebrations of African American heritage or with aspects of race in America, and I think that HASA members seemed slightly more inclined to participate in BSA events than the other way around. But some Africans lamented that they did not often share the preoccupations of their African American counterparts.

As in New Mexico, however, experiences with racism helped to cement racial unity on campus. There were frequent reminders of the seemingly precarious position of blacks in America, examples that underlined the common interest of black people who felt targeted by racism. Though I had grown up with American racism in Waltham and West Newton and had undergone a refresher course in New Mexico, I, like many newly arrived Africans, was still a little unprepared when it came to appreciating the depth and scope of American racial attitudes.

During my sophomore year at Harvard, Boston became obsessed with a case in which a white man named Charles Stewart claimed that a black man had murdered his pregnant wife. The passions the case whipped up were palpable; the horror of the crime offended most Americans, and enraged calls for swift, vengeful justice proliferated. But unfortunately, the many voices raised in understandable fury helped to create an almost hysterical climate; the suspicion and hostility often seemed fueled by racial undertones. Just as the image of black convict Willie Horton, who during the 1988 presidential campaign leered out of Republican ads claiming that Democrats were soft on crime, had played on the fears of white Americans terrified by the prospect of victimization by black criminals, so the black apparition that Stewart conjured took fearsome shape in local white imaginations. Mrs. Stewart's killer seemed the stereotypical embodiment of all that law-abiding white folks feared: a young, violent black male with a taste for killing white people and no respect for the rule of law. And the prospect of having such a monster loose on the streets of Boston triggered the frenzy of a Salem witch-hunt or a Scottsboro lynching party. Prompted by the widespread outrage and eager to find a suspect, the city unleashed its police force in a frantic manhunt in which officers seemed to round up all the young black men they could find who fit Stewart's vague description.

At the time I was teaching at an after-school program in Roxbury, one of Boston's predominantly black communities, where the police action caused turmoil and a great deal of resentment. Many of the teens I worked with, high school kids who came to voluntary weekly tutoring sessions, told me how they or their friends had been harassed by police who seemed to have free rein to stop, search, and interrogate young black men on the slightest pretext. It's a drill that many black people are familiar with: walking down a street or standing on a corner and being approached and interviewed by police who only sometimes bother to make an excuse for why they stopped you. Some kids said they had just been asked a few questions; others said they were frisked and told to get off the streets. I resented the authoritarian tactics the police were using, but I did feel sympathy for Stewart's loss and hoped that the police would find the man they were looking for soon. I never once supposed that Stewart might be lying.

"I think he did it," an African American friend told me soon after the murder made local headlines. Such a possibility hadn't occurred to me, perhaps because it seemed almost unthinkable. I could not see how anyone could do such a heinous thing. And my friend's suspicions struck me as slightly paranoid.

I was dumbfounded and disgusted when Stewart was arrested after confessing that he had killed his expectant wife for the insurance money. And my stunned anger was all the more bitter because he had blamed the crime on an imaginary black man, the stereotypical bogeyman always lurking threateningly on the edges of the white American consciousness, whose automatically presumed guilt had prompted few people to question Stewart's accusations. Jaded by this case, I grew suspicious some years later when Susan Smith, a white woman in South Carolina, said a black man had stolen her car and kidnapped her children. Sure enough, she eventually confessed to drowning her sons, and the fictitious black culprit was cleared.

Despite gaining a dose of cynicism from observing episodes like the Stewart case, I was still completely unprepared for the explosive outcome of the trial of the four Los Angeles police officers who beat Rodney King so savagely in 1991. I, along with millions of other television viewers around the world, had repeatedly seen the videotape of the officers clubbing and kicking King's prostrate form, and

I could not see how anyone could possibly side with the police. The day the officers were acquitted, I answered the phone to hear an African American friend say, "They fucking got off." Though I immediately knew what she was talking about, her words did not compute. I could not believe that such a thing was possible. In terms of American race relations, the acquittal of the Los Angeles police officers who had pummeled Rodney King on videotape was my ultimate loss of innocence.

Besides reading and hearing about racism in the media, I sometimes experienced it in my daily life around Cambridge. My African friends and I were often followed by security guards around stores where we shopped, so much so that we sometimes made a game of it, accelerating suddenly or stopping abruptly and whirling on our pursuer, who often tried to act as if he were just minding his own business. On trips to other colleges in New England in rented cars, we had been stopped by police while driving below the speed limit and asked whether we were transporting drugs. I noticed that white women would sometimes hold their bags closer and quicken their pace or cross the street if they saw me approaching them, especially after dark. Some would even cower in doorways until I walked by, and I even learned to herald my approach with a cough if I was coming up behind a white woman on the sidewalk, so that she wouldn't cry out in fright when I suddenly appeared beside her. When an African friend and I started looking for an apartment off campus, a landlady who had initially been friendly and welcoming on the phone quickly changed her mind about scheduling an appointment to meet us when my friend said we were from Africa. And in another memorable incident, a South African student and close friend who had never been harassed by the apartheid authorities at home was arrested by Harvard police while sorting laundry at his job in the campus linen service. Though my friend had a set of keys to the building and often worked alone there after hours, the police accused him of breaking and entering, and held him in a cell overnight; the charges were ultimately dropped, but my friend never received an official apology.

Some of my academic experiences at Harvard also made me feel rather marginalized. I had arrived at college intending to study political science, but I changed my mind when I realized the U.S.-centric thrust of Harvard's government program; I was interested in African and Third World politics and international relations, and didn't want to have to take classes like "The American Presidents" before I got a chance to specialize. I considered doing a degree in African studies, but found that no department existed, just an academic committee offering courses through other departments. I thought of doing Afro-American studies, but the department was in disarray, staffed by just a couple of full professors and offering only a handful of courses (this, of course, was before the arrival of Dr. Henry Louis Gates, Jr., and his academic "Dream Team" of black professors like Cornel West and K. Anthony Appiah in the mid-1990's). So instead, I pioneered my own course of study, becoming Harvard's first history and literature major to focus on African, African American, and Caribbean literature. The history and literature department administrators were verbally supportive, but I had trouble finding appropriate classes and professors, and it was a struggle just to keep my focus before an academic establishment that sometimes seemed skeptical.

I was offended when a professor who lectured on T. S. Eliot to an English class of mine said that while there were ethical reasons for reading and studying literature by women and nonwhites, there were no literary ones—it was as though he felt reading a Toni Morrison novel was an act of some sort of intellectual charity. Another professor claimed that Harvard's academic standards had dropped dramatically since black students had been admitted in large numbers, because liberal instructors shied away from giving poor grades to blacks. The implication, of course, was that black students who received good grades did not really earn them. And Harvard's then embattled Afro-American studies department was often ridiculed by conservative professors who dismissed it as the irrelevant product of black complaints and said it should cease to exist. I, a black student in what I sometimes saw as an intellectually hostile academic environment, often felt an obligation to prove myself. I felt that in addition to having to perform so as to pass, I had to show that I and other blacks had a right to be there.

In fortifying myself against what I regarded as the psychological assault of people who second-guessed my worthiness, I learned to carry myself with a slightly adversarial arrogance. I took all of the African- and African American–oriented courses I could, and delighted in celebrating the historical and cultural achievements of people of color and exposing the racism of some of the classic texts of Western civilization. I twisted my hair into tiny dreadlocks to express my outspoken pride in my African heritage, earning the disapproval of my Zairean relatives in Lynn, but somehow making myself feel more powerful and less invisible.

I was seduced by the "Afrocentric" scholarship of black academics like Prof. Tony Martin, who spoke at a campus conference I attended, and whose work seemed to attribute most of Western thought and civilization to African sources, ridiculing white myths of African backwardness by simply reversing the stereotypes. I read and relished *The African Origins of Civilization* (1974) by Cheikh Anta Diop, the Senegalese godfather of the Afrocentrism movement, and tracked down books on ancient African mysticism by scholars like Dr. Yosef Ben-Jochannen. But as I read more and more claims of the essential unity and superiority of African culture, and as I met black Americans in Roxbury who wore African robes and used ancient Egyptian greetings but seemed to know little about contemporary African politics, I became increasingly skeptical. I eventually came to regard many Afrocentric ideas as the height of African American mythmaking; I felt that as a philosophy Afrocentrism tended to ignore too much of Africa's historical and cultural complexity, and I couldn't really see how ceaselessly trumpeting the splendor of ancient Egypt and Nubia would serve to empower modern Africans to deal with modern African problems. But in my early undergraduate years, when I felt like my background and culture were devalued by a predominantly white academic establishment, Afrocentric stories that juxtaposed ancient African grandeur with European savagery provided a satisfying, if fleeting, feeling of vindication. When I moved beyond the feel-good simplicity of Afrocentrism, I hungered for more fulfilling fare.

Despite what I often saw as Harvard's Eurocentric biases, I availed myself of an excellent education. I tried to squeeze everything I could out of an environment that afforded valuable opportunities to learn from outstanding instructors. I absorbed the history of the Southern civil rights movement from Professor Julian Bond, a veteran of the marches and demonstrations of the 1960s, whose lectures were more like personal recollections than historical surveys. I took a class on African anti-colonial movements with Professor Martin Kilson, a distinguished African American historian, who always burst into class late in a flurry of papers, corduroy and tweed, perching his cowboy hat on his desk and combing his hair as he began his lecture. I struggled in a class on Francophone African literature conducted in French by Professor Etienne Tchimbembe, a visiting lecturer from Congo-Brazzaville, who was pleased to have a fellow Mukongo among his students even though my command of the language was so shaky. I discussed the history and theory of West African folklore in a seminar with Professor Isidore Okpewho, a Nigerian writer and scholar, who once caught me napping in class and sternly suggested I go home to rest, to my great embarrassment. And I spent long hours crouched between the stacks of Widener Library, poring over books that unlocked precious secrets. It was rewarding but difficult work, especially when my studies competed with my numerous jobs for my time and attention.

At various times during my undergraduate experience, I cleaned bathrooms, supervised the campus video game room, put up flyers, filed documents, answered phones, worked as a research assistant, tutored children, and volunteered for psychological experiments to earn money for my tuition and assorted bills. Still, I always had financial problems and became accustomed to being unable to register immediately at the start of each semester because I hadn't paid off the previous year's balance or because my financial aid and loans had not yet been credited. My parents provided as much support as they could, and I avoided asking them for money, keeping it to myself when I faced financial crises. At the close of one tax year, when I was adding up all of my meager earnings from my handful of odd jobs, I was appalled to discover that when I converted my father's African university salary to U.S. dollars, my own pitiful income was larger than his. I resolved to suffer through my student poverty as best I could alone and found creative ways of saving money and surviving.

In those difficult early undergraduate years I sometimes yielded to depression and thought often and wistfully of my family and friends back in Tanzania. In a process probably experienced by all travelers who leave their homes for long periods of time, my recollections of Dar es Salaam began to be colored by romantic and exaggeratedly positive nostalgia. I longingly recalled landscapes, friendships, and foods, while images of the widespread economic hardship and the difficulties of day to day life receded from my memory. I couldn't wait to go back. Fortunately, the African companionship of the extended Harvard African Students Association family and visits to the homes of my Zairean relatives nearby helped to ease some of my longings. To confront my sense of feeling racially marginalized on campus and in American society in general, I often looked for support from African and African American peers who experienced the same pressures.

For myself and other African students, the examples of racism covered by the American media, as well as incidents we experienced every day, demonstrated the extent of the social obstacles that confronted us as blacks in America. In response to the perceived threat, blacks in HASA and the BSA collaborated in efforts to combat racism on campus and in America at large. After the acquittal of Rodney King's torturers, some black students rallied in protest, angrily shouting our solidarity with those venting their frustrations in L.A. And we found plenty to complain about right at Harvard. We marched to protest the harassment of black students by white Harvard policemen, we demonstrated in support of the beleaguered Afro-American Studies Department, and we called for more faculty hiring of women and minorities.

Despite feeling encouraged by the black student solidarity that grew around such issues, I remained frustrated by my own perception of African American indifference to Africa and African affairs. Continuing the political activism I'd begun in New Mexico, I became involved in local anti-apartheid initiatives, campaigning for Harvard's divestment from companies doing business in South Africa and raising money for South African refugees, and I also worked on campaigns targeting other African countries where dictatorships held sway. But though the anti-apartheid movement in the United States was led by prominent black American leaders, I found less enthusiasm for the struggle among my black student peers. I was always puzzled and saddened by the fact that so few black American students actively supported us in our campus activities. Too often it seemed as though black Americans were mainly preoccupied with their lot in America and did not see events in Africa as relevant. More than anything else, it was ignorance and apathy that kept many students from greater participation in political activism on Africa.

The most memorable political campaign of my student activist career brought me up against the despotism that had imprisoned my father. If Harvard students seemed to pay little attention to events in South Africa, they cared even less what happened in less celebrated tyrannies like Zaire. But when President Mobutu Sese Seko was invited to speak at Harvard's John F. Kennedy School of Government in the spring of 1990, SASC, the local anti-apartheid group to which I belonged, and other political organizations mobilized to protest the visit.

A coalition of campus and community organizations joined together to denounce Mobutu and the college administrators who had invited him, arguing that by hosting Mobutu's speech Harvard was needlessly legitimizing his brutal politics. The coalition organized rallies at which I spoke of my experiences in Zaire and my father's detention; we canvassed the campus dormitories, informing students about Mobutu's speech and our protest against it; and we wrote letters expressing our disappointment that Mobutu had been invited, delivering them by hand to seemingly indifferent administrators at the Kennedy School.

The students we met on our canvassing expeditions had often never heard of the Zairean strongman. I told many African American acquaintances about our scheduled rally, but some admitted to me that they didn't know anything about Zaire and said they'd have to hear "the other side of the story" before they agreed to participate. We distributed as much information on Zaire as we could, but it was difficult to prove to a skeptical and completely uninformed audience that millions of people in a distant African country were suffering under the iron hand of a tyrant. I felt that the black students we spoke to were especially wary of accepting our indictments of Mobutu at face value, perhaps with good reason; black people are used to hearing criticism of black leaders and have learned to treat much of the fault-finding as hostile white propaganda. Ultimately those who took an interest would have to educate themselves, seeking the truth independently from sources that they trusted. But I knew it was probably more likely that in many cases ignorance would become an excuse for inaction.

In light of the widespread unawareness, some rally organizers and I tried to come up with ways of making our protest more meaningful to those unfamiliar with the political situation in Zaire. Since the American media and an international movement had made South Africa's anti-apartheid struggle so well known to most Americans, we decided to try to link the injustice in South Africa to that in Zaire. A friend and I printed a few T-shirts with the slogan "Free Mandela" above the words "Free Tshisekedi," a reference to a prominent Zairean opposition leader then imprisoned by Mobutu. It seemed unfortunate that we were reduced to such a clumsy and superficial way of publicizing our cause, but I suppose the shirts we managed to distribute helped to bring the issue home to American students more familiar with apartheid than what was happening in Zaire.

The day of Mobutu's speech found two groups of demonstrators positioned in front of the Kennedy School building: students and community activists who had come to denounce Mobutu, including some Boston-based Zairean dissidents, and a group of pro-Mobutu Zaireans from the Boston area who chanted their support for their president in French and Lingala. I picked out several faces that I recognized from the occasional Zairean parties at my uncle's home in Lynn. It hadn't really occurred to me that some of them would defend

Mobutu, and I saw their actions as a traitorous insult to all of those who still languished under Zaire's repressive government. When I later told my uncle about the Zaireans' presence at the protest, he laughed bitterly and told me that some days previously one of Mobutu's aides had contacted members of the Zairean community in Boston and offered them money to show their support at his speech. My uncle had also been approached with the offer but had flatly refused to get involved.

At the protest scene, police barricades separated the hundreds of demonstrators from Mobutu's convoy as it entered the parking lot at the rear of the building. Men in suits stood behind the police lines, coolly eyeing the protestors, and a man within the cordoned-off area snapped pictures of us, perhaps with which to open classified files in some shadowy government department. I led students in the South African shuffling stomp of the "*toyi-toyi*," the protest dance of anti-apartheid youth, and some of the Zairean dissidents began a call-and-response chant in French: "Mobutu, Mobutu—Assassin!" Inside the building, the demonstrators who had managed to get inside interrupted Mobutu's speech by unfurling a large banner that read END THE OPPRESSION NOW and were promptly ejected.

The demonstration made the local television news and was covered in the city papers. Veteran Cambridge activists said that it was the largest protest in recent memory, and student activists returned to their dorms satisfied that they had helped to discredit a dictator. But I left the demonstration alone, feeling empty, plagued by the same sense of discouragement that burdened my political activism throughout my college years. Was this really the best I could do? It was easy to see the protest as little more than a bunch of rebellious college students having fun disrupting the affluent calm of Harvard Square; it was much harder to keep the wider context in mind, to somehow link my activities in Cambridge with the suffering that continued in Zaire. But when I discussed the protest with my father I felt that he was proud of me and that maybe I had actually managed to emulate some of his courage and conviction.

Despite the gradual return of my political resolve, the African American disinterest in African political issues that I had encountered continued to perplex me. I could see how ignorance bred apathy, but I didn't understand why more black students did not seem to take more of an interest in Africa, why more did not seem to take it upon themselves to become informed about events on the continent. The realization of African American indifference to African realities was disappointing and jarring to me at first, but I eventually came to accept that I could not expect black Americans to automatically share African passions for African struggles. I resolved to encourage those black Americans I met who were interested in Africa but was no longer surprised when many were not. And I came to understand that much of the time, on politics as on many things, African Americans and Africans had entirely different perspectives.

On one occasion, an African American dean who often offered logistical support for HASA events called a Ghanaian friend and me into his office. After briefly discussing arrangements for an upcoming HASA function, he asked if he might elicit our comments on an idea of his. He said that he and a number of other black American academics were concerned that the significant legacy of W.E.B. Du Bois, Harvard's first black Ph.D. and one of the century's most prominent black intellectuals, was being lost on a new generation of African Americans who were too young to appreciate Du Bois's role in black history. The dean said he realized that Du Bois had become so disillusioned with America that he had opted to emigrate to Ghana, where he died in 1963, but he was convinced that the old scholar would have taken heart from the tremendous strides that had been made in American race relations since the 1960s. For this reason, and to revitalize Du Bois's image for young African Americans, the dean proposed to have Du Bois exhumed from his grave in Ghana and transported across the Atlantic for burial in the United States, amid appropriate ceremony and fanfare. He eagerly claimed to have had the plan approved by members of Du Bois's family. Now he was interested in hearing some African reactions to the proposal.

My Ghanaian friend and I looked at each other a bit incredulously. After a short silence, my friend replied politely that she didn't think Ghanaians would be overwhelmingly supportive of the idea because they had loved and respected Du Bois and considered him one of their own. And she wondered aloud if digging up the man's body in the interests of reclaiming his legacy wasn't a bit extreme. I echoed her sentiments, adding that I wondered whether it was fair to assume that reburial in America was what Du Bois would have wanted. Though our response was obviously lukewarm, the dean thanked us for our comments and we left his office.

Once outside, my friend and I gave voice to our astonishment. Though we were uncomfortable saying so in the dean's presence, we both found his idea bizarre. For my part, I also found it a little sad. I had come to regard Du Bois's move to Ghana as the reinforcement of an important link between black American and African communities, the appropriate finale to a career spent in defense of black people everywhere. That a group of African American leaders would want to wrest his body from African soil, and in so doing symbolically sever the transatlantic ties he had spent a lifetime creating, struck me as regressive. Ultimately, it was a difference in perspective; to African Americans like the dean, it must have seemed that Africans had enticed Du Bois, a black American activist and scholar, from his rightful home, and prevented his legacy from serving the community from which he sprang. I chose instead to regard Du Bois as a black man whose self-conscious identification with an African heritage had led him to Africa, and whose legacy transcended borders and belonged to the worldwide pan-African family. I was to find that such subtle but crucial distinctions in outlook have often complicated relations between Africans and black Americans. Not only do Africans who make it to the United States have to contend with an entire new culture and society, they also have to come to terms with the often bewildering attitudes of their distant American cousins.

In the same way that many of my interactions with black Americans in college were puzzling, when Kunta Kinte, perhaps America's best-known African transplant, had his first contact with American-born blacks he was confounded, confused and mystified. Kinte's experiences as a Mandinka youth abducted in Africa and enslaved in America are artfully explored by Alex Haley in *Roots*, a painstakingly researched but largely reconstructed account of the author's family history from Kinte's childhood in the Gambia through the Middle Passage, slavery, Reconstruction, and several generations. While mainly fictionalized, Haley's convincing and deeply moving narrative depends on historical research to depict the experience of slavery from Kinte's perspective and rings true in its imagination of his sufferings, trials, and triumphs as a despairing yet defiant young slave in eighteenth-century Virginia.

Kunta initially felt race-based kinship with the black American slaves he met, but then came to see them as different from himself because of their seeming support for his white oppressors, and also because their cultural practices are different from his own. And this tension between his strong sense of identification with American blacks and simultaneous hopeless alienation from them plagued Kunta for years. As he adapted to his new environment and he came to resign himself to his condition of servitude, sheer loneliness drove him to establish friendships with some of the slaves on his plantation, and though he became grateful for the company, the differences between his new friends' background and his own often seemed an insurmountable obstacle.

After more than a decade in Virginia, Kunta came to accept that after generations spent in America, the blacks there had become culturally distinct from Africans. And, with horror, he was forced to confront his own gradual alienation from the cultural traditions into which he was born; he began to lose his grasp of the Mandinka language, and though he never ate pork, he gradually became more and more lax in his maintenance of Islamic customs. He became more and more acculturated to his plantation environment and eventually became an integral member of the black slave community, marrying into it, learning its language and traditions. But he never forgot his original homeland and never lost the "Africanness" that set him apart from his African American peers.

Kunta Kinte's fictionalized experience as a transplanted African followed a pattern that closely resembles actual accounts by African slaves in the Americas. They describe a process of identification, alienation, and eventual assimilation. In more recent eras, the circumstances under which Africans travel to America have changed significantly, but in many ways this process has endured. Many Africans arriving in the United States identify with American black communities readily and seemingly automatically, but often end up having to reassess their relationship to African Americans. And many African U.S. arrivals ultimately succeed in establishing positive ties to, or integrating themselves within, black American communities, even if more recent African experiences with African Americans are sometimes as confounding as were those of their predecessors in centuries past.

Ota Benga, a pygmy from the forests of Congo, was one African traveler who explored America around the turn of the century, and, like Haley's Kinte, found himself having to negotiate the tension between finding a home in America's black communities and feeling excluded from them. Benga was born into a communal pygmy clan in the Congo Free State and captured by African slave catchers as a young man. He was purchased by S. P. Verner, an American missionary and explorer traveling in Congo on a mission to find a group of pygmies to exhibit in the 1904 World's Fair in St. Louis. The way Verner later told it, Benga agreed to travel to St. Louis with him and several other pygmy men, and created a sensation as the star of the fair's "Anthropology Exhibit," a collection of representatives of various nonwhite ethnic groups from around the world. Benga and his peers were impressed by the technological resources and infrastructure of the white man's country but resented being exhibited like animals for the amusement of huge crowds of prodding white people. They were relieved when the fair closed after four months during which they had been housed in "authentic" huts and gaped at by thousands of awestruck fairgoers.

There is no record of how many American blacks attended the fair, and the pygmies did not apparently have any significant contact with African Americans while on display. (Interestingly, though, a group of Zulus who were also exhibited at the fair rebelled after a dispute over their wages and are said to have "escaped into the black community never to be found.") Verner, however, did describe an encounter between the Africans and some local blacks when the Africans stopped in New Orleans on their way home. Benga and his comrades are said to have been moved to participate in an impromptu parade by the strains of jazz performed by the procession's black musicians, who were ironically dressed in carnival costumes meant to represent traditional "Zulu" garb. It must have been a curious scene, a group of African American musicians from New Orleans masquerading as African tribesmen when they were suddenly confronted by the "real thing," a troupe of Africans who were in turn impressed by the improvised quality of the Americans' jazz rhythms, which apparently reminded them of African music.

Verner returned his pygmy charges to Congo, but Benga, apparently curious enough about America to wish to explore it more fully, is said to have asked to return to the United States to learn more about the white man and his country (he was specifically interested in learning to read). With Verner as his initial guide, Benga embarked on a journey through America that would last for more than a decade. Unlike most African travelers to the New World before him, who were brought to America by force and prevented from leaving, Benga was evidently something of a tourist. He intended only to visit the United States, collecting impressions, knowledge, and experiences like snapshots and souvenirs, and to return home when he was ready.

On this second trip to America, Benga first came into significant contact with American blacks as the focal point of a shameful spectacle that highlighted the racism and arrogance of early twentieth-century America. Verner, Benga's American "host," fell on hard times and had difficulty gaining the recognition he had hoped for as an important African explorer and collector. While he sought employment, he "housed" Benga first at the New York Museum of Natural History and then at the Bronx Zoo. At the zoo, Benga, an authentic African anthropological curiosity, was eventually placed in a cage in the Monkey House and exhibited as an exotic oddity, a primitive savage whose teeth were filed to a point and who wrestled with his chimpanzee cellmates. Crowds were amazed by his antics and he quickly caused a sensation; he was easily the most popular attraction at the zoo for the duration of his stay in the Monkey House.

The few voices raised in protest at the idea of a human being displayed like an animal were rooted in the New York black community. A Baptist minister, the Reverend R. S. MacArthur, went to see the pygmy in the zoo for himself and registered outrage. "The person responsible for this exhibition degrades himself as much as he does the African," he complained. "Instead of making a beast of this little fellow we should be putting him in school for the development of such powers as God gave him. . . . We send our missionaries to Africa to Christianize the people and then we bring one here to brutalize him." MacArthur and other black ministers vowed to see to it that Benga was released from his cage and housed elsewhere, and they demanded that the mayor and the zoo's director put an end to the exhibit.

James H. Gordon, a minister and the administrator of a black orphanage in Brooklyn, denounced Benga's exhibition on the grounds that blacks were fed up with racist comparisons to monkeys, ideas that would only damage black self-esteem and that were an obstacle to black self-improvement. "Our race, we think, is depressed enough, without exhibiting one of us with the apes," he said. "We think we are worthy of being considered human beings, with souls. . . . You people are on top. We've got to rise. Why not let us, and not impede us? Why . . . show that Negroes are akin to apes? Give us opportunities." He offered to let Benga stay in his orphanage or even in his own home, and insisted that the pygmy no longer be caged. But he seems never to have explicitly challenged the idea that Benga was "akin to an ape."

There was another, barely articulated, reason why many blacks opposed the exhibition: those who uncritically accepted the dominant view of Africans as "primitive savages" were uncomfortable at being associated with Benga; they worried that the exhibition of his "backward" ways would stigmatize all blacks. Proponents of this view, expressed in black newspapers like the *Journal*, pointed out that Benga was hardly representative of all Africans, much less of all blacks. The *Journal* was expressing an attitude common among American blacks,

whose beliefs about Africa were tainted by decades of American propaganda that depicted Africa as an uncivilized wilderness. Many
blacks sought to distance themselves from what they had been told
was a barbarous place, a frighteningly foreign continent they saw personified in Benga, with his sharpened teeth and bow and arrow. Their
embarrassment at his presence was similar to the discomfort some
white-aspiring upwardly mobile blacks felt when lower-class blacks
acted "too black" (too loud, too sensual, too uninhibited) in the presence of whites.

Unfortunately, however, even those blacks whom Benga did not
embarrass seemed ready to accept the notion of his primitiveness. As
pressure from black ministers mounted on the zoo authorities, Benga
was eventually released and lodged at the Howard Colored Orphan
Asylum in Brooklyn, where he was welcomed as James Gordon's guest.
Gordon aimed to "civilize" the pygmy by teaching him to read, write,
and speak English. "As far as I can see, this little black man is capable
of development," he told reporters when Benga was released to his
care. "Indeed he seems bright to me. We think we can do better for
him than make an exhibition of him."

It was never suggested that Benga, who was around twenty-eight
years old by now and an accomplished hunter, tracker, and herbalist,
might already be "developed" or that he was anything other than
primitive. Thus, when the African traveler was finally adopted by a
New York black community, it was so that they could civilize him.
Ministers like Gordon were willing to recognize a kinship between
Benga and American blacks, but most felt that their duty to their
African cousin involved teaching him to be an American. In fact,
Gordon felt that Benga would serve as an important test case in the
eyes of white America. If he could educate the pygmy, it would
demonstrate American blacks' worthiness of equal access to education
and social services—for if an African primitive could be Christianized
and domesticated (transformed from a heathen savage into a civilized and productive Westerner), so the reasoning went, then surely
more evolved American blacks deserved the rights of full citizenship.
It's an argument that echoes Phillis Wheatley's 1773 reminder in "On
Being Brought from Africa to America": "Remember, Christians, Negroes, black as Cain, / May be refin'd, and join th' angelic train."

Despite his good intentions, Gordon's efforts to educate and "civilize" Benga were less than successful. Benga learned some English,
learned to write a few words, voluntarily underwent a Christian baptism that did little to change his behavior and outlook, and even came

to enjoy playing baseball, but that was essentially the extent of his Americanization. Gordon finally gave up trying to reform him. "His age was against his development," bemoaned the minister. "It was simply impossible to put him in a class to receive instructions, from a literary point, that would be of any advantage to him." In fact, Benga's example threatened to subvert the orphanage's order and discipline; he became so popular among the institution's boys that when he dropped out of classes some of the other students wished to follow suit. Benga had spent one semester of his time at the orphanage studying at a Baptist seminary in Lynchburg, Virginia; Gordon was probably relieved when Benga decided to return permanently to the South.

In Lynchburg, Benga continued to strike a precarious balance between assimilating into the black community that welcomed him and retaining the distinctive "Africanness" that set him apart from it. He occasionally attended classes at the Lynchburg Seminary; at his hosts' encouragement, he had his sharpened teeth capped; and his name was gradually Americanized into "Otto Bingo." Curious strangers were told he was from New York. But while he usually lived in town, ran errands, and even worked for a time in the local tobacco factory to earn money, Benga spent much of his time in the Virginia woods, hunting the local game, puffing on marijuana he cultivated there, gathering plants, dressing himself in a bark loincloth, and performing the dances of his youth around a campfire. Sometimes he was accompanied by neighborhood children, and he would often instruct them in the finer points of pygmy culture. In short, Benga sought to reproduce elements of the culture he was born into on American soil.

Yet at the Lynchburg Seminary, Benga also forged friendships with some of the most prominent black leaders of the era. The seminary's director, Dr. Gregory W. Hayes, was a leading black educator and an early proponent of pan-Africanism and became a close friend of Benga's. Hayes, along with John Chilembwe, an African who had studied at the seminary in the 1890s, had helped found the African Development Society, which sought to mobilize African American support for African political and economic independence. Benga also established a close relationship with Anne Spencer, a black poet who contributed significantly to the literary flowering of the Harlem Renaissance. Spencer's work and outspoken defiance in the face of Jim Crow segregation earned her the friendship of other black leaders, and through her Benga was introduced to W.E.B. Du Bois and Booker T. Washington. In Lynchburg, Benga hobnobbed with the elite of the

American black community, all the while maintaining a part-time pygmy lifestyle in the woods outside town.

Despite seeming to have mastered this sort of selective assimilation, and despite appearing to have adjusted to life in Lynchburg and being surrounded by supportive friends, apparently Benga became more and more unhappy. It's important to remember that he had always intended to return home once he had had his fill of traveling in the land of the whites. Benga had assumed that Verner would help him to find his way home, but he had lost contact with Verner when he left New York. Benga must have despaired of ever making his way back to the Congolese forest. He checked the price of steamship passage to Africa and returned disheartened, realizing he was unable to afford the voyage. Desperately homesick and telling no one of his intent, Benga acquired a revolver and set out for his woodland retreat. After one last dance around a campfire, he turned the white man's weapon on himself.

Ota Benga's biography, by Harvey Blume and Phillips Verner Bradford, a descendant of Benga's missionary companion, is unavoidably flawed in that, based on Verner's own writings and secondary source material, it is unable to present events from Benga's perspective. How did he really feel about life in America? What did he really think of his "friend" Verner? When he posed for photographs, grinning to show off his sharpened incisors for titillated audiences, what was going through his head? Who was really mocking whom? And what were his perceptions of this tribe of Africans displaced in America, the people among whom he lived at the end of his life?

We will never know the answers to these questions, but however successfully Benga appeared to have settled in Lynchburg, clearly his new friends and home could not provide him the emotional support and solace he needed to live. Even though Benga was embraced by a black community that practically considered him one of its own, there had been social costs for his acceptance, and he felt isolated and lonely enough to prefer death to life away from home. His friend Anne Spencer had trouble explaining his suicide to her son, who had often accompanied the pygmy on hunting trips in the woods, but eventually she told him that Benga "had sent his spirit home to Africa."

Benga's experience in America is tragically instructive. In the specter of an African pygmy adopted into an African American community yet unable to overcome unbearable loneliness, we find an unfortunate reminder of the often seemingly unbridgeable cultural gap separating black Americans from their African counterparts. Benga's sense of isolation is a common theme among African travelers to the United States, even if their sojourns abroad don't usually end so disastrously.

Though a unique visitor, Benga—as a student who ventured to the United States partly to acquire an education—was in some ways a fore-runner of the wave of Africans who began traveling to America to study in greater and greater numbers as the twentieth century progressed.

Akinsola Akiwowo, a Nigerian who studied at the historically black Morehouse College in Atlanta in the early 1950s, spoke for many African students in America when he wrote the poem "Song in a Strange Land" expressing his homesickness and disappointment with black Americans' lamentable ignorance of Africa:

> *Shall I sing your song, Africa,*
> *In this strange land of hate and love?*
> *Shall I sing to them whose forebears*
> *Were torn away from you long ago?*
> *For they know you not, but believe*
> *All the strange and gory stories*
> *They oft have read and seen in films:*
> *Apes, thick jungles and men with spears,*
> *And nude women with pancake lips.*
> *They have not seen how, what you are;*
> *That long estrangement shuts their eyes.*
> *Some see no beauty in our songs;*
> *Some mock the gorgeous robes we wear.*
> *Some say you are a thing of shame!*
> *But some are kind, understanding, good;*
> *Eager of hearts, or purpose true.*
> *But these are few, painfully few!*

Though most Africans who studied in the United States experi-enced at least some of this disillusionment when they first met black Americans who looked on their African heritage with shame, many also felt the elation of establishing valuable friendships with the "painfully few" black Americans who took an interest in Africa. If "long estrangement" had "shut the eyes" of many black Americans, many others had begun to gaze at Africa with curiosity. When African students began to be enrolled in U.S. universities in large numbers, intimate cultural and intellectual exchanges took place between black Americans and Africans. Consequently, universities became locales where blacks from both sides were forced to revise their unreal expectations and stereotypes of their counterparts, and sites where pan-African networks took root and flourished.

Benjamin Nnamdi Azikiwe, the first president of independent Nigeria, studied at American universities in the 1920s and 1930s and forged important links with black Americans with whom he came into contact. Azikiwe first became aware of black Americans as a youth in Nigeria, when a classmate informed him of "a great Negro who was coming with a great army to liberate Africa." Though the young Azikiwe, who had grown up as the privileged son of a civil servant, didn't even know that Africa needed liberating, he became inspired by the legend of Marcus Garvey, and read his ideas in contraband copies of the *Negro World* that circulated among his classmates. After reading Garvey's words and assessing the British-run colonial society around him, Azikiwe realized that Africa did indeed require "redemption" and dreamed of becoming a leader of the cause.

He decided on a means of acquiring the training he would need to fulfill this ambition when he heard a 1920 speech by J. E. Kwegyir Aggrey, a minister from the Gold Coast who had studied at black colleges in the United States. "If I, one of you, could go to the new world, and make a man of myself, then you can too," Aggrey concluded in his lecture. "From that day I became a new man," Azikiwe wrote later. "My ideas of life changed so much that I lived in daydreams, hoping against hope for the time when it would be possible for me to be like Aggrey."

Azikiwe began corresponding with professors at black schools—Howard University in Washington, D.C., and Storer College in West Virginia—attempting to secure funding and admission to an American school. Though the responses he received were encouraging, financial constraints prevented him from actually embarking for America for some years. He finally succeeded in 1925. Through his familiarity with the work of Marcus Garvey and the example of J. E. Kwegyir Aggrey, Azikiwe arrived in America secure in the knowledge that he could expect the friendship and assistance of American blacks whom he had come to regard as members of an extended African family.

He was therefore unprepared for the comments of the first black American he actually spoke with, a man he met on a New York subway a mere day after arriving on American soil. When he introduced himself as an African, his new acquaintance "became very curious and asked me why I was not naked," Azikiwe reported later. "Would I oblige by telling him about the lions and elephants which were supposed to roam the streets of Africa and made human life unbearable. Before I could answer, he interrupted: 'I beg your pardon, mister, do you belong to dem cannibal tribes who used to eat people? How does human steak taste? How does elephant steak taste? I betcha a dime to a dollar that lion steak ain't so tough but juicy!' " Though angrily taken aback, Azikiwe quickly regained his composure. "To me, it was a revelation of a strange mentality; but to him, it was stranger still, for he could not believe that Africans were civilised enough to wear trousers, coats, ties, shirts and shoes, much less to speak English," Azikiwe wrote. "When I looked at him crossly for some time without uttering a word, he told me that he meant no harm. He said that most of the missionaries whom he had heard and the Hollywood films he had seen had given him the impression that Africans were still in a savage and primitive state. I pitied his ignorance and told him that I was shocked to hear a gentleman of African descent, in an advanced country like America, ask me such foolish questions; but because of what seemed to me mitigating circumstances, I took no offence."

Azikiwe's interactions with fellow black students at Storer College, where he enrolled in the fall of 1925, were more positive. His classmates were full of questions about Africa, but none seemed to display the sort of ignorance he had run into on the subway. He taught his new colleagues a few African songs, and in turn they introduced him to jazz and dances like the Charleston and the Black Bottom. Though he soon realized that most black Americans were not very interested in Africa and were often somewhat ambivalent about their African heritage, Azikiwe seized every opportunity for cultural exchange and education.

After a year at Storer, Azikiwe enrolled at Howard, where he was privileged to study under Alain Locke, chief scholar and theorist of the New Negro Movement. From his vantage point at Howard, Azikiwe was exposed to many of the Harlem Renaissance's most prominent thinkers. He was especially impressed with classes taught by William Leo Hansberry, an anthropologist who pioneered Afrocentric readings of African history. Through the problack outlook of professors like Locke and Hansberry, Azikiwe acquired the intellectual foundation and perspective that would equip him to lead Nigeria toward independence. While some black Americans whom Azikiwe met were convinced of African backwardness and inferiority, others instructed him in African history and stressed that Africa *had* a history and heritage of which Africans could be proud. Ironically,

Azikiwe learned more about general African history in America than he had in Nigeria.

Azikiwe followed his stint at Howard with studies at Lincoln University, a black school near Philadelphia. There, he continued to establish close friendships with his black American peers and to develop his ideas on international black nationalism. Azikiwe's classmates included future U.S. Supreme Court justice Thurgood Marshall and others who would later rise to positions of considerable prominence. The interaction of African students like Azikiwe and Kwame Nkrumah (who later attended Lincoln and taught there) with future black American leaders like Marshall made Lincoln a breeding ground for a nascent pan-Africanism that would flourish in the 1960s. When Azikiwe was inaugurated in 1963, a number of former colleagues from his Lincoln days were in enthusiastic attendance. Thus, for Azikiwe, undergraduate study in the United States provided not only an education but also a forum for establishing a pan-African intellectual and political network.

In the early 1930s Azikiwe taught history and political science at Lincoln, and devoted himself to educating his black American students about the African past. After years of living in America, where he frequently confronted black Americans' ignorance of their African heritage, an attempt to fill in the gaps in historical knowledge about the continent seemed necessary. "Noticing how students of African descent, American and British or otherwise by nationality, were ignorant of their past, it dawned on me that research into the origins and development of the African in the stream of history should be a definite contribution in the field of learning," Azikiwe wrote of his decision to craft a syllabus for an African history course. His lectures "probing the dark mist which hung over the history of African peoples" were his final contribution to black American–African relations in America, for a few years later he returned to Nigeria to involve himself in the anticolonial struggle. At times his stay in the United States had been bewildering and difficult, and he had actually attempted suicide at one dangerously lonely point. But Azikiwe was doubtlessly enriched by the entire experience, twelve years in which he was able to bridge gaps of ignorance and misunderstanding to establish important links with his transatlantic cousins.

Kwame Nkrumah had a similar experience in the mid-1930s. Like Azikiwe, he was influenced in his decision to pursue higher education in America by J. E. Kwegyir Aggrey, who taught at Nkrumah's secondary school in the Gold Coast. Nkrumah was also inspired by

Azikiwe himself, who by 1934 was the editor of the *Africa Morning Post*, a regional newspaper. He applied to Lincoln University and left for America in 1935. His immediate impressions were positive. Initially received by a Sierra Leonean acquaintance in New York, Nkrumah quickly warmed to his new surroundings. "I felt immediately at home in Harlem and sometimes found it difficult to believe that this was not Accra," he wrote of his introduction to the world's most famous black community. Later, at Lincoln, Nkrumah became a popular addition to the freshman class, competing in speech-making contests, joining a fraternity, attracting female admirers, and earning pocket money by writing economics reports for other students. When he graduated with a bachelor's degree in economics and sociology in 1939, Nkrumah was voted Lincoln's "most interesting" student. He returned to teach at Lincoln in the early 1940s, lecturing in philosophy and black history. He enjoyed a number of friendships with black Americans during his years in America, and he became a supporter of the anthropologist Melville Herskovits's assertion that African Americans retained strong African cultural practices, a thesis Nkrumah once defended in a lecture at Howard University.

In addition to providing the opportunity to establish close personal ties with black Americans he met and worked with, Nkrumah's time in the United States provided the context in which his early political ideas first began to take shape. Of the books he read as a student, he credited *The Philosophy and Opinions of Marcus Garvey* (1923) with having had the most significant impact on his own thinking, and Garvey's calls for African self-determination informed Nkrumah's development of an anticolonial political stance. Eventually leaving the United States for London, Nkrumah began to refine his political ideas and started working with other African students and activists to try to coordinate independence movements on the continent. And his political activities consistently stressed a pan-African outlook. He learned much about political organizing from the West Indian writer and activist C.L.R. James, and worked closely with W.E.B. Du Bois, Jomo Kenyatta, and others to sponsor the fifth Pan African Congress in Manchester in 1945. Later he published an anticolonial magazine, *The New African*, and attempted to mobilize united political action by Africans and New World blacks in Africa and overseas. Nkrumah ultimately took the independence struggle back to his homeland, but he consistently drew support from and maintained strong ties to his black allies in the United States and Europe.

When Nkrumah's anticolonial efforts bore fruit in 1957, as Ghana became the first independent country in Africa, the victory was due in part to the international support of the pan-African network Nkrumah had established in his ten years abroad. Recognizing the important role that diaspora blacks had played in his country's fight against colonialism, Nkrumah welcomed many African Americans and West Indians to live and work in independent Ghana, including his old mentor Du Bois. Nkrumah's decade of study and work in America and England helped equip him with the knowledge and pan-African political contacts he would later use to help liberate his country.

Like Nkrumah, the Kenyan writer Mugo Gatheru first dreamed of studying in the United States as a young man in the 1930s. In an era when Kenyans looked up to the United States as a paradise where even blacks could rise to positions of prominence, Gatheru was inspired to travel to the United States by the accomplishments of a number of world-famous black Americans. "Educated Africans knew of individuals like Booker T. Washington, George Washington Cárver, Paul Robeson, Joe Louis, Dr. Ralph Bunche, Richard Wright, Langston Hughes, and Marian Anderson," Gatheru wrote in his autobiography. "However, for Africans, such people were symbols only of the success which a black man might achieve when given a proper chance to develop his natural abilities. . . . We thought of them merely as more emancipated members of the same community as ourselves." Thus, for many Africans like Gatheru, and many others who would later travel to the United States, the "American Dream" was actually more of an "African American Dream."

Modeling himself on idols like Robeson and Bunche (who was something of a folk hero in Kenya after a 1938 trip to the region during which he was hailed by crowds of enthusiastic locals), Gatheru decided to enroll in an American university to acquire the tools he would need to emulate the black Americans he admired. He also hoped that studying in the United States would enable him to meet some black Americans. "I was determined to go to America for higher education, especially to obtain the B.A. degree in History and Politics which would enable me to contribute something to Kenya's advancement," he wrote. "I was interested in seeing and meeting American Negroes, and Red Indians. Particularly, I had a tremendous curiosity about the Negroes and their progress in the United States. I am certain, even now, that this curiosity is being shared by many Africans in Kenya and in East Africa in general."

Through the international image of figures like Jesse Owens and Marian Anderson, and visits to Africa by black Americans like Ralph

Bunche, Kenyans like Gatheru had come to regard black Americans as "big brothers" whose access to ample American educational opportunities had allowed them to progress further than their African counterparts. Despite the acknowledged discrepancy, however, Africans still looked to black Americans as distant relations from whom they could expect assistance and to whom they owed racial allegiance. Though Gatheru met his first black Americans in Kenya, where American military units including black soldiers were stationed during World War II, he did not really have an opportunity to test his assumption of racial affinity with American blacks until he reached the United States.

Gatheru's quest for an American education encountered obstacles, but he eventually made it to the United States, arriving in New York City around 1944. He caught his first glimpse of blacks in America on their home turf while driving through Harlem with the white American acquaintances who first hosted him. And, seeing the much fabled American blacks, he was possessed of an elated feeling of kinship. "I saw many Negroes on the road," he reported eagerly. "When we drove through Harlem I was surprised to see so many. I wanted to stop and go over to one of them and say: 'I am your brother.' I was naïve. I felt like I'd like to start telling them about their brothers in Kenya. But I did not want to bother my friends to stop. Having seen them, I felt that I was not alone now, that if I got lost I could go to them and could get what I wanted."

Though Gatheru was pleased to see black Americans even from a distance, he didn't have his first conversations with any until he moved on to Chicago, where a black professor with whom he had corresponded had promised assistance in gaining admission to a college. The professor, St. Clair Drake, a prominent black scholar who had taken a strong interest in Africa and in establishing ties with the continent, helped to enroll Gatheru in Roosevelt College, where he soon began taking classes. Though the school was predominantly white, there were a few black students in Gatheru's classes and he enthusiastically introduced himself to them, anticipating an immediate sense of identification and friendship. He soon realized, however, that his expectations were slightly misplaced. "Instinctively, perhaps, I thought, wrongly, I would feel more at home if I made more friends among the American Negroes than the other Americans." Instead, however, he found that "they all behaved alike. I had then to start approaching all of them on the basis of human beings, white and black, and not on the basis of race. In other words, the very fact that the American Ne-

groes looked like my tribesmen did not imply that I could understand
them automatically." It was the classic realization shared by so many
African travelers to America.

Later in his autobiography, he reflects: "When I arrived in America
I had a vague expectation that they [black Americans] would act
much like my fellow tribesmen in Kenya. I was disappointed to find
that they did not and that they were in my inexperienced eyes more
like white men of a different colour." Gatheru was forced to confront
his own misperceptions and unfulfilled expectations, and was also appalled by many black American ideas about Africa: "However naïve I
may have been about them, I was still more surprised to find how little the Negroes knew about my people. Often enough, their knowledge of us was as primitive as the conditions in which they imagined
the whole of Africa was still living and many indeed were ashamed of
our common ancestry. At college, the Negro students were very keen
to know about African customs which I would attempt to explain to
their utter amazement and sometimes incredulous laughter. One particular student from Nigeria with particularly heavy tribal marks on
his face was the centre of great curiosity in the dining hall and on the
college campus. Many of the Negro students seemed incapable of understanding why intelligent people should wish to 'disfigure' themselves in this way: it was certainly not an 'American' thing to do!"

Gatheru also describes an incident in which some black Americans
failed to support him in a confrontation with institutionalized American racism. After entering a segregated bar with two black American
servicemen he met in the street, Gatheru was asked to leave, to his
own chagrin and his new acquaintances' seeming indifference. "As we
entered, the barman came directly to us," Gatheru narrates. "They
asked him if they could have some beer. He said: 'Yes, I can serve you
two because you're in uniform, but I can't serve him,' referring to
me. . . . I left the two G.I.s drinking beer. They did not protest against
this incident or say anything about it." Gatheru seems quietly offended that his American brothers did not stick up for him. Once
again, he was forced to revise his expectations in the face of experiences that were quite different from those he had anticipated.

After years in the United States, studying and living alongside
black Americans, Gatheru made some close friends among them and
learned to lower his expectations of automatic unity. And while he
maintained a sense of racial identification and saw the benefit of encouraging pan-African sentiments and a working unity among blacks
around the world, he came to understand that relations between

Africans and black Americans were more complicated than he had once thought. "For some reasons which must be obvious, all people of African descent are united by a bond of mutual sympathy," he writes. "I was therefore well-disposed towards 'my brothers' but it was not until I went to America that I realized that sympathy and good will alone do not necessarily make for true understanding. We had some curious ideas about each other."

Gatheru, like many other African travelers to the United States, arrived in this country with a perhaps naïve expectation of instinctive kinship with black Americans, only to have his optimism tempered by black Americans' obvious cultural differences and their often ignorant attitudes toward Africa. Gatheru's disillusionment at first led him to regard black Americans as "white men of a different colour." But after the initial shock, and after he got to know black Americans over an extended period, Gatheru's faith in the existence of important commonalities of experience between blacks in America and Africa returned. Though he realized that there was much that separated black Americans from Africans in cultural terms, he retained a belief in the value of pan-African unity. "The American Negro of today is undoubtedly a man of the West who stands as little chance of successful assimilation into African society as his white fellow countryman, a Chinaman or European so born," he concludes. "We shall always be most happy to welcome him in Africa, he is indeed our brother, but, as present Negro leaders realize, their true hope for equality must lie in the dynamic fight now being waged for complete integration in American society."

By the 1960s, when Mugo Gatheru completed his studies in America, the number of African students attending American universities had increased dramatically, and still more began to find their way to the United States as more African countries became independent. For many new African nations, especially those that aligned themselves with the West in the 1960s Cold War world, the United States became the prime training ground for a generation of professionals. And as more Africans made it to America, many of them began to remain in the United States after they earned their degrees; many others settled in the U.S. in search of jobs or to escape political upheaval, and the influx of Africans, which increased through the 1970s and 80s, prompted the formation of new African communities on American soil, especially in large metropolitan areas. Like all American immigrant groups before them, African permanent residents of the United States attracted and encouraged further African immigration. African families in America helped relatives back home to come over and join them, and soon various national African communities took root in different cities.

Many American immigrant groups have historically had an uneasy relationship with the African American community, for various reasons. Typically, many immigrants intent on material advancement in the United States have seen it as in their interest to keep their distance from American blacks, the stereotypical bottom rung of the American ladder. And African Americans have often resented the new competition for jobs and resources. Unfortunately, relations between African and black American communities have sometimes reflected similar tensions. By the 1970s, Africans had formed their own subcommunities within black American neighborhoods, but these largely remained socially distinct. Though important ties have always existed between black American communities and those of African immigrants, in general the two groups have tended to go their separate ways, sometimes regarding each other suspiciously across the invisible social barriers. Although Africans in America and African Americans have sometimes united to combat American racism, a common enemy, since the rise of African immigration in the 1960s and 1970s black Americans and African residents of the United States have often seen their interests, concerns, and agendas as distinct.

The stories of African travelers and students like Ota Benga, Azikiwe, Nkrumah, and Gatheru speak to a common experience of adjustment and assimilation for Africans transplanted in America, and though the context has shifted and changed through time, many of the sorts of issues Africans have confronted in the United States have not. The accounts of African students, travelers and immigrants who made their way to the United States in the 1960s, '70s, and '80s all seem to echo the same basic themes; indeed the stories of African American ignorance and the shock of unfulfilled expectations seem almost identical. More than a century after Kunta Kinte first wondered what to make of the strange community of American blacks he encountered as a slave in Virginia, I found myself wrestling with many of the same issues and concerns as an African student in the United States in the 1990s.

When the social politics and academic grind at Harvard became too oppressive, I would seek refuge at my uncle's home in Lynn, an hour-long train and bus ride from Cambridge. Lynn had been known as the raucous "city of sin" in the nineteenth century, but by the 1990s it had become a lower-middle-class enclave that was home to long-time white and black American residents and growing immigrant communities from Africa and the Caribbean. At my uncle's house I was always assured of a good meal and the affectionate company of a family.

In the mid 1970s, when my immediate family was living in West Newton, my father had helped his sister and her family to come to the United States from Zaire to attend university, find jobs and raise a family, and to avoid Zaire's increasingly difficult economic and political climate. Aunt Anne, Uncle Bawa, and my cousin Dina had settled in Lynn soon after their arrival from Kinshasa, and by the time I returned to the Boston area in 1989, they had already been there for over fifteen years. Although my aunt visited family members in Africa whenever she could, she and her husband were in the United States to stay. After completing their degrees, she and her husband had gone to work (she as a clinical psychologist, he as an auditor); they had had two more children, purchased a home, and had eventually received their green cards, which enabled them to help other relatives in Congo to come to the United States as well.

Over the years they made friends with their neighbors, Americans as well as immigrants from Jamaica and the Dominican Republic, but mainly they socialized with members of the Boston area's growing Congolese community. And like most immigrants, even while they looked forward to and worked toward a future in America, they maintained strong ties to their homeland. They learned to speak fluent American English, even picking up Bostonian slang expressions, but they retained Congolese accents and still spoke Kikongo and French around the house. They acquired a taste for American food and celebrated Thanksgiving with a turkey and stuffing (as well as white beans and salt fish) but still mainly cooked Congolese meals at home. They adopted American lifestyles, but remained rooted in a Congolese past.

For my cousins, one born in Kinshasa and brought to the United States as a child, the other two born in Lynn, the Congolese culture that still anchored their parents' lives was less significant. Adjustment had been difficult for Dina at first. When he first started public school in Lynn, black and white kids alike jeered and teased, shouting insults like "African monkey" or "African booty scratcher." He had eventually adjusted, making friends among the kids in his classes and neighborhood, learning the niceties of American culture and speaking American English with a Boston-area accent. He had arrived in the United States speaking French and Lingala, but he soon lost most of his knowledge of these languages as he focused on learning English. He quickly became fond of hamburgers, french fries, submarine sandwiches, and candy, and learned to play baseball, basketball, and football. And as he became more American, his memories of Africa and his love of African food and culture began to fade. He retained a conscious knowledge of his land of origin and draped his bedroom wall with the Zairean flag, and his parents were quick to stress his familial ties to Africa. But in many ways Dina began to self-identify primarily as an American. And for my cousins Konzo (who would eventually prefer to be called Antoinette) and Sivi, both born in the United States, this process was even more automatic.

My aunt and uncle consciously sought to recreate elements of their culture in America, decorating their homes with Congolese art, compiling huge collections of Congolese popular music, and serving American adaptations of Congolese dishes. But as their children became more familiar with American youth culture, they became Americans in culture and outlook, even though they acknowledged their African roots and expressed an interest in visiting Congo. And while my aunt and uncle, like many other African immigrants of their generation, tended to stick within insular African communities in America, their children and a new generation of Africans born in the United States increasingly ignored such boundaries. Dina's circle of friends incorporated African Americans, Jamaicans, Dominicans, Puerto Ricans, and African immigrants like himself, and while they all reflected the cultural specificities of their individual backgrounds, they were united by the commonalities of contemporary American youth culture. At home they might hear different languages and eat different foods, but at parties where they danced to hip hop, on basketball courts, at shopping malls, and in school, they all found common ground.

Dina, Antoinette, and Sivi, and even my brothers and I, represent a new generation of African immigrants to America: young, assimilated "African" Americans who straddle the Atlantic in their remembrance and conscious retention of an African cultural heritage. I met many others at Harvard and other American campuses, Africans who were born in America or had lived there for much of their lives; often they had only dim recollections of the countries and cultures of their parents, but they were eager to rediscover themselves by learning about their roots. We were tied to Africa by ancestry and family, and to America by experience and culture. So we were uniquely poised to mediate between Africans and black Americans and to recognize the cultural features, concerns, and interests common to both groups. Perhaps it is we who represent the best hope for greater closeness between Africans and African Americans, in the United States and around the world.

8

DRUMBEATS FROM
ACROSS THE ATLANTIC

The essential Pan-Africanism is artists relating across conti-
nents their craft, drumbeats from across the aeons, sounds that
are still with us.
                                              —Ishmael Reed

Once, in a music store near the Harvard campus, I stumbled on an
album by Remmy Ongala, a Tanzanian musician of Congolese
origin who was popular in Dar es Salaam, known for his poignant
songs about the plight of the poor. In the depths of my freshman-year
depression, when I was desperately disoriented and lonely and wanted
badly to return to Africa, Remmy's music was a lifeline linking me to
my home. When my roommates weren't around I'd crank it up and sing
along, especially to a song called "Kifo" (Death), a mournful lament
on the sad, indomitable power of death: "Kifo, oh, kifo," Remmy's
clear, warm tenor would intone, "kifo hakina huruma" (Death, death
has no mercy). I would shake my head, *sikitika* regretfully (that "tsk,
tsk" sound many Africans make to express sympathy and sadness) and
feel plaintively overwhelmed by the elegant poetry of the Kiswahili
verses, but the songs actually made me feel better. Though I usually
ended up even more homesick, it was a yearning tempered by nostalgia and affection, psychological insulation from the cold New England winter.

Music has always played an important role in my family's life, and
now, when I was on my own on unfamiliar terrain, it was music that
helped to keep me going. Remmy's songs provided only one of the

various rhythms to which I lived my life in Cambridge. The universe of music that flavored and nourished my existence was vast and eclectic, but rooted quite firmly in traditions that began in Africa but have been echoed all over the world. My education in rhythm began with my parents, who passed down an appreciation of soul, jazz, reggae, and African pop. Later, my own musical exploration led me to rock, funk, hip-hop, dancehall reggae, and various other flavors of the black diaspora, and it was as a youth in Tanzania that I began to see the diverse interconnections linking black music from around the world in an international cultural system.

When my family moved to Dar es Salaam, friends and local media outlets introduced us to the vibrant Tanzanian popular culture. As we learned Kiswahili, my brothers and I began to decipher and appreciate the popular songs that blared out of every radio, local classics like "M.V. *Mapenzi*" (a song about the merchant vessel *Love*, which "sails the sea between us") and "Shauri Yako" (It's Your Fault). And at neighborhood parties we learned to gyrate to "chakacha," upbeat dance music that combined aspects of modern disco music and taarab, a Swahili musical form that fuses African and Arab traditions. These songs always made clever use of language and often used suggestive metaphors and lewd puns to comment on social issues and aspects of sexuality. When we knew enough to understand the double meanings, we would giggle appreciatively at each ribald reference, singing the seemingly innocent words with loud abandon: "Leo, ni leo, nimempata dereva mjuwaji, gari langu huenda mbiyo" ("Today I found an experienced driver, and my car goes fast," a reference to the virtues of a sexually skilled woman). Whenever the first recognizable strains of a favorite song played at a party, people would flood the dance floor, chanting and singing and grinding their hips in time to the drums.

We also listened and danced to a lot of African imports. Zairean pop music, the driving dance numbers and smooth ballads that had passionate followings all over Africa, was especially popular in Tanzania. My teenage Tanzanian friends called it "Bolingo," because the word seemed to figure so prominently in the Lingala lyrics they could repeat but not understand; my Dad told me it meant "love." Friends were always asking to borrow tapes from my father's large Zairean collection, and many of the local Tanzanian bands seemed to have been influenced by popular Zairean singers and "orchestras." My friends and I tended to regard Zairean hits by musicians like Franco or Tabu Ley as old people's music, but we knew and liked many of the songs, and they featured prominently at most parties. Performers from South Africa like Yvonne Chaka Chaka, whose R&B-inflected pop enjoyed constant airplay in Dar in the mid-1980s, were also popular. And West African songs from Mali or Ghana would also find their way into Dar es Salaam homes and night clubs.

Though African musical fare made up a large part of our cultural diet, and though there was a widespread local attraction to American country music that I was never quite able to fathom, West Indian and African American popular music always occupied a privileged position among my Tanzanian friends and with me. I was largely introduced to reggae music in Dar es Salaam, where many young people embraced the genre with all of the enthusiasm of the ghetto youth of Kingston, Jamaica. Among many Tanzanian young people Bob Marley was popularly revered as a prophet, musical genius, and black hero, and I was first exposed to his amazing oeuvre by my father, who began acquiring Marley tapes through a colleague of his shortly after we moved to Dar es Salaam.

When I first heard the complex beauty of the albums *Burnin'* and *Catch a Fire*, I was enchanted. The music fit so perfectly together, plaintive vocals and inspired lyrics over steady bass lines and a network of seamless percussion. I eagerly worked my way through the albums *Kaya*, *Exodus*, *Survival*, *Uprising*, and *Confrontation*, and soon couldn't hear one song conclude without having the next one begin in my mind before the music actually started playing. I felt transported and uplifted by songs like "Rastaman Chant," "Small Axe," and "Natty Dread," and wondered at the poetic mystery of classic lines like "but the stone that the builder refuse shall be the head cornerstone." I was filled with revolutionary fire when Bob and Peter Tosh traded incendiary lyrics on "Get Up Stand Up" ("You can fool some people sometimes, but you can't fool all the people all the time"), I felt Bob's pain when he poured out his anguish on "She's Gone" ("Oh mockingbird, have you ever heard the words that I never heard?"), and became religiously introspective at the profound faith professed on "We'll Be Forever Loving Jah" ("We won't worry, we won't shed no tear, we've found a way to cast away the fear, forever yeah"). Bob had songs for every mood, thoughtful lyrics for every occasion.

It was only in college that I realized the debt Marley owed to the Old Testament, Marcus Garvey, Karl Marx, and other sources. In addition to many phrases culled right from the Bible, I found Bob lines in *Capital* ("the capitalist [read 'Babylon'] system is a vampire, sucking the blood of the sufferer") and learned that one of his most famous lyrics, "Emancipate yourselves from mental slavery," quoted Garvey.

"Bobu," as he was often affectionately known in Dar, was perhaps the most popular non-African musician in Africa, and when I was growing up his songs played frequently on Tanzanian radio and often blasted from buses, the music of choice for hundreds of conductors and drivers around the city. If my friends and I ever got tired of dee-jaying at the neighborhood parties we threw, we would just let a Mar-ley album play, and watch the crowd go wild, bobbing up and down in time to the peerless Wailers rhythm section and trying to sing along with Bob when he got to the familiar chorus. Although virtually all Bob songs were embraced, the Dar youth had their favorites: on "Rasta-man Live Up!" Bob sang the line "Bongoman, don't give up," which some local fans took as a special dedication since "Bongo" was a slang name for Tanzania. And the classics "Buffalo Soldier" and "Bad Card" were well-loved hits as well. Bob Marley became my favorite singer of all time, but my friends and I were also fans of Gregory Isaacs, who specialized in reggae love songs, Eek-A-Mouse, whose "Ganja Smug-gling" was regarded as a "national anthem" in some teenage circles in Dar (when it played you *had* to stand up), as well as I Jah Man, Yellow-man, Alpha Blondy, Steel Pulse, Aswad, UB40, and many others.

Of course, reggae, like all diaspora music, has obvious African rhythmic roots that are recognized and embraced by African fans. But it also made sense that many young Tanzanians would be attracted to reggae music, because Africa was so often a focus of the genre's songs. Reggae—which emerged in urban Jamaica in the 1960s, a blend of African-influenced folk music and more recent Caribbean styles like rock steady and ska—found early lyrical inspiration in Garveyism and Rastafarianism and often championed the idea of black repatriation. Songs like Marley's "Exodus: Movement of Jah People," Burning Spear's "We Are Going," and Gregory Isaacs's "The Border," all spoke to the desirability of black resettlement in Africa and painted an idyl-lic vision of a peaceful and bountiful "motherland," a representation that appealed to many African reggae enthusiasts. The fact that reggae claimed to speak for the poor and disenfranchised "ghetto youth" also helped to popularize it among Dar es Salaam street kids, many of whom imitated elements of reggae fashion and culture, growing dreadlocks, wearing red, gold, and green tams, T-shirts, wristbands, hats and bracelets and smoking copious quantities of marijuana.

A university colleague of my dad's, a Jamaican political scientist, told me that Rastas in Jamaica may have been partly inspired to grow dreadlocks by the Mau Mau, Kenyan freedom fighters whose distinctive locks were said to strike fear in the hearts of English settlers. Yet most young "dreads" in Dar wore their locks in imitation of Jamaican reggae singers, in particular Bob Marley. And while Jamaican musicians often celebrated Africa as a perfect homeland to which diaspora blacks would one day return in a final escape from the evils of Babylon, the contemporary residents of the motherland felt Babylon's oppressive presence in their lives every day, and celebrated the music as a statement against their disenfranchisement. Also, as with the early pan-African movement of the nineteenth century, in the 1980s it was often diaspora blacks who popularized the idea of black unity in Africa: Marley's "Africa Unite" ("Africa unite, 'cause we're moving right out of Babylon, Africa unite, 'cause we're moving right back to our fatherland") probably did more to spark the consciousness of Dar's youth than any of the pronouncements of the OAU.

Though reggae had a fiercely loyal following in Tanzania and across Africa, if Marley had a rival for the devotion of Dar es Salaam's youth, that rival would have had to be Michael Jackson. The Jackson Five were popular in Tanzania throughout the 1970s, but "Maiko," as we affectionately called him, earned himself special recognition for the albums *Off the Wall* and *Thriller*, which became staples on Radio Tanzania and at parties around Dar as soon as they hit town. Though most people in Dar es Salaam speak at least a little English, a language barrier does prevent most people from learning all the lyrics to most popular American songs, but that never stopped anyone from enjoying the music. In our neighborhood the kids would improvise Kiswahili lyrics to sing along with American songs, and these usually nonsensical versions would sometimes become as well known as the originals. Michael Jackson's songs yielded especially memorable Kiswahili renditions: the chorus of "Wanna Be Starting Somethin' " ("So you wanna be startin' somethin'?") evolved into "Unataka binzari sasa?" ("Would you like some saffron powder now?"), for example.

We rewrote other American songs as well, and some seemed to especially lend themselves to this sort of reinterpretation. Lionel Richie's "All Night Long" had a chant in it that sounded like Kiswahili to us, although the words hardly made sense: "Jambo, nipe senti moja, oh, jambo, jambo" ("hello, give me one cent, hello, hello"). And Dennis Edwards and Siedah Garrett's "Don't Look Any Further," a local favorite, had a line that actually fit the rest of the song quite appropriately when we sang it in Kiswahili: "Leo, leo, mambo si hayo? Don't look any further" ("Today, today, isn't everything right there? Don't look any further").

Dar es Salaam's Michael-mania was fueled by his music videos, which were bootlegged in the United States and brought or sent into the city, where they became hot commodities. On some nights my friends and I would trek over to the university campus auditorium, Nkrumah Hall, to watch screenings of movies and videos for twenty shillings (about a dollar at the time, now barely a penny). Hundreds would gather for these shows, peering eagerly at two television screens at the front of the large hall, cheering, laughing, and offering expert analysis and commentary on the action onscreen. Usually a single movie would be advertised on the flyers announcing the event, perhaps Sylvester Stallone in *First Blood* (always a crowd pleaser), a James Bond film, or maybe Charles Bronson in *Mr. Majestyk*, but you never really knew what else you were going to get on movie nights. In addition to the main event, we were treated to bits of international soccer, enigmatic Eastern European cartoons, American sitcoms like *The Cosby Show*, and music videos. Lionel Richie, Whitney Houston, New Edition, Chaka Khan, Colonel Abrams, Jeffrey Osbourne, Janet Jackson, Diana Ross, and Donna Summer (as well as Madonna, Gloria Estefan, and Kenny Rogers) all gained substantial followings in Tanzania, but nothing like Michael's.

My friends and I marveled at the videos for "Billie Jean," "Beat It," and "Thriller," and, along with practically every other kid in Dar, devoted considerable energy to imitating Michael's moves. Kids would hike up their pants to expose two inches of white sock the way he did, and I even saw some teenagers sporting single white gloves, a serious expression of devotion in Dar's wilting temperatures. At the height of Jackson's popularity, people would sit in the shade at the side of the road and describe his videos to each other in detail, jumping up to act out scenes to fully capture the narrative. And they took pride in Michael as a black man who had somehow managed to become the most popular entertainer in the world.

Unlike the reggae we listened to so often, Jackson's music had little overtly Africa-oriented content. Many Tanzanians suspected there was an African inspiration for songs like "Wanna Be Startin' Somethin'," which featured a very African-flavored beat and a chant ("Mamasay, Mamasa, Mamakusa") in what sounded like an African language. Manu Dibango, a Cameroonian saxophonist who has recorded numerous albums of funk-flavored African jazz in his thirty-year career, thought so, too: he accused Jackson of copying the African chant in

"Wanna Be Startin' Somethin' " from his "Soul Makossa," a song with a strikingly similar chant that was a crossover hit in the United States in 1973. Jackson denied the allegation, but my friends and I were tickled by the notion that our favorite Jackson song might have been copied from an African musician.

There were other undisputed examples of African influence in Jackson's music, however. Fans in Tanzania were especially pleased when he used a Kiswahili phrase in one of his later songs, never mind that the song perhaps exposed more ignorance of Africa than it did pan-African sentiment. "Liberian Girl," a ballad on Jackson's *Bad* album, featured a whispered declaration of love, "Nakupenda pia, nakutaka pia, mpenzi we!" ("I love you too, I want you too, you lover"). Jackson didn't seem to realize that Kiswahili is spoken neither in Liberia nor in South Africa, the homeland of the singer hired to recite the words on the song (which she did with a notably inauthentic accent). Nonetheless, East African fans were happy for the acknowledgment.

Michael Jackson's reputation in Tanzania became slightly tarnished as he escalated his experimentation with plastic surgery, a process of self-mutilation many saw as an effort to rid himself of black features. Like many African Americans, Tanzanians wondered why he felt the need to so drastically alter himself (the very concept seemed so strangely American), and whether he was ashamed to be black. The last straw came when Jackson actually visited Dar es Salaam in the early 1990s as part of an international tour. He arrived at Dar es Salaam airport to great local excitement, but sparked considerable controversy when he repeatedly squeezed and brushed his nose with his hand, a gesture many Tanzanians took to mean that he found the scent of the damp East African air distasteful. Jackson later insisted that he had a nervous habit of touching his nose, but many Dar residents remained skeptical. A rumor circulated that Jackson had expressed an interest in visiting one of the game parks in northern Tanzania but had changed his mind when told that he would not be permitted to land his private jet in the park, and his public estimation suffered dramatically.

Along with Michael Jackson, hip-hop became a cherished import among Dar es Salaam teenagers. Early raps by hip-hop pioneers like the Sugarhill Gang reached Dar in the early 1980s, but the genre didn't really become popular until breakdancing overtook the city in the middle of the decade, gaining popularity through the films *Beat Street* and *Breakin'*. I was introduced to breakdancing through my cousin Chris, who taught me new moves and updated me on the music when my family visited the United States every second summer. I would return to Dar with new musical acquisitions and clothes, well versed in the latest dance moves, and share my fresh cultural knowledge with my friends. I competed in breakdancing competitions around the city, and established a self-styled hip-hop crew with my friends. With hip-hop music came hip-hop fashion, and soon teenagers all over Dar were wearing sweat suits, parachute pants, and high-top sneakers, and sporting high-top fade haircuts with creative parts carved into them. They bought their imported clothing cheap from *mitumba* salesmen, who sold piles of secondhand clothes brought in from the United States. I would painstakingly write out the lyrics to songs by Run-D.M.C. and Eric B. & Rakim for my friends, who attempted to memorize them. Hip-hop videos circulated among rap fans all over the city.

We missed many of the cultural references in Rakim songs like "Follow the Leader" or "Microphone Fiend" (two favorites), but that did not stop us from appreciating the insistent lyrical flow and the irresistible beats. More than understand it, my friends and I *felt* it.

My friends and I took a special interest in the representations of Africa that sometimes crept into rap songs. Rap references to Africa were usually depictions of a glorious African past or grim descriptions of contemporary Africa, and while neither entirely resembled our reality in Dar es Salaam, Tanzania, we were struck by the fact that the continent was even mentioned at all. In the title track from the film *Beat Street*, for example, rapper Melle Mel described an Africa gripped by famine and poverty, painting a generalized image of stereotypical despair: "The children in Africa don't even eat, / Flies on their faces, / They living like mice, and the houses even make the ghetto look nice / The water tastes funny, / It's forever too sunny, / And they work all month and don't make no money." Rap groups like Stetsasonic, Public Enemy, and Boogie Down Productions (BDP) provided more favorable depictions, but in the end the positive interest in Africa shown by many black entertainers of the 1980s was a temporary fad. As the ever-insightful KRS-One of BDP rhymed on "Stop the Violence," "You could talk about Nigeria, / People used to laugh at ya, / Now I take a look and I see USA for Africa?"

My friends and I were also impressed by the Afrocentric turn black fashion took in the late 1980s, at the peak of hip-hop's black nationalist phase. Africa medallions, Afrocentric T-shirts featuring figures like Malcolm X, and the pan-African colors black, red, and green became more and more prominent in the rap videos we watched, and many

Tanzanian hip-hop fans took the cue. I often reflected on the irony of urban African youth eagerly outfitting themselves in "African" clothing and accessories created and popularized by African Americans.

An entire industry grew out of the local demand for African American music. Tanzanians abroad would send records and videos to their friends and relatives back home, and anyone who traveled to the United States or Europe returned to Dar with an ample supply of the latest musical goodies. As soon as the new music arrived it became a valuable commodity. My friends and I used to collect music for our own enjoyment and for the university campus parties or neighborhood get-togethers we occasionally hosted. Our techniques were rather primitive: we would cobble together a music system out of various components (one tape deck from my house, another from somewhere else, and an amplifier and speakers on loan from a family friend), and traverse the city to record new music from friends who had just received records from abroad. Sometimes local deejays would guard popular new songs jealously, and we would have to settle for less celebrated tracks or else record songs from the unlabeled, anonymous tapes that circulated along the city's underground musical grapevine. We were often reduced to guessing at the artists or titles of the songs we played at parties, but we managed to keep our audiences happy by sticking to the mix of black American R&B and hip-hop, Caribbean reggae and calypso and African pop that was the standard fare at Dar es Salaam dance parties.

We never thought it remarkable that so much of the music we loved came from overseas, and I don't think we ever really wondered why songs in a language that many could not understand would be so popular among African audiences. It was obvious that locals responded enthusiastically to music by black artists like Michael Jackson and Lionel Richie, while white rock by groups like Van Halen usually left us cold. But I don't know that we really understood the power of Africa's legacy in African American music, or the extent of the informal musical dialogue between African and diaspora that helped to produce our favorite songs. I only really came to appreciate the existence of a global cultural network in which aspects of culture are circulated between international communities when I left Tanzania to study in the United States.

As a college student in Cambridge, I often devoted my Saturdays to exploring a musical heritage. During my sophomore year, I became a staff deejay at WHRB-FM, Harvard's student-run radio station.

"Werb," as some called it, mainly featured classical, jazz, rock, and news shows, and coverage of Harvard sporting events. But on Saturday afternoons and evenings, black music took over the airwaves.

Various cohorts and I were first up at one p.m. with *Dub Frequency*, a four-hour reggae show in which we spun reggae classics and new hits for appreciative audiences in Cambridge and Boston. In addition to the foundational staples of Bob Marley, we played hypnotic dub tracks by Mikey Dread and Prince Far I, melodic masterpieces by groups like Culture and the Mighty Diamonds, and roughneck dancehall gems by Shabba Ranks and Ninjaman. Drawing from the considerable collection of albums that the radio station had assembled over the years, and buying new records at area stores every week, I learned much about the genre and its diversity. And the show gained a following among local reggae lovers, who would call up to make requests, applaud our selections, and ask us to make "shout outs." Almost every Saturday a guy with a heavy Jamaican accent would call up asking us to "big up" Eaton Street (apparently the haunt of a group of Rastas who always tuned in to the show), and one caller once even asked up to repeat a song we had played because he had been taping the show but his cassette ran out.

After *Dub Frequency*, I would sometimes sit in on *Street Beat* at five, a tremendously popular hip-hop program that received even more calls than the reggae show. My college years coincided with an especially fertile period in hip-hop history, and the deejays at *Street Beat* always did their best to showcase much of the rich new talent. Favorites of the day included "How I Could Just Kill a Man" by Cypress Hill, "The Choice Is Yours" by Black Sheep, "Scenario" by A Tribe Called Quest, "O.P.P." by Naughty by Nature, "They Want Effects" by DAS EFX, and "Know the Ledge" by Rakim. These were the songs I heard at the radio station on Saturday evenings, and danced to at clubs and campus parties. Contemporary hip-hop, the reggae I played on *Dub Frequency*, and the African music I listened to in my room formed the life-sustaining soundtrack of my undergraduate career.

If Africans, African Americans, and West Indians at Harvard tended to have many separate interests and concerns, we always came together to party. "Black" parties, whether sponsored by the BSA, HASA, the Caribbean Students Association, or individuals, attracted students from all of the area colleges' black subcommunities. And they all seemed hungry for hip-hop, reggae, and R&B, and for the sweaty intimacy of darkened rooms jammed with dancing bodies pressed hotly against one another, with no choice but to move as one to the pumping music. Many African Americans may have taken little interest in African politics, and many Africans may have been bewildered by black American preoccupations, but the boundaries seemed to dissolve on dance floors fueled by the driving rhythms of contemporary black music.

There was of course a diversity of regional tastes. If Africans hosted a party, in addition to the customary R&B, hip-hop, and reggae, it would tend to feature segments of Ghanaian highlife, Nigerian juju music, South African township pop, or Zairean soukous, interludes in which many Africans would whoop excitedly and gyrate with even greater intensity while many non-Africans left the dance floor. At times, Caribbean-sponsored dance parties would deluge partygoers with blocks of carnivalesque calypso that would eventually sideline non–West Indians who couldn't stand dancing to more than a couple of the high octane songs in a row. And at African American–organized events, Africans and Caribbeans would sometimes tire of an undiversified diet of rap, R&B, or house music, or would be reduced to looking on as black Americans zealously shouted the lyrics of an old-school favorite. Still, all of the various musical traditions that came together at pan-African parties seemed somehow related, all at least partly derived in some way from the pulse of African rhythms. By being exposed to different rhythmic flavors we learned about each other and ourselves. And in sharing our celebrations of different sounds with one another, we participated in a process of cultural mixing and exchange that had helped to shape all of the various musical styles that we cherished.

Music has always played a central role in the international black experience. Richard Jobson, an English seaman who explored West Africa in the 1620s, was prompted to observe, "There is without a doubt, no people on earth more naturally affected to the sound of musicke than these people." In traditional African societies, music served a variety of functions in everyday life, as a medium for communication and an important part of ritual and recreation rooted primarily in the rhythmic power of the drum. Though musical styles and forms varied greatly among the hundreds of West African ethnic groups, there were certain commonalities that would later find expression in the musical heritage of displaced Africans in the Americas. In particular, African Americans held on to specific forms of polytonality and syncopation, harmonic conventions, call-and-response singing, and the "ring shout," a mode of musical performance in which dancers formed a circle and sang while shuffling in a (usually) counter-clockwise motion. Mindful of the communicative and therefore subversive potential of African drums and music, slaveowners in America forbade their slaves from using drums. However, Africans' "natural" musicality was recognized and even appreciated; male slaves with good singing voices fetched higher prices at market because overseers had noticed that slaves seemed to work faster when their labor was accompanied by a rhythmic work song. Without access to drums, the cornerstone of African musical innovation, enslaved Africans in the Americas relied on practices like the ring shout to pass on modified cultural knowledge in the form of music. Through the ring, Africans in the Americas used an African musical tradition to create American musical forms that reflected the new social context and that borrowed elements from the European cultures to which the slaves were exposed. But at the music's heart was the throbbing beat of Africa.

Spirituals, the earliest documented African American musical form, were heavily African in flavor, often using a call-and-response structure that demonstrated the influence of West African musical conventions, though they also reflected European choral traditions. And as religious songs that envisioned a place where slaves could be free of the burdens of bondage, they evoked idealized visions of the American North and perhaps recalled freedom in Africa.

In the post-Emancipation period, black spirituals and work songs gave rise to the blues, a genre that became popular in the Reconstruction era and bore a striking resemblance to West African musical forms, adopting similar structural and stylistic conventions. The blues thrived among poor rural blacks, and during the great black migration of the late nineteenth century moved to the cities, where it continued to evolve and gained commercial success with singers like Bessie Smith. But the music was often looked on with disdain by upper-middle-class blacks who regarded it as common, crude, and far too "black" for polite circles. As one blues musician of the period commented, "When we played for the black people it would depend on what element we played for. Because there were the upper class, or elite, black people. We would call them 'siddity,' which is black chat for highfalutin', high strung, or elite. That means high brow. And you couldn't play no low-down funky blues for them neither. We'd have to play basically what we had to play for high-brow white people."

Black spirituals, too, fell victim to these class tensions. After Emancipation, many upwardly mobile, educated blacks sought to uplift the race by demonstrating their "civility" and eligibility for polite American society. Ensembles like the Fisk Jubilee Singers toured the United States and Europe and won international acclaim for their renditions of black spirituals, but their versions, largely stripped of African flavor and adapted to European choral conventions, were quite different from the spirituals devised and performed by slaves in the antebellum South.

Efforts by certain segments of the black community to distance themselves from more "African" styles of musical expression were in part a backlash against the enormously popular (among white audiences) minstrelsy of the nineteenth century, in which white musicians performed whitened versions of slave songs while wearing blackface makeup in a parody of black musical performance. Many black composers of the late nineteenth century understandably sought to disassociate themselves from this stereotypical "black" music, but, unfortunately, to many musicians making black music "respectable" meant stamping out its Africanisms.

When heroic black involvement in World War I did little to earn African Americans the full rights of citizenship in the United States, and when white resentment mounted as thousands of Southern blacks moved to urban centers in the North, more nationalistic and less assimilationist voices began to assert themselves among the black elite. This newly outspoken attitude found expression in the New Negro movement, and the new appreciation for the cultural distinctiveness of African American music became a hallmark of the era.

As Langston Hughes declared: "Let the blare of Negro jazz bands and the bellowing voice of Bessie Smith singing Blues penetrate the closed ear of the colored near-intellectuals until they listen and perhaps understand. . . . We younger Negro artists who create now intend to express our dark-skinned selves without fear or shame. If white people are pleased we are glad. If they are not, it doesn't matter. We know we are beautiful. And ugly too. The tom-tom cries and the tom-tom laughs."

Some of the pan-Africanist ideas that found expression in the New Negro movement were the product of the late nineteenth century, when blacks from around the world crossed paths in Europe, fanning the flames of pan-African consciousness and resulting in the first Pan-African Conference, in 1900. Many of these international travelers were entertainers and musicians; from the very inception of the pan-African movement music played an important role as a unifying medium and a forum through which blacks around the world shared ideas and expressed commonalities. Marcus Garvey and his UNIA emerged in this political climate, and the organization's theme song, the "African National Anthem," with its references to "the land of our fathers" and its demand to "let Africa be free," expressed the UNIA message in music.

Black composers who studied and performed in Europe also paid tribute to Africa in their work. Samuel Coleridge-Taylor, an African American composer who became famous internationally around the turn of the century, often wrote music with a "black" theme, such as *Symphonic Variations on an African Air* (1906), *The Bamboula* (1910), and *Twenty-four Negro Melodies* (1905), while William Grant Still, a Coleridge-Taylor disciple, penned *Africa* and *Afro-American Symphony* (the first symphony by an African American) in 1930. The titles of compositions by artists like Coleridge-Taylor and Still often referred explicitly to Africa, but although they experimented with the blues and spirituals, in musical terms the pieces bore a stronger resemblance to European orchestral suites than to African forms. With the advent of jazz, African American music began to seek to evoke Africa in style as well as in name.

Jazz, a new genre that became increasingly popular in the early twentieth century, had emerged from blues and ragtime in the 1890s, and rose to world prominence by the 1920s through the influence of performers like Joe "King" Oliver and Louis Armstrong. Early on a debate raged between music critics on the extent to which jazz reflected African stylistic influences; while critics were divided on this point, many early jazz musicians seemed to acknowledge a debt to Africa, at the very least in the titles of early jazz tunes. Though jazz is an American invention that borrows from diverse European traditions, it exhibits numerous musical Africanisms that survived the slave experience, perhaps most significantly in its heavy use of improvisation, syncopation, and polyrhythms. And throughout jazz's history, explicit efforts have been made by African American musicians to evoke Africa and establish a musical and cultural link to the continent through their music.

Late-nineteenth-century ragtime compositions by musicians like Eubie Blake, H. B. Newton, and Leo Berliner bore titles like "Sounds of Africa" (1899), "An African Reverie" (1900) and "Africana: A Ragtime Classic" (1903); between 1899 and 1934 more than forty rags and jazz tunes by various composers referred to Africa in their titles. This was partly because of African Americans' new interest in Africa, prompted by the back-to-Africa rhetoric of figures like Bishop Turner and Marcus Garvey. But African American composers who came up with song titles like "Zulu's Ball" or "Ethiopian Nightmare" were also undoubtedly influenced by the white tastes for the unfamiliar exoticism of "black" music. Eubie Blake admitted that his manager and co-composer Will Marion Cook helped sell the song "Sounds of Africa" (later renamed "Charleston Rag") by telling the white music publisher who bought it that it was "*genuine* African music," a label that supposedly served to explain the piece's less "conventional" musical devices.

While few, if any, African American jazz composers of the early twentieth century knew much about "genuine" African music, their ignorance did not stop them from imagining Africa through their own compositions, which often seemed to represent Africa as a heavily mythologized and savage place overrun with jungles and inhabited by "Hottentots," "Head Hunters," and "Pharaohs." Such imaginings often reflected ambivalence toward Africa on the parts of the musicians who sought to evoke it in song.

With the advent of the Harlem Renaissance, many jazz musicians exchanged this ambivalence for a positive identification with Africa, even if some remained as ignorant of the continent as ever. In 1927, Edward Kennedy "Duke" Ellington, a young pianist from Washington, D.C., became the bandleader at the Cotton Club in Harlem, a venue that would become a focal point of American jazz during the swing era. Ellington was influenced by the rhetoric of the Harlem Renaissance and applied some of its ideas to his music. As he said early in his career, "We must be proud of our race and our heritage, we must develop the special talents which have been handed down to us through the generations, we must try and make our work express the rich background of the Negro."

In his efforts to evoke a sense of black heritage and cultural distinctiveness, Ellington created a style of jazz that became known as "jungle music," a highly improvised big-band style that self-consciously harked back to an African past. Ellington's band was known for sprinkling its compositions with trombone and trumpet grunts, tweets, growls, and wails that were meant to evoke a jungle scene, and Ellington employed a number of West Indian musicians whose style was regarded as richer in African elements than that of their American counterparts. As Ellington said, "A whole strain of West Indian musicians came up who made contributions to the so-called jazz scene, and they were all virtually descended from the true African scene." Ellington's own interest in Africa, and black America's preoccupation with the continent in the 1920s and 1930s, found expression in the titles of such Ellington songs as "Menelik (The Lion of Judah)," a tribute to the Ethiopian ruler written around the time of the Italian invasion in 1935.

In 1973 Ellington and his band toured West Africa in a fitting culmination to a career spent exploring the black heritage in song. Ellington was appropriately moved by the experience: "After writing African music for thirty-five years, here I am at last in Africa," he wrote during the trip. "When the time for our concert comes, it is a wonderful success. . . . It is the acceptance at the highest level, and it gives us a once-in-a-lifetime feeling of having truly broken through to our brothers."

Ellington's efforts to capture Africa in his music can be seen as a musical corollary to much of the literary output of Harlem Renaissance poets like Claude McKay, whose work invoked images of Africa that were inspired more by American popular culture than by any real knowledge. The jazz musicians who followed in Ellington's footsteps did explore more sophisticated ways of evoking Africa in their music, but these still often retained a sense of imagined connection to the continent.

For John Birks "Dizzy" Gillespie, a pioneer of bebop in the 1940s, the exploration of African themes in his music was more a personal musical quest than a political or ideological one: he was looking for a specific type of sound, and his search led him to Africa. As he wrote in his autobiography, "Very early in my career I realized that our music and that of our brothers in Latin America had a common source. The Latin musician was fortunate in one sense. They didn't take the drum away from him, so he was polyrhythmic. My conception was, 'Why can't our music be more polyrhythmic?' In 1941 I wrote 'A Night in Tunisia' where the bass says, 'do-do-do-do-do-do' and 'daaanh-da-da-da-da-da-da' was being played against that. That was the sense of polyrhythm."

Although Gillespie had never been to Tunisia, let alone Africa, when he wrote "A Night in Tunisia," he did eventually make it to the continent and had a chance to interact with African musicians. At the Dakar Jazz Festival in 1980, Gillespie joined the Senegalese group Xalam and other African and African American musicians for an impromptu jam session on Gorée Island, where, during the Atlantic slave trade, captives had been stockpiled in notorious dungeons before being transported to the Americas. After playing alongside the Africans at the historic setting, Gillespie had a heartfelt message for his fellow musicians. "As a black American, I know my music comes from this land," he told them.

Another major jazz artist to experiment with African rhythms in the 1940s was Art Blakey, a drummer who, ironically, saw jazz as a distinctly American genre with little relation to Africa. Blakey's interest in the continent was more spiritual than musical, and when he traveled to Africa in 1948 it was not for musical instruction. "I went to Africa because there wasn't anything else for me to do," he said. "I went over there to study religion and philosophy. I didn't bother with the drums." Still, it seems as though he did find musical inspiration, for he recorded the song "Message from Kenya" in 1953, and then released a series of African-flavored drum ensemble albums, most notably *The African Beat*, which featured drummers from Nigeria, Senegal, Jamaica, and the United States.

The great John Coltrane, a saxophonist on a perennial search for spiritual enlightenment through music, also took an interest in the sounds of African music and sought to infuse his work with African stylistic elements. Coltrane played with a number of important jazz ensembles in the 1940s and 1950s, and by the time he started heading his own bands around 1957, he was striving to find innovative new ways of expressing himself musically and had begun to explore the African roots of jazz, a heritage he sought to capture in his compositions. In so doing Coltrane became a standard-bearer of the black cultural revolution of the 1960s; as his colleague and contemporary Miles Davis said, "[Trane] was expressing through music what H. Rap Brown and Stokely Carmichael and the Black Panthers and Huey Newton were saying with their words, what the Last Poets and Amiri Baraka were saying in poetry. . . . It was all about revolution for a lot of young black people—Afro hairdos, dashikis, black power, fists raised in the air. Coltrane was their symbol, their pride—their beautiful, black revolutionary pride."

While Dizzy Gillespie was inspired by Latin American musicians to experiment with African rhythms, Coltrane went directly to the "source." He began to collect recordings of African music and used some of the rhythms he heard there as foundations for compositions like "Dial Africa," "Tanganyika Strut," and "Dakar." In the 1960s Coltrane's musical exploration of African themes became even more pronounced. "Liberia" (1962) was a tune inspired by a chance meeting with some Liberians in New York City, "Dahomey Dance" sought to duplicate the vocal improvisation of some Dahomeyan singers on an anthropologist's field tape, "Africa" was a horn adaptation of pygmy vocal melodies, and "Ogunde," "Kulu Se Mama," and "Afro Blue" also reflected prominent African influences.

Coltrane also became interested in the work of African musicians like the Nigerian drummers Chief Bey and Babatunde Olatunji, whose *Drums of Passion* album influenced a number of American musicians of the era. Coltrane saw both drummers perform in New York and spoke to them about collaborating on an album that unfortunately never materialized; however, Trane paid tribute to Olatunji in the song "Tunji" and supported him in his efforts to open a Center of African Culture in Harlem. And he reportedly spoke to his Nigerian friend about visiting the continent: "Next time you go to Africa, I'm going with you," he told Olatunji. "I gotta go over there. I want to go over there with someone like yourself." As Coltrane's biographer C. O. Simpkins writes, "John spoke of 'having to get to the source,' feeling that Africa contained the throbbing heart from which all music came." Though Coltrane died before he could make the trip to West Africa, the continent remained an important influence in his music and in the spiritual quest that dominated his later life.

In Coltrane's friendship with Olatunji, we see the beginnings of a new phase in African American musicians' efforts to express an African heritage in their work. While black American composers of the early twentieth century tried to evoke Africa with little knowledge or understanding of actual African musical conventions, using their inherited cultural knowledge and imaginations to conjure musical jungle scenes, by the 1950s African American musicians had gained access to actual African music and to African musicians. Musicians like Coltrane explored African rhythms in recordings and actually played with African performers like Olatunji, to produce a more "authentic" version of musical pan-Africanism. And African American musicians like Art Blakey learned even more about African music by traveling to the continent itself. Also, with advances in recording and broadcasting technologies, musicians in Africa in their turn were increasingly exposed to, and influenced by, African American music. Thus, as actual contacts and collaborations between African and African American musicians expanded, so did a pan-African musical dialogue that spanned the Atlantic in a complex musical give-and-take.

In 1956 the trumpeter Louis Armstrong, who all but personified jazz in the 1920s, traveled to Ghana and performed for a crowd in Accra that included soon-to-be prime minister Kwame Nkrumah, a jazz fan since he was exposed to the genre as a college student in the United States.

It was a symbolic moment layered with meaning and emotion. "I want to lay this one on the prime minister," Armstrong said in his famous growl, announcing and dedicating the song "Black and Blue." "What did I do to be so black and blue?" Armstrong sang gruffly. Ralph Ellison had referred to the famous song in *Invisible Man* (1952), poignantly playing on its allegorical meaning as a reference to the existential "social condition" of blackness. Perhaps with this rendition in Accra, Armstrong was sending a specific message to his audience, hinting at a racial experience that he, Nkrumah, and the thousands of assembled Africans all seemed to share. "I'm white inside . . . so what did I do to be so black and blue?" he continued the almost jarring lyrics. Nkrumah, the pan-Africanist who had spent several formative years in America, probably knew just what Armstrong was talking about. He sat listening with the slightest of smiles playing across his face. Armstrong called the experience the "second happiest moment of my life" (the happiest being his first performance alongside the legendary bandleader "King" Oliver), and it was a milestone in the history of black music and pan-Africanism. Armstrong was met by a joyous throng at the airport and the crowd he performed for was estimated at one hundred thousand. He was struck by his own physical resemblance to the Ghanaians he met, and when he saw a woman who looked just like his mother he became convinced that Ghana was his ancestral home. "My ancestors came from here and I still have African blood in me," he said.

He communed with his newfound kin during his concert, trading trumpet licks with local musicians, on whom he had a significant impact. E. T. Mensah, a prominent Ghanaian musician and pioneer of "highlife," a popular West African dance music that borrowed from ragtime, was enthralled. "Louis was a great player and put all his energy in, from his head to the tip of his toes," Mensah reported of the historic jam session. "We could see everything quivering, sweating all around, and saliva coming out. I observed that if he wanted to play a note, he must force the note to come, come what may. So we could see him pitching high. He found my range and started above it, so that his trumpet sounded like a clarinet. He was pitching high all the time, his lowest note was my top G. We jammed for about a half an hour playing 'Saint Louis Blues.' Then he left the stage and listened to us playing highlife." With the advent of African American musical performances in Africa and the collaborations of artists like Coltrane and Olatunji, Africa and her diaspora began to participate in a global ring shout in which musical ideas and musicians circulated and bounced off one another to forge new and rich musical creations.

Interestingly, though it was a rewarding encounter for himself and his hosts, Louis Armstrong did not decide to travel to Africa independently. He performed in Ghana at the request of the U.S. State Department, which sponsored international tours featuring a number of American "goodwill ambassadors" in the 1950s, sending musicians and athletes abroad as representatives of American democracy in an effort to combat communism. At the time Soviet propaganda often focused on U.S. racism to discredit American claims of leading the "Free World," and the United States hoped that its black "jambassadors" would help to demonstrate America's social progress and that dedicated African Americans could flourish in America. The State Department attempted to shape the interaction of black American performers with international audiences and essentially sought to deploy the creativity of jazz musicians and sports stars for U.S. political ends.

Despite the official political purpose of the visits, black American performers were often able to use the platform to serve their own interests and did not always articulate the political message that they were expected to. Dizzy Gillespie toured Asia and South America as a State Department emissary in 1956 and established relationships with Brazilian musicians that would later influence his work. However, as he put it, "I sort've liked the idea of representing America, but I wasn't going to apologize for the racist policies of America." In at least one case, a musician even angrily refused to cooperate with the U.S. agenda. In 1957, after violent mobs in Little Rock, Arkansas, resisted federal orders to desegregate a public school, Louis Armstrong was upset enough to call off a scheduled State Department tour of the Soviet Union. "The way they are treating my people in the South, the government can go to hell," he told the press, an uncharacteristically harsh statement from a man famous for his uncomplaining graciousness. He also lashed out at Orval Faubus, Arkansas' segregationist governor, calling him an "uneducated plow-boy," and said President Eisenhower was "two-faced" for not standing up to Faubus. "It's getting so bad, a colored man hasn't got any country," Armstrong lamented.

Though Armstrong's denunciations were embarrassing for the State Department, the government soon seemed to get its revenge. Having recovered from his anger over the Arkansas desegregation debacle, Armstrong eventually agreed to represent the U.S. on another State Department tour to Africa and visited the Congo in 1960. He was welcomed enthusiastically by Congolese, who carried him triumphantly around Leopoldville (later renamed Kinshasa) in a sedan chair. Armstrong clearly relished the adoration, waving at cheering crowds with his handkerchief and flashing his famous grin, but what he did not know was that his visit provided cover for a much more sinister U.S. government initiative. The happy commotion on the streets of Leopoldville may have been engineered by the State Department as the perfect distraction from a conspiracy unfolding at around the same time: the assassination of prime minister Patrice Lumumba.

Despite the role of Cold War intrigue in the State Department jazz tours of the 1950s, as evinced by the impact of Armstrong's visit to Ghana, concerts in African nations often afforded African American musicians with opportunities to build on and explore processes of pan-African cultural exchange.

After Louis Armstrong and E. T. Mensah shared the stage in Ghana, many other transatlantic collaborations followed, with mixed results. In 1960 Max Roach, a drummer who rose to prominence during the bebop era, recorded his *Freedom Now Suite*, a musical exploration of the black experience that celebrated black liberation struggles in America and Africa. The large ensemble that performed the composition included Coltrane's old friend Babatunde Olatunji and the vocalist Abbey Lincoln, who engaged in a musical dialogue that explicitly underlined the link between African American and African musical traditions and liberation struggles. As much a political manifesto as a musical expression, the *Freedom Now Suite* chronicled the African American fight for civil rights and the triumphs of Africa's independence movement, and denounced apartheid in South Africa, where it was promptly banned. Following up on his interest in African music, Roach later became a professor of jazz and spent a summer in West Africa doing research for a course he wanted to teach on the history of African music, returning to the United States with a firm grasp of African musical styles and with a number of African instruments, with which he set up a "drum choir."

In 1960, in the heyday of the African decolonization process, the African American jazz pianist Randy Weston celebrated the emergence of independent Africa in *Uhuru Africa* (*uhuru* means "freedom" in Kiswahili), a multimovement composition for a large ensemble made up of a number of African American and African musicians (including the ubiquitous Olatunji). The piece fused a number of

African American genres, making wide use of African rhythms, and the music was complemented by a poetic text on the black experience by Langston Hughes.

However, when the ensemble performed the composition at a festival of black arts in Lagos in 1961 it was not well received, by some local accounts. Despite hostile reviews by some writers in the Nigerian press, one of whom denounced the performance as "repulsive," Weston was unfazed, returning to Nigeria in 1963 to lecture on music at local universities. "I gave demonstrations on the piano and I would tape Nigerian folk music, then take the same melodies and the same rhythms and play it on the piano, and explain to them that this music that is called jazz . . . for me is an extension of African culture," he said.

Though some Nigerian music critics had rejected *Uhuru Africa*, Weston was able to open a valuable dialogue with musicians and musical students in West Africa, and his own work reflected the experience. "I've been going through a period of heavy concentration on rhythm," he said during a later phase of his career. "Using a lot of traditional rhythms and also playing the blues, so people can recognize that there's actually no difference in the musics. It's like I'm developing the language of the African talking-drums on piano."

The African American drummer Ronald Shannon Jackson had a similarly positive experience on his visit to the Congo in the 1960s. He was drawn to Africa out of a lifelong sense of identification and a desire to further explore the African-derived rhythms that dominated his drumming, and he was not disappointed.

"What I saw and heard was unbelievable," he said of his arrival in the Congo. "I heard some of the most fantastic drumming I've ever heard in my life. . . . I was like a sponge soaking up new experiences." Jackson's exposure to African drummers and drumming styles subtly affected his own playing, but more than that it confirmed for him the cultural and musical link between Africans and African Americans. "The African trip didn't change my way of drumming," he said. "It just verified a lot of things I intuited, and truthfully, I knew, but I had no verification in reality until then." Perhaps most edifying for Jackson was the realization that music was often the only language he needed to converse with African musicians. "Most of the places I went to, the people who did speak any Western language spoke French. And I don't speak French or any African language," he recalled. "Certain places you go you're on a certain communications level where you don't have to use words. We communicated through the music. That's it." Jackson's trip had such a profound impact on him that when he returned to the United States he recorded a musical tribute to his experiences. "This music is a reflection of a person who went on a journey," he wrote in the album's liner notes, "a soul searching historical perspective, an identification, and who found those things."

Even while musicians like Ronald Shannon Jackson exulted in being able to converse with Africans through the mutually understood language of music, other black American musicians who collaborated with Africans acknowledged that understanding on nonmusical matters was often more elusive. In 1973 the clarinetist and composer John Carter recorded *Roots and Folklore: Episodes in the Development of American Music*, an extended meditation on the African roots of African American folk music, and he employed a number of Ghanaian drummers on the composition. But he found that he shared little with the African musicians besides an understanding of the music itself. "That was heavy," he said of the pan-African recording session. "I'm sitting there listening to them translate my English into Ghanaian, thinking: 'You know, these people look like me, and we are undoubtedly from the same place—yet they were Eastern people. The difference between us culturally was very glaring. They were Africa—I was America—and there was no mistake about it'."

The 1960s was a decade of cultural revolution for African Americans and Africans alike, and while it wasn't always an "authentic" Africa that was celebrated in the compositions of many black jazz musicians, the period afforded African American musicians an opportunity to explore the African roots of their music by visiting and studying in Africa and by collaborating with African musicians in the United States and abroad. As one African American composer of the period put it, speaking some years later, "During the 60's the prevailing opinion seemed to be that free playing was a return to African roots, a rejection of Western criteria. But while we were busy feeling that we were returning to our roots, it would have been better to say we were looking for those roots. In fact we're just now learning what African music is all about and how to perform it."

If we think of Africa and the diaspora as being involved in a transatlantic ring shout in which musical ideas are circulated, the pan-African outlook of African American music from the 1940s onward can be seen as a "call" to the motherland. The "response" from African artists was swift and profound. As communications technology and swifter global transportation made the world a smaller and smaller place, African American music spread across the world and was eagerly absorbed by African communities.

As early as the 1890s, we find evidence of African American musical forms carrying special cultural and political weight with audiences in South Africa. In 1890 the Virginia Jubilee Singers, a touring troupe of African Americans, performed a selection of spirituals in Kimberley, South Africa, as part of a regional tour, and were lauded by the local newspaper for their efforts. The singers "not only sang the Negro spirituals, the heartpiece of the oppressed culture of America's black slaves, deep into black South Africans' hearts," gushed one enthusiastic listener, "the tours also set ablaze the minds of South Africa's black population with a vision of black pride and dignity more powerful and clear than had ever been voiced before from a South African theatrical stage."

In the early 1900s ragtime and minstrelsy reached Africa, gaining a local following and spawning imitators. The vaudeville music of J. Turner Layton and Willie Johnson and the minstrel films of Al Jolson became especially popular, and in the early 1920s the African American minstrel team Glass and Grant were well received on a tour of West Africa. By the 1920s, Africans were creating their own ragtime bands and vaudeville troupes; Ghana boasted the Two Bobs and Carolina Girl, and a minstrel team called Williams and Marbel (all equipped with appropriately "American" names), while South Africa produced the Dark Town Strutters and the Hivers Hivers. Though they initially imitated the American models wholesale, African ragtime and minstrelsy soon incorporated local elements; in West Africa, the clownish antics of minstrels were soon identified with Anansi, the trickster figure of Ghanaian folklore, a familiar jester who often appears in traditional festivals and performances, and ragtime soon absorbed local instrumentation and conventions to generate highlife. And in South Africa, ragtime fused with local beer-hall songs to yield marabi, an urban pop that dominated the 1920s and 1930s, while local composers like Reuben Caluza combined ragtime with Zulu choral traditions to create a new indigenous musical blend.

In the post–World War II years, the dominant musical import in Africa were the cha-chas, mambos, and rumbas of Afro-Cuba, which flooded the continent in the 1940s. Essentially African in rhythm, Cuban music by bands like the Orquestra Casino Havana and Trio Matamoros quickly took over nightclub soundtracks from Congo to Senegal. The styles were picked up quickly by local groups, especially in francophone African countries like the French and Belgian Congos, where elaborate dance orchestras played music that closely resembled the Latin dance numbers of 1940s Havana.

Africans who traveled abroad were also exposed to and influenced by diaspora music. Manu Dibango, the Cameroonian saxophonist and sage veteran of African popular music, left Douala in 1950 to attend secondary school in France. Like many African students in the West, he often confronted feelings of isolation and loneliness, but he found some solace in the African American music he listened to on the radio. "What happiness . . . when I first heard Louis Armstrong humming on the radio!" Dibango exclaimed in his autobiography. "Here at last was a black voice I recognized, a voice singing songs like the ones I learned in church. . . . Armstrong, Sidney Bechet, the Lesters [a reference to saxophonist Lester Young] were like gods to us—more to us than to their fans in Saint-Germain-des-Prés, where they would give concerts. . . . Count Basie, Duke, Coltrane, Parker—some of their songs marked me for life. I ended up discovering the world through music." Part of the music's strong impact, Dibango noted later, was due to its unexpected familiarity: to him, Coltrane's playing sounded like oboists he had heard in Cameroon.

Encouraged in his own interest in music by listening to these artists, Dibango referred to them for inspiration when he began his own musical career. It was Armstrong's trademark singing that convinced Dibango that he, too, could sing as well as play his horn: "Louis Armstrong haunted me as a model. He played trumpet like a god and used his voice to give his music a human touch the cold metal instrument couldn't give. I had all his records. Before I ever understood English, Armstrong's voice and trumpet had blown me away. So why not try to follow his example? Even if the public couldn't understand my Douala, voices could be a connection to instruments."

Dibango's reasoning paid off in 1973, when he scored a huge international hit with "Soul Makossa," a delicious blend of funk, soul, jazz, and African rhythms that garnered a Grammy nomination for best R&B Instrumental Performance of the year. "The piece was released at the perfect moment," Dibango said of its success. "Afro wigs were all the rage. We felt as if we were back home with the Zulus. The Americans appreciated harmonies and vocal timbre close to their own. So what if they didn't understand the words? For them, 'Soul Makossa' evoked the Africa of the cities, the Africa they imagined when they thought of the continent. . . . For Uncle Sam, I was an

African making African music. In fact, it was no such thing . . . it was just my response to Louis Armstrong."

In addition to highlighting the ongoing process of pan-African musical dialogue, "Soul Makossa," a dance favorite in U.S. discos in the 1970s, was a breakthrough in that it was a rare case in which the African American public responded with widespread enthusiasm to music by an African musician. While African American music often seemed to flood into African cities, where it found eager consumers, African popular music did not usually enjoy wide distribution and rarely sneaked onto American radio stations or into U.S. record stores. And though the African songs that did hit U.S. markets didn't often become popular, some, like Dibango's answer to Armstrong, did make it onto U.S. charts and had an impact on African American audiences.

Though "Soul Makossa" was Dibango's only U.S. hit, his illustrious career produced many acclaimed albums that made him a popular star in Africa, Europe, and among international jazz and world music aficionados. And his music was often informed by explorations of various black musical traditions, experimenting with African melodies and rhythms, and mixing in jazz, soul, funk, and even reggae. In 1979, for example, he recorded an album in Jamaica, playing with well-known reggae musicians and producing a jazzy, reggaefied, and distinctly African musical mixture. And in 1985 he cut the album *Electric Africa* with Herbie Hancock, a high-tech mixture of African dance funk, techno-rock, and synthesized scratches and loops along the lines of Hancock's "Rock It," a breakthrough single that was a favorite amongst African American and Latino breakdancers in the mid-1980s.

African American music continued to have a significant impact in Africa in the 1960s, when rock 'n' roll by artists like Fats Domino became popular around the continent. Inspired by the rock 'n' roll they heard at sources like the United States Information Service offices in capitals all over the continent, youthful African musicians began putting together their own rock bands, at first usually based on white models like Elvis Presley, the Beatles, and the Rolling Stones. One of the earliest and most influential African rock bands was the Heartbeats, formed by Geraldo Pino in Sierra Leone in 1961. A number of groups were formed in the wake of the Heartbeats' success; the Echoes, the Golden Strings, and the Red Stars offered Pino's outfit competition in Sierra Leone, while the Avengers, the Road Runners, Blues Syndicate, Circuit Five, and the Phantoms emerged on the

Ghanaian scene in the early 1960s. In Nigeria the top rock groups were the Cyclops, the Clusters, the Hot Four, and the Spiders, all playing approximations of Chuck Berry, Cliff Richard, and other Western pop icons. As rock 'n' roll by African American performers like Chubby Checker began to dominate the American music scene, African rock musicians began to model themselves after black stars.

The soul music of Wilson Pickett, James Brown, Otis Redding, and Ray Charles swept Africa during the mid-1960s. James Brown quickly became the definitive model for African solo performers, and was widely imitated. The Heartbeats brought Brown-style soul on tour with them around West Africa, and seemed to inspire the creation of new soul bands in all of the cities they performed in; the El Pollos, the Black Beats and the Barbecues heated things up in Ghana, while the Hykkers, the Strangers and Joni Haastrup (the "Nigerian James Brown") made it funky in Lagos. And "Sukki Sy Man," a Congolese soul number, became a huge hit across West Africa.

Early attempts at African rock and soul were basically straight imitations that fell short of the originals. But by the late 1960s, with the proliferation of African American soul in addition to other musical imports (in 1966, for example, the Jamaican singer Millicent Small toured West Africa, introducing ska to the region, while the Latin rock of Santana and the blues-laced rock of Jimi Hendrix also became popular), African musicians began to create new fusions that went beyond the standard soul or rock recipes. And as soul songs like James Brown's "Say It Loud—I'm Black and I'm Proud (Part I)" became popular and helped to usher in a new era of politically charged lyrics, African musicians began to tackle topics of local importance in their songs. Also, with the intensification of the African independence movement, the rise of cultural nationalism all over Africa prompted many musicians to infuse African elements into their music.

By the late 1960s the stage had been set for the creative innovations of artists like Segun Bucknor, a Nigerian musician who headed the Soul Assembly (later renamed the Revolution), a soul outfit that was one of the first to experiment with African rhythms, lyrics of local relevance, and new musical combinations. As Bucknor states, "After the Assembly, I changed the name to Revolution as I was experimenting with pop music but using the real basic African beat, the African jungle-beat which we call the kon-kon, in 6/8 time. We did something like Santana did with Latin music and pop." The Revolution's early hits included "Who Say I Tire," a song about the harsh reality of life in Lagos, and "Pocket Your Bigmanism," a scathing condemnation of the arrogance of Nigeria's economic elite.

An even more significant departure from simple mimicry was made by Nigeria's Fela Kuti, who, until his death in 1997, was one of modern African music's senior statesmen. Kuti's musical journey is a chronicle of the evolution of contemporary African popular music. A saxophonist educated in England, Fela began his musical career in a highlife band in Lagos, the Cool Cats, and later headed another highlife ensemble while studying in London, where he was introduced to the music of Miles Davis and John Coltrane. He returned to Nigeria and, straying from his highlife roots, began to play jazz. When he had little commercial success in Nigeria, he traveled to the United States, where his musical (and political) horizons continued to expand.

In addition to being influenced by African American musicians he met in the United States, he absorbed the black nationalistic rhetoric of the Black Power movement and returned to Africa with a new pan-Africanistic cultural outlook. "You see, at the beginning, my musical appreciation was very limited, but later I got opened to many black artists," he said. "It was after I was exposed I started using jazz as a stepping-stone to African music. Later, when I got to America, I was exposed to African history which I was not even exposed to here. It was then that I really began to see that I had not played African music, I had been using jazz to play African music, when I really should be using African music to play jazz. So it was America that brought me back to myself."

After this musical revelation, Fela tried to move away from the imitation soul that dominated the Nigerian music scene in the late 1960s, an often frustrating though ultimately fruitful endeavor. "Every other band was playing soul music but me," Fela later remembered. "The attack was heavy, soul music coming in the country left and right. Man, at one point I was playing James Brown tunes among the innovative things because everybody was demanding it and we had to eat." Despite the prevailing preference for mimicry over homegrown creativity, Fela created a new musical style he called Afrobeat, a mixture of African rhythms, jazz, and soul replete with politically outspoken lyrics chanted in pidgin English. His work won a wide following, and helped to encourage other local artists to experiment with their own music instead of copying American imports.

It's an interesting irony that Fela found himself imitating James Brown before he could find acceptance for his own compositions. James Brown, whose music is filled with recognizable Africanisms (in his songs he usually plays the role of "master drummer," repeating shouted instructions against a polyrhythmic background and directing musical traffic with call-and-response phrases—"Can I take it to the bridge? Shall I take it to the bridge? Hit me now!"), said that some of his songs were inspired by East African rhythms. So while James Brown looked to Africa for musical inspiration and imitated African rhythms in his music, African musicians looked to his songs as models of African American soul that they copied for local consumption. By the late 1960s, the transatlantic ring shout had turned in on itself— the barking dog was chasing its tail.

This active musical syncretization helped to fuel events like FESTAC (the second World Black and African Festival of Arts and Culture) in 1977, an event in which black delegations from sixty-two countries gathered in Nigeria to celebrate the cultural achievements of black people around the world.

In attendance were the Ghanaian "Afro-rock" band Osibisa, Miriam Makeba (the South African singer who became world famous in the 1960s), Bembeya Jazz, Trinidad's Mighty Sparrow, Brazil's Gilberto Gil, Stevie Wonder, Donald Byrd, Tabu Ley (Zaire's top star) and many, many others. It was a truly pan-African gathering, in which musicians and artists were able to exchange and share ideas as well as showcase the diaspora cross-fertilizations that had already taken place. And FESTAC helped to herald the rapid shrinkage of the black musical universe; by the 1970s more musicians from Africa and the diaspora were crossing paths, on the continent and in the West, than ever before, and the music began to reflect this increasing contact. English-speaking musicians congregated in cultural centers like New York, London, and Los Angeles, while Paris became a focal hub for artists from Zaire, Senegal, Mali, Cameroon, and the French Antilles. With an irony that has often been repeated in the history of the black diaspora, the West, not Africa, became the primary locus for meaningful pan-African dialogue and exchange.

In addition to heralding unprecedented pan-African explorations of Africa's musical heritage, the 1970s and '80s also saw the rise of a number of African female artists. Miriam Makeba, who embraced an eclectic range of musical influences and styles, and whose life seemed to embody the world's increasing internationalism, became a model for many of the singers who would follow. In keeping with the long tradition of transatlantic exchange, artists like Mpongo Love, Angelique Kidjo, and Sally Nyolo referred to African, Caribbean, and African American vocal and musical styles to forge new mixtures, often providing specifically female perspectives to the social issues they examined in song, a foil to the masculinist work of singers like Fela, who was for some time married to twenty-seven of his backup singers and who expressed his disdain for notions of female equality in hits like "Lady." In this way, not only did music provide a medium for exploring pan-African culture, for a number of women it afforded the opportunity for a rich, gendered musical dialogue.

Hip-hop, the most significant development in black music since the 1970s, also emerged from and participated in the diaspora ring shout. Rooted in the toasting techniques that Jamaican sound-system deejays brought to New York City, rap music was created in the South Bronx by disenfranchised black and Latino youth in the late 1970s. A genre consisting of chanted rhymes backed by "break" beats made from fragments of prerecorded songs, rap has long been likened to West African praise-singing griot traditions and embodies elements of other African and African American oral conventions, such as playing the dozens. And early in its young history, rap pioneers looked to Africa for musical and cultural inspiration.

Afrika Bambataa, legendary Bronx deejay and one of hip-hop's leading pioneers, traveled to Africa as a high school student after winning the trip in an essay contest. The visit had such a strong impact on him that he changed his name to that of a nineteenth-century Zulu chief. And after watching a British movie set in South Africa, he felt inspired to form the Zulu Nation, a Bronx-based youth organization that played an important role in popularizing hip-hop culture. "I got the idea [for the group] when I seen this movie called *Zulu* which featured Michael Caine," Bambataa remembers. "It was showing how when the British came to take over the land of the Zulus how the Zulus fought to uphold their land. They were proud warriors and they was fighting very well against bullets, cannons and stuff. They fought like warriors for a land which was theirs. When the British thought they'd won the next thing you see is a whole mountain full with thousands of Zulus and the British knew they was gonna die then. But the Zulus chanted—praised them as warriors and let them live. So from there that's when I decided one of these days I hope to have a Zulu Nation too."

In its infancy most rap was basically party music, but the early success of a few "message" raps in the early 1980s (most notably "The Message," by Grandmaster Flash and the Furious Five, a bleak tale of urban poverty and hardship that became an international hit in 1982) set the stage for the emergence of an entire genre of rap music that took its cues from the politically outspoken black music of the 1960s. Though most of these songs provided descriptions of inner-city squalor or lectured listeners about staying in school, black nationalism did find its way into many raps.

Black nationalist groups such as Public Enemy rose to prominence in the mid-1980s. Public Enemy, a rap ensemble from Long Island whose musical innovations and radical politics helped change the face of hip-hop, used symbolism that recalled the Black Panther Party, and rhetoric influenced by figures like Malcolm X and Louis Farrakhan, to protest racism and promote black pride and unity. Sampling speeches by black leaders and layering siren screeches and bass and drum barrages under the rapid-fire lyrics of rapper Chuck D, Public Enemy sparked controversy but helped revolutionize rap music by making black nationalist "message" rap the most significant hip-hop genre of the late eighties. PE also influenced hip-hop's aesthetic shift from gaudy gold chains and glamorous leather suits to African jewelry and pendants and casual sweatsuits.

Other Afrocentric and black nationalist rappers followed. The Jungle Brothers, a trio from Brooklyn, brought a problack sensibility and style to a laid-back brand of funk-inflected rap and chose their name to demonstrate a positive reevaluation of Africa, their ancestral "jungle" home. X-Clan, a New York ensemble, pushed a black nationalist agenda and appeared onstage in African robes and red, black, and green bead necklaces; "I'm that kind of nigga that they can't stand / The one that taught African how to say Black Man," went a verse in the song "Fire and Earth." "The one you can plainly see / With nationalist colors of red, black and green / The one who cut Tarzan's vine / And ran his ass out of the jungle with his homeboy swine."

The New Jersey rappers Poor Righteous Teachers took a similar approach. "I see rap as being a gardening tool due to the fact that we are planting seeds," said group member Wise Intelligent of the group's philosophy. "We are trying to plant seeds in the minds of black youth. We are tying to tell the black youth that they are more than what they are being presented as. We're teaching black youth that their history goes beyond slavery. Their history goes beyond Africa. Black people are the mothers and fathers of the highest forms of civilization ever built on this planet. . . . We've been living amongst Americans for so long when we find out that we're not Americans it's time to take off the red, white and blue. Time to put on the red, black and green."

Some rappers even traveled to Africa on pan-African missions of self-education and brotherhood. Doug E. Fresh, a veteran Bronx rapper whose rhymes were usually more about partying than pan-Africanism, claimed to be the first African American rapper to visit Africa, an experience he found moving. "I felt like I was honored," he said of his visit to Gambia and Senegal. "I felt that it was a blessing to be there. I felt like I was touching history. I felt like I was doing something that a lot of people don't get the opportunity to do in a lifetime. Here I am in Africa. It was like, yo, this is no joke. I went to Senegal and I saw Gorée island, where the slaves were taken from. . . . I definitely made a record about that whole experience. It was called 'Africa: Going Back Home.' "

Rapper Daddy-O of the Brooklyn group Stetsasonic, which expressed Africa's important psychological impact in the song "A.F.R.I.C.A.," had a similarly positive experience when he visited Senegal in the late eighties. "We just played one venue. It was the football stadium there, it was like 77,000 people. It was incredible. It was the first time they had ever heard rap music. It was incredible. . . . By the time I was a day and a half into it, it was the most incredible experience in my life."

The pro-Africa rhetoric of many hip-hop groups did not go unchallenged, however. African American culture has always been characterized by a dialogue on Africa and on black people's relationship to it, and the Afrocentric rhymes of groups like Public Enemy eventually prompted a backlash.

With the rise of gangsta rap, usually associated with the West Coast and often preoccupied with urban crime and violent tales of gangster glory, the pro-black messages of black nationalist rappers began to be displaced by the gun-toting image and outlook of groups like Niggaz With Attitude, who often spoke disparagingly of other rappers' preoccupation with Africa. As NWA member Ice Cube complained on "Endangered Species," "You want to free Africa, I'll stare at ya, Cause we ain't got it too good in America. / I can't fuck with them overseas / My homeboy died over kee's." Similarly, in "The Nigga You Love to Hate," Cube lashed out against proponents of repatriation: "All those motherfuckers who say they're black / Put 'em overseas, they be beggin' to come back." NWA founder Eazy E was even blunter in his disdain for the pro-Africa hip-hop set: "Fuck that black power shit," he once said in an interview. "We don't give a fuck. I bet there ain't nobody in South Africa wearing a button saying 'Free Compton' or 'Free California.' "

Rap's pan-African and black nationalist outlook declined with the rise of other subgenres in the 1990s, but an interest in Africa as a source of spiritual or historical inspiration lingered in the work of some hip-hop artists. The Fugees, a Haitian–African American group, brought a pan-diasporean sensibility and feel to hip-hop that often sampled from reggae and other Caribbean sources, and identified with an African heritage. And all three Fugee members also launched solo careers that evolved into distinct New World African flavors. Wyclef Jean's solo effort explored his Haitian folk roots and an eclectic range of black musical traditions; Lauryn Hill created rap-laden masterpieces of '70s-style hip-hop soul and revisited a New York–Kingston musical axis; while Pakazrel Michel concocted pumping hip-hop dance jams.

In 1997, Erykah Badu, a hip-hop-influenced R&B singer from Texas, infused sensitive soul songs with Afrocentric mysticism and introduced a new sense of "African" spirituality to black popular music, and various African-oriented strands appeared in other contemporary work. The Brooklyn duo Black Star recalled the teachings of Marcus Garvey and invoked a vision of pan-African upliftment in classic hip-hop rhyming displays, while the Queens-based rapper Nas sometimes sounded a utopian note of Afro-escapism in reflective rhymes on the black American ghetto experience. "If I ruled the world," Nas rhymed in 1996, "I'd open every cell in Attica, send them to Africa." With the explosion of the African immigrant populations in large U.S. cities since the 1970s, African youth in America who grew up with hip-hop also began to produce rap music in the 1990s, often adding their own African cultural perspectives to the lyrical content as well as the backing beats. Perhaps African emcees will emerge as a new force in hip-hop in the twenty-first century.

Though only a handful of rappers actually traveled to Africa to visit or perform, rap music became immensely popular on the continent. In urban African centers where the music and videos were circulated (particularly in anglophone countries), many African youth became committed hip-hop fans and soon began making their own rap music.

By the 1990s, hip-hop-influenced performers like Prophets of da City, Zimbabwe Legit, and Too Proud had emerged in South Africa, Zimbabwe, and Tanzania, and there were rap ensembles in other countries, adorning hip-hop songs with lyrics in Zulu, Kiswahili, French, Shona, and other continental languages. African American hip-hop icons have large fan bases in many African cities: youth in Africa mourned the death of the Notorious B.I.G. in 1997 and rumors that Tupac Shakur had in fact feigned his death a few months earlier ran as rampant among African rap fans as they did among their counterparts in the United States. But despite the strong identification with American hip-hop, regional musical, cultural, and political influences have crept into the various African rap strands. As the manager of South Africa's Prophets of da City, one of the nation's leading rap crews, said in 1997, "If we're going to succeed in building a hip-hop identity here, the sounds have got to be South African and pertain to what's happening here."

In the 1990s, France-based rappers and singers of African descent like MC Solaar, Les Nubians and Bisso Na Bisso, an accomplished crew of Congolese MCs from Paris, also pioneered new and culturally distinctive responses to African American hip-hop and looked to both Africa and America for inspiration. American hip-hop has also influenced other genres of African pop music, which have sometimes featured rapping in addition to the usual singing, and whose artists often exhibit the influence of hip-hop fashion in their wardrobes. The Senegalese singing star Baaba Maal began mixing his native Fulani music with rap and reggae in the 1990s and became one of many self-conscious African participants in a process of pan-African musical innovation and exchange. "I'm sure that all the music that we hear from all over the world comes, in some way, from Africa—especially all the music that is coming from black communities in the Caribbean and the United States. They have their roots in Africa," he said in 1998, expressing a view shared by many African and diasporean musicians alike. "The music we play went out of Africa and got some experiences out in the world. And now it's coming back to Africa."

As Baaba Maal and so many other black cultural artists attest, the first Africans enslaved in America brought with them musical forms and cultural practices that mutated, evolved, and were combined with other traditions to yield new cultural offspring. Like ripples in a pond bouncing back toward their source, elements of African American culture later made their way back across the Atlantic to Africa, where they were in turn reworked and sent back, in an ongoing process of cultural cycling.

After four years in New England, during which I often found comfort in the emotionally reassuring strains of my favorite music, I graduated from Harvard in 1993, and said good-bye to Cambridge, Boston, and a large circle of friends who had seen me through the best and worst of my hectic college experience. My graduation was attended by the same family members who had dropped me off at my freshman dormitory when I first arrived, and their presence helped

give the event even more of an appropriate sense of closure. I was glad
to be finished, and proud to have done well. I had earned a bachelor's
degree in history and literature with honors.

As my senior year was drawing to a close, I had applied to the Columbia Graduate School of Journalism in New York City, hoping to
earn a master's degree in journalism and possibly embark on a writing
career. As the sun set on graduation day and my undergraduate years,
I already began to look forward to living and studying in New York in
the fall of 1993.

My year in graduate school proved even more chaotic than my four
years at Harvard. The Columbia workload threatened to smother me,
and though I had won a small scholarship and worked part-time, I
was constantly strapped for cash. A friend and I rented a cheap but
freezing hovel in Harlem, and pretty soon I was lunching on Snickers
bars and walking forty blocks in snow to save token money. I had become good friends with the Chinese restaurateurs on the corner
("Chicken wings and fried rice?" they'd say expectantly as I walked up
to the counter). The adversity fueled my homesickness. It had been
over six years since I had first arrived in the United States to pursue a
higher education, and in that time, I had returned to Tanzania twice.
But I still found myself dreaming of home. And as they had on lonely
evenings in Cambridge, music and the companionship of friends nurtured me through good and bad times in the Big Apple.

It was my Walkman that provided the nourishing background
rhythms of my life. As usual, it was hip-hop and reggae that kept me
going, the lyrical stylings and urban folklore of A Tribe Called Quest,
De La Soul, or Nas, the gravel-voiced reggae pronouncements of Buju
Banton and Terror Fabulous, or, as ever, the higher learning and biblical poetry of Bob Marley. I'd unwittingly mouth lyrics with Q-Tip
while headed uptown on the D train and wonder if Nas was deliberately quoting a Kikongo proverb when he said, "Sleep is the cousin of
death." I'd feel a bittersweet empathy when I listened as Buju yearned
for the Africa of his imagination ("Oh what a beauty my eyesight behold, / holy Ethiopia, protect me from the cold"), and it would get
me to thinking when Bob sang a line that seemed contextually meaningful ("the rich man's wealth is in his city"). And I savored the uplifting exaltation of emerging from the subway on a clear blue night,
when the song in my headphones would sound as if it were swelling to
fill the sky, so much so that I'd wonder why the people around me
weren't bobbing their heads too.

Music has helped to sustain me throughout my life, as it has for millions of black people throughout history. Even as Remmy Ongala's songs linked me to my home as a freshman at Harvard, African rhythms and melodies have historically served to evoke an ancestral home for blacks in the diaspora. Imagine the nostalgic emotional power carried by even a few strains of a favorite song from your childhood. Now imagine if that song recalled a home you had been stolen from and would never see again, or conveyed a sense of a place your parents had come from but you had never seen. Such is the power of Africa's musical legacy in the New World. The songs of Africa survived to nurture the descendants of Africa on foreign shores and still echo in a transatlantic cycle of black creativity, a medium for pan-African communication that inspires new cultural possibilities. These are the sounds that are still with us, the drumbeats from across the aeons, the "remembering song" that has helped to bind black people together.

STRETCHING HANDS UNTO GOD

I would go back to darkness and to peace,
But the great western world holds me in fee,
And I may never hope for full release
While to its alien gods I bend my knee.
                        —Claude McKay "Outcast"

My father stepped forward and addressed the smooth gray headstone, raising his arms in greeting. Nearby, a flock of Canada geese grazed in the grass, sticking their bills into the dirt and honking softly when they got in each other's way. Dragonflies flitted through the still, warm air, darting about in the rich orange glow of the twilight sun. The late-summer aromas of mown grass and sod hung in the air, and the headstones, dappled yellow in the fading light, looked unearthly and beautiful. I stood behind my father, flanked by my father's younger brother, my uncle André, and my two younger brothers, Kolo and James. I felt strangely proud, standing there in that place that brought back so many memories, surrounded by men representing two generations of my family, each of us so different from what we had been the last time we were there together. I felt I was attending a reunion of some sort, and was glad that my old friends would see how far I had come. And I felt at once sad and solemn, in light of what we had come to do.

My father spoke. "Remy Datave Wamba," he said formally, "this is Ernest Wamba-dia-Wamba, your father. We have come to feel your spirit and be with you." He said he knew Remy could hear him, and told him that we were fine. He told him that his uncle and brothers had also come, and then he beckoned to André. André said a few words, updating Remy on recent events in his life, including the recent birth of his baby boy, Kiese, and then was silent. I stepped forward.

"Remy, this is your brother Philippe," I said. "I'm sorry I haven't come to see you in a long time, but I think of you every day." It had been years since I had spoken directly to him. I had come to the cemetery in Waltham, Massachusetts, a few times while I was at Harvard, but in the four years since I'd graduated and moved to New York I hadn't made it back. And this was the first time in my memory that we had been there together, my father, my brothers, and I. It wasn't often that we were able to assemble in one place. My father had come to the United States for a conference and to spend some time with family, and Kolo and James had been going to school in the States for almost a year. We had all converged on my uncle's house in Lynn. Unfortunately my mother had been unable to come, but I was glad that the rest of us had been able to make this pilgrimage together. It was long overdue.

I told Remy that I knew he would always be with us. I said that I was doing well. And I told him that I knew he could see all that we had accomplished and that I hoped he was proud of us. Suddenly my voice caught in my throat and I could no longer speak. I felt long-buried emotions erupting to the surface as images and memories crowded my mind and spilled out of my eyes. I tried to continue, but everything that occurred to me to say seemed woefully inadequate and trivial, and every time I opened my mouth I tasted salty tears trickling into my throat. My father waited for me to speak, but I shook my head. My father gestured to Kolo and he stepped forward. As he began to speak, I gave myself over to tears, my first in many years.

* * *

My father keeps a thick photograph album bound in a speckled red cover on a shelf in the living room of the house in Dar es Salaam, Tanzania, we've lived in since we moved there from Boston in 1980. It chronicles a life.

The album opens with the first photograph ever taken of Remy, a baby picture mounted on white card, taken at the Kalamazoo hospital where he was born. The pudgy-faced infant is shrouded in a white hospital blanket and his tongue sticks out between his tiny brown lips. My mother often points proudly to the fact that the newborn sports a full head of curly black hair.

Flip through the pages and watch Remy grow from a solemn little boy in overalls, his large dark eyes peering out questioningly at the viewer, to a buck-toothed and gangly youth, the even tan of his smooth skin broken only by the dark scar on his forehead he got from walking into a wall when he was ten. Mixed in with the pictures are pieces of his schoolwork written on yellow-lined exercise paper in his distinctive dyslexic script, rough drawings and sketches he did at home and a typewritten note addressed to my parents, composed after Remy was grounded for smoking when he was eleven. "Dear Mom and Dad," the first line of the letter reads, "I promise I will never put another cigarette in my mouth again."

The pictures illustrate my close relationship with my brother, whom I referred to as my best friend though he was five years my senior. In one photograph he teaches me to fly a model airplane; in another, he helps me set up an electric car-racing set, a Christmas gift from our parents. The photos remind me of going fishing and trick-or-treating, riding bicycles or cutting school in the cemetery, where we attempted to smoke cigarettes in spite of my brother's promise not to.

The last section of the album consists of pictures taken in the children's cancer ward of the Boston hospital where Remy spent most of the last year of his life. Remy lying in bed wearing a brown bathrobe, his chemotherapy-ravaged hair sticking out unevenly from his scalp. Two-year-old James sitting on a bedpan, looking up and wondering why everyone is laughing. A Polaroid of Roberto, the hospital laboratory rat Remy named after a friendly technician who used to draw Remy's blood.

These photographs trigger recollections of curling up on the living room couch with James, Kolo, and my mother, as she read to us from *Helping Children Understand Leukemia*, a book in which cartoon figures of scowling leukemia cells stole oxygen from hardworking red blood cells. I remember visits to the hospital, the most disturbing of which was interrupted by a frantic group of nurses and orderlies armed with an oxygen mask and syringes, swarming around my brother while I looked on.

In the album there is also a Christmas card addressed to all of us from a hospital-bound Remy, with the words "I love you" painfully written in the unsteady scribble of a hand immobilized by IV drips, and a Christmas wish list scratched in the same strained scrawl on lined notebook paper. "First of all," the list starts, "I want *out*."

And loose inside the back cover, not placed under the sticky cellophane of the album's pages, are photographs from the funeral: my mother posing with her siblings and parents in unsmiling formality on the steps of our house on Cherry Street; the plot in which Remy was buried in the cemetery in Waltham. I remember our living room clogged with mourning friends and relatives, my mother disappearing into the bedroom while my father was led away by my aunt Anne. I remember confusedly welcoming the legions of dutiful well-wishers. It was the only time I had ever seen my father cry, and the image almost frightened me more than Remy's death.

I have selective but intense memories of Remy's illness and death. The images I recall of his suffering and its effect on my family stand out in my mind with a raw and still painful immediacy. Its impact was devastating and wrenching. When I consider the tragedy now, I realize that two things that sustained us through those traumatic years were the support of concerned family and friends and a strong faith. In attempting to make sense of the senseless passing of a child, my family almost unconsciously relied on a spiritual view of the universe that assumed the immortality of the human spirit and understood death as an inevitable transition in life. We took unspoken solace in the notion that Remy's soul would never be far from us and would find guidance and peace in its travels through a nonearthly realm. If these convictions can be called a religion, it is a religion without a formal name. But if religion is a system of beliefs with which people interpret and relate to spirituality, my family found religious ways to come to terms with Remy's death.

I would hardly call my family religious, but certain quasireligious beliefs and practices found their way into my family's everyday life and became almost second nature to my brothers and me. I think we all accepted the idea of a spiritual afterlife and had a sense of the existence of larger-than-human cosmic forces at work in the universe. My mother was essentially born and raised in the Congregational church, and has less than fond memories of Sunday worship in uncomfortable clothes, of saying grace before every meal, and of the strict moral authority of a God-fearing and quick-handed father. My father's father was a Protestant pastor of considerable influence in his rural Congolese community. On a visit to Zabanga, my brother Kolo was permitted to enter the region only when my aunt told the doubtful border guard that she was the daughter of "le pasteur." My father grew up in an intensely religious environment of stern ethical discipline and faithful fatalism.

Both my parents strayed from their Christian roots as young adults, my father learning to critique the church as the masses' opiate when he became interested in leftist ideas and politics, my mother abandoning her experience with organized religion and teenage "born again" piety in favor of a more relaxed, generalized sense of spirituality. Neither I nor any of my siblings has ever been baptized, and I don't believe I have ever attended a church service with either of my parents. We have never said grace at our dinner table (unless a guest suggested it), and if either of my parents has ever sat down to read the Bible, I have never seen it. Nevertheless, my childhood was informed by strong spiritual convictions and an amalgam of religious ideas and practices unself-consciously drawn from various traditions.

I have very early memories of my mother singing a mournful song in which a little girl asks her mother what heaven was like and why her dead father had gone there. "Heaven, my child, is a beautiful place, where there's a smile on everyone's face," my mother would sing the sad response to the child's innocent questions. "Daddy loved us so, but he had to go. We needed him so, but they needed him more." I was haunted by the lyrics and melody of the song, and would ask my mother to sing it again and again, grappling with the meaning of the words, furiously conjuring images to accompany the descriptions.

My father provided slightly different conceptions of an afterlife. His stories about his childhood in "the Village" took for granted the existence of a spiritual domain where the nonliving dwelled. In the world he described, the physical and spiritual realms often seemed to overlap; in one story he told of how a village man whose wife had died recently was suddenly taken ill. The local herbalist was consulted, and after examining the sick man he filled a large basin with water and displayed it in the compound. My father says he gathered around the basin with other curious villagers and peered into the water. There, like a picture on some surreal television screen, he saw the image of a woman who was clearly very angry, gesticulating aggressively and speaking rapidly and venomously. The herbalist said that the angry woman was the sick man's departed wife, and that she was furious because her husband had not bought her a *kitenge* (a bolt of colorful fabric) she had been promised before she died. The herbalist instructed the sick man to buy the *kitenge* in question and present it as an offering to his dead wife. My dad says that when the man followed the herbalist's instructions, he quickly recovered from his sudden illness.

Another story my father used to tell was about a little girl, one of his nieces, who one day accompanied his mother to the fields where the family grew cassava and other crops. While my grandmother worked in the field, the child playing contentedly nearby, she began to sing a traditional folk song in time to her labor but was interrupted by the little girl. "That's not the way we used to sing it," she said mysteriously. Intrigued, my grandmother asked, "How did you used to sing it?" The child launched into an archaic version of the song, singing in a dialect of Kikongo that was no longer in wide use. My grandmother questioned the little girl, asking her name and those of her family members and quizzing her on antiquated cultural knowledge. On the basis of the child's responses, my grandmother concluded that she was the reincarnated spirit of a long-deceased ancestor.

To hear my father tell it, this was not an entirely uncommon occurrence in Congo of his childhood, and he always told this story, and others like it, matter-of-factly, with little sense of drama or exaggeration. My father would also tell us about services in his father's church, so we never felt that the idea of ancestral spirits returning to earth, or of the actions of the dead affecting the living, were at odds with Christianity. I came to understand what little Christian rhetoric I was exposed to as just another way of talking about spirituality and the existence of realms beyond our physical reality.

Later, when I was old enough and interested enough to ask my father pointed questions about the various religious ideas that informed his upbringing, I learned that the balance between African and Christian belief was an important theme of his childhood. My father was born in a transitional period in Congolese religious history. Christian missionaries from Europe had preached the gospel among my father's Bakongo countrymen since the fifteenth century, when the Bakongo king Affonso I was baptized by Portuguese explorers. Though the king's conversion was generally thought to be a political move, European evangelism along the Congo River continued through the sixteenth, seventeenth, and eighteenth centuries, intensifying in the late nineteenth century especially. Despite the continued presence of missionaries in Congo throughout the colonial period, the European and American missions that carried Christianity to the Congolese countryside did not realize their greatest impact on Bakongo society until the post–World War II era. During the late 1940s, in my father's youth, Bakongo villages became stages for a confrontation between Christianity, as represented by various foreign missions, and Bakongo religious traditions.

My father's father was born into a traditional Bakongo household; his father had two wives, and my grandfather was raised with respect for traditional beliefs and customs, taught to revere Nzambi, the supreme creator god of Kongo religion, and to accept that prayers and offerings to lesser gods and ancestors could help one overcome misfortune and obstacles in life. Nonetheless, my grandfather's father seemed to early on see value in Christianity and Western schooling; although he himself never became a Christian, he sent my grandfather to be educated in Swedish mission schools. My grandfather joined the church as a young man and eventually became a catechist.

As a Christian, he learned to spurn polygamy and witchcraft, and raised his children with a strict Christian morality, passing on bits of religious wisdom with adages and sayings. "We found money here and we will leave it here," he used to tell his children to discourage them from stealing. "The most stupid person is the one who steals for the stomach." A well-respected leader in the community, my grandfather lived by the Golden Rule, paying school fees for village children whose parents could not afford them, providing food for those who lacked it, and encouraging his children to love their neighbors as themselves. The household my father grew up in often seemed like a "guest house," what with all the transients who constantly sought shelter there. In addition to earning a reputation as a man of God within his own community, my grandfather carried his Christian ideas to other villages in the area on preaching trips, on which my father would sometimes accompany him. As a youngster, my father attended church regularly, singing solos in the church choir organized by his musically gifted brother Daniel, and he received instruction in Christian dogma as part of his missionary education.

My grandfather and his family represented a growing trend in rural Congolese communities being transformed by new social forces. As Protestant missions began to have a greater impact, Christian values began to gain ascendancy: monogamous marriages began to be more favored and more common, and the education offered at mission schools began to be regarded as a valuable social resource. And as the society began to change, new conflicts and tensions began to arise.

Despite my grandfather's conversion and his role in the church, my father remembers that in some ways he struck a balance between traditional and Christian beliefs. Though he denounced witchcraft and taught his children to regard it as "worthless," as a child my father often suspected that his father possessed some sort of protective charm that shielded him and his family from hostile magic. That members of the community should seek to harm my grandfather through sorcery did not seem unreasonable to my father, for witchcraft was often one way in which the confrontation between tradition and "modernization" found expression. Older "protradition" members of the community sometimes denounced those who seemed too quick to accept Christianity and the new values that were transforming the society, and were sometimes thought to channel their frustration through destructive sorcery.

My father's uncle, a traditionalist and herbalist, came into frequent conflict with my grandfather, and my father has vivid memories of their intense quarrels and of having to calm my grandfather after particularly upsetting arguments. Their disputes embodied a struggle then engulfing the society at large, a confrontation between a younger generation that embraced "modernization" and an older generation that was not in tune with new developments and was losing control, using witchcraft and the threat of it in an effort to hang on. The most "modernized" members of the community—Christians, teachers, pastors, and young people who left their villages to seek employment in the cities—were often targeted by hostile traditionalists, who accused them of being "no longer of us," of having "ceased to be real people" or having "sold out to white people." My father remembers that he and his siblings were sometimes taunted as the "children of *muzungu*" (whites), but though the words stung, his family never seemed to fall victim to sorcery.

Though my father never confirmed his suspicions regarding his father's use of magic, he came to see him as a man who, despite being the catechist of a European church, was firmly rooted in his ancestral culture and had succeeded in articulating the two cultural dimensions. Though as a Christian he frowned on some traditional practices, he seemed completely at home with both Christianity and tradition. In addition to Christian morality and biblical teachings, my grandfather taught my father how to hunt and fish, told him stories about the clan and its organization, instructed him in proper traditional politeness and conduct, and passed on some of the values he had learned from his father.

Even if my grandfather had sought to shield his children from traditional customs and practices, he would have had difficulty. The daily life of Zabanga was dominated by tradition—at the fireplace, where villagers took their meals and discussed social issues; in the fields, where they tended their crops; in the forest, where groups of men and boys hunted or cut wood for carpentry and sang lewd songs about women and sex; and in the river, where the young people swam in the evenings. My father remembers that there were always occasions to celebrate life, and that singing, drumming, and dancing always commemorated the first harvest and other major events. When he accompanied her to the fields, my father's mother offered lessons on the natural environment, and taught him traditional songs that contained messages on morality and social conduct, and instructed him in what would be expected of him as a man and his role within the community. And his uncle, the philosopher who so often argued with his father, taught him about Kongo cosmology and traditional beliefs. Other community members whom he saw and spoke with every day helped fill in his cultural education. The religious dogma he received at school, imposed from without and not rooted in local experience, seemed artificial by comparison.

Despite my grandfather's religious zeal, my father's Christianity didn't really stick. Not only did he begin to associate a stigma with Christianity after being mocked as "the pastor's son" by his youthful peers, but also his experience with missionary education soured his relationship with organized institutional Christianity. He grew to hate school as a young student, and would often run and hide in the forest to avoid class. And even after he learned to enjoy academics and to take pride in his work and performance, he never really warmed to the religious aspect of his studies. Bible study was based on memorization, and not made to at least appear related to local life, and unimaginative missionary teachers used corporal punishment as the main technique for motivating students. By the time he reached secondary school, when he began to be influenced by the growing anticolonial movement, which included a critique of the role of evangelism in colonial subjugation, my father had lost patience with what he saw as missionary paternalism and racism. He noticed that in church the missionaries always sat in the front seats, and generally refused to mix with blacks. By the time my father won his scholarship to study in the United States, where he became an avid reader of leftist political thought, he, like many other African nationalists, had come to see institutionalized Christianity as part of the problem facing African nations struggling to free themselves from European imperialism.

In my father's adult estrangement from the Christianity of his youth, he found a like mind in my mother, a recovering Presbyterian by the time she reached college. My mother's father had grown up Baptist, while her mother came from a family of Christian Scientists. Neither of her parents was especially religious when she was growing up, but her family did occasionally attend Congregational church service together. My mother and her sisters also attended a Christian Science church every Sunday when they were staying with their maternal grandmother, but overall my mother could hardly be said to have had a strict religious upbringing. When she was seventeen, she independently decided to join the Presbyterian church in her family's Detroit neighborhood, but for social more than religious reasons.

Though she was somewhat active in the church as a teenager, by the time she went to college her interest in religion had diminished considerably. Since her experience with religion in childhood and adolescence had been lukewarm, she was perhaps especially susceptible to the reevaluation of religion that characterized the Black Power movement of the 1960s. For her, as for many African American young people at the time, the reclamation of a black identity and the cultural nationalism that found expression in Afro hairstyles also incorporated a move away from Christianity and toward more "authentic" forms of black religious expression and the secularism of leftist political thought. When my mother met my father in college, she had already dispensed with institutionalized Christianity, although she kept the basic belief in God and an afterlife that she had been taught as a child.

When my parents were married, they made a conscious decision not to baptize their children and to raise us with a more fluid, informal set of spiritual values than the Christianity they had been raised in. And they resolved to approach spirituality as a general outlook and a way of life, not as a discrete institution to which one paid homage on certain days of the week.

Remy's illness and death brought my family's peculiar spiritual synthesis to the fore. When Remy was in the hospital, he was visited by many relatives from both sides of the family, and many would pray for him. The Zaireans would gather in the small hospital room, bow their heads, and join hands, sometimes even kneeling while a prayer was recited loudly in Kikongo; sometimes they laid hands on my brother's body to transmit God's healing power. Religious members of my mother's family, such as my mother's youngest sister, Frances, whose deep and personal attraction to the Catholic church had led her to the final steps towards becoming a nun in her early twenties, would sit by Remy's bed and pray silently, perhaps holding Remy's hand and whispering words of encouragement. My brothers and I looked up to Frances, who was young and pretty and filled with a calm radiance and gentle goodness, like an older sister. I remember her as a warm and calmly reassuring presence at Remy's bedside as he neared the end of his life.

I knew nothing of it at the time, but years later I learned that during Remy's illness debate raged among my father's family regarding witchcraft or the displeasure of powerful ancestors as possible causes of the disease. Apparently traditional "alternative" treatments were employed to fight the illness, but none was successful. I have met many strictly Christian Africans who have taken serious offence at having traditional remedies used on their behalf, but my family have never been such purists. When Remy was sick, my family mustered all the spiritual armament at our disposal, sampling from various religious traditions for answers—sadly, in the end, to no avail.

My brother's funeral was attended by hundreds of family members and friends, and the two sides of Remy's heritage were easily distinguishable in the crowded church. The ceremony itself was a study in cultural duality. My mother's sister Anne read a eulogy written by my maternal grandmother about how Remy's spirit would live eternally. My father's uncle Fukiau, a dignified scholar and expert on Kongo culture and philosophy, read a tribute to Remy in French, punctuated by African exclamations of agreement from the Zaireans in the audience and greeted with polite applause by those who couldn't understand the words. Others, from both sides of the family, read from the Bible and led the church in prayer. All of the speakers stressed that the end of Remy's earthly life was but a transition from one state to another.

Before the funeral, my parents had selected an unembellished gray granite headstone, and my father had drawn a symbol on some paper for the stonemason to carve into the stone's facade. The symbol, a circle around a square crossed by two lines at right angles like the points of a compass, was drawn from Kongo cosmology and represented the universe and the human cycle of life:

In, perhaps, an unwitting example of religious syncretization, many of the American family friends who later visited Remy's grave assumed that the symbol was a version of the Christian cross, which it indeed resembles. So in a strange way it came to embody an appropriate double meaning for the mourners.

I think it was my family's faith in Remy's entry into a boundless spiritual state that enabled us to move to Tanzania less than a year after his death, for we believed his spirit would travel with us to Africa. Maybe this belief was an unconscious echo of the faith many African American slaves had that their souls would return to Africa after death. Once in Tanzania, I often felt certain that Remy's presence was with me, that I could communicate with him, and that he watched over us. It was a belief that was encouraged by my parents, and it seemed especially plausible in an African environment in which spirituality was an integral part of everyday life.

While my brothers and I did not receive religious instruction as children, our parents did provide spiritual guidance, mainly through the example of their own beliefs and practices. In Kongo cosmology, for example, dreams are one of the gateways between spiritual realms, and my father used to offhandedly mention his dreams, probing for spiritual meaning in the dreamtime appearance of a deceased relative or friend. Sometimes his dreams proved prophetic; once he awoke recalling an inexplicable image of a female colleague dressed only in a cloth wrapped around her body. The next day we coincidentally ran into her at the beach, where, sure enough, she wore a colorful cloth over her bathing suit. On other occasions he would dream of a friend or relative he had not seen or heard from in some time and shortly afterward would receive a letter or call from them.

Sometimes my father would link phenomena in the earthly world to events "elsewhere" and find telling spiritual symbolism in seemingly everyday occurrences. When an otherwise sunny day was accompanied by gentle rain showers, he would half-jokingly remind us that simultaneous sun and rain heralded the birth of a spirit. And he became visibly perturbed when he was told after his detention in Kinshasa that a large owl had stationed itself on a tree just outside our home many times during his absence. In many African cultures the owl is a symbol of sorcery; it is thought to be one of the most favored forms for a sorcerer's spirit to take on nighttime flights of mischief. My father never voiced his obvious concern after being informed about the mysterious feathered interloper, but he consulted with relatives in Zaire who were knowledgeable about such matters, and perhaps he even took herbalistic precautions to prevent the return of the unwanted visitor.

The stories he told us when we were children also proved rich in Congolese folk beliefs. In one of our favorites, the family of a man called Petelo was harassed by a festive group of ghosts every night while he was away. When Petelo returned from his trip and was told about the nocturnal callers, he loaded a rifle with hot red peppers, a sure ghost repellent, and fired on the reveling spirits as soon as they appeared. The ghosts never returned to bother Petelo's family again.

Stories about my father's family proved equally informative on matters of Kongo belief and tradition. He spoke often of the mysterious abilities of his uncle, who used to unexpectedly appear at my father's mission boarding school, a good three days' journey from his village by bus, claiming to have left the village on foot the night before. My father suspected that like the herbalists of African and African American legend, his uncle knew how to fly, but he never heard the evasive old man admit it. My father also often told stories about the activities of traditional healers in his community who treated people's illnesses with spiritual and herbal cures, and he described many scenes he had witnessed but could not explain. And he sometimes shared with us the opinions and explanations of a sort of family diviner whose prophecies and warnings often found their way to him through letters from Zaire. When my father's father died in 1987, a period in which it was unsafe for my father to travel to Zaire for fear of detention, she said that the clan might suffer misfortune if my father failed to pay his respects at his father's grave and make the required offerings to his father's spirit, in keeping with Kongo tradition. My father took her words to heart, especially after being visited by his unhappy father in dreams. When he finally made it to his village to perform the necessary libations in 1990, when the weakening of the Zairean government made it possible to visit without complication, I think my whole family heaved a collective sigh of relief.

A body of African American folk and religious beliefs was passed on by my mother. Though her experiences had left her disillusioned with institutionalized worship and suspicious of the motives of evangelists, she retained a belief in God, and seemed to enjoy a somewhat casual and friendly relationship with the Creator. "God don't like ugly," she would often say by way of criticizing meanness in my brothers and me, sounding as though she was speaking of an acquaintance or older relative and frowning reproachfully. I have never seen my mother attend church services, but I do believe I have seen her worship. Her altar consisted of the record player in our living room, and her sermons were the devotional songs of Stevie Wonder, Aretha Franklin or Sweet Honey in the Rock, music rooted in black religious tradition. "When you feel your life's too hard, just go have a talk with God," she would sing along with Stevie, seeming to mean every word.

She would shake her head slowly in support and agreement when De-
niece Williams reached for the high notes on "He Is Amazing," and
she'd nod in answer to Sweet Honey's query about the biblical gospel,
"Ain't that good news?"

In addition to maintaining vestiges of the African American religious outlook she had grown up with, my mother absorbed elements
of my father's traditional beliefs, so her conception of God and spirituality became a highly hybridized one. While she agreed with the
Bible's message of fraternity, kindness, and social justice, she also accepted the existence of a spirit world and its interaction with humanity. In addition to identifying with the soulful gospel of Aretha,
she found special meaning in songs like Sweet Honey in the Rock's
"Breaths," a family favorite that the African American vocal group
adapted from a French poem by the Senegalese Negritude writer Bi-
rago Diop:

> *Listen more often to things than to beings,*
> *Listen more often to things than to beings,*
> *'Tis the ancestors' breath when the fire's voice is heard,*
> *'Tis the ancestors' breath in the voice of the water*
> *Those who have died have never ever left.*
> *The dead are not under the earth.*
> *They are with us in the home,*
> *They are in the wailing rocks.*
> *The dead have a pact with the living.*

The fact that my parents took a tolerant, relaxed view of religion
and sampled somewhat freely from different traditions meant that my
brothers and I had considerable latitude to explore religion and spirituality on our own terms. Our mother and father provided spiritual
support and guidance in times of need, and they passed on certain beliefs and values, but I think that when we became old enough to take
an interest in such matters, my brothers and I were free to seek spiritual truth on our own. And the Dar es Salaam in which we came of
age proved full of possibilities.

Tanzania's coastal areas and the islands of Zanzibar, Mafia, and
Pemba off the coast of Dar es Salaam are heavily Muslim, a legacy of
the thirteenth-century sultanate of Oman, which was headquartered
in Zanzibar. Conversely, the Tanzanian interior is largely Christian,
because of the proselytizing of Catholic and Protestant missionaries
who established themselves in the area in the nineteenth century.

(David Livingstone, who set up missions and died in western Tanzania, was probably the most famous of the region's European evangelists.) But I quickly learned that most people in Tanzania, even those who considered themselves devout Muslims or Christians, also incorporated elements of traditional African religious beliefs and practices into their lives. Like my family, many Tanzanians saw no contradiction in sampling from a number of religious traditions to seek spiritual fulfillment and solve spiritual problems.

My uncle Ray, a middle-aged white man who married my mother's sister Anne after over thirty years as a Catholic priest, was, quite coincidentally, a missionary in northern Tanzania during the 1960s. He was stationed among the Maasai, the legendary nomadic herders and warriors of the East African savanna, and also worked with other tribes in the area, including the WaChagga, who live in the vicinity of Mount Kilimanjaro. My uncle has very fond memories of his time in Africa, but not because his missionary activities were greatly successful. He developed a deep respect and love for the land and the people he met, learning to speak fluent KiMaasai and Kiswahili and educating himself about local culture. He would spend evenings around a fire with Maasai elders, philosophizing and learning about their religion, which they outlined for him in simple terms, describing humanity as a knife that could cut for good or evil. He was ridiculed for his celibacy, and learned to appreciate his hosts' quick wit and humor, even though he was often the butt of the jokes. And as he grew closer to his new friends and learned more about their culture, he began to take issue with some of the activities of his fellow missionaries, who discouraged traditional African religious practices and would not permit worshipers to attend services in their traditional dress. In the end, Ray puts it, instead of being converted by him, the Maasai converted him. He decided that the church had no right to attempt to destroy traditional African ways of life, and that it could learn much from the peoples it sought to convert. He returned to the United States disillusioned with organized religion and quit the church.

I have always felt that Uncle Ray should have taken some heart from the fact that Christianity did not really succeed in entirely displacing traditional African religion in Tanzania; instead, it merged with local traditions, rituals, and beliefs. Shortly after my family moved to the University of Dar es Salaam campus, my mother hired a young Mchagga woman named Franciska to baby-sit James and keep house while she was at work. Like many WaChagga, Franciska considered herself a Catholic, but I wonder if the pope would have approved of her brand of Catholicism. Franciska told my brothers and me stories about witches who would steal children and about evil "djinis" who roamed the night in search of unsuspecting victims; she warned us not to walk near baobab trees after dark, because they often housed hostile spirits. When her daughter, Zwena, was sick, Franciska would take her to the university dispensary for treatment, and would also consult a traditional healer for an alternative cure. And every Sunday, without fail, she would scrub herself clean, rub her skin shiny with Vaseline, and put on her best clothes to go to mass with her daughter in tow.

Other Christian churches were also popular in Dar es Salaam. Fairly close to my family's home was a Pentecostal church that attracted thousands of the faithful every Sunday. On still, quiet evenings you could hear the congregation's voices raised in song or shouts of religious ecstasy for miles. Popular lore held that the church's preacher could channel God's power through his hands into worshipers afflicted by illness or bad luck, and every week people came from all over the city seeking the Lord's regenerative blessing.

In addition to being introduced to African versions of Christianity in Dar es Salaam, my brothers and I had our first real exposure to Islam. In the States I had had some conception of Islam thanks to figures like Muhammad Ali and Malcolm X, and I realized that the religion's popularity among African Americans was somehow related to the pro-Africa rhetoric that colored my childhood. But I knew next to nothing about Islam itself. Though Tanzania is a nation forged from an alliance between the Christian mainland and Muslim Zanzibar, Dar es Salaam is a visibly Muslim city, filled with mosques and Koranic schools, and some areas are home to women in veils, and men in Muslim caps. There was a mosque on the university campus, and in the evenings and early mornings we could hear the muezzin calling the faithful to prayer, a haunting, musical sound that always struck me as very mournful.

Muslim holy days were national holidays and my brothers and I would listen to the radio on the eve of possible days off from school to see if anyone had sighted the moon, which would determine when the holiday would fall. During Ramadan, the holy month of fasting, I felt admiration and sympathy for my Muslim friends, who went without food or drink all day and sometimes had to sit through class or take exams on empty stomachs. Even though I never fasted, I would sometimes join friends for nighttime feasts that were like parties. It was also easy to get caught up in the general festivities associated with major holidays like Eid el Fitr, which marks the end of Ramadan; on that day Muslims all over the city would walk from house to house sharing gifts and eating food provided by fellow Muslims, often complete strangers. In heavily Muslim parts of the city, during Eid the streets would seem awash in the white Muslim robes locals called *kanzu*.

Tanzanian friends invited me to attend the university campus's nondenominational church with them and I accepted their offers on a number of occasions, on which I listened to the English and Kiswahili sermons with interest and sang hymns with the rest of the flock. Organized religion didn't appeal to me much, however, and eventually I stopped going to church altogether. When Tanzanian friends asked me what my religion was, I would answer that I didn't really have one, a response that was entirely novel and usually unacceptable. To most of my friends, you were either *Mkristo* (Christian), *Mwislam* (Muslim), or maybe *Mhindi* (Hindu) if you were an Indian, but you had to have a religion. I would usually merely shrug or laugh. I preferred to think of my spirituality as a matter between my own vaguely conceived God and myself.

While I decided early against making organized religion a fixture in my life, Kolo and James took more of an interest in going to church. In their early teens they became close friends with the children of a deeply religious family and began accompanying them to church, Sunday school, and Bible study quite regularly. My parents didn't mind, although I suspected they were unimpressed by some of the Christian dogma that my brothers sometimes repeated around the house. Kolo and James attended church for a few months before they lost interest.

Kolo, who has always been extremely sincere and thoughtfully moral, seemed to take to heart much of what he heard at church and read in the Bible, but in the end I guess he didn't entirely buy it. I remember on one occasion he returned from services bewildered by a conversation he had had with a fellow worshiper. Shortly after introducing herself, the woman had told Kolo that she loved him, apparently not with lust but in that Christian, "love thy neighbor" way. Kolo was very disturbed. "How can she love me when she doesn't even know me?" he asked me later. He was also unsettled by something he learned at a Sunday school class he attended with some friends: the teacher said that Christianity was the only true and acceptable religion, which put him off because his two closest friends at school were Muslim and Hindu. I think my parents might have actually been a little relieved when Kolo and James stopped going to church.

I never understood clearly why James started going to church in the first place, and I wasn't surprised when he stopped. But I was a bit taken aback when he converted to Islam at eighteen. He had been something of a rambunctious teenager, intelligent but often uninterested in schoolwork, popular and well liked among his peers but a disciplinary challenge for teachers and my parents. Then he began discussing religion with some close Muslim friends; I think he may have felt that Islam offered the order and purpose he was missing. In any case, after extensive discussions with Muslim friends and imams, and after finding out all he could about the religion, he converted.

Ever since he was a small child, James's life had been marked by periodic obsessions to which he would devote himself wholeheartedly until his interest waned: airplanes and buses as a kindergartener, martial arts as a young teen, basketball as a young man, and drawing and painting throughout. It was easy to dismiss his conversion to Sunni Islam as yet another obsessive phase—and some did, but I think everyone in my family was impressed with the zeal with which James took to his new faith. He learned to read and write some Arabic; he read extensively about the religion, sharing anecdotes about the exploits of Muhammad with anyone who would listen; he attended the mosque regularly; and he changed his name to Saleem. I think he felt purified by the rigid discipline and inspired by the Koran's glorious depictions of Allah and the heroic prophets of the past. And I know he relished his admission into an international club that is a source of great pride and strength to millions of Muslims worldwide. James's conversion seemed to improve his grades and strengthen his seriousness of purpose. Though four years after becoming a Muslim he no longer prayed as regularly as he had at first, I could see that his eyes still lit up with boyish excitement when he spoke about his religion or listened to a recital of the ninety-nine names of Allah on Islamic programs that appeared on Tanzanian TV. While Kolo and I seemed to have inherited our parents' relaxed and somewhat fluid sense of religion and spirituality, James seemed to have found spiritual fulfillment in organized Islam.

Before the introduction of Christianity in many parts of Africa, traditional Africans believed that worldly events were controlled by the actions of powerful gods and ancestors, and they conceived complex cosmologies to explain and influence the interaction between the earthly and spiritual universes. The majority of African slaves abducted from West Africa and enslaved in the New World were adherents of traditional African belief systems, and they drew on their faith for strength and comfort in order to survive the traumas of slavery. Some slaves were said to have carried protective amulets or "fetishes" to the New World with them, hoping that the symbols of spiritual power would help to deliver them from their terrible predicament. And in addition to prompting Africans to invoke the guidance of their traditional beliefs, slavery provided many Africans' first exposure to Christianity.

Since its inception in the fifteenth century, the European slave trade was closely intertwined with Christianity. Many European slave traders considered it their duty to convert the slaves they purchased, and early on the Christianizing mission became a favored excuse for the trade among slavery apologists, who argued that enslavement benefited heathen Africans because it brought them into contact with Christianity. While this hardly seemed a convincing excuse for the brutalization of millions of Africans by Europeans who called themselves Christians, it is true that through slavery Africans were exposed to a new religion, Christianity, and adopted elements of it to serve the specific spiritual challenges of their peculiar situation.

Though European proponents of the evangelization of African slaves hoped that new converts would abandon their traditional beliefs and practices, in reality newly Christianized Africans did not turn their backs on their gods and religious traditions. Instead, the slaves brought specifically African perspectives and styles of worship to Christianity. A debate has long raged as to the degree of African retention present in African American religious belief and expression, but most historians seem to agree that Africans enslaved in the New World did keep something of their religious heritage. This was, of course, most obvious in Brazil and the Caribbean, where large populations of slaves practiced African religions that remained strikingly similar to traditions in West Africa, but African religious practices and beliefs endured in North America as well. For this reason, even if slave owners and their slaves on American plantations of the eighteenth century had the same religion in name, Christianity as understood and practiced by slave and master usually differed considerably.

Charles Ball, a former slave who recorded his experiences in the nineteenth century, described a slave funeral that seemed to draw heavily from African belief and tradition. According to most West African religious traditions, death marks a spirit's transition from the world of the living to that of the dead, a realm in which the spirit may still have use of earthly possessions. For this reason, in some parts of

Africa the dead are buried with personal items, and gifts and offerings are sometimes placed near grave sites. During the slave funeral in America that Ball depicted, various implements that the dead child's spirit would need on its journey to the African spirit world were placed in the grave: "a small bow and several arrows; a little bag of parched meal; a miniature canoe . . . and a little paddle." In addition, the corpse was accompanied by a small symbolic fetish that was supposed to enable the child's spirit to be recognized by its relations in Africa. Satisfied with his handiwork, the dead child's father completed the ritual with one further addition. "He cut a lock of hair from his head," we are told, "threw it upon the dead infant, and closed the grave with his own hands. He then told us the God of his country was looking at him, and was pleased with what he had done."

Not only did specifically African ideas about death and the afterlife endure in the New World, so did the ritual ceremonies that reinforced them. And by maintaining African beliefs and customs in the New World, Africans transplanted to American soil were able to retain and strengthen spiritual ties to the land of their ancestry. In the example provided by Ball, an African slave buried his American-born child according to African tradition, secure in the knowledge that its spirit would return to Africa to be welcomed by the spirits of its African ancestors and relations.

The ceremony Ball described would doubtless have been among the religious practices slave masters frowned on and forbade. Though American slave masters tried to stamp out traditional African religious practices, many traditions continued in secret. In public, however, slaves prevented from reproducing African religious traditions Africanized Christian worship instead, bringing an African sensibility to (predominantly) Baptist and Methodist sermons and camp meetings.

John Watson was only one of the many white ministers who disapproved of the slaves' approach to worship. "In the blacks' quarter, the coloured people get together, and sing for hours together, short scraps of disjointed affirmations, pledges, or prayers, lengthened out with long repetitious choruses," he complained in 1819. "With every word so sung, they have a sinking of one leg of the body alternately; producing an audible sound of the feet at every step. . . . the evil is only occasionally condemned and the example has already visibly affected the religious manners of some whites."

Watson here was unwittingly describing the ring shout, an African-derived practice common in eighteenth-century African American religion. In the absence of the drums and songs of African ritual, the ring, in which worshipers circled rhythmically, singing and praying in time, became an American adaptation of an African style of religious expression. Though many white ministers, like Watson, thought of singing and dancing as sinful and tried to discourage it in their black converts, slaves continued to infuse the religion they learned from whites with a flavor and sensibility they brought from Africa. Another often noted example of an African style of worship, one that appears in black American Christianity, is the "baptism by the Holy Spirit" that takes place in Pentecostal and Sanctified churches; it closely resembles the "spirit possession" that is a common feature of some West African religious traditions.

In addition to the ring shout and "possession" by the Holy Spirit, other Africanisms characterized black religion and folk belief in eighteenth-century America. Areas like the Sea Islands of coastal Georgia and South Carolina, where there were relatively many blacks in comparison with whites and African cultural survivals were more prevalent, maintained an especially rich supply of African-derived folk beliefs, but African traditions survived in other parts of the United States as well. In the rural South, for example, a common belief persisted that an ax could be used to "cut a storm in two" and rob it of its power. Some black Southerners probably still wave an ax in the air or prop one against the wall when rain threatens. This practice is thought by many scholars to correspond to a similar practice among believers of Yoruba religion in West Africa, where an ax is a symbol for Shango, the god of thunder and lightning.

Many scholars also believe that African slaves who converted to Christianity did so because they recognized similarities between Christian ritual and symbolism and religious traditions in Africa. Slaves brought into the Baptist church in ceremonies conducted in rivers or streams might have been reminded of similar rituals performed by African religious "water cults." And the ubiquitous symbol of Christian belief and dogma, the cross, might have struck a familiar chord among slaves from the Bakongo culture of central West Africa, where a symbol resembling a cross signifies the life cycle of birth, death, and regeneration. In this way, American evangelists who converted newly arrived slaves may have unwittingly provided them with ways of interpreting Christianity in specifically African terms.

In addition to Africanizing Christian worship through practices like the ring shout, black slaves in America who took Christian ideas to heart looked to the Bible for messages relevant to their situation. Though masters and preachers intent on keeping their slaves passive steered them towards scriptural directives ordering them to be obedient and cooperative, the slaves were much more taken with Old Testament references to the enslavement of God's chosen people and their ultimate liberation and redemption. Also, the notion of Exodus as a religious journey from bondage, the portrayal of Jesus as the ultimate spiritual liberator, and the Christian emphasis on social justice seemed especially relevant. In fact, many of the slaves who led revolts against the slave system in the nineteenth century, including Denmark Vesey and Nat Turner, were religious leaders who used the rhetoric of the Bible to communicate their message of liberation. It wasn't difficult for African slaves who already possessed the concept of a supreme creator being (known variously in Africa as Nzambi [Kongo], Olorun [Yoruba] and Chukwu [Igbo], among many other names) to accept the basic principles of Christianity, especially when, despite the distortions of ministers and slave masters, Christianity presented itself as a sufferer's religion, offering comfort in adversity and deliverance from bondage.

Though through this process of syncretization the Christianity practiced by blacks in eighteenth- and nineteenth-century America was somewhat "Africanized," by the nineteenth century a class and geographical distinction had come to characterize black religion. While plantation slaves in heavily black areas of the American South were more likely to express African cultural and religious features in their approach to Christianity, free blacks often attempted to distance themselves from an African religious heritage. Worshiping in separate pews in segregated white churches, many free black communities in the North adopted white versions of Christianity and white styles of worship. Though by the 1800s some free black congregations decided to strike out independently, it was to seek greater autonomy in their interpretation and practice of Christianity, not to "Africanize" their religion. The "African" in the titles adopted by the independent black African Methodist Episcopal Church (founded in 1816) and African Methodist Episcopal Zion Church (founded in 1821) referred to the fact that their congregants were of African descent, not to any desire to create an "African" version of Christianity. In fact, in the nineteenth century the AME and AME Zion churches tended to look down on the Christianity practiced by slaves and lower-class blacks, because it bore too much of a resemblance to traditional African religion.

The AME bishop Daniel Alexander Payne complained disgustedly in the late nineteenth century when a group of ex-slaves at an AME camp meeting in the South insisted on performing the ring shout.

"Sinners won't get converted unless there is a ring," one of the ring shouters explained when Payne voiced his strong disapproval. "The Spirit of God works upon people in different ways. At camp-meeting there must be a ring here, a ring there, a ring over yonder, or sinners will not get converted." To Payne, such African-oriented religious displays were "disgusting," but he was forced to admit that to "the ignorant masses . . . it was the essence of religion."

"He who could sing loudest and longest led the Band, having his loins girded and a handkerchief in hand with which he kept time, while his feet resounded on the floor like the drumsticks of a bass drum," Payne goes on, describing the religious practices of the ex-slaves. "In some cases it was the custom to begin these dances after every night service and keep it up till midnight, sometimes singing and dancing alternately—a short prayer and a long dance. Someone has even called it the 'Voodoo Dance.' I have remonstrated with a number of pastors for permitting these practices, which vary somewhat in different localities, but have invariably met with the response that he could not succeed in restraining them, and an attempt to compel them to cease would merely drive them away from our church."

So there was an obvious division between an American black elite, who embraced a more European version of Christianity, and a "lower stratum" of blacks, whose Christianity had an African flavor. Interestingly, however, even among the Christian black elite, religion still acted as a vessel for pan-African sentiments and as a medium through which ties to Africa were established and strengthened.

Northern independent black churches of the nineteenth century became rallying points for black political empowerment and forums for early pan-African ideas. For black preachers who struck out on their own to form independent churches, specifically black American readings of the Bible and Christianity were a central preoccupation. And in nineteenth-century America, in which a free black population and sympathetic whites campaigned against slavery, a black interpretation of Christianity that stressed the humanity and admirable history of Africans was especially advantageous.

In defense of blackness, nineteenth-century African American ministers and theologians scoured the Bible for positive references to blacks. Sermons by black preachers made frequent mention of King Solomon's Egyptian wife, whose virtues and beauty are lauded in the Song of Solomon (1:5–6). And Jeremiah 13:23, which asked "Can the Ethiopian change his skin, or the leopard his spots?" was cited by some religious scholars as evidence of the black man's acceptability in the eyes of the Lord.

While white apologists for slavery had used the Bible to justify the subjugation of black people, arguing that blacks, descendants of Noah's son Ham by one common reading, deserved ill treatment because of Ham's sin against his father, black theologians like the Reverend Rufus L. Perry looked to the Bible for evidence of the black man's past glory. "If it be shown here beyond reasonable doubt . . . that the ancient Egyptians, Ethiopians and Libyans . . . were the ancestors of the present race of Ham, then the Negro of the nineteenth century may point to them with pride," wrote Perry, a former slave who ministered to a Baptist congregation in Brooklyn, New York. "And with all who would find in him a return to racial celebrity, when in the light of a Christian civilization, Ethiopia shall stretch out her hands unto God." The image of Ethiopia stretching out her hands to God comes from Psalm 68:31, a verse that became a favorite of nineteenth-century black American ministers, who saw the words as proof of a great and holy destiny for Africa and the children of Africa around the world.

Martin Delany, an AME theologian who became one of the most outspoken supporters of black emigration to Africa in the nineteenth century, used the psalm to encourage blacks to move to Sierra Leone in 1852: " 'Princes shall come out of Egypt; Ethiopia shall soon stretch out her hands unto God,' " he said in one sermon. "With the fullest reliance upon this blessed promise, I humbly go forward in—I may repeat—the grandest prospect for the regeneration of a people that ever was presented in the history of the world." For theologians who, like Delany, had grappled with trying to find a religious explanation for the horrors of slavery, the idea that the enslavement of millions of Africans in America was all part of a divine plan for Africa's redemption was a welcome one.

If black Americans were the "princes" that the psalm referred to, and "Egypt" was America, the land where God's chosen people had languished in bondage before returning in glory to the promised land of "Ethiopia," then perhaps God's purpose in allowing the slave trade to take place was to introduce Africans in America to Christianity so that they could spread the gospel in Africa. Thus, Delany—a member of the African Civilization Society, a black organization formed to promote "the civilization and christianization of Africa and of the descendants of African ancestors in any portion of the earth, wherever dispersed"—used Christianity to provide a reassuring religious read-ing of black American history and to generate pan-African enthusi-asm. He sought to encourage black Americans who were "practically qualified and suited to promote the development of Christianity, mo-rality, education, mechanical arts, agriculture, commerce and general improvement" to move to Africa to offer their services. "God himself as assuredly as he rules the destinies of nations, and entereth measures into hearts of men, has presented these measures to us," Delany once wrote. "Our race is to be redeemed; it is a great and glorious work, and we are the instrumentalities by which it is to be done."

Alexander Crummell's was another voice raised in favor of black American emigration to Africa to bring Christianity to the continent. A zealous supporter of the proposal of African colonization and chris-tianization by a black American advance guard, Crummell even com-plained in the 1870s that black Americans took the responsibility of providing religious enlightenment too lightly. "The difficulties in the way of our brethren doing a goodly work for Africa, are more subjec-tive than objective," he once complained. "One of these hindrances is a want of missionary zeal. . . . This is our radical defect." Crummell likened the destiny of black Americans to that of Joseph, who was sold into slavery by his brothers but later found redemption through God's plan for him. Joseph's experience, wrote Crummell, was similar to "the forced and cruel migration of our race from [Africa], and the wondrous providence of God, by which the sons of Africa . . . trained, civilized and enlightened, are coming hither again; bringing large gifts, for Christ and his church, and their heathen kin!"

Though pan-African in his desire to promote unity between blacks in America and indigenous Africans, Crummell was Eurocentric in his disdain for African culture; he was certain that the continent could only profit from exposure to Western civilization. Emigrating to Liberia in the 1850s, Crummell wholeheartedly supported the often crude methods of Americo-Liberian settlers and saw military cam-paigns against hostile locals as justifiable means to the end of civiliz-ing a backward, heathen people—necessary "to set up a civilized nationality . . . amid the relics of barbarism, and to extend the bless-ings of Christian enlightenment among those rude people, their, and our own kinsmen."

Crummell essentially saw nothing in African culture worth pre-serving (unlike Martin Delany, who was well versed in African history and wished to retain elements of African tradition) and actually went so far as to claim that "so far as Western Africa is concerned, there is no history. The long centuries of human existence, there, give us no intelligent disclosures. 'Darkness covered the land, and gross darkness the people.' " Such self-hatred and blind certainty of the superiority of Western culture afflicted many blacks of the nineteenth century. Despite Crummell's negative view of his own heritage, he was committed to uplifting black people around the world through religion, and was one of the century's most significant champions of pan-Africanist sentiment and black American emigration to Africa.

Edward Wilmot Blyden, a theologian and scholar who was born in Barbados and is sometimes called the "father of pan-Africanism," also subscribed to the "Divine Providence" idea that God had seen fit to enslave millions of Africans in the Americas in order to position them for conversion to Christianity and enable them to lead Africa to redemption. Despite his Christian orientation, however, Blyden had great respect for African traditions and cultures, and was also impressed with the important role of Islam in West African cultural history. He felt there was much that blacks of the diaspora could learn from Africans and, unlike Crummell, he did not wish simply to create in Africa a civilization that mimicked the West. He said that Americo-Liberians and other diaspora blacks who returned to Africa to lead the continent to glory should "amalgamate with [their] aboriginal [siblings] and carefully study [their] 'social organization,[their] religion, [their] politics' which, though they might be modified somewhat, must form the basis of a distinctive African culture."

Though supportive of African religious and cultural traditions, Blyden used the religious language of the Christian tradition he was born and trained in to encourage black Americans to move to Liberia, his own adoptive home. In addition to the oft-quoted Psalm 68, in his sermons of the 1870s and 1880s Blyden was partial to Deuteronomy 1:21, "Behold, the Lord thy God hath set the land before thee: go up and possess it, as the Lord God of thy fathers hath said unto thee; fear not, neither be discouraged." He regarded the verse as a divine directive to New World blacks to return to Africa.

As well as putting a black spin on biblical verses, black theologians of the nineteenth century sought to change the image that blacks had of God himself. Henry McNeal Turner, AME church bishop and proponent of black emigration to Africa, was one of the earliest black scholars to suggest that Christians of African descent should pray to an African God. "We have as much right biblically and otherwise to believe that God is Negro, as you buckra or white people have to believe that God is a fine looking, symmetrical and ornamented white man," he declared. "This is one of the reasons we favor African emigration . . . for, as long as we remain among the whites, the Negro will believe that the devil is black and that he (the Negro) favors the devil and that God is white and that he (the Negro) bears no resemblance to Him." Other black religious leaders, too, regarded the christianization of Africa by black Americans as part of a general Africanization of Christianity that often included recasting God as a black figure.

By the early 1890s, the bishops of the African Methodist Episcopal Church regarded the establishment of black-run missions in Africa as a priority. "Africa is the largest and most important of the fields that lie before us," they wrote in 1892. "First, because of the number of persons involved in the work; second, on account of the relationship that exists between our race and the inhabitants of the Dark Continent; third, because our church is better adapted to the redemption of Africa than any other organization among the darker races for the moral and religious training of the people." Although black American emigration to Africa did not become as popular as proponents like Turner might have hoped, the activities of churches like the AME and AME Zion in setting up missions in Africa and providing educational and religious instruction to Africans did have a significant impact. Some scholars have even attributed the rise of certain nationalistic ideas that would later find expression in anticolonial movements to concepts popularized by black American missions in Africa.

Though enthusiasm for missionary activity in Africa dwindled somewhat among black Americans after the turn of the century, black American efforts to create Africa-oriented theologies or interpretations of Christianity did not. The most significant example of religious pan-Africanism of the post–World War I period was undoubtedly embodied in the back-to-Africa movement of Marcus Garvey's Universal Negro Improvement Association. Though the UNIA was essentially secular and political in outlook, Garvey often made his case for black repatriation to Africa in religious terms. "Our cause is based upon righteousness," he said in one speech in the early 1920s. "And anything that is not righteous we have no respect for, because God Almighty is our leader and Jesus Christ our standard bearer. We rely on them for that kind of leadership that will make us free, for it is the same God who inspired the Psalmist to write 'Princes shall come out of Egypt and Ethiopia shall stretch out her hands unto God.' At this moment . . . methinks I see the Angel of God taking up the standard of the Red, the Black and the Green, and saying 'Men of the Negro Race, Men of Ethiopia, follow me.' "

In addition to featuring such Christian rhetoric, UNIA meetings had a distinctly religious tone. The *Negro World* reported that a typical meeting opened with "the customary religious service of congregational singing of anthem and prayer, followed by all repeating the Twenty-third Psalm." What's more, while Garvey did not wish to alienate blacks of any religious persuasion by naming an official organization religion, the UNIA was affiliated with the independent Christian African Orthodox Church and did have a chaplain-general in Reverend George Alexander McGuire, chosen by Garvey in 1920. The African Orthodox Church promoted an Africanized version of Christianity, complete with a black messiah. "Erase the white gods from your hearts," McGuire urged his followers. "We must go back to the native church, to our own true God."

With the dramatic urbanization of African Americans through the Great Migration from the rural South to the industrial North, new religious alternatives to the black church, in addition to Garvey's African Orthodox Church, proliferated in the growing black communities in Northern cities in the 1920s. The Church of God (also known as the Black Jews), which emerged in New York City around 1919, taught that white Jews were frauds, and that blacks were God's true chosen people. The group's leader, Prophet F. S. Cherry, preached from the Bible and the Talmud and asserted that "Jesus Christ was a Black man." The rather flamboyant Cherry would make his point while waving one of the standard blond-and-blue-eyed depictions of Christ, saying, "I'm offering fifteen hundred dollars cash to anyone who could produce an authentic likeness of Jesus Christ and show me I'm wrong! Who the hell is this? Nobody knows! They say it's Jesus! That's a damned lie! Jesus was black!" By 1931 there were as many as eight Black Jewish sects in Harlem, each espousing a rewriting of religious history that placed blacks at the center of the biblical narrative and stressed black Americans' ties to Africa and the African origin of Judaism and Christianity.

Another example of an Afrocentric alternative to the black church was the Moorish Science Temple of America, founded in 1913 by Timothy Drew, who moved to the Northeast from North Carolina. Drew, who renamed himself Noble Drew Ali the Prophet, established the first Moorish Science Temple in Newark, New Jersey. His followers proudly traced black American origins to Africa and referred to themselves as Asiatics or Moors. Although they regarded themselves as Muslims, the Moorish Scientists followed the teachings of Confucius, Buddha, and Jesus, as well as those of Muhammad. The Moorish Science movement quickly spread to New York, Detroit, Chicago, Philadelphia, and a number of Southern states before the organization fell apart after Ali's death. A number of Moorish Science spinoffs maintained the Temple's ideas and practices, however, including the Five Percent Nation of Islam, a movement that has become increasingly popular in urban black communities in the 1980s and 90s, where it has found an effective means of proselytization in hip-hop lyrics.

Probably the most famous alternative to the traditional, mainstream black churches was the Nation of Islam. The NOI was founded around 1930 by Wallace Fard Muhammad (also known as Wallace D. Fard or Wali Fard), an enigmatic figure who claimed he was an Arab from Mecca and appeared in Detroit, seeking to reacquaint American blacks with Islam, their "true" religion. Fard dropped from view around 1934; he was succeeded by Elijah Poole, a black Southerner who had early on become Fard's second in command. Poole, who changed his name to Elijah Muhammad, recruited numerous converts and by 1962 the movement had spread to twenty-two cities. The NOI taught that the God of the "Black Nation" (the "Mahdi" or Savior) was black and that Islam was the true religion of black people. Though Africa was revered as the site of powerful ancient black civilizations, NOI lore placed the origin of black people even further back, teaching that blacks inhabited the moon trillions of years ago and that a black scientist caused the Tribe of Shabazz, the black first earth-dwellers, to move to Earth.

Although NOI sermons combined this sort of fantastic history with Christian ideas as well as Koranic insights, Elijah Muhammad called the Bible "a poisoned book" of a "slave religion" and ridiculed black Americans for putting their faith in Christianity, which he saw as designed by whites to keep blacks enslaved. "You have made yourselves the most foolish people on earth by loving and following after the ways of the Slavemasters, whom Allah has revealed to me to be none other than real devils," Muhammad wrote in the NOI paper, *Mr. Muhammad Speaks.* "Their so-called Christianity is not His religion of Jesus or any other prophet of Allah."

Malcolm Little, a Michigan-born New York street hustler who became a follower of Elijah Muhammad while in a Massachusetts penitentiary, used his time in jail to educate himself and emerged as Malcolm X, the well-read, charismatic orator who became the Nation of Islam's premier spokesman in the 1950s. As head of the Nation's New York temple, Malcolm X did much to popularize the NOI among Northern blacks and helped to build the movement's reputation for strength, discipline, and organization, qualities that won the admiration of many black Christians as well as Muslim converts. A fiery and effective speaker, Malcolm X frequently denounced Christian black clergymen and the "slave religion" they represented. "My brothers and sisters, our white slavemaster's Christian religion has taught us black people here in the wilderness of North America that we will sprout wings when we die and fly up into the sky where God will have for us a special place called heaven," he used to say bitterly. "This is the white man's Christian religion used to brainwash us black people! We have accepted it! We have believed it! We have practiced it! And while we are doing all of that, for himself, the blue-eyed devil has twisted his Christianity, to keep his foot on our backs. . . . to keep our eyes fixed on the pie in the sky and heaven in the hereafter . . . while he enjoys his heaven right here . . . on this earth . . . in this life." Such attacks were very effective in exposing the seeming hypocrisy inherent in the Christian churches to which the majority of black Americans belonged.

The Nation of Islam's most famous minister left the organization in 1963 when he learned that his mentor, the Honorable Elijah Muhammad, was guilty of some of the sins he preached against, having fathered several children by a number of NOI secretaries. Malcolm X's defection cost the NOI some popularity, and it freed Malcolm from the rigid constraints of NOI dogma. He began to take radical strides in his thinking on race and religion. In 1964 he made the Islamic pilgrimage to Mecca, taking the name El Hajj Malik Shabazz, and toured a number of African states. Malcolm's experiences in Africa and the Middle East (Africans lauded him as "the son who has returned," while Muslims of various races welcomed him as a spiritual brother) prompted him to take a more international view of black people's struggle against racism and oppression worldwide; he began to think in global pan-Islamic and pan-African terms. Upon returning to the United States, he formed the Muslim Mosque, Inc., a religious group, and the Organization of Afro-American Unity, a political vehicle for black empowerment. Though Malcolm's efforts to address the spiritual and political needs of his community were cut short when he was assassinated in 1965, he remains one of the most influential black leaders of the twentieth century. And, like many black American religious leaders before him, he used religion as a springboard for exploring and promoting pan-African ideas and sentiments.

While Malcolm X and the Nation of Islam gained adherents in the 1960s as an alternative to the traditional black church, the main-stream of black American religion was led by Dr. Martin Luther King, Jr., and the Southern Christian Leadership Conference, which had risen to prominence in the 1950s as the vanguard of the civil rights movement. King stressed the doctrine of Christian social justice and, like many black preachers of the nineteenth century, often cited the Hebrews' deliverance from slavery in Egypt as inspiration for black American struggles for freedom and equality. King's vision was one of black integration into mainstream white society; he shied away from specifically black interpretations of Christianity and did not explicitly identify with Africa or African anticolonial movements. King, like Frederick Douglass a century before, strove for full African American inclusion in American society; he insisted that blacks in the United States were American, and he rejected the back-to-Africa rhetoric of some contemporary Black Power spokesmen.

Though Dr. King is arguably the most well-respected black Ameri-can leader of the century, revered in Africa as well as the rest of the world, as the civil rights movement began to lose steam in the mid-1960s, many black Americans began to become disillusioned with what they criticized as the movement's turn-the-other-cheek ap-proach and its long-suffering appeals to white love and goodwill. When African American impatience with the slow pace of political gains erupted in the Black Power movement, many black theologians began to feel that their religion needed to reinvent itself to remain vi-able in the new, radical political and social climate. "Black theology," the brainchild of a group of African American ministers critical of the black church's failure to make Christianity more relevant to the needs of the contemporary African American community, became one radi-cal effort to Africanize Christianity in the service of the black freedom struggle. Black theology as defined by theologians like Gayraud Wil-more and James Cone, leading black religious scholars since the 1960s, stressed black political liberation in its revision of white Chris-tianity. "Black Theology is saying that the God who spoke to us out of our African past and out of the religion of the slaves is speaking to us today in the accents of the contemporary Black community—and his message is Liberation," Wilmore and Cone wrote of the new ideology.

Such radical black approaches to Christianity helped to revolutionize black religious theory and practice.

Albert B. Cleage, Jr., a minister from Detroit who preached at the "Shrine of the Black Madonna," became one of black theology's outspoken proponents. In 1967 he introduced his congregation to some theological revisions of Christian thought; like nineteenth-century religious leaders trying to "Africanize" Christianity, Cleage and other supporters of black theology promoted the idea that biblical figures were actually black and had been misrepresented by white Christians. "You are a Christian, and the things you believe are the teachings of a Black Messiah named Jesus, and the things you do are the will of a black God called Jehovah," he told the members of his church. "And almost everything you have heard about Christianity is essentially a lie."

According to Cleage, lies that Western Christianity had perpetrated included the notions that Jesus and his followers were white and that whites are favored by God: "Jesus was a Black Messiah. He came to free a black people from the oppression of the white Gentiles. . . . Our religion, our preaching, our teachings all come from the Old Testament, for we are God's chosen people." Having unearthed such truths, Cleage argued that it was the duty of black preachers and theologians of the 1960s to bring black nationalist readings of the Bible to the black church to forge a "new-time religion" that would complement the political revolution of Black Power by revising the lies of white Christianity. "The Black Church," he said in one sermon, "must speak to the needs of black people who are proud of their African heritage."

Other black American activists who were influenced by the civil rights and Black Power movements sought to create new, more "authentic" black-oriented religious traditions outside of the black church. Ron Karenga, a California professor and civil rights activist, created Kwanzaa, an "African" celebration, in the mid-1960s. Kwanzaa borrowed symbolism and ritual from African traditions and black history, and while not specifically religious (it was meant to transcend religious denominations and boundaries) it was designed to enhance spiritual ties between African Americans and Africa. "I created Kwanzaa in the context of the Black Freedom Movement," Karenga, who later adopted the first name "Maulana," explained. "An organization I formed named Us, which means Us Black people as opposed to our oppressors, began observing it in Southern California in the mid-1960s. We wanted to speak our own truth to the world. We argued that culture is a fundamental way of being human in the world. . . . [Kwanzaa] reaffirms our rootedness in Africa. It's stepping back to Black! That was a strong push in the 1960s, getting back to roots."

"Kwanzaa" (Kiswahili for "first fruit") was conceived as a seven-day celebration beginning on December 26, with each day devoted to a different "principle" and marked by the burning of a candle (the candles, three red, three green, and one black, borrowed their colors from Garvey's UNIA flag). The principles resembled social ideas and were known by Kiswahili names: "Umoja" (Unity), "Kujichagulia" (Self-determination), "Ujima" (Collective Work and Responsibility), "Ujamaa" (Cooperative Economics), "Nia" (Purpose), "Kuumba" (Creativity) and "Imani" (Faith). Kwanzaa was embraced by black Americans of various religious backgrounds and for some it became a sort of substitute Christmas, even though it was never intended to serve as an alternative to any religious holiday. And though it was self-consciously Afrocentric, Kwanzaa even found followers among non-blacks and earned mainstream recognition: the U.S. Postal Service issued a commemorative Kwanzaa stamp in 1998. "It's an African holiday created for African people," Karenga said of the celebration. "It speaks to me in a way it can't speak to people outside our culture. We honor and reaffirm our family, community and culture. But other people can and do celebrate it."

Though Kwanzaa is essentially a secular celebration of culture and spirituality, Karenga was later involved in an academic "quest for an authentic African spirituality," delving into ancient Egyptian history in search of the African roots of monotheism and Christianity. By finding evidence of the theological underpinnings of Western monotheism in the writings of Kemet (ancient Egypt), Karenga laid claim to Judeo-Christianity as the religious legacy of Africa, a theory controversial among black and white theologians alike. In this way, like other black theologians before him, Karenga sought both to reclaim and recreate an African spiritual heritage and to "Africanize" Christianity by rooting it in an African historical experience.

The 1960s were regarded as something of a high point for black American religion, what with the rise of the Nation of Islam, the black minister–led civil rights movement, the radicalization of the black church, and the emergence and popularity of Afrocentric spiritual traditions like Kwanzaa. Since the 1960s, however, religious pan-Africanism has continued to exist in diverse forms.

In the mainstream black church, the legacy of ministers like Albert

Cleage, Jr., has been upheld by preachers like Dr. Johnny Ray Youngblood, a Baptist minister who brought an Afrocentric outlook to readings of the Bible in his sermons at his Brooklyn church. Youngblood often wore African clothing, incorporated African ritual into his services, and he made liberal use of the Akan "sankofa" symbol, which expresses the importance of acknowledging the past. In the spirit of "sankofa" is Youngblood's aphorism "The Way Out Is the Way Back Through" (that is, the path to the future must lead us back through our ancestral heritage), and organized commemorations of the "Maafa" (a Kiswahili word for the Middle Passage) which featured a reenactment of the horrific sea voyage by costumed children from his church and a ceremony in which wreaths were placed in the Atlantic to honor the African slaves who died there. Youngblood was one of many contemporary black ministers who continued a tradition of applying an African sensibility to spiritual leadership in various African American communities in the 1990s.

The Nation of Islam underwent an internal crisis after the death of Elijah Muhammad in 1975 when his son, Wallace Muhammad, assumed leadership of the organization and began to revise many of its teachings. Wallace Muhammad eventually discarded his father's racial ideas and disbanded the organization in 1985, encouraging its followers to integrate themselves into the international Orthodox Muslim community. Nonetheless, despite the dissolution of Wallace Muhammad's NOI, a branch of the Nation has continued to thrive in the 1990s under the leadership of Louis Farrakhan, who has remained true to the ideas of Elijah Muhammad.

Farrakhan, ever a controversial figure, has earned mainstream notoriety for anti-Semitic remarks, but proved his high standing in the American black community at the Million Man March, a historic gathering of black men in the nation's capital. The march was Farrakhan's idea, and although many marchers were probably attracted by the event and not necessarily by its organizer, many noted that few contemporary black leaders would have been popular enough to conceive and pull off such a significant assembly. Also, in recent years Farrakhan had distinguished himself as one of the most internationally minded American black activists, reaching out to leaders around the world, including nations in Africa and the Caribbean, and touring various countries as an official state guest. Farrakhan's internationalism often seems more pan-Islamic than pan-African, as his closest relationships seem to have been forged with Arab Muslims in the Middle East and North African leaders on the continent. And his goodwill tours, which have included trips to Sudan (whose Islamic government has long been denounced by international human rights groups for perpetuating slavery and waging a bloody war against the people of the country's predominantly non-Muslim southern region), have prompted widespread criticism.

Since the 1970s, black Americans in search of spiritual alternatives to the Christianity of the mainstream black churches have also become practitioners of African religions. Yoruba religion, with its array of gods, its divination system, and its spirit-possession rituals, has become one of the most popular African religions in the New World. Having thrived in South America and the Caribbean for centuries, more recently it has made its way to the United States as well. Though there is little published information on black Americans who worship the Yoruba gods, in some major U.S. cities Afrocentric black professionals in search of "authentic" models of black spirituality have become adherents of the religion, often receiving spiritual instruction from Nigerian Yoruba priests. While what is practiced in the United States has been adapted to a modern American context and is substantively different from the version practiced in rural West Africa, black American practitioners of the Yoruba religion attempt to remain faithful to the essence of its spirituality. For example, some worshipers of Ogun, the god of iron, view the god as something of a patron saint, invoking his protection and aid by wearing heavy iron bracelets. Many black Americans in recent years have also come to identify themselves as "African spiritualists." Their belief system borrows from various African traditions. African spiritualists often revere their ancestors, possibly performing ritual ablutions and making offerings for their benefit, and appreciate the interaction between the living and spirit worlds.

In addition to finding expression in the efforts of black Americans to find spirituality systems that link them to a nurturing African heritage, pan-African religious outlooks have also spawned initiatives at the institutional and theological levels. In attempting to find ways of suiting Christianity to the black experience, black Christian theologians in America and Africa have collaborated on the conception of a black Christian theology at various points in history.

Though the dialogue between African and African American theologies has sometimes highlighted more ideological differences than similarities, the spirited exchange of ideas that took place through the 1970s and '80s underlined a shared African-centered approach to

Christianity that often served to strengthen pan-African spiritual ties. African American theologians like Wilmore and Cone traded ideas with receptive African religious scholars like the South African Bishop Desmond Tutu, and together they explored shared approaches to black Christianity in a meaningful and mutually rewarding discourse.

"There exists between us a mysterious bond of blood brotherhood, a common past and a common experience of suffering and subjugation which God can use to his own good purposes as we come together in faith and life," Wilmore and Cone wrote of the appropriate partnership. "The old Black theologians . . . used to talk about the destiny of the Black race and how the sons of Ham would be a blessing to the world. . . . It is not racist madness to believe that Africa shall again have one of the greatest civilizations the world has ever known and that long-separated brethren, weary of bruising their fists upon doors that will not fully open, will come home by the millions to contribute to and share in the building of that greatness. It is not too much to believe that God wills to use the churches of Africa and Black America to give the sublimity and spiritual depth to that historical process that will make it minister to the humanization and redemption of the world." Having identified such common interests and lofty goals, Wilmore and Cone stressed the need for continued dialogue and collaboration. "We must talk to one another, for we have much to talk about," they concluded. "But we must hear one another with sympathy and understanding."

And in the assertion by African American and African theologians like Cone and Tutu that God has special plans for the redemption of blacks in Africa and around the world, these thinkers have continued a long tradition in black religious thought and practice, three hundred years of stretching hands unto an African God.

Two years after I cried over my brother's grave, I returned to the cemetery. This time I was with my mother. She had spent her summer vacation visiting various relatives around the United States and would soon be returning to Dar es Salaam. I had come up from New York to meet her in Boston, and had already spent two days with her and my aunts, uncles, and cousins in Lynn, shopping, talking, and just getting caught up. My mother had reserved this third day for a visit to the cemetery, and while it was too bad that I was the only one who was able to accompany her, I welcomed the chance to spend some time alone with her. I usually only got to see her and my father once a year, whenever they or I made the transatlantic crossing. And I always found there was much I had stored up and wanted to tell her.

We took the train to Waltham and walked to the cemetery. It was a bright, warm day, and we strolled slowly and talked. We made our way leisurely to Remy's grave and sat comfortably in the grass in front of his headstone. My mother kicked off her sandals and stretched her toes in the sod. I scraped some lichen from the stone and cleared a few pebbles from the vicinity, running my fingers over the deeply etched lettering and admiring the speckled gray color and the smooth cool feel of the granite against my hand. My mother and I chatted idly, remembering people, places, and events from the past, laughing easily and enjoying the sun, warm and friendly on our skin. A lawn mower sounded in the distance, and a man walked past us.

"Lovely afternoon," he said pleasantly, smiling.

"Yes, it's beautiful," my mother replied. The man continued on his way and my mother and I lapsed into silence, lost in our own thoughts, feeling a gentle breeze dancing around us and quietly taking in the sky, the trees, the grass, and the gray headstone. I ran my hand over it once more.

"Do you think you'll ever see him again?" I asked my mother suddenly.

"I'm sure of it," she said immediately.

I nodded and leaned back in the grass, digging my elbows and fingers into the soil and feeling warmed by the sun.

CONCLUSION: THE LAND OF THE FUTURE

How good and how pleasant it would be,
Before God and man,
To see the unification of all Africans.
—Bob Marley

The old woman was tired. Since her husband's death she had been shunted from relative to relative, and even though living with her daughter's family in Kimpese was an improvement over the cramped quarters she had shared with another daughter at her brother's cinder-block home in Kinshasa, she was weary. Of course it was good to be surrounded by grandchildren and to once again live in a quiet rural area after the impersonal loneliness and oppressive hubbub of the big city, but she still felt listless. Despite her now regular visits to a physical therapist and her improved country diet of fruits, vegetables, and other fresh farm produce, it was becoming more and more difficult to get around on her own. In Kinshasa, as the pain in her increasingly brittle legs had gradually incapacitated her, she had taken to crawling and was helped in and out of bed by her daughter. Now she barely made the effort to crawl unless she had to. And she was too frail even to use the four-legged metallic contraption that was supposed to help her walk. Her grandson had sent it for her from America, but while it was good that her children in foreign lands thought about her and wanted to help, the gesture had come too late. At least she could wear the pagne and scarf he had brought her when she saw him in Kinshasa, for the only time.

She sighed, thinking about her scattered children. She especially missed her son Ernest, who had left Congo many years before to study in the white man's country. He had returned to Congo with an American wife and son and had gotten a good government job that had made her very proud of him. But then he had left again, and she had had to make do with letters that her daughter read for her and with photos of his children, two of whom she had never met. Ernest visited sometimes, but not as frequently as she would have liked, and he had only brought one of her grandsons with him on that single brief visit to Kinshasa. She always enjoyed his visits; she sometimes called him by the name he had originally been given when he was born, Bazunini (They Now Have Peace) because he did indeed have a soothing effect on her. She wished he would just come home to be near her. There was still much she wanted to tell and teach him.

They said that she had many other grandchildren in foreign lands, and she felt sad that she would probably never meet most of them. Things had changed a great deal since the days of her childhood, when most of her extended family had lived within shouting distance, in the same village, and other relatives were a short journey away. Back then there had been little need for children of the clan to travel far away to study in the white man's schools to learn the skills required of the new society, or to leave the village to find work in the city. Back then the clan had been strong and united, and the villages of the area where they lived had been prosperous. Now it seemed as if the clan was in turmoil, its children dispersed, its leadership in crisis, its bond with the ancestral lands of Bas-Congo weakened. Now, with most of her generation already dead, she was the senior member of the clan, but she felt too exhausted to offer the leadership her family sorely needed.

She thought of her late husband. She had known him her entire life. They had grown up together, surrounded by numerous other siblings and cousins and village children, but a special bond had formed between them alone. They had loved each other very much, and had built an admirable life together. They had been very happy. She had borne him ten children, and only one of them had died before reaching adulthood. She had tended the large fields that yielded much of the family's food, while he had set traps for fish in the river near their home and earned money teaching primary school for the Swedish mission and traveling from village to village as a catechist. He had seen to it that she acquired an education as well, and they sent most of their children to school, too. The educated children were able to find jobs in the city, but the search for better opportunities also caused the family to scatter all over the world in pursuit of further education and employment. The family had already begun to lose its cohesion by the time her husband died, a tragedy that had further disrupted the clan. She had felt so alone when he died.

She sighed again. She had already outlived her husband by more than ten years, but now she was getting tired. Perhaps she would be seeing him soon.

Three years after I met my father's mother for the first and only time, she stopped eating. When her daughter became alarmed and demanded to know why she refused her food, my grandmother simply said that it was time for her to go. Her grandchildren in the household confronted her and pleaded with her to start eating again, but she declined. And when they insisted, she lapsed into obstinate silence and stopped responding to their entreaties altogether. One of her brothers was sent for and he traveled hurriedly to Kimpese to try to reason with her. When she remained deaf to his pleas to eat, he grudgingly accepted that she had decided her course and would not be deterred. He suggested that if she wanted to die, she should at least have her children summoned so they could see her one last time. She agreed, but she was already so weak that it was questionable whether she would last until her sons and daughters abroad had a chance to reach Kimpese.

My grandmother died on April 16, 1998. It was my father's birthday. He received the news that day, and instead of celebrating his fifty-sixth year he sorrowfully found himself making plans to travel to Congo for his mother's funeral. Through his grief, he wondered if the date was purely coincidental or if his mother had selected it deliberately, wanting to make sure he would always remember her death. Perhaps one day he will ask her.

I met my paternal grandparents only once before they died. When my grandfather passed, I was seventeen, in my second year at the United World College in New Mexico. I had met him when I was ten years old, on my second visit to Kinshasa, while my father was under "city arrest." Though the circumstances surrounding our introduction were less than ideal, it was still a momentous occasion. I remember that he was tall and thin and seemed very kind, with soft dark eyes, a gentle smile, and short silver hair. When I received news of his death, I secluded myself in my dormitory's deserted laundry room and cried for a loss I barely understood. My grief was partly out of sympathy for my father, who, for months after his father's death, would sit silently on his bed, gazing at a photo of his parents cradled tenderly in his hands. But I also wept for my own sense of deprivation and missed opportunity, for the sadness of realizing that it was now forever too late for me to know my grandfather.

I was equally moved when my grandmother died, perhaps even more so since I had firmer, more recent memories of her, and because I had felt when meeting her that I was forging an important, belated connection. My brothers, like my American-born Congolese cousins, never had the opportunity to meet our grandmother, so I had also felt a sense of responsibility to share my experience of her with them. "Now you have seen your grandmother," she had said to me when I met her, "and when you go home you will tell the others about me." I have tried to do as she instructed. But I have not always felt equal to the task.

How can I speak of eighty-some years of a life that I shared for just a few moments? How do you convey a sense of a person's spirit and being to those who have only seen photographs? How could I put into words the emotion I felt when I met her? Or convey the unmistakable love I saw on her face when she gazed on my father and me? I fear that whatever I say or write will appear simplified and sentimental, sweetened with nostalgic honey. Still, I hope my words will allow my grandmother's memory to endure as a source of affection, reverence, and pride. I want my brothers, cousins, and children to think of their ancestors and feel proud of whom and where they came from. As my grandmother said, our "species" has spread far, and will probably continue to scatter. But, I hope, not so far that we can no longer recall our origins.

*   *   *

A Kikongo proverb states, "A tree cannot stand without its roots." It seems such obvious wisdom now, a well-worn cliché in our era in which everything truly insightful has already been said. But all clichés derive their endurance from their truth, and my ancestors who coined this adage were sending a clear and powerful message to their descendants: a people cannot flourish without their life-giving foundations in the past. The ties between those who came before and those who live now must be maintained and nurtured if a people is to survive. It's a truth that my grandmother understood when she made a point of directing me to "tell the others" about her. And it's a truth that has been well recognized by successive generations of black people in America. Another Kikongo proverb reminds us that "one can only steal a sleeping baby; once awake, she will look for her parents." It's a maxim that conveys the seemingly instinctive pull of one's heritage, our inborn curiousity in our origins, the quest we all share for self-identification and self-knowledge.

Black Americans, the tribe of Africans marooned on American soil, have managed to sustain links with the continent of their origin, against tremendous odds and despite deliberate efforts to sever them from their past. Through ingenuity and dogged determination, in calculated symbolism and unwitting remembrance, for over three hundred years African Americans have kept various ties to Africa intact. The bond has frayed and stretched, it has become twisted and contorted, and some, black and white, have tried to cut it altogether, while others have attempted to strengthen it. Through it all, the bond has not been broken. And for as long as blacks in America have reached back to Africa to offer and receive reassurance, reaffirmation, fraternity and strength, Africans have reached to blacks in the Americas, "those who were taken," for the same reasons.

We have fascinated each other ever since we were separated so long ago. For centuries, we have gazed at one another across the transatlantic divide like a child seeing itself in the mirror for the first time. And, unable for so long to reach behind the glass and touch the strangely familiar face we saw staring back, we filled in all that we did not know with all that we could imagine. And we anxiously anticipated the day when we would be reunited.

When we finally met, in Africa and America, we were sometimes disappointed. Shadowy imaginings do not usually hold up in the light of real experience. We wondered if we hadn't been mistaken, if the kinship we could feel more than describe was really there, if the roots that had once bound us together had not already withered and died. But time and again we were reminded of what we shared. Africa has left her mark on all of us, in the skin and features that supposedly justified our oppressors' contempt, and in the souls that survived it. Africa is alive in her children's laughter, in a sensation tugging at our hearts, in the curve of our backsides, the rhythm of our songs, and the ecstasy of our worship. We have reached out to one another through literature, politics, music, and religion, and whenever we've made contact, the world has been forced to take note.

I, like many, have explored the dynamics of this bond throughout my life, and in many ways my family and I are products of the historical yearning of blacks divided by an ocean to reach out to one another.

In testing the limits of transatlantic kinship I, too, have been disillusioned and bewildered, by Africans who have felt alienated by my Americanness, and black Americans who have seen my Africanness as cause for mistrust or derision. But despite these experiences, which have tried my faith in the potential of international black brotherhood, after periods in which I have despaired of ever finding common ground within my dual heritage, I have found myself back where I started. I have discovered that African Americans and Africans *are* culturally distinct in most ways, and centuries of separation *have* made them strangers. But through the evidence of history and my own personal experience, I have learned that Africans and black Americans can move beyond their real and perceived differences to celebrate and build on what they share.

Anyone can claim Africa as a "motherland." But only black people are claimed by Africa so powerfully, whether we like it or not. Africanness has been called a stain, a stigma, a mark, a curse, a sable hue, a tawny front, and a funky suntan, but whatever it's called, "black" people of various complexions all carry the conspicuous evidence of our heritage on our faces. And for this reason, all black people have been forced to contend with Africa and what it means to them. Some may conclude that it holds no importance to them, but all feel pressured to decide one way or another. The Harlem Renaissance poet Countee Cullen wondered in verse what Africa meant to him, but perhaps more significant than the ambiguous answers he explored was the fact that he felt compelled to pose the question at all.

Similarly, Africans confronted with the existence of blacks overseas have historically had to find ways to come to terms with them. Like black American responses to Africa, African attitudes towards black Americans have run the gamut. In Africa, American blacks have been variously regarded as long-lost kin, powerful potential saviors of the continent, a strange tribe of Africans on American soil, and "black whites" with American cultural values. But whatever their opinion of their counterparts in America, Africans have always been preoccupied with finding out more about the mysterious blacks of the New World. Like most Africans who visit the United States, African students at American universities in the 1940s and 1950s made a point of seeking out black Americans, and African American visitors to Africa have always sparked tremendous interest and curiosity among the locals, whatever their eventual conceptions of the newcomers.

These efforts by black people on both sides of the Atlantic to struggle to come to terms with what they mean to one another has produced much of interest and import. Black American efforts to re-discover Africa helped spawn one of America's most important literary movements, generating work that so resonated with African writers that it helped in turn to spark some of Africa's best-known writing. Alarmed by the unchecked expansion of white supremacy, African Americans teamed up with Africans to help rid the world of colonial-ism, and a mass movement led by an Africa-obsessed Jamaican based in New York became poised to change the face of the planet. African and African American musicians and artists, working separately and in collaboration on two continents and invoking common musical roots and idioms, have produced some of the world's most memorable art. And the challenges of racism have prompted blacks on both sides of the Atlantic to collectively conceive new black approaches to spirituality.

In my own experience, I've seen how Africans and Americans have been able to transcend different cultural perspectives to unite in bat-tles against racism, and I've seen how efforts at cultural exchanges have enriched and educated both black Americans and Africans. In Africa, I've seen black Americans assimilate aspects of African culture to claim identities that span two continents, and I've seen Africans in America mirror that process. I've seen Africans look to African Ameri-cans for reaffirmation and cultural inspiration, and black Americans look to Africa for the same. And I've watched the black world get smaller and more intermingled. I've danced alongside African Ameri-cans and Africans at African clubs in New York, and bobbed to hip-hop with black Americans and Africans at discos in Dar es Salaam and Johannesburg.

As it has at other times and places, the potential of black unity came into sharp focus for me at the Million Man March in Washing-ton, D.C., in 1996. I attended the march by myself, somewhat spon-taneously taking the day off from work, but I hardly felt alone when I arrived. Disembarking from the bus with two dozen other black men, I was greeted by a sea of brown faces everywhere I looked. I was pos-sessed of an excited, exhilarated feeling, like the glee of my first trip to Harlem after years of study in predominantly white Cambridge, Mas-sachusetts. I felt powerful, proud, and safe, at home among my own.

I worked my way toward the front of the crush of black bodies, of-fering and returning happy greetings, grasping hands and smiling as I wove through the massive crowd and took up a position close to the podium where speaker after speaker addressed the throng. I didn't pay all that much attention to most of the orators, and as far as I could tell, not many other people did, either. Instead, I turned from the Capitol building and gazed in awe at the assembled multitude behind me. I am hard pressed now to remember the names of even ten out of the many who made speeches, or what exactly they had to say. But I will never forget the feeling of gazing out across that vast plain of people. Commentators would later argue about just how many people turned out for the event, but I couldn't have cared less how many were actually there. I don't know what an assemblage of a million people looks like, but I do know that there were black men as far as I could see from where I stood. It was as if brothers had taken over the city. Black men in all their strength and diversity: young men with jeans and dreadlocks, Muslims in suits and bow ties, grandfathers in polyester slacks and hats, Africans and Afrocentrists in bright embroidered shirts and robes. It gave me a sense of our tremendous potential to see hundreds of thousands of us gathered like that.

I noticed that some men were draped in national flags (I picked out the red Trinidadian flag and the red, gold, and green of Ghana); others held banners proclaiming their affiliation with clubs or civic organizations, or announcing the cities they had come from. While some critics later dismissed those who attended the march as merely zealous followers of Minister Louis Farrakhan, the event's chief organizer, I found that to be a gross oversimplification. I certainly hadn't traveled to D.C. simply to hear Farrakhan speak, and I felt that the opportunity to commune, as people sharing a specific identity and faced with specific problems, motivated most participants' attendance. And the fact that the march attracted black men of such varied experience and background was to me a testament to how much we shared in spite of our differences. At the Million Man March, many celebrated the specificity of their region, religion, and nationality, but all had assembled as black people.

I was even more encouraged by the pan-African flavor of the gathering when friends in Africa later asked me eager questions about the march. Apparently news of the historic assembly had reached across the ocean, and Africans had followed the event with interest. One friend in Tanzania had been very surprised that black Americans would even stress their black identity enough to gather as self-consciously black people, and he and other Africans felt encouraged by the demonstration of black solidarity. The agenda put forward at the march seemed secondary; most people were just impressed that blacks in the United States had come together in a positive and empowering way.

And the participation in the march of black people from various parts of the world underlined for me how much America's black communities have changed. Today unprecedented numbers of Africans and West Indians live in the United States, adding further diversity and color to an already varied black population. And, faced with many of the same issues as American-born blacks in the United States, many feel motivated to collectively address common problems and add their voices to a black chorus calling for change. If the tensions I have observed between Africans and African Americans have shaken my faith in the validity of transatlantic kinship, events like the Million Man March (and the Million Woman March in Philadelphia a year later, which went even further in demonstrating a pan-African outlook by selecting Winnie Mandela as the keynote speaker) have provided cause for optimism.

We now find ourselves at the dawn of a new century, and Africans and the descendants of Africa around the world once again have the opportunity to make the world take note of us. My father keeps a small wooden carving in the shape of the African continent on his desk in my family's home in Dar es Salaam. It bears the words "Africa: Land of the Future." This is a common sentiment among many African scholars these days, observers of Africa who have been heartened by political changes, economic growth, and increasing stability across the continent. The old guard of African leaders, born under colonialism and in power during an era when African politics was dominated by the imperial interests of the Cold War, are dying off, literally and politically, and a new generation of "born free" Africans are poised to take over the reins of leadership. Despite the persistent, nagging civil wars and the continuation of nondemocratic rule in a number of countries, Africa's future now looks brighter than it has in some time.

My uncle Fukiau shares my father's optimism, but for slightly different reasons. Diagramming his points on a napkin at a family gathering, he explained to my brother and me that in Kongo philosophy, history is regarded as cyclical, with all of the world's civilizations going through periods of evolution and decline, rising to power and prominence as other nations fall. By his calculation, Africa is due for its turn as the most prosperous continent on earth, a position it occupied in the distant past, and it is the duty of concerned Africans around the world to hasten her toward her destiny. "Rise up ye mighty race!" Marcus Garvey urged in the 1920s. Perhaps he was merely a century too early to witness the fulfillment of his dream.

If we are indeed on the cusp of a new era in Africa, I hope that blacks in America, equipped with a new appreciation of their place in an international black community, will be closely involved, and there is much to suggest that they will. Today black Americans and Africans have access to more information about each other, and have more contact with each other, than ever before. They study together in American universities more than ever in the past; more Africans than ever before now live in the United States; more African Americans now travel to Africa; and the 1990s have seen the advent of a new "back-to-Africa" movement in the hundreds of black Americans who have flocked to South Africa since the dismantling of apartheid. Record numbers of African Americans now occupy positions of power in the American foreign affairs establishment and are poised to influence U.S. policy on Africa. And black entrepreneurs on both continents are now reaching out to one another in unprecedented economic initiatives.

There was a reggae song called "Radio Africa" by a British group called Latin Quarter that my friends and I used to dance to as teenagers in Tanzania. "I'm hearing only bad news on the Radio Africa," went the tune's somber refrain. I am tired of hearing so much bad news come out of Africa. I'm tired of countries like Nigeria, where a military dictator made himself the sole candidate in ludicrous "multiparty" elections, becoming the laughingstock of Western foreign affairs officials. I'm tired of only hearing mention of Africa on the American evening news when a massacre, famine, or natural disaster has occurred. I'm tired of the images of black skeletons with distended bellies queueing for food at hunger relief centers, and of the pictures of pint-sized African child warriors clutching rifles that dwarf them. I'm tired of Africa being synonymous with poverty, war, and mismanagement. And I'm tired of black people around the world looking on the land of their ancestral origin with shame and embarrassment. I'm weary of blackness being regarded as a "stain" linking a person to the most wretched continent on earth.

Similarly, I am fed up with the bad news that too often seems to define African America. To many observers around the world, African Americans are identified with crime, violence, poverty, sexual irresponsibility, and professional and academic underachievement. Far too many African Americans die young or end up in prison, and too many black children are being left behind as America's most privileged look forward to a brave new technological world.

Of course, we know that Africa and black America are much more than what the international media consistently reduces us to, that the popular images of our degradation are only amplified part truths. But the fact that depictions of black misery are even partly accurate underlines the depth and breadth of our very real problems; as I once heard Cornel West so eloquently put it, "black folks are catching hell all over."

If we cannot count on predominantly white media outlets to present more balanced images of us, we also cannot rely on others to solve our problems. If there is one lesson to be learned from the struggles of our ancestors, it's that the burden of progress rests on our shoulders, that we can count on no one but ourselves to build our future. Only Africans can take responsibility for redeeming Africa; only African Americans can uplift black America. But by linking these two fronts in a single black battle for worldwide empowerment, we can tap our most valuable resource—the incredible human potential of our sheer weight in numbers; the children of Africa have spread throughout the world and stand more than a billion strong, to update Garvey. By standing together and reaching out to one another there is much we have accomplished throughout history. But so much remains to be done.

What if black people around the world could marshal our considerable talents and resources to attempt to find solutions to some of the problems facing us as black people? What if African economies could be made to flourish, and African governments made to serve their people? What if African leaders were in a position to offer assistance and support to embattled blacks around the world, pressing Western governments to improve the condition of their black minorities? What if Africa could become synonymous with prosperity and peace and act as a source of pride and stature for black people around the world, and what if blackness were a badge of honor? I believe that through coordinated efforts, these things are possible.

As Bob Marley wrote and sang in 1979, a time of great optimism for pan-Africanists around the world as the last vestiges of colonialism in Africa seemed poised to fall,

> *Africa Unite, 'cause the children wanna come home. . . .*
> *Unite for the benefit of your children,*
> *Unite, for it's later than you think. . . .*
> *Unite for the Africans abroad,*
> *Unite for the Africans a yard [at home].*

Marley, whose music was both a product and driving force of the international ideal of black kinship, was looking to the future, shortly after the end of Portuguese rule in Angola and Mozambique and in the midst of the war that would end white rule in Rhodesia. He was anticipating Africa's full independence and looking forward to "moving right out of Babylon" to "our father's land," the mobilization of the black diaspora for the cause of Africa's redemption and a return to the ancestral homeland. He was envisioning a strong and unified Africa, a source of power and pride for Africans around the world, and hoping for the growth of a sense of common purpose among the beleaguered descendants of Africa worldwide. Twenty years later, we are still struggling to free Africa from colonialism's legacy and to promote greater pan-Africanism on the continent and around the world. Africa still occupies the bottom rung in the world's hierarchy, and has yet to harness the energies and initiative of the African diaspora. But perhaps things are about to change. And as Bob would say, how good and how pleasant that would be.

EPILOGUE

In August 1998, as I was writing this book, I received some news that was cause for shock, concern, and ultimately, hope. I was in Boston visiting relatives at the time, and my uncle André, my father's younger brother, casually handed me a printout of a news story he had just taken off the Internet. The international press report informed me that my father was leading a revolution.

"Leaders of the ongoing rebellion in the Democratic Republic of Congo have formally announced details of their movement and its principal members," the article read. "The Rwanda News Agency, reporting the rebels' announcement, said the movement would be known as the Rassemblement Congolais pour la Democratie (RCD), whose chairman was Ernest Wamba dia Wamba (an academic and member of the Bakongo people from the Matadi area)."

Because I was so familiar with my father's political views and his history of involvement in Congolese struggles against dictatorship, I was not entirely unprepared to find out that he was in the thick of this latest political upheaval. But the revelation of the extent of his involvement, mentioned so matter-of-factly in the stream of journalistic prose, took me, and many other members of my family, completely by surprise. The "formal announcement" of my father's leadership of the rebel movement in the international press was also my father's "formal announcement" of his involvement to many of his relatives and friends.

Though surprised by my father's central role in the events in Congo, I was already aware of the war's outbreak and of the circumstances which had led up to it. Like many Africans around the world, I had closely followed the tumultuous situation in the Congo since the mid-1990s, a period of unprecedented change in the entire region. So I understood that the hostilities of 1998 were rooted in the unresolved issues of another war, one that had left a million people dead in 1994.

The Rwandan genocide of 1994, in which so many hundreds of thousands of ethnic Tutsis were beaten, bludgeoned, and hacked to death by Hutu mobs and militias deployed by a criminal and corrupt Hutu government, had left me feeling stunned and disheartened, as much by the killing itself as by the international indifference. The slaughter was not stopped by the international community, despite its long-standing pledge to prevent and punish genocide, but by the Rwandan Patriotic Army, a Tutsi rebel group that attacked from Uganda, overthrowing the genocidal Hutu government and prompting the Hutu Interahamwe militias, which were responsible for the massacres, to flee to Zaire. President Mobutu had considered the deposed Rwandan Hutu government an ally, and he readily welcomed the killers, who took up residence in the refugee camps set up and supplied by international aid organizations. Many international observers suspected that the presence in Zaire of an army of trained killers would later lead to crisis, and of course it did.

By 1996, the thousands of Rwandan "refugees" still in Zaire had begun to clash with the local Banyamulenge population, who, though Zairean by birth and residence, were ethnic Tutsis and resented the Hutu incursions on their land. Mobutu exacerbated the tensions by attempting to expel segments of the Banyamulenge population to make way for the newcomers, denying the citizenship of the long-term residents. In response, Banyamulenge rebels staged a revolt against the Mobutu regime, fighting the Zairean army and its Interahamwe allies in defense of their land and rights. The rebellion gained the support of much of the Zairean population and the governments of Rwanda, Uganda, and other regional powers who were fed up with Mobutu's antics, which had long destabilized the entire region. The rebel movement gained momentum and acquired a spokesman and leader in Laurent Kabila, a longtime anti-Mobutu dissident and onetime associate of Patrice Lumumba. In just seven months, the rebel alliance overcame the disinterested opposition of a weak Zairean army, marching triumphantly into Kinshasa in April 1997.

Mobutu had already fled for Morocco, where he was the guest of his fellow authoritarian King Hassan; he later succumbed to the prostate cancer that had afflicted him for some time and was buried in Morocco. Few of the allies who had stood by him while he ran Zaire to suit their needs and enrich himself bothered to send representatives to his funeral. Back in Kinshasa, Kabila, who became known as the man who had finally rid the nation of its dictator, declared himself president and was hailed as a conquering hero.

Zaireans at home and abroad greeted the news of Mobutu's ouster with jubilation. It seemed as though, after so many years of disastrous governance, Zaire would finally see the political changes that so many had craved for so long. I was working and living in Boston at the time, and the Zaireans in the area, including my aunts and uncles in Lynn, Massachusetts, were possessed of the same optimism and exultation that was gripping Zaireans all over the world. Many who had left the country for political reasons looked forward to being able to return to the land of their birth one day soon. And since the war that had overthrown Mobutu had been supported by a pan-African coalition of nations, Africans on the continent and in the diaspora celebrated the initiative as a rare case of Africans assuming control of their own collective political destiny.

My father felt the same sense of elation and hope. After years of fruitless opposition to the tyranny of the Zairean state, after his own detention, and after the genocide in Rwanda, a tragedy that had affected him deeply, here finally was a positive political development on a continent that often seemed dominated by bad news. He had spent a career championing the cause of democracy in Zaire, and now his efforts, and those of millions of Zaireans who had opposed Mobutu throughout his reign, seemed to have finally been rewarded. His exuberant optimism bubbled over in the letters he wrote me from Dar es Salaam, where he followed events in Zaire closely, often receiving reports from his family, friends, and colleagues within the country.

Despite my father's hopefulness, there was also just the hint of omen in the midst of his celebratory enthusiasm. Ever the conscientious academic, and ever mindful of the lessons of history, my father was quick to identify the pitfalls that could befall this promising movement for change. He had seen the hopes of the Congolese people betrayed before, and even while he celebrated the downfall of a regime that had all but wrecked his homeland, he was wary of the possible emergence of a new dictator. "We must avoid a coup d'état and a 'red Mobutu' replacing a 'green one,' " he wrote me in one letter, referring to Kabila's self-identification as a "red" leftist, versus Mobutu's "green" money-obsessed kleptocracy. "In that sense, the attitude of saying that 'any change is good' is self-defeating."

My father had met Kabila before (as apparently had I, for the dissident visited our home when I was a young child) and had considered him a comrade in a common battle against the Zairean dictatorship. But he wasn't sure that the new rebel leader necessarily represented the best choice to lead the country into a new era. Kabila had already exhibited signs of a repressive leadership style, banning political parties from operating in the areas the rebels controlled during the march to Kinshasa. My father also told me that when Kabila was a Lumumbist rebel in the 1960s, he had hosted Che Guevara, who was then touring Africa in an effort to promote revolution on the continent, but that the Argentine revolutionary had expressed serious reservations about the young Congolese leader, a damaging judgment from a man my father regarded as a hero. And my father wondered if the fact that the rebels were so heavily reliant on foreign (particularly Rwandan) assistance would pose problems later when the movement tried to present itself as homegrown and legitimately Congolese.

As the rebel alliance began to set up a post-Mobutu government, my father's worst fears seemed to prove justified. To begin with, Kabila prohibited political activity, saying that during the delicate period of reconstruction following the war, political campaigning would be a disruption. He then moved to dominate the rebel alliance that had put him in power, pushing through statutes that gave him wide dictatorial powers.

Though Kinshasa was the base of a number of opposition parties that had peacefully struggled against Mobutu for years, Kabila refused to consult with local political opposition forces; save for some token political appointments, he derisively dismissed the demands of opposition politicians to open the new government to the full spectrum of Congolese political tendencies. He also began to eliminate rival leaders within the AFDL (Alliance of Democratic Forces for the Liberation of the Congo), the rebel coalition. Of three other leaders with whom he had shared power when the movement was formed, one died under murky circumstances, one was arrested, tried on dubious charges and imprisoned on Kabila's orders, and the third survived a mysterious assassination attempt before being progressively stripped of his responsibilities.

The political situation in the newly rechristened Democratic Republic of the Congo continued to worsen, to the growing alarm of many of Kabila's colleagues and a Congolese political class that had hoped that the AFDL's victory would result in greater democracy and openness. Instead, Kabila seemed to be reproducing some of Mobutu's worst practices. He began to reserve key positions in the government for family members, people from his ethnic group, and associates from his home region, Katanga province. And in addition to being president of the AFDL and the country, Kabila made himself minister of defense.

He adopted other Mobutu-style tendencies as well. To package his image for mass consumption, Kabila recruited a public relations expert who had worked for Mobutu and began erecting large billboards emblazoned with his visage beaming down on his subjects. He reportedly paid thousands of citizens to march in the streets in massive rallies in which they sang his praises. And from his alleged tendency to command a hefty percentage of almost all international mining contracts, he acquired among some Kinshasa residents the nickname "Mr. Thirty Percent"; the joke on the streets of Kinshasa was that while Mobutu used to demand fifteen percent of all foreign investment profits, Kabila had doubled the obligatory presidential cut.

Despite Kabila's consolidation of power, his extensive reliance on Rwandan assistance made it difficult for him to win over the masses of the Congolese people after the euphoria of Mobutu's flight began to wear off. Rwandan armed forces had remained in Congo after the AFDL conquest and formed a visible presence in some areas, to the chagrin of some Congolese. Rwandans, and even Congolese ethnic Tutsis from the east, were often regarded with mistrust by many western Congolese (in Kinshasa especially), and the prominence of Rwandans and Banyamulenge in Kabila's rebel army and the AFDL led some xenophobic Congolese to denounce Kabila as a puppet of Tutsi interests. In response to the criticisms, Kabila began to turn on his erstwhile allies.

Playing on the anti-Rwandan, anti-Tutsi sentiments that were partly causing his unpopularity in much of Zaire, Kabila began using anti-Tutsi rhetoric to express his independence from his former allies and to try to whip up nationalist Congolese enthusiasm. He purged and politically neutralized Banyamulenge AFDL members, but since the Banyamulenge rebels who had first rebelled against Mobutu still formed the backbone of his army, Kabila realized that he would need to construct an alternate military force. So, in his most sinister move, Kabila began courting the Interahamwe, the thousands of Hutu "genocidaires" still scattered through eastern Congo and central Africa. In preparing to break ties with Rwanda and his Banyamulenge colleagues, Kabila began to seek out and re-arm the militias that had killed a million people in 1994.

Banyamulenge members of the AFDL coalition and the soldiers they commanded interpreted Kabila's rapprochement with the Interahamwe as a dangerous act of betrayal—these were the very forces that had committed genocide, the very enemies allied with Mobutu's army against whom they had fought in the rebellion that put Kabila in power. The government of Rwanda was similarly alarmed; it had supported Kabila's rebellion because it was counting on him to secure Rwanda's border with Congo and to flush out its enemies in exile—now, instead, Kabila had begun to ally himself with those very adversaries. For many Congolese who opposed Kabila, the move raised the haunting specter of another anti-Tutsi genocide, this time in eastern Congo.

In a final break with his former allies, Kabila ordered the Rwandan soldiers still in Congo to leave the country at the end of July 1998. A few days later, a mutiny broke out in eastern Congo, pitting Banyamulenge and other Congolese soldiers disenchanted with Kabila against troops who remained loyal to the government. The rebellion quickly spread to other parts of eastern Congo, with the rebels taking the cities of Goma and Bukavu on the Rwandan border from government control. AFDL members who opposed Kabila's abandonment of the principles and objectives for which they had originally supported him began to leave Kinshasa, convening in eastern Congo. Congolese opposition politicians, military commanders, civic leaders, and intellectuals, including my father, joined the other rebel leaders gathering in the east, and together they began to set up a political movement.

Mindful of the way in which Kabila had emerged to dominate the rebel alliance that had put him in power, the Rally for Congolese Democracy (RCD) embraced a principle of "collective leadership," whereby all important decisions were to be debated and discussed. It attempted to spread power among a generalized authority. Although my father had been elected chairman, he shared leadership with a number of vice presidents and coordinators, whose authority was in turn balanced by other members of the RCD general assembly. To guard against the sort of exclusivity that characterized Kabila's government, the RCD proclaimed itself "open to all active democratic forces in the Congolese society" and welcomed members with various political perspectives, drawing the line at Mobutu-era political criminals. And lest anyone assume that membership in the RCD would automatically lead to a post in government if Kabila were successfully ousted, all of the positions within the organization were identified as provisional. To most of the movement's members, the goal was not to conquer Kinshasa and put the RCD in power; they hoped instead to force Kabila to the negotiating table, convening a national conference to discuss the country's political future and pave the way for truly free and open elections. Uganda and Rwanda, fed up with Kabila's failure to curb the activities of rebel groups that had long used the friendly haven of eastern Congo as a base for launching attacks on them, threw their support behind the rebels. Kabila, on the other hand, whose mining and arms deals with a number of regional powers made him a financial asset to some foreign leaders, enjoyed the military backing of Zimbabwe, Angola, and Namibia.

As the RCD released its political declaration in Goma, in the capital, state radio began to call on Congolese to take up clubs and machetes to kill the "Tutsi invaders." Unfortunately, some xenophobes seemed all too willing to comply, and there were Tutsi witch hunts on the streets of Kinshasa, where many who were felt to match the stereotypical physical appearance of a Tutsi (tall, light-skinned, with a "long nose") were rounded up and killed. Some African Americans in Kinshasa were even mistakenly set upon until they managed to identify themselves. When I heard this from my shocked vantage point in New York I couldn't help thinking that the angry mobs shown throwing people off bridges on CNN would probably have seen my mother, and perhaps even myself or my brothers, as fair game.

My father had been kept apprised of the situation throughout its deterioration by his close contact with progressive members of the AFDL, some of whom were colleagues he had worked with before, and a network of academic and political contacts in the region. He was horrified by Kabila's alliance with forces that had committed genocide. The genocide itself had had a devastating impact on my father. He had been appalled by the killing and furious that the world had looked on and done nothing to stop it. He was outraged when reports surfaced that UN "peacekeepers" in Rwanda at the time had been ordered to avoid confrontation and had had their hands tied by a seemingly indifferent bureaucracy while a million people were murdered. In early 1997, he, my mother, and Jacques Depelchin, a Congolese colleague, had written and circulated a fiery document entitled "The African Declaration for an End to Genocidal Violence," which railed against the international apathy, denouncing "the lukewarm efforts to deal with a 'yet again,' more than fifty years after the entire world had said 'never again' after the Nazi extermination of Jews."

"If we do not change radically the dominant and dominating structures which govern our relations, if we do not rapidly attend to the direct and indirect causes of the genocidal violence which has plagued the countries of the Great Lakes, we shall be preparing a perfect stage for the next onslaught," the declaration warned. "We refuse to be accomplices to such a scenario, not only because it will eventually explode in the countries which see themselves as totally immune from such tragedies, but also because we see it as a duty dictated by our conscience."

With Kabila's alliance with the Interahamwe and his open declaration of war on Tutsis, the Congo seemed primed for the "onslaught" my father had dreaded. My father's concern about the ominous turn of events was also fueled by his patriotic feelings for his country and his decades of disgust with the way it was being run. Just when Mobutu's tyrannical career had finally come to an end, the land of my father's birth had become saddled with a new dictator, and a rebellion had begun in which Congolese hopes for a free society and perhaps the lives of thousands hung in the balance. My father felt that he had to act. "I couldn't just stay in Dar es Salaam and read books," he said later. He left Tanzania for Goma, the eastern Congolese city that became the rebel headquarters, and joined Congolese colleagues with a range of political perspectives and backgrounds. He was elected to lead the fledgling political movement that dedicated itself to establishing democracy in the Congo and eradicating dictatorship once and for all.

It seemed as if within a week my father had gone from being a committed historian little known outside Africanist academia and Congolese political circles (he had emerged from "relative obscurity," in the words of several newspaper articles) to assuming chairmanship of a movement that could change the face of Africa.

In the weeks that followed I would hear from my father occasionally, speaking to him briefly when he would call from Goma, Lusaka, Pretoria, Tripoli, Ouagadougou, or Dar es Salaam, as he traveled the continent as a rebel shuttle diplomat. On the phone he was the same old Dad, calm, reassuring, and often even jocular. He would update me on the movement's progress, ask how the war was being covered in the international press, how my work was going, and how my brothers and our relatives in Boston were doing. Occasionally he sounded drained and tired, burdened with too much to do on too little sleep, and sometimes I'd hear flashes of annoyance as I told him bits of the anti-rebel propaganda that circulated on the Internet. But he was always optimistic.

Even while I was reassured in late night phone conversations that my father was essentially the same person, at the same time, as I kept abreast of events in the Congo through the world media, I watched a strange, new public persona of my father develop. It was odd reading his name in newspapers, and especially strange to see him described as a "rebel leader." The words conjured images of beards, berets, and bravado, a picture laughably distant from my bookish, mild-mannered father. My father, who concentrated so hard when he was reading that he was often oblivious to loud, violent childhood disputes between my brothers and me. My father, who liked to buy the most unusual and exotic fruits he could find at Kinondoni market and bring them home for us to try. My father, who relished Sunday afternoons spent with a game of chess, a bowl of peanuts, a beer, and a worthy opponent. My father, the "rebel leader."

It's difficult to explain how it made me feel to learn of my father's role in the Congo's latest insurrection. My pulse quickened and my mind started racing as soon as I read his name in the article my uncle showed me, and I rushed through several conflicting emotions. I immediately worried about his safety, a concern that would grow in the coming months, especially at times when I heard that Kabila and his allies were bombing cities in eastern Congo, my father's base of operations. Familiar with the history of Congolese politics, which is fraught with assassinations and political betrayals, I also worried about more veiled threats to my father's security. I was also nervous about my mother, who was on her own in Dar es Salaam, and about the family members in Congo who might be within Kabila's vindictive reach. It was always obvious that the personal and political stakes were tremendously high. But my father had clearly considered the potential costs and, courageously, I thought, committed himself to his course.

Though I was concerned for my father's safety and that of my family, and lamented the war's inevitable price in human lives and aspirations, amid my reservations there were glimmers of pride and hope. I felt proud that my father was trying to help transform his country, to put what he believed were the interests of the Congolese people first. "People make history," my father had once written to me in a letter. "When occasions offer themselves, we must do so." He had clearly taken his own advice to heart, and viewed his involvement in the quest for Congolese freedom and reconstruction as an obligation he accepted with all of the risks it embodied.

I, in turn, saw it as my duty to support my father, but my position was not solely informed by a sense of filial loyalty. Congo has seen many wars seeking to end the oppression that has been a way of life for the majority of Congolese since before the turn of the century. The rebellion that had put Kabila in power had been claimed by those who fought it as a war of liberation and had been hailed as such by many observers around the world. Kabila had been seen as the man who rid the Congo of Mobutu, and though to many an unknown quantity, he had been widely expected to strive to put right much of what had been wrong under Mobutu. But the truth is that no one, including the allies who helped to put him in power, really knew what to expect from a career rebel who had spent the last thirty years commanding guerillas in the bush and, reportedly, dealing in gold in Tanzania. I had cautiously applauded Kabila's ascension to power and felt as betrayed and disappointed as anyone when he began to behave as badly as his predecessor.

This time around, I had complete faith in the leader of the rebellion that aimed to bring democracy to the Congo. My deeply patriotic father had spent decades studying the processes that had resulted in his country's history of exploitation and misery. And he believed he saw solutions. He had always struggled against imperialism, dictatorship, and neo-colonialism and for the rights and interests of the masses of Congolese people, using his position as an academic as a platform for his ideas. He was well respected in his field and had distinguished himself as a capable leader as the president of one of Africa's largest academic research organizations, the Dakar-based CODESRIA. He had received prestigious awards for his scholarship and earned the respect of political colleagues in his work with other Congolese pro-democracy activists. He had written extensively on Congolese history, politics, and philosophy, taking a special interest in indigenous forms of democracy, collective leadership, and decision-making processes, all ideas he applied to building this new political movement. He had visions of a popularly elected Congolese government that was accountable to its citizens and a Congolese nation that actually realized its full potential. He had only embraced armed struggle as the means to liberating his country after all other political alternatives had been exhausted, and even while the fighting continued he insisted that the country's problems were political and begged a political solution.

I knew my father very well and had total confidence in his intelligence, integrity, and sincerity; in some ways, I felt that his role in the rebellion seemed the appropriate culmination of a career of engagement in Congolese struggles for change. It was not difficult for me to decide that I supported what he was doing. I regretted the fact that war seemed the only recourse, but I was glad and inspired that my father and other progressive Congolese were attempting to influence its outcome.

But at the same time, I wasn't so naïve as to think that the good intentions and personal virtue of a few would be enough to save an entire country. And I knew enough about Congolese history to know that wars had devastated the country for much of its existence. And that betrayals had claimed the lives of too many Congolese martyrs.

During my childhood years in Dar es Salaam, my family often played host at our home on the university campus to people my parents knew and sometimes people they did not. Some were neighborhood friends or colleagues who had stopped by to say hello, others were visiting from much farther and had come to Tanzania on vacation or business. Many stayed for a meal, others settled for tea, peanuts, and conversation. Some stayed a few minutes, some a few nights. Most arrived unexpectedly, and all were welcomed.

Mr. Masamba was one occasional houseguest. He was a Congolese trader who traveled between western Tanzania and the capital buying and selling goods and eking out a living. He would stay with us on some of his Dar trips, spending a few days in town, making his sales and purchases, and then going home to do the same. I don't know how my father knew him or even if he had met Mr. Masamba before he first appeared at our home. But as a Congolese in Dar, Mr. Masamba didn't need to know my father to expect and receive his help and hospitality.

There were quite a number of Congolese in Dar es Salaam, students, businesspeople, permanent residents, and refugees, and many of them often found their way to our living room for animated discussions about Congolese politics or to ask for the *Professeur*'s help. Some of the younger guys, many of them students who had come to Tanzania to try to complete their education after having had to leave Zaire for political reasons, respectfully addressed my father as *"Grand-frère"* and became quite friendly with my brothers and me. Congolese residents in Dar who were associated with the Zairean government were less likely to be as amiable, since my father made no secret of his opposition to Mobutu, and most knew that he had been detained by the Zairean regime in 1981. But most of those who came by the house either shared my father's views or seemed apolitical—just pleased to have been received by a Congolese "brother" in Dar es Salaam.

Mr. Masamba clearly cared little for politics. He seemed to spurn the inevitable discussions between my father and Congolese friends who stopped by while he was a guest in our home. He seemed much more intent on his business activities than on his home country's political future, a topic that sparked endless debates among many of my father's Congolese visitors.

Mr. Masamba was a short, somewhat round man in his fifties with thinning hair and a ready smile that revealed a large gap in his teeth. He would respond affably when my brothers and I greeted him respectfully, asking how we were in his accented Kiswahili from eastern Congo. Although he shared a room with me whenever he showed up in Dar and his snores sometimes startled me awake in the middle of the night, I liked Mr. Masamba. He always seemed cheerful and friendly, and rarely betrayed any bitterness at the unfortunate circumstances that afflicted his life.

And to me, there was much he could have chosen to be bitter about. What fascinated my brothers and me most about Mr. Masamba was not his traveling salesman lifestyle or his easy good humor; it was the fact that he only had one arm. His left arm looked as if it had been severed right above the elbow, and his left biceps tapered down into a blunt little nub, the rounded outline of a bone protruding under the taut, scarred skin. I used to try to be surreptitious with my stares, but it was difficult, especially when he was maneuvering his arm to perform the tasks of his missing hand.

If Mr. Masamba ever noticed us gawking, he never said so. He approached his disability with the confident independence of one who took pride in his capacity to adapt and an unspoken insistence on his own self-sufficiency. Often refusing offers of assistance, he would iron his own clothes, stooping over the ironing board and pinning a shirt or pair of trousers in place with his bad arm while ironing with his right hand. When his right hand was occupied, he would sometimes carry a newspaper or pen under his left armpit, trapping the items against his left side. And he would deftly and efficiently tie his shoelaces with his single hand, manipulating the laces with the practiced dexterity of one who had performed the task for years. My brothers and I would watch these performances with wide-eyed curiosity and sympathy. It taught me something about dignity, seeing Mr. Masamba uncomplainingly coping with his difficult destiny. I wondered what had caused the horrible injury that changed his life forever. And I marveled at how he had apparently made his peace with it.

I only once heard Mr. Masamba refer directly to his missing arm. When it happened, he and my father were sitting in the living room, talking with some Congolese guests who had stopped by. As usual, the conversation turned to politics, and the debate started to heat up as different perspectives competed for the floor. Mr. Masamba sat back in his chair with typical disinterest, sipping his beer and occasionally reaching for a handful of peanuts, just listening to the various monologues on what was afflicting Zaire and the different opinions on how to solve the problems.

At the time, in the mid-1980s, the Zairean dictator, Mobutu Sese Seko, was playing his usual games, promising reform to the activists at home and abroad who demanded change, even while he continued to jail and eliminate political opponents and to bankrupt the country, amassing a personal fortune in foreign bank accounts. My father had not returned to Zaire since his release from detention in 1982, but he had remained engaged in the cause for Congolese democracy, publishing scathing critiques of the Mobutu regime and conferring with other Congolese dissidents, like those who gathered in our Dar es Salaam home on this particular afternoon.

As my father and his Congolese companions traded perspectives on the Zairean conundrum over beers and peanuts, one of the guests eventually opined that armed struggle was the only means to effecting meaningful political change in Zaire. He said that Mobutu would never give up power unless he was forced to, and that an opposition movement that relied on articles, petitions, speeches, and demonstrations had no teeth and would never be taken seriously. The only viable solution, he concluded, was violent insurrection, a popular rebellion to take power from the dictator by force.

Some of the assembled Congolese nodded in agreement, but before anyone could respond, Mr. Masamba sat up in his chair as though jolted from slumber and snorted disdainfully.

"Don't tell me about war," he said bitterly, his voice rising. "You are young. You know nothing about war. It changes nothing. I lost my arm in a war, and nothing changed. So don't tell me about war."

He slumped back in his chair and was silent. The room grew quiet for a moment as Mr. Masamba's words hung in the air. Then, slowly, the discussion began again, as others weighed in with other ideas on the Zairean problem and its possible solutions. Mr. Masamba did not contribute again, but sat quietly, sporadically raising his beer glass or some peanuts to his lips with his right hand, the stump of his left arm resting heavily on the arm of his chair.

Mr. Masamba lost his arm and optimism in the early 1960s, when he fought alongside other supporters of Patrice Lumumba against the forces of the Congolese traitors who had killed him. The rebel patriots were vanquished in 1965 when Mobutu took power in a CIA-backed coup. Perhaps partly due to my knowledge of the experiences of Africans like Mr. Masamba, I can suffer no illusions about the costs and stakes of war.

Whenever I read about new political strife in central Africa in the international media, I am sure to hear follow-up stories from my relatives on the ground. In 1996, when the war that toppled Mobutu began in eastern Congo, I received a firsthand account of its initial human impact from a childhood friend who was in boarding school in Bukavu at the time. Mobutu's forces had started shelling the city, and my friend and his younger brother had fled along with everyone else. They had walked northwest along muddy roads with hundreds of other people, with no money, carrying nothing, eating whatever they could find along the way. They had marched all the way to Kisangani, a distance of almost five hundred miles, and had somehow managed to find a family friend who helped them get a ship along the Congo River to Kinshasa, where their father was. When the war ended, my friend had decided not to go back to school. After all he had seen and experienced, he said he no longer saw the point. Maybe it's just as well—war was to overrun eastern Congo again in less than two years.

After civil war broke out in Congo-Brazzaville (the Democratic Republic of the Congo's neighbor to the west) in 1997 and fighting had raged in the capital city, my ten-year-old cousin solemnly recounted how her family had fled to Kinshasa, leaving their home during a lull in the shooting and picking their way around corpses lying in the street. Though her brother had tried to cover her eyes, she had still seen the *"cadavres,"* she told me. And a year later, when an insecure government was rounding up young men in the capital who were accused of being rebels, I heard from family members in Brazzaville that a cousin, a young student in no way involved in the rebel militias, had been abducted by the military. He was held for three days, during which he was beaten and forced to witness the executions of other prisoners, and had feared that at any moment he would be next. He was only released when family members paid the soldiers ransom money, partly raised through contributions by relatives in the United States.

The region has seen so many wars; and, as Mr. Masamba remonstrated, most have not succeeded in changing the living conditions of the masses of African people. But there are just and unjust wars. And in the fall of 1998, as I watched the progress of a new offensive in Congo, a rebellion against dictatorship and genocide in which my father was integrally involved, I hoped that this war would succeed where others had failed.

I shared my father's optimism. Whenever he'd call and I'd ask him how it was going, he would usually say, "I think we're going to make it." And I knew that he didn't just mean the war or the negotiations that would have to precede a cease-fire, or even the ouster of Kabila. He meant he believed that we would all make it: that the Congolese people would finally have the opportunity to elect a popular government that strove to serve the interests of all Congolese and worked to eradicate poverty, disenfranchisement, and unemployment; that the country's resources would be utilized for the benefit of its people; and that the Congolese people would unite in building a society based on human rights, democracy, and social justice.

Perhaps then, by addressing the root causes of the country's endless succession of wars, we could end the constant cycle of violence. We've had far too much war and militarism in Congo and the region. And we will still be reaping its effects for some time to come.

I've tried to do my part to make a contribution to the struggle. I've disseminated information about the war and the rebels' aims, and attempted to build support for the movement among concerned academics, African American activists, and Africans in the United States. I helped to organize a conference to mobilize African American and African perspectives on the war and the history of the Congo's struggle for freedom and self-determination, trying to build a unified constituency for the Congo and Africa out of a sorely divided diasporean activist community. I was struck by the level of passion and interest in the war among many African Americans but realized that much more political organizing and work would be needed to generate galvanized, coherent support for the Congolese people from the black diaspora. To have an impact, we will need to build a mass movement of the sort that existed in the 1940s, when organizations like the Council for African Affairs underlined the linkages between struggles for black freedom in America and Africa and fought for the liberation of all black people.

As war rages in the Congo once again, I hope desperately that the damage it causes will not be in vain. For my family, for all Congolese, for the millions of Congolese who have died for their freedom in the past, and for the patriots fighting for it now, I hope my father and his colleagues are successful. I feel the urgency of the work at hand and realize the challenges of the many obstacles ahead. There is much to do, and I feel the pull of Africa, the call to throw my shoulder behind the aspirations of the Congolese people. I sense that it's time to go back home.

Perhaps this war will do what no other war in the Congo's history has: silence the guns once and for all by returning power to the Congolese people, allowing them to take control of their own destiny. If the much-touted "African renaissance" is to become a reality, if the twenty-first century is to be the moment of Africa's triumph, perhaps it begins here.

NOTES

Chapter 1: Middle Passages

"Hope surged in Kunta"   Alex Haley, *Roots,* 220.

"I've been to Africa"   Whoopi Goldberg, stand-up comedy performance, U.S. national television, 1995.

"I think the single greatest mistake"   Alex Haley, *The Autobiography of Malcolm X,* 347.

"All of us are bound to mother Africa"   Desmond Tutu, "Black Theology/African Theology—Soul Mates or Antagonists?" in James H. Cone and Gayraud S. Wilmore (eds.), *Black Theology: A Documentary History, Volume One: 1966–1979,* 386.

"No matter where you come from"   Peter Tosh, "African."

"They face each other"   James Baldwin, *Notes of a Native Son* (1955), quoted in David Jenkins, *Black Zion: The Return of Afro-Americans and West Indians to Africa,* 58.

"Psychologically, we've been brainwashed"   Kenneth Noble, "A Meeting Place for Africans and U.S. Blacks," *New York Times,* April 18, 1991, p. A8.

"When Black Americans believe"   "What Black Americans and Africans Can Do for Each Other," *Ebony,* April 1986, p. 158.

"more opportunities for us to develop"   Ibid., p. 162.

"first-ever African–African American summit"   Noble, "A Meeting Place."

"Home of our heritage" Neil Henry, "Meeting Seeks to Bind U.S., Africa," *Washington Post,* April 18, 1991, p. A31.

"Martin's presence is surely with us" Neil Henry, "Meeting of Africans, U.S. Blacks Ends with Vow to Boost Aid, Ease Debt," *Washington Post,* April 20, 1991, p. A18.

"That is not the real Africa" Henry, "Meeting Seeks to Bind," p. A41.

"I wish some of these Americans" Ibid.

"We have to move beyond romance" Kenneth Noble, "U.S. Blacks and Africans Seek Stronger Ties," *New York Times,* May 27, 1993, p. A10.

"We represent a potent political force" Neil Henry, "Discovering 'the Worst Place on Earth,' " *Washington Post,* April 19, 1991, p. A14.

"surprised to see the wide gap" Pamela A. Keels, "Afrocentricity: The Real Deal," *Essence,* July 1995, p. 116.

"harassed by a bunch of neighborhood kids" Mukami Ireri, "The Other Racism," *Essence,* February 1992, p. 124.

"At a time when Ethiopia" Djibril Diallo, "African Drought," *Essence,* April 1985, p. 136.

"there were friendly greetings" Howard W. French, "On Slavery, Africans Say the Guilt Is Theirs, Too," *New York Times,* December 27, 1994, p. A4.

"Black Americans make noise" Ibid.

"Until there is an admission" Ibid.

"The average Ghanaian" Stephen Buckley, "U.S., African Blacks Differ on Turning Slave Dungeons into Tourist Attractions," *Washington Post,* April 17, 1995, p. A10.

"hypocrites and damn liars" "The Fruit of Islam?" *Boston Magazine,* September 1996, p. 14.

"It's a shame I have to stand" Ibid.

"If [my] original ancestor hadn't been forced" Keith B. Richburg, "Continental Divide," *Washington Post Magazine,* March 26, 1995, p. 18.

"Talk to me about Africa" Keith B. Richburg, *Out of America: A Black Man Confronts Africa,* xii.

"My skin is black" Eddy L. Harris, *Native Stranger: A Black Man's Journey into the Heart of Africa,* 311.

"Africans could learn more" Alexis Sinduhije, "Welcome to America," *Transition,* Issue 76, fall 1999, p. 6.

"I was terrified" Ibid., p. 23.

"My tie to Africa is strong" W.E.B. Du Bois, *Dusk of Dawn* (1940), quoted in Jenkins, *Black Zion,* 270.

"it is not culture" Ralph Ellison, *Shadow and Act* (1964), quoted in Penny M. Von Eschen, *Race Against Empire: Black Americans and Anti-Colonialism, 1937–1957,* 1.

"All of us have roots" Tutu, "Black Theology/African Theology" in Cone and Wilmore, *Black Theology,* 385.

"a gulf of three hundred years"   Baldwin, *Notes of a Native Son* (1955), quoted in
    Jenkins, *Black Zion,* 58.
"Thank God"   Richburg, *Out of America,* xiv.
"The sun never sets"   Ali Mazrui, public address at Harvard University, 1990.

Chapter 2: The Joining of Africa and America

"I want my children to straddle"   Bernadette G. Kayode, "African–Afro-American
    Marriages: Do They Work?" *Essence,* July 1979, p. 106.
"I am only teasing"   Lorraine Hansberry, *A Raisin in the Sun* (1959), in Henry
    Louis Gates, Jr., Nellie Y. McKay, William L. Andrews, Houston A. Baker, Jr.,
    and Barbara T. Christian (eds.), *The Norton Anthology of African American
    Literature,* 1748.
"Lord, that's a pretty thing"   Hansberry, in Gates et al., *Norton Anthology,* 1749.
"wriggle . . . as she thinks"   Hansberry, in Gates et al., *Norton Anthology,* 1750.
"It's a dance of welcome"   Hansberry, in Gates et al., *Norton Anthology,* 1755.
"Three hundred years later"   Hansberry, in Gates et al., *Norton Anthology,* 1782.
"I will show you"   Hansberry, in Gates et al., *Norton Anthology,* 1782.
"The man was blue-black"   Maya Angelou, *The Heart of a Woman,* 112.
"He pulled me to him"   Angelou, *Heart,* 113.
"Maya Angelou Make"   Angelou, *Heart,* 115.
"to picture those exquisite hands"   Angelou, *Heart,* 118.
"When I knew I was coming"   Angelou, *Heart,* 117–18.
"This is the joining of Africa"   Angelou, *Heart,* 120.
"I would bring to him"   Angelou, *Heart,* 123.
"He's serious about the struggle"   Angelou, *Heart,* 127.
"Glories stood in thrilling array"   Angelou, *Heart,* 128.
"I am an African"   Angelou, *Heart,* 140.
"It seemed to me"   Angelou, *Heart,* 141.
"That African's got her jumping"   Angelou, *Heart,* 142.
"Vus is teaching you"   Angelou, *Heart,* 143.
"If you chippie on me"   Angelou, *Heart,* 187.
"You must call . . . and explain"   Angelou, *Heart,* 227.
"I am a man"   Angelou, *Heart,* 245–46.
"flashing, endless moment"   Marita Golden, *Migrations of the Heart,* 14.
"I was no longer a Negro"   Golden, *Migrations,* 22.
"enveloped in the aura"   Golden, *Migrations,* 50.
"He etched verbal pictures"   Golden, *Migrations,* 51.
"Already I had left"   Golden, *Migrations,* 53.
"how is it to live here?"   Golden, *Migrations,* 85–86.
"Belligerently patriarchal"   Golden, *Migrations,* 84.
"Uncle will never"   Golden, *Migrations,* 102.
"Iyawo—wife to husband"   Golden, *Migrations,* 143.

"Oyingbo [foreign] wife"   Golden, *Migrations,* 177.

"For the sin of questioning"   Golden, *Migrations,* 178.

"a clan in exile"   Golden, *Migrations,* 141.

"Foreign wives"   Golden, *Migrations,* 181.

"I spoke to black American women"   Golden, *Migrations,* 202.

"You have to work at a marriage"   Golden, *Migrations,* 193.

"Does it always end"   Golden, *Migrations,* 205.

"straddle the Atlantic"   Kayode, "African–Afro-American Marriages," p. 106.

"[My wife] and I are developing"   Jere Smith, "South Africa's New 'Mixed' Marriages," *Ebony,* November 1996, p. 88.

Chapter 3: What Is Africa to Me?

"What is Africa to me"   Countee Cullen, "Heritage" (1925), in Henry Louis Gates, Jr., et al. (eds.), *The Norton Anthology of African American Literature,* 1311.

"It was now between two and three years"   Olaudah Equiano, *The Interesting Narrative of the Life of Olaudah Equiano, or Gustavus Vassa, the African, Written by Himself,* excerpted in Gates et al., *Norton Anthology,* 164.

" 'Twas mercy brought me"   Phillis Wheatley, "On Being Brought from Africa to America" (1773), in Gates et al., *Norton Anthology,* 171.

"I have for some years"   Adelaide Cromwell Hill and Martin Kilson (eds.), *Apropos of Africa: Sentiments of Negro American Leaders on Africa from the 1800s to the 1950s,* 11.

"In Africa we shall be freemen"   Hill and Kilson, *Apropos,* 35.

"We are of the opinion"   Hill and Kilson, *Apropos,* 39.

"I see nothing for the Negro"   Hill and Kilson, *Apropos,* 47.

"as a class they are averse"   Hill and Kilson, *Apropos,* 49.

"It is lamentable"   Hill and Kilson, *Apropos,* 51.

"The books I read"   Elliott P. Skinner, *African Americans and U.S. Policy Toward Africa, 1850–1924: In Defense of Black Nationality,* 165.

"a big-nosed white man"   Skinner, *African Americans and U.S. Policy,* 159.

tall tales of African bounty   Robert G. Weisbord, *Ebony Kinship: Africa, Africans and the Afro-American,* 24.

"have no conception of any land greater"   Hill and Kilson, *Apropos,* 58.

"fruits of every beauty,"   Weisbord, *Ebony Kinship,* 29.

"gold dust can be switched up"   Weisbord, *Ebony Kinship,* 31.

Africa as a paradise   Weisbord, *Ebony Kinship,* 36.

"too rich"   Weisbord, *Ebony Kinship,* 91.

"the United States as Hades"   Skinner, *African Americans and U.S. Policy,* 155.

"If native Africans are unable"   Marcus Garvey, in Hill and Kilson, *Apropos,* 64.

"Our race gave the first great civilization"   Weisbord, *Ebony Kinship,* 53.

"The old time stories"   Marcus Garvey, in Gates et al., *Norton Anthology,* 974.

"The American Negro must remake"   Arthur Schomburg, in Gates et al., *Norton Anthology*, 942.

"Something is lost in me"   Claude McKay, "Outcast," in Gates et al., *Norton Anthology*, 987.

"Africa? A book one thumbs"   Cullen, "Heritage," in Gates et al., *Norton Anthology*, 1311.

"Why do our black faces search"   Arna Bontemps, "Nocturne at Bethesda," in Gates et al., *Norton Anthology*, 1242.

"The low beating of the tom-toms"   Langston Hughes, "Danse Africaine," in Gates et al., *Norton Anthology*, 1255.

"Feasting on a strange cassava"   Jean Toomer, "Conversion," in Gates et al., *Norton Anthology*, 1105.

"the chanting / Around a heathen fire"   Gwendolyn Bennett, "Heritage," in Gates et al., *Norton Anthology*, 1227.

"The white people had held my people"   Zora Neale Hurston, in Gates et al., *Norton Anthology*, 1063.

"The young Negro artist"   Wallace Thurman, in Gates et al., *Norton Anthology*, 1235.

"only Black Sovereign in the world"   Weisbord, *Ebony Kinship*, 101.

"the ruler of a country where"   Weisbord, *Ebony Kinship*, 101.

"secret Mau Mau society"   Penny M. Von Eschen, *Race Against Empire*, 166.

Chapter 4: And Lo! I Was in Africa

"When shall I forget the night"   W.E.B. Du Bois, quoted in David Jenkins, *Black Zion*, 134.

"I must leave you to guess"   Jenkins, *Black Zion*, 14.

"Smeathman's humane plan"   Jenkins, *Black Zion*, 18.

"I am sorry, and very sorry"   Jenkins, *Black Zion*, 20.

"Alass! alass! in place of growing better"   Jenkins, *Black Zion*, 66.

reunited with his mother   Jenkins, *Black Zion*, 68.

thanked God for bringing them to their "mother country"   Robert G. Weisbord, *Ebony Kinship*, 15.

"The sun had far mounted the sky"   Jenkins, *Black Zion*, 80.

"What my sensations were"   Jenkins, *Black Zion*, 81.

"I am an African, and in this country"   Adelaide Cromwell Hill and Martin Kilson (eds.), *Apropos of Africa*, 79.

"There never has been an hour"   Jenkins, *Black Zion*, 80.

"We know nothing of that"   Jenkins, *Black Zion*, 81.

"dirty and contemptible rag"   Weisbord, *Ebony Kinship*, 28.

"Something to eat is scarce"   Weisbord, *Ebony Kinship*, 31.

passengers had died of fever   Jenkins, *Black Zion*, 100.

"I am sorry to say that this Negro"   Jenkins, *Black Zion*, 107.

"Long may the links"   Jenkins, *Black Zion*, 47.

"When Ghana became free"   Jenkins, *Black Zion*, 134.

"I was gazing upon a world"   Jenkins, *Black Zion*, 139.

"When you *really* realize you are not African"   Jenkins, *Black Zion*, 165.

"Before I came here I thought"   Ernest Dunbar (ed.), *Black Expatriates: A Study of American Negroes in Exile*, 57.

"It means 'stranger' "   Dunbar, *Black Expatriates*, 61.

"I really don't fit"   Dunbar, *Black Expatriates*, 64.

"I discovered that this emotional idea"   Dunbar, *Black Expatriates*, 97.

"I am simply not interested"   Jenkins, *Black Zion*, 130.

"Give us a dollar"   Jenkins, *Black Zion*, 140.

"[African Americans'] problem is to 'acculturate' "   Jenkins, *Black Zion*, 147.

"If you really want to belong"   Dunbar, *Black Expatriates*, 82.

"They didn't ask the news"   Jenkins, *Black Zion*, 78.

"The longer I live here"   Jenkins, *Black Zion*, 169.

Chapter 5: Our Fellow Blacks in America

"There are legends among the tribes"   Robert G. Weisbord, *Ebony Kinship*, 132.

Refusing American requests to extradite the refugees   Weisbord, *Ebony Kinship*, 137.

Tanzanian women discouraged from wearing their hair in Afros   Weisbord, *Ebony Kinship*, 195.

"You know, for the last three hundred years"   David Jenkins, *Black Zion*, 168.

Angelou was embraced as a lost descendant   Maya Angelou, *All God's Children Need Traveling Shoes*, 206.

"The people who were taken away"   Melville Herskovits, *The New World Negro*, 84.

"At these customs"   Herskovits, *New World Negro*, 85.

"Oh, ancestors, do all in your power"   Herskovits, *New World Negro*, 87.

"You have nearly all the people"   Herskovits, *New World Negro*, 87.

"This family has strong men"   Herskovits, *New World Negro*, 87.

"When Gezo became king"   Herskovits, *New World Negro*, 89.

Visiting black Americans were given the status of "honorary whites"   Yekutiel Gershoni, *Africans on African-Americans: The Creation and Uses of an African-American Myth*, 20.

"Their visit will do their countrymen"   Gershoni, *Africans on*, 20.

"You are the first black man"   Gershoni, *Africans on*, 21.

"Bishop H. M. Turner . . . was welcomed"   Gershoni, *Africans on*, 21.

"that the black man was not the incapable"   Gershoni, *Africans on*, 23.

"Our fellow blacks in America"   Gershoni, *Africans on*, 25–26.

"divine purpose in permitting their [African-Americans'] exile"   Gershoni, *Africans on*, 61.

"I believe that the Negro was brought"   Gershoni, *Africans on,* 65.

"America is not the destined home"   Gershoni, *Africans on,* 62–63.

"The Afro-American has lost"   Gershoni, *Africans on,* 69.

"Indeed we are bound to say"   Gershoni, *Africans on,* 69.

"America as far as I am aware"   Gershoni, *Africans on,* 13.

"Blacks in America were economically"   Gershoni, *Africans on,* 14–15.

"For days afterwards [he] lived"   Gershoni, *Africans on,* 15.

"Natives received impressions"   Gershoni, *Africans on,* 15.

"There looms up before us now"   Gershoni, *Africans on,* 16.

"The Negro race is a great and growing race"   Gershoni, *Africans on,* 16.

"I am just as much opposed"   Gershoni, *Africans on,* 17.

"If the President had gone to them"   Gershoni, *Africans on,* 84.

"The Negro race in America has been successful"   Gershoni, *Africans on,* 29.

"our asylum where the hunted"   Gershoni, *Africans on,* 116.

"our intelligent brethren"   Gershoni, *Africans on,* 83.

"well-deserved homage to the poets"   Gershoni, *Africans on,* 108.

"Studying at the Sorbonne"   Gershoni, *Africans on,* 109.

"It is evident that for a time"   Gershoni, *Africans on,* 83.

"was supposed by some to be the herald"   Gershoni, *Africans on,* 51.

"God sent the black man"   Gershoni, *Africans on,* 63.

"It is but asserting the commonplace"   Gershoni, *Africans on,* 63.

"the voice of God now seems"   Gershoni, *Africans on,* 31.

"in those days we read"   Gershoni, *Africans on,* 9.

"excited by rumors that a black king"   Gershoni, *Africans on,* 9.

"the young men of Sierra Leone"   Gershoni, *Africans on,* 32.

"Moses Garvey"   Gershoni, *Africans on,* 32.

"Before the American Negro can hope"   Gershoni, *Africans on,* 88.

"Suppose for a moment"   Gershoni, *Africans on,* 88.

"In fact our brethren"   Gershoni, *Africans on,* 88.

"Marcus Garvey is trying to light"   Gershoni, *Africans on,* 98.

"Some of us Negroes did not know"   Gershoni, *Africans on,* 32.

"The white men dumped these Africans"   Kimpianga Mahaniah, "The Presence of Black Americans in the Lower Congo, from 1878–1921," in Joseph Harris (ed.), *Global Dimensions of the African Diaspora,* second edition, 407.

"There shall be conquests o'er militant forces"   Gershoni, *Africans on,* 46.

"the negroes of America had heard"   Gershoni, *Africans on,* 47.

"waited everyday for those Americans"   Gershoni, *Africans on,* 47.

"In about six months a flight"   Gershoni, *Africans on,* 48.

"The time is at hand, America"   Gershoni, *Africans on,* 52.

"Nigger or even Negro"   Weisbord, *Ebony Kinship,* 169.

"in a derogatory and humiliating manner"   Weisbord, *Ebony Kinship,* 169.

"American Negroes are always crude"   Angelou, *All God's Children,* 34.

"I don't think they would fit in"   Weisbord, *Ebony Kinship,* 156.

"do not . . . even like to be called Africans"   Weisbord, *Ebony Kinship*, 161.

"the black American's complete loyalty"   Weisbord, *Ebony Kinship*, 156.

"There had been a great deal of alienation"   Ernest Dunbar (ed.), *Black Expatriates*, 96–97.

outrage at the mistreatment of American blacks   Weisbord, *Ebony Kinship*, 172.

"would not be surprised if before long"   Weisbord, *Ebony Kinship*, 161.

"Although material opportunities"   Randall Robinson, *Defending the Spirit: A Black Life in America*, 73.

"true that after slavery"   Angelou, *All God's Children*, 65.

Chapter 6: Africa's Tyranny

"In every family, bad boys"   Michael Schatzberg, *The Dialectics of Oppression in Zaire*, 1.

"the Siberia, of the African continent"   Elliott P. Skinner, *African Americans and U.S. Policy Towards Africa, 1850–1924*, 225.

"disenchanted, disappointed and disheartened"   Skinner, *African Americans and U.S. Policy*, 226.

"I now appeal to the Powers"   Skinner, *African Americans and U.S. Policy*, 226.

"I indulge the hope that"   Skinner, *African Americans and U.S. Policy*, 227.

"My cry is for *Africa for the Africans!*"   Skinner, *African Americans and U.S. Policy*, 230.

"in calling the attention of the country"   Skinner, *African Americans and U.S. Policy*, 234.

"Wherever the white man"   Skinner, *African Americans and U.S. Policy*, 235.

"The oppression of the colored race"   Skinner, *African Americans and U.S. Policy*, 233.

"armed sentries of chartered"   Skinner, *African Americans and U.S. Policy*, 238.

circulation of the *Negro World* in Congo   Kimpianga Mahaniah, "The Presence of Black Americans in the Lower Congo, from 1878–1921," in Joseph Harris (ed.), *Global Dimensions of the African Diaspora*, second edition, 414.

concern of Belgian colonial administration   M. W. Kodi, "The 1921 Pan-African Congress at Brussels: A Background to Belgian Pressures," in Harris, *Global Dimensions*, 267.

"If the king of the Americans comes"   Kodi, in Harris, *Global Dimensions*, 278.

"Our fight for Negro rights"   Penny M. Von Eschen, *Race Against Empire*, 20.

"interested in Africa for the wealth"   Von Eschen, *Race Against Empire*, 104.

"extremely active in behalf"   Von Eschen, *Race Against Empire*, 1.

"Negroes are American"   Von Eschen, *Race Against Empire*, 97.

"increasing the purchasing power"   Von Eschen, *Race Against Empire*, 161.

"progressing slowly without bias"   Von Eschen, *Race Against Empire*, 161.

"You must understand that"   Von Eschen, *Race Against Empire*, 161.

"Africans built America"   Robert G. Weisbord, *Ebony Kinship*, 187.

"The 20 million Americans"   Karl Evanzz, *The Judas Factor: The Plot to Kill Malcolm X,* 86.

"surely among the most sinister"   Weisbord, *Ebony Kinship,* 187.

"You cannot understand"   David Jenkins, *Black Zion,* 47.

"The interests of twenty million"   Weisbord, *Ebony Kinship,* 170.

"the deep concern aroused"   Weisbord, *Ebony Kinship,* 171.

"our kith and kin"   Weisbord, *Ebony Kinship,* 171.

"continuing manifestations of racial bigotry"   Weisbord, *Ebony Kinship,* 171.

"have been a matter of as much concern"   Weisbord, *Ebony Kinship,* 172.

"The United States condemned"   Evanzz, *Judas Factor,* 241–42.

"had the opportunity to raise questions"   Weisbord, *Ebony Kinship,* 174.

"congenial and responsible,"   Tejumola Olaniyan, "The Return of the Native Son," *Transition,* issue 72, vol. 6, no. 4, winter 1996, p. 61.

Chapter 7: In the White Man's Country

"Shall I sing your song, Africa"   Akinsola Akiwowo, "Song in a Strange Land," *Phylon,* 12, no. 1, First Quarter, 1951, p. 36.

"escaped into the black community"   Phillips Bradford Verner and Harvey Blume, *Ota: The Pygmy in the Zoo,* 114.

"The person responsible for this"   Verner and Blume, *Ota,* 182.

"Our race, we think, is depressed"   Verner and Blume, *Ota,* 183, 186.

"As far as I can see"   Verner and Blume, *Ota,* 192.

"Remember, Christians, Negroes, black as Cain"   Phillis Wheatley, "On Being Brought from Africa to America" (1773) in Henry Louis Gates, Jr., et al. (eds.), *The Norton Anthology of African American Literature,* 171.

"His age was against"   Verner and Blume, *Ota,* 203.

"had sent his spirit home to Africa"   Verner and Blume, *Ota,* 218.

"Shall I sing your song, Africa"   Akiwowo, "Song," p. 36.

"a great Negro who was coming"   Nnamdi Azikiwe, *My Odyssey,* 32.

"If I, one of you, could go"   Azikiwe, *My Odyssey,* 37.

"From that day I became a new man"   Azikiwe, *My Odyssey,* 37–38.

"became very curious and asked"   Azikiwe, *My Odyssey,* 80.

"To me, it was a revelation"   Azikiwe, *My Odyssey,* 80–81.

"Noticing how students of African"   Azikiwe, *My Odyssey,* 158.

"I felt immediately at home"   Kwame Nkrumah, *The Autobiography of Kwame Nkrumah,* 24.

"Educated Africans knew"   Mugo Gatheru, *Child of Two Worlds,* 207–208.

"I was determined to go to America"   Gatheru, *Child,* 115.

"I saw many Negroes on the road"   Gatheru, *Child,* 145.

"Instinctively, perhaps, I thought"   Gatheru, *Child,* 147–48.

"When I arrived in America"   Gatheru, *Child,* 208.

"However naïve I may have been"   Gatheru, *Child,* 209.

"As we entered, the barman came" Gatheru, *Child,* 157.

"For some reasons which must be obvious" Gatheru, *Child,* 207.

"The American Negro of today" Gatheru, *Child,* 209.

Chapter 8: Drumbeats from Across the Atlantic

"The essential Pan-Africanism" Norman Weinstein, *A Night in Tunisia: Imaginings of Africa in Jazz,* 1.

"There is without a doubt, no people" Ronald Segal, *The Black Diaspora,* 375.

"When we played for the black people" Samuel A. Floyd, *The Power of Black Music: Interpreting Its History from Africa to the United States,* 90.

"Let the blare of Negro jazz" Floyd, *Power of Black Music,* 133.

"*genuine* African music" Weinstein, *Night in Tunisia,* 5.

"We must be proud of our race" Weinstein, *Night in Tunisia,* 37.

"A whole strain of West Indian" Weinstein, *Night in Tunisia,* 41.

"After writing African music" Weinstein, *Night in Tunisia,* 37–38.

"Very early in my career" Weinstein, *Night in Tunisia,* 50.

"As a black American, I know" Manu Dibango (in collaboration with Danielle Rouard, translated by Beth G. Raps), *Three Kilos of Coffee: An Autobiography,* 128.

"I went to Africa because" Weinstein, *Night in Tunisia,* 51.

"[Trane] was expressing through music" Floyd, *Power of Black Music,* 190.

"Next time you go to Africa" Cuthbert Ormond Simpkins, *Coltrane: A Biography,* 232.

"second happiest moment of my life" Weinstein, *Night in Tunisia,* 178.

"My ancestors came from here" Laurence Bergreen, *Louis Armstrong: An Extravagant Life,* 461.

"Louis was a great player," Lewis John Collins, *African Pop Roots: The Inside Rhythms of Africa,* 55.

"I sort've liked the idea" Penny M. Von Eschen, *Race Against Empire,* 178.

"The way they are treating" Von Eschen, *Race Against Empire,* 179–80.

"I gave demonstrations" Weinstein, *Night in Tunisia,* 113.

"I've been going through a period" Weinstein, *Night in Tunisia,* 107.

"What I saw and heard" Weinstein, *Night in Tunisia,* 172.

"The African trip didn't change" Weinstein, *Night in Tunisia,* 174.

"This music is a reflection" Weinstein, *Night in Tunisia,* 166.

"That was heavy" Weinstein, *Night in Tunisia,* 89.

"During the 60's the prevailing" Weinstein, *Night in Tunisia,* 182.

"not only sang the Negro spirituals" Joseph K. Adjaye and Adrianne R. Andrews (eds.), *Language, Rhythm, and Sound: Black Popular Cultures into the Twenty-first Century,* 249.

"What happiness . . . when I first" Dibango, *Three Kilos,* 13, 17, 21.

"Louis Armstrong haunted me" Dibango, *Three Kilos,* 75.

"The piece was released"   Dibango, *Three Kilos*, 88.

"After the Assembly, I changed"   Collins, *Africa Pop Roots*, 62.

"You see, at the beginning"   Collins, *Africa Pop Roots*, 78.

"Every other band was playing"   Chris Stapleton and Chris May, *African All-stars: The Pop Music of a Continent*, 65.

"I got the idea when I seen this movie"   David Toop, *Rap Attack 2: African Rap to Global Hip Hop*, 57.

"I'm that kind of nigga"   William Eric Perkins, *Droppin' Science: Critical Essays on Rap Music and Hip Hop Culture*, 159.

"I see rap as being a gardening tool"   Joseph D. Eure and James G. Spady (eds.), *Nation Conscious Rap*, 68, 75.

"I felt like I was honored"   Eure and Spady, *Nation Conscious*, 9.

"We just played one venue"   Eure and Spady, *Nation Conscious*, 137–38.

"You want to free Africa"   Robin D. G. Kelley, *Race Rebels: Culture, Politics and the Black Working Class*, 212.

"All those motherfuckers"   Kelley, *Race Rebels*, 212.

"We don't give a fuck"   Kelley, *Race Rebels*, 212.

"If I ruled the world"   Nas, "If I Ruled the World," *It Was Written*, Columbia Records, 1996.

"If we're going to succeed"   Farai Chideya, "Africa's Hip Hop Generation," *Vibe*, August 1997, p. 67.

"I'm sure that all the music"   Charles Sugnet, "I Sing All the Spaces" (interview with Baaba Maal), *Transition*, Issue 74, vol. 7, no. 2, fall 1998, p. 193.

Chapter 9: Stretching Hands unto God

"I would go back to darkness and to peace"   Claude McKay, "Outcast," in Henry Louis Gates, Jr., et al. (eds.), *The Norton Anthology of African American Literature*, 987.

"a small bow and several arrows"   Albert Raboteau, *Slave Religion*, 44.

"In the blacks' quarter"   Raboteau, *Slave Religion*, 67.

"Sinners won't get converted"   Raboteau, *Slave Religion*, 69.

"He who could sing loudest"   Raboteau, *Slave Religion*, 69.

"Can the Ethiopian change"   Gayraud S. Wilmore, *Black Religion and Black Radicalism: An Interpretation of the Religious History of Afro-American People*, second edition, 121.

"If it be shown here beyond"   Wilmore, *Black Religion*, 99.

"With the fullest reliance upon"   Wilmore, *Black Religion*, 113.

"the civilization and christianization"   Wilmore, *Black Religion*, 111.

"God himself as assuredly as he rules"   Wilmore, *Black Religion*, 112.

"The difficulties in the way"   Wilmore, *Black Religion*, 115.

"the forced and cruel migration"   Josiah U. Young III, *A Pan-African Theology: Providence and the Legacies of the Ancestors*, 28.

"no less than to set up"   Young, *Pan-African Theology,* 31–32.

"So far as Western Africa"   Young, *Pan-African Theology,* 42.

"amalgamate with [their] aboriginal"   Young, *Pan-African Theology,* 68.

"Behold, the Lord thy God"   Wilmore, *Black Religion,* 118.

"We have as much right biblically"   Wilmore, *Black Religion,* 125.

"Africa is the largest"   Wilmore, *Black Religion,* 127.

"Our cause is based upon righteousness"   Leonard Barrett, *Soul Force,* 144.

"the customary religious service"   Randall Burkett, *Garveyism as a Religious Movement,* 20.

"Erase the white gods"   Wilmore, *Black Religion,* 150.

"Jesus Christ was a Black man"   Wilmore, *Black Religion,* 157.

eight Black Jewish sects in Harlem   George E. Simpson, *Black Religions in the New World,* 269.

"You have made yourselves"   Wilmore, *Black Religion,* 173.

"My brothers and sisters"   Wilmore, *Black Religion,* 184.

"Black Theology is saying"   James H. Cone and Gayraud S. Wilmore, "Black Theology and African Theology: Considerations for Dialogue, Critique and Integration," in James H. Cone and Gayraud S. Wilmore (eds.), *Black Theology: A Documentary History, Volume One: 1966–1979,* 372.

"You are Christian"   Wilmore, p. 212.

"He came to free a black people"   Albert B. Cleage, Jr., *The Black Messiah,* 111.

"The Black Church"   Cleage, *Black Messiah,* 103.

"I created Kwanzaa"   Aldore Collier, "Maulana Karenga: The Man Who Invented Kwanzaa," *Ebony,* January 1998, p. 116.

"It's an African holiday,"   Ibid., p. 120.

"quest for an authentic African spirituality"   Young, *Pan-African Theology,* 189.

"There exists between us"   Cone and Wilmore, "Black Theology," 378.

"We must talk to one another"   Cone and Wilmore, "Black Theology," 377.

Conclusion: The Land of the Future

"How good and how pleasant it would be"   Bob Marley, "Africa Unite," *Survival,* Island Records, 1979.

Epilogue

"Leaders of the ongoing rebellion"   *IRIN* (United Nations electronic news bulletin), "Rebellion in the Democratic Republic of Congo," August 17, 1998.

BIBLIOGRAPHY

Joseph K. Adjaye and Adrianne R. Andrews (eds.). *Language, Rhythm, and Sound: Black Popular Cultures into the Twenty-first Century.* University of Pittsburgh Press, Pittsburgh, 1997.

Akinsola Akiwowo. "Song in a Strange Land." *Phylon,* 12, no. 1, First Quarter, 1951, p. 36.

William L. Andrews, Frances Smith Foster, and Trudier Harris (eds.). *The Oxford Companion to African American Literature.* Oxford University Press, Oxford, 1997.

Maya Angelou. *The Heart of a Woman.* Random House, New York, 1981.

———. *All God's Children Need Traveling Shoes.* Random House, New York, 1986.

Nnamdi Azikiwe. *My Odyssey.* Praeger, New York, 1970.

Leonard Barrett. *Soul Force.* Anchor, New York, 1974.

Laurence Bergreen. *Louis Armstrong: An Extravagant Life.* Broadway Books, New York, 1997.

J. W. E. Bowen (ed.). *Africa and the American Negro: Addresses and Proceedings of the Congress on Africa, 1895.* Mnemosyne, Miami, 1969.

Stephen Buckley. "U.S., African Blacks Differ on Turning Slave Dungeons into Tourists Attractions." *Washington Post,* April 17, 1995, p. A10.

Randall Burkett. *Garveyism as a Religious Movement.* Scarecrow, London, 1978.

Farai Chideya. "Africa's Hip Hop Generation." *Vibe,* August 1997, p. 67.

Albert B. Cleage, Jr. *The Black Messiah.* A Search Book: Sheed and Ward, New York, 1968.

Aldore Collier. "Maulana Karenga: The Man Who Invented Kwanzaa." *Ebony,* January 1998, p. 116.

Lewis John Collins. *African Pop Roots: The Inside Rhythms of Africa.* W. Foulsham, London, 1985.

James H. Cone and Gayraud S. Wilmore (eds.), *Black Theology: A Documentary History, Volume One: 1966–1979; Volume Two: 1980–1992.* Orbis Books, Maryknoll, NY, 1993.

Bernard Dadié. *One Way: Bernard Dadié Observes America,* tr. Jo Patterson. University of Illinois Press, Urbana, 1994.

Djibril Diallo. "African Drought." *Essence,* April 1985, p. 136.

Manu Dibango (in collaboration with Danielle Rouard). *Three Kilos of Coffee: an autobiography,* tr. Beth G. Raps. University of Chicago Press, Chicago, 1994.

Ernest Dunbar (ed.). *Black Expatriates: A Study of American Negroes in Exile.* E.P. Dutton, New York, 1968.

Olaudah Equiano. *The Interesting Narrative of the Life of Olaudah Equiano, or Gustavus Vassa, the African, Written by Himself.* Excerpted in Gates et al. (eds.), *Norton Anthology* (q.v.).

Joseph D. Eure and James G. Spady (eds.). *Nation Conscious Rap.* PC International, New York, 1991.

Karl Evanzz. *The Judas Factor: The Plot to Kill Malcolm X.* Thunder's Mouth, New York, 1992.

Samuel A. Floyd. *The Power of Black Music: Interpreting Its History from Africa to the United States.* Oxford University Press, New York, 1995.

Melvin P. Foote. "Opening Doors to Africa." *Emerge,* June 1998, p. 36.

Howard W. French. "On Slavery, Africans Say the Guilt Is Theirs, Too." *New York Times,* December 27, 1994, p. A4.

"The Fruit of Islam?" *Boston Magazine,* September 1996, p. 14.

Henry Louis Gates, Jr., Nellie Y. McKay, William L. Andrews, Houston A. Baker, Jr., Barbara T. Christian (eds.). *The Norton Anthology of African American Literature.* W.W. Norton, New York, 1997.

Mugo Gatheru. *Child of Two Worlds.* Heinemann, London, 1964.

Yekutiel Gershoni. *Africans on African-Americans: The Creation and Uses of an African-American Myth.* New York University Press, New York, 1997.

Marita Golden. *Migrations of the Heart.* Anchor, Doubleday, Garden City, NY, 1983.

Philip Gourevitch. *We Wish to Inform You That Tomorrow We Will Be Killed with Our Families: Stories from Rwanda.* Farrar, Straus and Giroux, New York, 1998.

Alex Haley. *The Autobiography of Malcolm X* (1965). Ballantine, New York, 1992.

———. *Roots.* Doubleday, Garden City, NY, 1976.

Eddy L. Harris. *Native Stranger: A Black Man's Journey into the Heart of Africa.* Vintage, New York, 1992.

Joseph Harris (ed.). *Global Dimensions of the African Diaspora.* Second edition. Howard University Press, Washington, DC, 1993.

Neil Henry. "Meeting Seeks to Bind U.S., Africa." *Washington Post,* April 18, 1991, p. A31.

———. "Discovering 'the Worst Place on Earth.' " *Washington Post,* April 19, 1991, p. A14.

———. "Meeting of Africans, U.S. Blacks Ends With Vow to Boost Aid, Ease Debt." *Washington Post,* April 20, 1991, p. A18.

Melville Herskovits. *The New World Negro.* Minerva, 1966.

Adelaide Cromwell Hill and Martin Kilson (eds.). *Apropos of Africa: Sentiments of Negro American Leaders on Africa from the 1800s to the 1950s.* Cass, London, 1969.

Adam Hochschild. *King Leopold's Ghost: A Story of Greed, Terror and Heroism in Colonial Africa.* Houghton Mifflin, Boston, 1998.

Mukami Ireri. "The Other Racism." *Essence,* February 1992, p. 124.

IRIN (United Nations electronic news bulletin). "Rebellion in the Democratic Republic of Congo." August 17, 1998.

David Jenkins. *Black Zion: The Return of Afro-Americans and West Indians to Africa.* Wildwood House, London, 1975.

Bernadette G. Kayode. "African–Afro-American Marriages: Do They Work?" *Essence,* July 1979, p. 81.

Pamela A. Keels. "Afrocentricity: The Real Deal." *Essence,* July 1995, p. 116.

Robin D. G. Kelley. *Race Rebels: Culture, Politics and the Black Working Class.* Free Press, New York, 1994.

M. W. Kodi. "The 1921 Pan-African Congress at Brussels: A Background to Belgian Pressures." In Harris (ed.), *Global Dimensions* (q.v.).

Kwabena Appiah Kubi. *In America in Search of Gold.* Pub. by author, 1985.

Kimpianga Mahaniah. "The Presence of Black Americans in the Lower Congo, from 1878–1921." In Harris (ed.), *Global Dimensions* (q.v.).

John Mbiti. "An African Views American Black Theology." In Cone and Wilmore (eds.), *Black Theology* (q.v.).

Kwame Nkrumah. *The Autobiography of Kwame Nkrumah.* Thomas Nelson and Sons, Edinburgh, 1959.

Kenneth Noble. "A Meeting Place for Africans and U.S. Blacks." *New York Times,* April 18, 1991, p. A8.

——. "U.S. Blacks and Africans Seek Stronger Ties." *New York Times,* May 27, 1993, p. A10.

Tejumola Olaniyan. "The Return of the Native Son." *Transition,* issue 72, vol. 6, no. 4, winter 1996, p. 50.

William Eric Perkins. *Droppin' Science: Critical Essays on Rap Music and Hip Hop Culture.* Temple University Press, Philadelphia, 1996.

Albert Raboteau. *Slave Religion.* Oxford University Press, New York, 1978.

Keith B. Richburg. *Out of America: A Black Man Confronts Africa.* A New Republic Book: BasicBooks, New York, 1997.

——. "Continental Divide," *Washington Post Magazine,* March 26, 1995, p. 17.

Randall Robinson. *Defending the Spirit: A Black Life in America.* Dutton, New York, 1998.

Michael Schatzberg. *The Dialectics of Oppression in Zaire.* Indiana University Press, Bloomington, 1988.

Ronald Segal. *The Black Diaspora.* Farrar, Straus and Giroux, New York, 1995.

Cuthbert Ormond Simpkins. *Coltrane: A Biography.* Black Classic, Baltimore, 1975.

George E. Simpson. *Black Religions in the New World.* Columbia University Press, New York, 1978.

Alexis Sinduhije. "Welcome to America." *Transition,* Issue 76, fall 1999, p. 4.

Elliott P. Skinner. *African Americans and U.S. Policy Toward Africa, 1850–1924: In Defense of Black Nationality.* Howard University Press, Washington, DC, 1992.

Jere Smith. "South Africa's New 'Mixed' Marriages." *Ebony,* November 1996, p. 85.

Chris Stapleton and Chris May. *African All-stars: The Pop Music of a Continent.* Quartet, London, 1987.

Charles Sugnet. "I Sing All the Spaces" (interview with Baaba Maal). *Transition,* Issue 74, vol. 7, no. 2, fall 1998, p. 184.

David Toop. *Rap Attack 2: African Rap to Global Hip Hop.* Serpent's Tail, London, 1991.

Desmond Tutu. "Black Theology/African Theology—Soul Mates or Antagonists?" In Cone and Wilmore (eds.), *Black Theology* (q.v.).

Phillips Bradford Verner and Harvey Blume. *Ota: The Pygmy in the Zoo.* St. Martin's, New York, 1992.

Penny M. Von Eschen. *Race Against Empire: Black Americans and Anti-Colonialism, 1937–1957.* Cornell University Press, Ithaca, NY, 1997.

Sheila Walker. "It Can Work." *Essence,* July 1979, p. 81.

Norman Weinstein. *A Night in Tunisia: Imaginings of Africa in Jazz.* Scarecrow, Metuchen, NJ, 1992.

Robert G. Weisbord. *Ebony Kinship: Africa, Africans and the Afro-American,* Greenwood, Westport, CT, 1973.

"What Black Americans and Africans Can Do for Each Other." *Ebony,* April 1986, p. 155.

Gayraud S. Wilmore. *Black Religion and Black Radicalism: An Interpretation of the Religious History of Afro-American People,* second edition, Orbis, Maryknoll, NY, 1983.

Josiah U. Young III. *A Pan-African Theology: Providence and the Legacies of the Ancestors,* Africa World Press, Trenton, NJ, 1992.

———. "God's Path and Pan-Africa." In Cone and Wilmore (eds.), *Black Theology* (q.v.).

INDEX